P9-AGU-346

# COPENHAGEN & BEYOND

MICHAEL BARRETT

# CONTENTS

**1** Roskilde Cathedral

**2** traditional herring restaurant in Nyhavn

**3** Kronborg's rooftops

**4** Amalienborg Slotsplads square

**5** restaurant in the town of Stege on Møn

**6** Langelinie

# DISCOVER
## COPENHAGEN & BEYOND

Denmark has always held a favorable reputation on the world stage, repeatedly topping "world's happiest country" lists, yet it has often remained off the beaten path, or at least down a side street, for many visitors to Europe. Copenhagen has no Big Ben, Eiffel Tower, or Colosseum to conjure up iconic images in travelers' minds, but the Danish capital has serious claims to be considered in the same tier as the famous cities these landmarks call home.

Copenhagen's accessibility, culture, nightlife, food, bicycle bridges, calming lakes, microbreweries, diversity, and healthy work-life balance are all part of its appeal. They are also part of the city's way of life and show that its "happiness" is more than just a vague idea. Don't rush your visit. Take your time to scratch under the surface and uncover what makes this city so special.

I once heard someone say, "There's Copenhagen, and then there's the rest of Denmark." It was meant to praise the capital, but I prefer to see it as a compliment to both. There are many treasures just beyond Copenhagen. To the north, in the suburbs, you'll find a giant deer park right next to Bakken, an ancient amusement park that brings out the child in everyone. And just across the Øresund—a strait that forms the Danish-Swedish border—is Malmö, where you can easily get a taste of Swedish life.

The southern island of Møn is only a couple of hours from Copenhagen, yet it feels like it's another world, with undulating countryside, dramatic cliffs, and a welcoming friendliness that's hard to find in any city. Helsingør and Roskilde are approachable small towns with spectacular historical edifices. The atmospheric harbor village of Dragør has a charm that cannot be denied. And, of course, there's the Louisiana Museum of Modern Art, a museum that ranks among the best in the world, located in a sleepy fishing village in north Zealand. If you're visiting Copenhagen, much of Denmark is truly within your reach.

# MY FAVORITE
## EXPERIENCES

**1** Spending the afternoon at **Tivoli Gardens**—a 19th-century amusement park—riding the "Demon," strolling through a Chinese bamboo forest, and dancing to a live swing band as the sun goes down (page 55).

**2** **Bicycling** on the specially designed twisting bridges across the harbor, and feeling the wind on your face on a two-wheeled trip around town. It's Copenhagen—you'll feel you've missed something if you don't (page 76).

**3** Climbing to the top of the **Church of Our Saviour** and admiring the panoramic views of Copenhagen from its gilded spire (page 69).

**4** Drinking a beer on Queen Louise's Bridge and watching joggers and lovers pass by at the **Lakes**—the best place to get a taste of everyday life in the Danish capital (page 61).

<<<

**5** Sampling the best of Copenhagen's **nightlife** at a hip club in **Vesterbro's Meatpacking District** or a microbrew pub in **Nørrebro** (page 130).

>>>

**6** Walking along the peaceful pebble beach and through the beech forest at **Møns Klint,** where white chalk cliffs glisten over the turquoise sea (page 241).

<<<

**7 Stargazing** on a secluded beach in the dark-sky preserves of Møn and Nyord (page 261).

>>>

**8** Finding your inner bard at **Kronborg Castle,** the magnificent Renaissance palace overlooking the crossing to Sweden (page 186).

>>>

**9** Taking a quick train ride across the dramatic Øresund Bridge to Malmö and going for *fika,* a Swedish coffee-and-cake break, after a stroll in one of the city's many parks (page 284).

**10** Going for a run in **Amager Nature Park,** a tranquil nature reserve where the evening sun glows orange through the reeds, birds sing, and the only sign of civilization is an aircraft on the distant horizon (page 222).

**11** Visiting **Louisiana,** a sprawling modern art museum and sculpture park, and soaking in creative and ever-evolving exhibitions that will put you in dreamland (page 171).

# EXPLORE
## COPENHAGEN & BEYOND

## BEST OF COPENHAGEN & BEYOND

To see the best of Copenhagen and its environs in five days, spend around three and a half days in the city and the rest exploring the surroundings. This itinerary is easy to follow using only public transportation.

### >DAY 1:

Spend your first day in Copenhagen getting oriented with the city's center, style, and café culture, and mix in a museum or two.

- Start the day with a **coffee** and *wienerbrød*—a Danish pastry—at a city center **café**.

- Stroll around the **Inner City's shopping streets**, taking in classic Danish designs and brands at places like **Hay**, **Royal Copenhagen,** and **Magasin du Nord**.

- Head to the **Round Tower (Rundetårn)**, steer up the cobblestone-spiraled walkway, and see the city from above.

- Grab lunch at a nearby restaurant or café such as **Schønemann** or **Democratic Coffee**.

- Walk off lunch in the **King's Garden (Kongens Have)**.

- Head into **Rosenborg Castle** to inspect the Crown Jewels or visit the **David Collection**, where a

shopping the Inner City streets, Amagertorv central square

## IF YOU HAVE...

- **One day:** Pick a main attraction like **Tivoli** and focus on that, then spend the evening in the **Meatpacking District** (Kødbyen) to get a feel for the city's exceptional food and nightlife scene.

- **A weekend:** Add two or three attractions in the **Inner City** with a thorough exploration of one or two neighborhoods away from the Inner City, such as **Nørrebro, Vesterbro,** or **Christianshavn.**

- **Five days:** Add a climb to the top of the **Church of Our Saviour** and visit **Christiania** and **Refshaleøen.** Don't miss **Louisiana,** and spend another day taking a side trip to **Malmö, Roskilde,** or **Helsingør.**

summer evening in the Meatpacking District, Vesterbro

- **One week or more:** With more than a week, spend a couple nights on **Møn,** where you can explore natural Denmark on two wheels or in a pair of hiking boots.

breathtaking collection of Islamic art awaits.

- In the evening, go for cocktails and nibbles at a local bar.

### >DAY 2:

Combine art and history on your second day in the city.

- After eating breakfast at your hotel, make your way to either the **National Museum of Denmark** for national history or walk across H. C. Andersens Boulevard to view classic art at **Ny Carlsberg Glyptotek**.

- These are both extensive museums, so you'll probably be ready for lunch afterward. Head to **Nyhavn** and get a bite.

- Walk around **Nyhavn** and be ready to photograph the harbor, then cross the **Inderhavnsbro** bridge to **Christianshavn**.

- Head to the **Church of Our Saviour**, the prettiest of all of Copenhagen's spires. If you have it

- Alternatively, if you have the funds and are able to prebook months in advance, spend your first night at one of Copenhagen's 15 **Michelin-starred restaurants**.

in you, climb the 400 steps to the top—the view is worth it.

- Enter nearby anarchist **Christiania**, and cross the lake for a pleasant walk alongside the reedy bank and improvised houses on the **Dyssen** pathway.

- Returning to Christianshavn, grab something traditionally Danish to eat at **Christianshavns Færgecafe** or get a homemade curry at **Curry Club**.

- If you're here in the summer, head instead to the **Reffen** street food market at **Refshaleøen**, with its atlas of different world cuisines. Stay for a craft beer at **Mikkeler Baghaven** and watch the sunset over the harbor.

## >DAY 3:

Head north to Helsingør and visit Louisiana Museum of Modern Art on the way back.

- Grab a to-go coffee and an almond croissant and take an early train to **Helsingør**.

- Spend the morning exploring **Kronborg**, the imposing, powerful 16th-century castle with royal chambers, a lookout tower, and (sometimes) Shakespearian actors. Be sure to seek out the mythical Danish hero solemnly waiting in the castle's darkest depths.

- Grab some lunch at **Elsinore Street Food**, where fish and chips, Brazilian tapioca, Indian butter chicken, and Syrian tapas are among the offerings.

- Take a bus or train the short distance back down the coast to Humlebæk and spend the rest of the afternoon and early evening at **Louisiana**, one of the world's leading modern art museums.

- Stay in the village for a traditional Danish dinner at **Gl. Humlebæk Kro**, housed in a building that resembles a charming, old hunting lodge.

## >DAY 4:

See some of Copenhagen's outer neighborhoods, and spend the afternoon at the city's iconic Tivoli amusement park.

- Start by bicycling or taking a bus to **Nørrebro**, where you can get Arabic-style breakfast at **Ali Bageri**

- Walk or bicycle down multicultural **Nørrebrogade** and soak up the atmosphere.

- Walk around **Assistens Cemetery** (Assistens Kirkegård), a historic cemetery that doubles as a park and is the resting place of many of Denmark's most famous daughters and sons.

- Make your way back to the Inner City, crossing the lakes at **Dronning Louises Bro**. Buy a coffee from a street wagon and

pause at a bench to watch the city move around you.

- Stop for lunch at **Torvehallerne**, the artisan food market next to Nørreport station, before you take a bus or S-train from here to **Copenhagen Central Station**.

- Leave the station and enter **Tivoli Gardens**—a legendary 19th-century amusement park—and enjoy rollercoasters, gardens, and entertainment. Stay until evening.

- From here, it's a short walk to the ultra-cool **Meatpacking District (Kødbyen)** in **Vesterbro**. Find a spot for food and drink such as **Kødbyens Fiskebar**, **Magasasa Dim Sum & Cocktails**, **Hija de Sanchez**, or **Warpigs**, or hop from one to the other.

- Weekend? End your night at **Jolene** and keep dancing until it's light.

## >DAY 5:

Spend a day breathing in the fresh air of the suburbs before finishing your stay at a famous sight back in town.

- Once you're up and ready (hopefully not too late), take the S-train to **Klampenborg** and go for a peaceful walk through **Jægersborg Dyrehave**. See how many deer you can spot.

various spices inside glass jars and in bulk inside the market of Torvehallerne

- Have lunch at the tranquil **Raadvad Kro.**

- Go to **Bellevue Beach** where in the summer you might be able to swim in the sea. Alternatively, take a **walk** along the **Strandvejen coast** and see the many buildings designed by famous Danish architect **Arne Jacobsen.**

- Back in Copenhagen, head out to **Langelinie** and walk along the promenade until you reach the famous **Little Mermaid** statue. If your timing is right, you might get the perfect photo opportunity.

- Go to **Nyhavn** and finish with wine and tapas near the waterfront, maybe at **Den Vandrette** or **Nebbiolo.**

# OUTSIDE COPENHAGEN

If you want to explore the areas outside Copenhagen, this itinerary will take you away from the city. A car is not essential for the trip but would be a useful asset, particularly if you are going to Møn and are not planning to bicycle or hike around the island.

## >DAY 1:

See some serious Danish history and a picturesque fishing village.

- Take an early train from Copenhagen to **Roskilde** and walk through the town and its park until you reach the **Viking Ship Museum** on the shores of Roskilde Fjord.

- After lunch at the museum's café or in town, head toward the towering **Roskilde Cathedral**—you can't miss it—and get lost in the legends of Danish monarchs from centuries past.

- Get a coffee or snack and take the train back to Copenhagen,

# WHERE TO GO FROM COPENHAGEN

| If You Want... | Destination | Why Go? | Distance and Travel Time from Copenhagen | How Long to Stay | Page |
|---|---|---|---|---|---|
| A quick trip outside Copenhagen | North of Copenhagen | Get a dose of nostalgia at a centuries-old amusement park or open-air museum in the suburbs | Klampenborg: 8 mi/13km; 25 mins by S-train Frilandsmuseet: 9.3 mi/15 km; 35 mins by S-train | ½-1 day | page 154 |
| World-class art | Louisiana MoMA | Explore one of the best collections of modern art in the world in a rustic coastal setting | 21.7 mi/35 km 35 mins by train | 1 day | page 168 |
| History and culture | Roskilde | See how the Vikings lived (and died) in the former capital | 21.7 mi/35 km 25 mins by train | 1 day | page 198 |
| | Helsingør | Immerse yourself in Shakespeare's *Hamlet* at the iconic Kronborg castle | 31 mi/50km 50 mins by train | 1 day | page 182 |
| A mix of history and nature | Dragør | Wander through the narrow alleys of the old town and the wide expanses of the Amager Nature Park | 9.3 mi/15km about 50 minutes by metro and bus; 25 mins by car | 1 day | page 215 |
| To see more of Scandinavia | Malmö | Get a taste of Swedish culture and enjoy an afternoon *fika*, just a short train ride away | 26 mi/42km 25 mins by train | 1-2 days | page 265 |
| Outdoor adventure | Møn | Spend a few days hiking, cycling, and stargazing in the wilds of Denmark, with dramatic white cliffs as a backdrop | 80 mi/128km 90 mins by car | 2 days | page 235 |

where you can change to a bus for **Dragør**, a small village on the south coast of the island of Amager.

- Walk through the timeless alleyways of Dragør's cobblestoned **old town** and stop for dinner.

## >DAY 2:

Cross the Øresund and discover Malmö, a Swedish little brother to Copenhagen.

- Take the train from Copenhagen to **Malmö**. Don't forget your passport.

- Spend the morning wandering the streets of **Gamla Staden** (the old town).

- Stop at a café for lunch before going to **Malmöhus Castle**, a 16th-century citadel with plenty of history about past fights with the Danes.

- Stroll the harbor with an ice cream in hand. From here you can see the Øresund Bridge and aircraft coming in to land at Copenhagen Airport. Consider staying the night in Dragør, although Copenhagen is close at hand, if there is no accommodation available.

- From there, the **Science and Maritime Museum** is just down the road. It looks a little worn from the outside but has some great collections of nostalgic pieces of engineering and a look back at the Øresund crossing in the days before the bridge was built.

- Get dinner and something to eat at food market **Malmö Saluhall** near the docks. It closes earlier on weekends, so if it's a Saturday or Sunday, head directly into town.

- Go for a drink at one of the old town's hotspots. **Lilla Torg** is where most of the action is.

Malmö Town Hall in Gamla Staden

## IF YOU LIKE...

### DESIGN AND ARCHITECTURE

The **Danish Architecture Center** showcases all that is good about new architecture and urban design. For some all-time classics, find the legacy of Arne Jacobsen around **Bellevue Beach** north of the city.

### FOOD AND DRINK

For fine dining, **Noma** and **Geranium** are the most famous of Copenhagen's restaurants and require advance planning. Alternatively, the **Meatpacking District (Kødbyen)** has some outstanding concept restaurants. Or head to a food market, such as **Reffen** or **Torvehallerne** in Copenhagen and **Elsinore Street Food** in Helsingør, to sample a bit of everything.

### POLITICS

**Slotsholmen,** the island separated from the Inner City by canals, exudes history, with **Christiansborg Palace,** an impressive palace that is the seat of Danish Parliament.

### OUTDOOR RECREATION

The island of **Møn** is an idyllic getaway for outdoor recreation, with activities such as sailing, stargazing, and bicycling, as well as easy access to the increasingly popular **Camøno** hiking trail. A little closer to Copenhagen, visit the massive **Amager Nature Park** for a peaceful getaway.

### ART

The classic Roman and Greek statues and French Impressionism at **Ny Carlsberg Glyptotek,** the outstanding **David Collection** of Islamic art, and the contemporary art at **Nikolaj Kunsthal** are all in Copenhagen. The crowning glory is **Louisiana Museum of Modern Art,** set in beautiful, modernist buildings and among spectacular rural coastline scenery.

### ROYALTY

**Amalienborg,** the royal residence where a changing of the guard takes place daily, and **Rosenborg,** the home of the Crown Jewels, are essential viewing. Head north to **Kronborg Castle** in **Helsingør** for some Shakespearean-style palace intrigue.

## >DAY 3:

Enjoy Malmö's many green spaces and proximity to the sea, while getting up close to Scandinavia's tallest building.

- After breakfast at your hotel or a café in town, head a little way out of the city center by bicycle or on foot and take a walk around **Pildammsparken**, where you'll find lakes, pavilions, a café, and an amphitheater.

- Head down to the harbor for lunch at **Saltimporten** and then walk off the meal by continuing toward Västra Hamnen.

- Spend a couple of hours walking along the promenade at **Västra Hamnen**, the rejuvenated former port, passing by the soaring, twisting **Turning Torso** skyscraper.

- If it's cold or windy, slip into the contemporary art museum **Moderna Museet Malmö**.

- Take a break in the afternoon for *fika* at the antique **Konditori Hollandia** or coffee bean specialist **Lilla Kafferosteriet**.

- Spend the evening back in the old town with dinner at **Bastard** or get a *döner* from **Jalla Jalla**—a kebab shop that is featured in a scene in the Nordic noir crime show *The Bridge*.

## >DAY 4:

Get away from it all by immersing yourself in the biosphere on the island of Møn.

- Travel via train and bus from Copenhagen, or rent a car from Copenhagen Airport and drive south to the island of **Møn**.

- Go directly to **Møns Klint** and visit **Geocenter Møns Klint** before taking a walk through the forest at **Klinteskoven**.

- Have lunch at the Geocenter's café before descending a long flight of stairs to the bottom of the seaside cliffs and walk slowly along the shore, taking time to enjoy the bright white of the chalky cliffs that are a quirk in Denmark's geology.

- Grab some delicious **Møn ice cream** before bringing out your romantic side at **Liselund**, an 18th-century landscaped park and accompanying manor house.

- Find a peaceful spot to stargaze, if the weather is kind enough to reveal Møn's **clear night skies,** before making your way to dinner and your accommodation in the town of Stege.

## >DAY 5:

Indulge in nostalgia and take in Møn's unspoiled marshlands and thriving nature.

- After breakfast at your accommodation or in Stege, spend a few hours deep in Danish nostalgia and chat with one of the volunteer staff members about island life in days gone by at **Thorsvang Samlermuseum**.

- Have coffee and an early lunch— traditional Danish, of course—in the museum's restaurant.

- Stop at Møns Museum and ask for directions to the first leg of the **Camøno** hiking trail, which leads to the stunning island of **Nyord**. It is connected to Møn by a narrow bridge, where you can birdwatch and stop for dinner at one of Denmark's smallest towns.

- Alternatively, **rent a bicycle** and ride to Nyord: the terrain on this side of the island is flat, and the destination is rewarding.

# BEFORE YOU GO

## WHEN TO GO

High season for tourism is during the European **summer** holiday months of **June**, **July**, and **August**. Many Danes have several weeks off work in July, which can swell crowds and make accommodations a challenge to find. Many museums and other sights extend their opening hours to cope with this, but popular spots such as Nyhavn and the Inner City's shopping streets can feel a little claustrophobic at times. Denmark's summer weather is consistently inconsistent, and recent years have seen both endless weeks of glorious sunshine and cold, gray washouts. It might be 15°C (59°F) one day and 30°C (86°F) the next.

In **winter**, be prepared for aching cold coupled with very short days in **December** and **January** and relentlessly freezing blasts of wind in February and March. The average temperatures for these months range between -1°C and -4°C (30°F and 25°F). The cold can easily be negotiated if you know what to expect and come equipped with plenty of warm layers. Danes are very good at compensating for the cold and dark by cranking up the *hygge*—it is at this time of year that the concept of lighting candles and hunkering down with friends and good food really comes into its own.

Some sights, particularly

deer in Jægersborg Dyrehave

## DAILY REMINDERS

- **Mondays:** Many museums are closed—double check before you go or plan a non-museum day if you're in town at the beginning of the week.

- **Weekends:** Shops and markets often have earlier closing times on weekends, and some are closed completely on Sundays.

ones with outside elements, have **shorter opening hours** in the winter season or even **close** completely: Tivoli, for example, shuts its doors outside of the warmer months, emerging from hibernation at Halloween and Christmas (although it did have a special 175th anniversary winter season in February 2018).

The fall and spring shoulder months—particularly **September** and **May**—can be great times to visit, hitting a good balance between crowd sizes, temperature, and daylight hours.

# WHAT TO PACK

The season will define much of what you pack for your trip to Copenhagen.

## FOR WINTER

Winters are harsh and long, and if you're out and about walking through town or by the harbor, the windchill factor is likely to make things feel even colder. Bring **warm, comfortable layers** like hoodies or sweaters, a good pair of **gloves,** and warm headgear. If you want to fit in with the Danes, include a stylish **scarf**. The winter months are December-March, but the temperature often drops in November, and it can still be quite cold in April, so check the forecast if you're planning to travel during these months.

## FOR SPRING AND FALL

Wet weather is common in the spring and fall, so bring a **waterproof jacket** and **footwear** to protect yourself from the elements. These are often useful during the summer, too.

## FOR SUMMER

Summer weather is unpredictable. You could find yourself needing both a jacket and swimsuit. **Sunscreen, a hat,** and **sunglasses** are useful on the brighter days: don't forget the sun stays up until approaching midnight from mid-June to mid-July.

## YEAR-ROUND

You'll need to bring **adaptors** to be able to plug your electrical devices into the round, two-pin sockets used in Denmark. American appliances run on 110 volts, while European appliances are **220 volts**. Modern electrics are dual voltage, so anything you bring should work on both American and European current. If you see a range of voltages printed on your device or its plug (something like "110–220"), then it will work in Europe.

Other things to remember include **medications** and a **small emergency kit**. In the summer, include **insect repellent**: mosquitos are common this time of year.

## WHAT YOU NEED TO KNOW

- **Currency:** Kroner (DKK)

- **Conversion Rate:** 1 kroner (DKK) = €0.13 (euro) = $0.15 (USD) = £0.12 (GBP) (exchange rate to dollar and British pound likely to vary)

- **Entry Requirements:** A valid passport that does not expire for the duration of your trip. Visitors from EU and Nordic countries do not need a visa. No visa is required for a stay less than 90 days if you are from the United States, the United Kingdom, Australia, New Zealand, or Canada. South African citizens who wish to travel to Denmark for 90 days or less must apply for a visa. U.K. travelers should check for new regulations post-Brexit. **Emergency Numbers:** Dial 112 for all emergency services.

- **Embassy Numbers:** U.S. Embassy Copenhagen, tel. 33 41 71 00; British Embassy Copenhagen, tel. 35 44 52 00; Australian Embassy in Denmark (Copenhagen), tel. 70 26 36 76; New Zealand Consulate-General Copenhagen, tel. 33 37 77 00; South African Embassy Copenhagen, tel. 39 18 01 85; Embassy of Canada to Denmark (Copenhagen), tel. 33 48 32 00.

- **Time Zone:** winter, CET/UTC+1; summer, CEST/UTC+2.

- **Electrical System:** 230V/50Hz, round two-pin outlets

- **Opening Hours:** restaurants, noon-10pm, some close later (11pm or midnight); shops, Mon-Fri 10am-6pm, some close earlier on Saturdays (between 2pm and 4pm), some open on Sundays; museums, 10am or 11am to 5pm or 6pm, and many are closed on Mondays.

Some extra **printed copies of your passport** are also good to have. If you want the extra feeling of security, you can leave your passport in a safety deposit box at your hotel while you're out and about and carry a copy with you, but remember you'll need your actual passport with you if you're going to Sweden (or crossing any border).

If possible, exchange a couple of hundred dollars for **Danish kroner** before departing for Copenhagen. Exchange booths at airports or train stations can offer poor rates, so it's also worth withdrawing cash you might need on hand for transportation or other last-minute costs from an ATM. Payment with Mastercard and Visa is available at the majority of shops, cafés and restaurants, and all hotels.

# GETTING THERE

## BY AIR

International flights arrive at **Copenhagen Airport**, also known colloquially as **Kastrup**. In October 2017, European Union rules were amended so that all passengers flying on routes between countries within the EU's Schengen Area of common visa policy must now have their passports checked.

Copenhagen Airport is the busiest airport in Scandinavia. **Scandinavian Airlines (SAS)** (www.flysas.com) operates services to

## KEY RESERVATIONS

Approximate times to reserve ahead for:

- **Michelin-starred restaurants:** 2-3 months

- **Popular or highly rated restaurants:** 1-2 weeks

- **Accommodation and tours:** in high season, 2-3 weeks; low season, 1 week

- **Camping:** high season, 1-3 days

a number of U.S. and Asian cities, including New York, Boston, Chicago, San Francisco, Beijing, Tokyo, and Hong Kong. **Ryanair** (www.ryanair.com), **Norwegian** (www.norwegian.com), and to a lesser extent **Easyjet** (www.easyjet.com) all operate low-budget flights to Copenhagen.

## BY CAR

Coming by car from either mainland Europe via Germany or from Sweden via the Øresund Bridge remains straightforward, given all three countries are within the EU's Schengen common visa policy area. Special **border controls**—in practice, random spot checks—were put in place in 2016 as a response to heightened arrivals of refugees and migrants, and these still apply at the time of writing, so it's essential to carry your **passport**.

**EU driver's licenses** are recognized in Denmark, as are driver's licenses from **non-EU (or EEA) countries**, provided they are printed with Latin letters or accompanied by a translation to Danish, English, or French. **International driver's licenses** are also valid. If you have a non-EU license and stay in Denmark for more than 90 days, you will need to convert your driver's license to a Danish license, which may require you to pass a theory and practical driving test, depending on where your original license was issued.

Most **car rental companies** require your **passport** and a credit card **deposit** in order to rent a car. You can reserve in advance using sites or apps such as www.rentalcars.com.

## BY TRAIN

**Copenhagen Central Station** (Hovedbanegården, often shortened to Hovedbanen) is linked to the **European train network** via Stockholm to the north and Amsterdam, Hamburg, and Berlin to the south and east.

International tickets can be booked via Denmark's state rail operator **DSB** (tel. 70 13 14 18; www.dsb.dk). If you are planning an extended trip around Denmark or further afield by rail, it is advisable to look into the two main European rail passes, **Eurail** (www.eurail.com) for non-Europeans and **Interrail** (www.interrail.eu) for European citizens. Both are particularly useful for travelers under 25.

## BY BUS

German company **Flixbus** (www.flixbus.com) operates international bus services into Denmark from both **Sweden** and **Germany**. **Gråhundbus** (http://graahundbus. dk) has three departures daily that serve the **Copenhagen-Malmö** route, and a 120kr return is a less-expensive, if also less-convenient, option than the train.

## GETTING AROUND

### BY CAR

Copenhagen is quite **driver-friendly**. Danes are defensive drivers and respectful of traffic laws—this is a generalization, of course, and there are exceptions. If I were to critique Danish driving traits, I would say the Danes can be impatient or selfish about giving way to other cars, cyclists, or pedestrians, but that is perhaps not everyone's perception. As a driver unused to the city, you will need to pay attention to the high volume of **bicycle traffic** and be aware that **bicyclists have the right of way** when you are turning right—have a long look in the rearview mirror and make sure it's all clear before you turn.

Cars are **not essential** for travelling around Copenhagen. The **bus, Metro, and metropolitan train (the S-trains) network** is comprehensive, efficient, and easy to use, and the city is compact. You could also opt to really get into the spirit of the city and use a **bicycle** during your stay, joining the hordes of two-wheeled Copenhagen commuters.

Outside of Copenhagen where distances increase, having a car can make travel more convenient. This is particularly the case on Møn, where public transport is far less exhaustive. Many people visit

Copenhagen metro train at a station

## BUDGETING

- **Cup of coffee:** 25-60kr

- **Beer on tap:** 45-75kr

- *Smørrebrød:* 40-75kr

- **Breakfast:** 70-100kr

- **Lunch:** 90-150kr

- **Dinner:** restaurant from 200kr, Michelin-starred restaurants 1,500-3,500kr

- **Entrance fees for museums or art galleries:** 50-150kr

- **Rejsekort travel card:** 80kr (plus 70kr credit) from machines at Metro and rail stations

- **Single Metro ticket with Rejsekort:** 15kr; standard ticket 24kr (zones 1-2)

- **Bike rental:** from 80kr for 24 hours

- **Hotel:** from 400kr per person per night

Møn specifically to experience the island's beautiful, natural terrain on foot or by bicycle, but if you're not doing this, consider renting a car.

### BY TRAIN
Denmark's state rail operator **DSB** (tel. 70 13 14 18; www.dsb.dk)

is responsible for all services between Copenhagen and the other destinations in this book, including the Øresundståg service to Malmö. Tickets can be purchased via the company's website or app. Travel to Møn involves changing to a bus at Vordingborg, the last town in Zealand before the Queen Alexandrine Bridge that connects Møn with Zealand, but you can purchase a ticket for the whole journey from DSB (the destination will be Stege, Møn's largest town).

### BY BUS
Visitors wishing to travel around Denmark may do so with **Sortbillet** (https://sortbillet.dk), **Kombardo Expressen** (www.kombardoexpressen.dk), or **Flixbus**. Buses from all three companies arrive and depart from the remarkably unglamorous **Ingerslevsgade** terminal, which is actually no more than a parking lane on a side road near the Copenhagen Central station. **Flixbus** and **Gråhundbus** have regular, daily departures from Copenhagen to Malmö, which are a little less expensive but not as convenient as taking the train.

# COPENHAGEN

## From the pomp and history of

the Royal Quarter to anarchist Christiania, from the shiny, clean lines of groundbreaking architecture and design to the gritty inner-city life and urban chic of Vesterbro and Nørrebro, the city of Copenhagen is a thrilling mix of the classic and modern, of expectations and surprises.

Visitors come to Copenhagen for a variety of reasons: to view epoch architecture, live a healthy lifestyle, eat at a Michelin-starred restaurant, shop for designer clothes, drink coffee by the canal, or even just to see the Little Mermaid statue up close

## HIGHLIGHTS

✪ **THE ROUND TOWER:** The dizzying medieval attraction in the center of Copenhagen is an architectural outlier and an easy stop on your way through the historical Inner City (page 51).

✪ **THE DAVID COLLECTION:** This impressive, comprehensive, and meticulously curated collection of Islamic Art is a labor of love and one of the underrated gems in a city with a strong museum game (page 53).

✪ **AMALIENBORG:** The old money of European regal tradition is on display daily during the changing of the guard at the official royal residence (page 54).

✪ **TIVOLI GARDENS:** The amusement park from the 19th century mixes modern thrills and old-school leisure, retaining the charm of its Victorian origins (page 55).

✪ **NY CARLSBERG GLYPTOTEK:** A supremely elegant museum that is home to the classics: Greek and Roman sculptures, Egyptian hieroglyphs, and paintings by Picasso and Monet (page 57).

✪ **CHURCH OF OUR SAVIOUR:** The church's gilded spire is like a daredevil version of the Round Tower, being considerably higher and with the last section of the climb to the top outside. It's not necessarily for the faint-hearted, especially on one of Denmark's many windy days, but you'll be rewarded with stunning panoramic views of Christianshavn (page 69).

✪ **REFSHALEØEN:** Listen to the wind rattle the old shipping containers as you bite into your pulled chicken burger from Reffen, the nearby food market, and enjoy the harbor view at this former industrial-area-turned-new-hip destination (page 70).

✪ **CHRISTIANIA:** This anarchist enclave is as unique an experience as you'll find in any European city since nowhere else has an entire community emerged from the same set of social, historical, and logistical circumstances. Independent traders, autonomous cafés, artistic spaces, and improvised houses on hidden, green pathways are integral to its vibe (page 71).

✪ **CAFÉ CULTURE:** Start your day slowly with coffee and *wienerbrød*. Enjoy them outside if the weather's fine or, in Copenhagen spring tradition (if it's warmish), even if it's not (page 98).

✪ **NØRREBRO AND VESTERBRO NIGHTLIFE:** Wash down your *döner* with a microbrew or two in gritty Nørrebro before heading across to Vesterbro's Meatpacking District for some seriously stylish Scandinavian nightclubs (page 130).

(and you'll need to get close to be able to see it).

Although these elements are part of its beauty, Copenhagen is more than what's advertised in tourism brochures and in "happiest city in the world" articles. It's looking up into a yellowing street lamp on a misty winter night, sitting on your bicycle waiting for the light to change and thinking it never will. It's emerging from the cemetery—reclaimed by Copenhageners as a park—where Hans Christian Andersen is buried and finding yourself in the middle of a flea market in Nørrebro, the most ethnically diverse neighborhood in the city. It's jogging with locals on quiet lakeside paths in the early morning, or mingling with them in the Friday night hustle of an earthy bodega—a pub where you don't have to be a local to feel like a regular. These small moments bring the stories of high-quality standards and discerning taste to life.

# Orientation and Planning

Copenhagen is administratively and in common parlance divided into Greater Copenhagen and the more central districts, which are normally referred to simply as Copenhagen. It is the latter that this chapter will primarily be concerned with.

Geography neatly divides the city into separate neighborhoods. Some, such as Nørrebro, are not technically districts in their own right, while others like Frederiksberg have their own municipalities and don't actually have Copenhagen postcodes. I will use the popular designations rather than the technical ones.

The names of the neighborhoods Vesterbro (West Bridge), Nørrebro (North Bridge), and Østerbro (East Bridge) come from their geographical relation to the Inner City. The Inner City refers to the area between Knippelsbro bridge in the east and the three lakes in the west, and from Copenhagen Central Station in the south to Østerport Station and the street of Dag Hammarskjölds Allé in the north. To the east and southeast

of the Inner City, separated by the Copenhagen Harbor, is the island district of Christianshavn. The southernmost part of urban Copenhagen is located on the island of Amager across the South Harbor, completing the broader set of neighborhoods.

## NØRREPORT AND AROUND

Visitors to Copenhagen are more than likely to spend time on the central Inner City streets around Nørreport, the primary hub for public transportation within Copenhagen. Strøget, the busy, high street-esque thoroughfare with its chain stores, souvenir shops and prestigious design outlets, connects the Town Hall Square to **Kongens Nytorv,** a large square at the opposite end of the Inner City from the City Hall, and the Nyhavn area, running almost east to west. Købmagergade, a bustling shopping street that passes the **Round Tower** and joins with the busy Nørreport area, bisects Strøget. From here, it is a short walk north to the **King's Garden** and **Rosenborg Palace**—a museum and culture-rich area.

## GREATER INNER CITY

Spreading out beyond the busiest areas around Nørreport, the greater Inner City stretches from Copenhagen Central Station bordering Vesterbro in the south to the Nordhavn harbor, the Lakes, and Kastellet (the Citadel) in the north. The chaotic area around **Copenhagen Central Station** and the nearby Ingerslevsgade bus terminal can feel a bit confusing to a newcomer. However, careful negotiation will bring you in no time at all to the pedestrian-friendly Halmtorvet and Sønder Boulevard or to the Fisketorvet shopping mall. Behind Fisketorvet, the "Cycle Snake," a bendy bike bridge, takes you across the harbor to the Islands Brygge neighborhood, a residential part of Amager (there's also a pedestrian bridge). **Tivoli,** opposite the Central Station, is a sight that can't be overlooked. The area stretching alongside the Lakes to the north and east is home to a number of first-class museums and open space. Bridges that lead into Frederiksberg, Nørrebro, and Østerbro span the Lakes themselves.

## SLOTSHOLMEN

Slotsholmen is actually a small island cut onto the edge of Zealand by canals. Translated literally, it means "the castle islet." It is one of the most commonly referred to subdivisions of the Inner City. The southern end of Købmagergade runs into Højbro Plads, an elongated square where buskers wait in line to play music in front of the Illum department store. Cross the bridge at the far end of Højbro Plads, and the impressive **Christiansborg,** the seat of the Danish Parliament, will stand imposingly before you.

Beyond Christiansborg, the **Royal Library** sits on the harborside part of Slotsholmen, facing Christianshavn on the other side of the water. From here, you can walk along the quay, with Nyhavn to the north and the **Danish Architecture Center** and Langebro (bridge) in the opposite direction.

## NYHAVN

Nyhavn is located directly to the east of the Inner City and the Kongens Nytorv public square, and north of Slotsholmen along Copenhagen Harbor, which is served by the harbor bus At Kongens Nytorv, the Royal Theatre faces Nyhavn, a postcard-maker's heaven with its row of 18th-century buildings in a rainbow of facades. Nyhavn's quay was dug out by Swedish prisoners of war in the 1670s and had an unfavorable reputation of housing a hive of rascals and tough seafaring types as recently as the 1970s. A regeneration project began to turn it into the powerhouse of tourism it is today. The eastern end of Nyhavn connects to Christianshavn via the new Inderhavnsbro bridge.

## VESTERBRO AND FREDERIKSBERG

Leave Copenhagen Central Station to the west and you will emerge on Istedgade, once the heart of a tough area at the center of a drug addiction epidemic. Traces of that time are still visible today, but the street, which marks the beginning of Vesterbro, does not feel hostile. Hip, smart, and cool, Vesterbro boasts arguably the prime food and nightlife destination in the city. Parallel to the north of Istedgade runs Vesterbrogade, a broad street lined with shops and businesses, while just south of Istedgade is Kødbyen, the **Meatpacking District,**

# Copenhagen

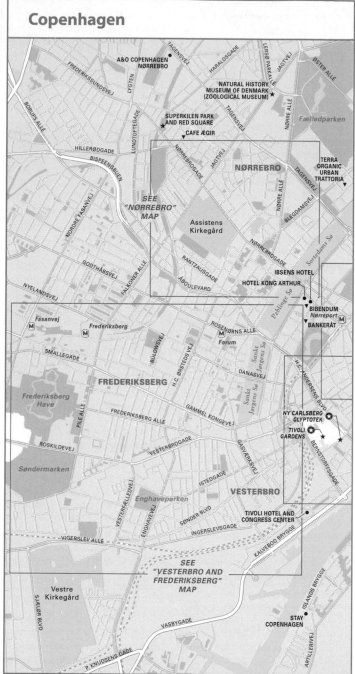

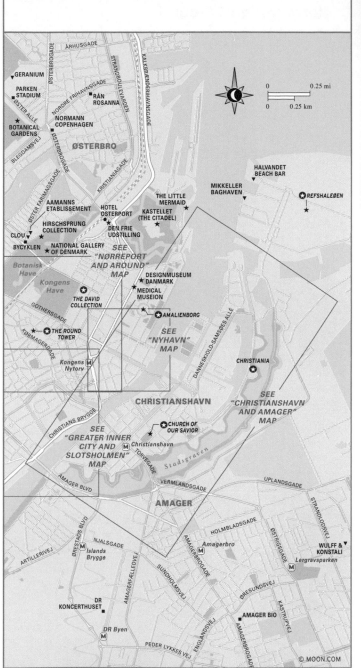

ÅRHUSGADE

★ GERANIUM

■ PARKEN STADIUM

NORDRE FRIHAVNSGADE

RÅN ■ ROSANNA

NORMANN COPENHAGEN

ØSTERBRO

BLEGDAMSVEJ

KRISTIANIAGADE

THE LITTLE ★ MERMAID

HALVANDET BEACH BAR

MIKKELLER ▼ BAGHAVEN

⊛ REFSHALEØEN ★

ØSTER FARIMAGSGADE

AAMANNS ETABLISSEMENT

HOTEL ØSTERPORT ●

HIRSCHSPRUNG COLLECTION

CLOU ★ BYCYKLEN ★

NATIONAL GALLERY OF DENMARK ■

KASTELLET (THE CITADEL) ★

DEN FRIE UDSTILLING ■

**SEE "NØRREPORT AND AROUND" MAP**

Botanisk Have

Kongens Have

GOTHERSGADE

❂ THE DAVID COLLECTION

DESIGNMUSEUM ★ DANMARK

MEDICAL MUSEION ■

⊛ ★ AMALIENBORG

**SEE "NYHAVN" MAP**

KØBMAGERGADE

★ ❂ THE ROUND TOWER

Kongens Nytorv Ⓜ

DANNESKIOLD-SAMSØES ALLÉ

CHRISTIANIA ❂

**CHRISTIANSHAVN**

CHRISTIANS BRYGGE

**SEE "GREATER INNER CITY AND SLOTSHOLMEN" MAP**

❂ CHURCH OF OUR SAVIOR

Ⓜ Christianshavn

TORVEGADE

Stadsgraven

**SEE "CHRISTIANSHAVN AND AMAGER" MAP**

AMAGER BLVD

VERMLANDSGADE

UPLANDSGADE

**AMAGER**

HOLMBLADSGADE

ARTILLERIVEJ

ØRESTADS BLVD

NJALSGADE

Ⓜ Islands Brygge

AMAGERFÆLLEDVEJ

SUNDHOLMSVEJ

AMAGERBROGADE

Amagerbro Ⓜ

ØSTRIGSGADE

STRANDLODSVEJ

WULFF & ▼ KONSTALI

Lergravsparken Ⓜ

ØRESUNDSVEJ

KASTRUPVEJ

DR ■ KONCERTHUSET

Ⓜ DR Byen

ENGLANDSVEJ

AMAGER BIO ■

AMAGERBROGADE

PEDER LYKKES VEJ

© MOON.COM

0      0.25 mi
0      0.25 km

# Nørreport and Around

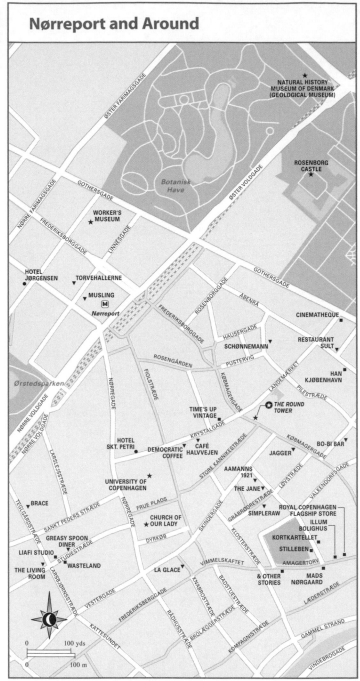

NATURAL HISTORY
MUSEUM OF DENMARK
(GEOLOGICAL MUSEUM)

ØSTER FARIMAGSGADE

ROSENBORG
CASTLE

GOTHERSGADE

Botanisk
Have

ØSTER VOLDGADE

NØRRE FARIMAGSGADE

FREDERIKSBORGGADE

WORKER'S
MUSEUM

LINNÉSGADE

HOTEL
JØRGENSEN

TORVEHALLERNE

GOTHERSGADE

MUSLING
Ⓜ
Nørreport

ROSENBORGGADE

ÅBENRÅ

FREDERIKSBORGGADE

CINEMATHEQUE

HAUSERGADE

SCHØNNEMANN

RESTAURANT
SULT

ROSENGÅRDEN

PUSTERVIG

Ørstedsparken

NØRREGADE

FIOLSTRÆDE

KØBMAGERGADE

LANDEMÆRKET

HAN
KJØBENHAVN

PILESTRÆDE

NØRRE VOLDGADE

TIME'S UP
VINTAGE

THE ROUND
TOWER

NØRRE VOLDGADE

KRYSTALGADE

KØBMAGERGADE

BO-BI BAR

HOTEL
SKT. PETRI

DEMOCRATIC
COFFEE

CAFÉ
HALVVEJEN

STORE KANNIKESTRÆDE

JAGGER

LARSLEJSSTRÆDE

AAMANNS
1921

LØVSTRÆDE

VALKENDORFSGADE

UNIVERSITY OF
COPENHAGEN

NØRREGADE

THE JANE

TEGLGÅRDSTRÆDE

BRACE

FRUE PLADS

GRÅBRØDRESTRÆDE

SIMPLERAW

ROYAL COPENHAGEN
FLAGSHIP STORE

SANKT PEDERS STRÆDE

CHURCH OF
OUR LADY

SKINDERGADE

ILLUM
BOLIGHUS

KLOSTERSTRÆDE

GREASY SPOON
DINER

DYRKØB

KORTKARTELLET

LIAFI STUDIO

STUDIESTRÆDE

STILLEBEN

THE LIVING
ROOM

WASTELAND

LA GLACE

VIMMELSKAFTET

AMAGERTORV

LARSBJØRNSSTRÆDE

& OTHER
STORIES

MADS
NØRGAARD

VESTERGADE

FREDERIKSBERGGADE

KNABROSTRÆDE

BADSTUESTRÆDE

LÆDERSTRÆDE

KATTESUNDET

RÅDHUSSTRÆDE

BROLÆGGERSTRÆDE

GAMMEL STRAND

KOMPAGNISTRÆDE

VINDEBROGADE

0        100 yds

0        100 m

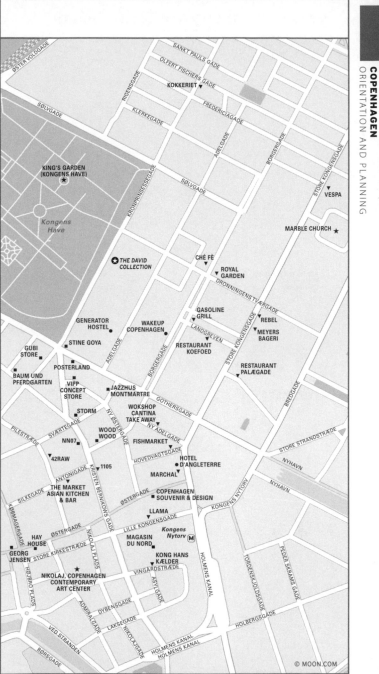

ØSTER VOLDGADE

SANKT PAULS GADE

OLFERT FISCHERS GADE

RIGENSGADE

KOKKERIET ▼

FREDERICIAGADE

SØLVGADE

KLERKEGADE

ADELGADE

BORGERGADE

STORE KONGENSGADE

KRONPRINSESSEGADE

SØLVGADE

VESPA ▼

KING'S GARDEN
(KONGENS HAVE) ★

MARBLE CHURCH ★

Kongens
Have

✪ THE DAVID
COLLECTION

CHÉ FÉ ▼

ROYAL
GARDEN ▼

DRONNINGENS TVÆRGADE

GASOLINE
GRILL ▼

REBEL ▼

GENERATOR
HOSTEL ●

WAKEUP
COPENHAGEN ●

LANDGREVEN

STORE KONGENSGADE

MEYERS
BAGERI ▼

STINE GOYA ■

ADELGADE

BORGERGADE

RESTAURANT
KOEFOED ●

RESTAURANT
PALÆGADE ▼

GUBI
STORE ■

POSTERLAND ■

BAUM UND
PFERDGARTEN ■

VIPP
CONCEPT
STORE ■

JAZZHUS
MONTMARTRE ■

BREDGADE

STORM ■

GOTHERSGADE

WOKSHOP
CANTINA
TAKE AWAY ▼

PILESTRÆDE

SVÆRTEGADE

NY ØSTERGADE

WOOD
WOOD ■

NY ADELGADE

STORE STRANDSTRÆDE

NN07 ■

FISHMARKET ■

NYHAVN

42RAW ▼

1105 ■

HOVEDVAGTSGADE

HOTEL
D'ANGLETERRE ●

KRISTEN BERNIKOWS GADE

ANTONIGADE

MARCHAL ▼

NYHAVN

SILKEGADE

THE MARKET
ASIAN KITCHEN
& BAR ▼

ØSTERGADE

COPENHAGEN
SOUVENIR & DESIGN ■

KONGENS NYTORV

KØBMAGERGADE

HAY
HOUSE ■

ØSTERGADE

NIKOLAJ PLADS

LILLE KONGENSGADE

LLAMA ▼

Kongens
Nytorv Ⓜ

TORGENSKJOLDSGADE

PEDER SKRAMS GADE

GEORG
JENSEN ■

STORE KIRKESTRÆDE

MAGASIN
DU NORD ■

HØJBRO PLADS

NIKOLAJ, COPENHAGEN
CONTEMPORARY
ART CENTER ★

KONG HANS
KÆLDER ▼

VINGÅRDSTRÆDE

ASYLGADE

HOLMENS KANAL

ADMIRALGADE

DYBENSGADE

NIKOLAJGADE

VED STRANDEN

LAKSEGADE

HOLMENS KANAL

HOLBERGSGADE

BØRSGADE

HOLMENS KANAL

© MOON.COM

# Greater Inner City and Slotsholmen

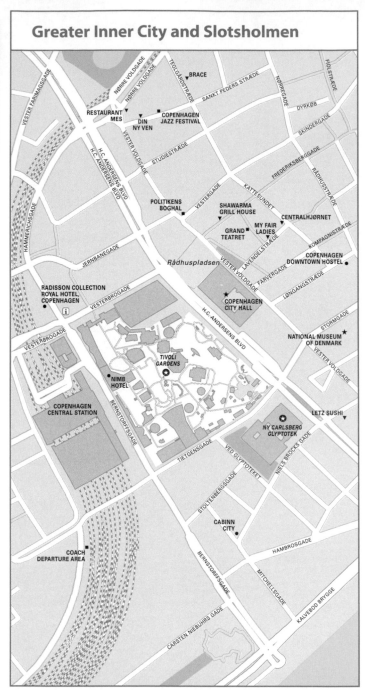

NØRRE VOLDGADE

TEGLGÅRDSTRÆDE

▶ BRACE

SANKT PEDERS STRÆDE

NØRREGADE

FIOLSTRÆDE

DYRKØB

SKINDERGADE

RESTAURANT MES

▼ DIN NY VEN

COPENHAGEN JAZZ FESTIVAL

STUDIESTRÆDE

VESTER VOLDGADE

H.C. ANDERSENS BLVD

FREDERIKSBERGGADE

RÅDHUSSTRÆDE

KATTESUNDET

VESTERGADE

POLITIKENS BOGHAL

SHAWARMA GRILL HOUSE

CENTRALHJØRNET

GRAND TEATRET

MY FAIR LADIES

KOMPAGNISTRÆDE

LAVENDELSTRÆDE

COPENHAGEN DOWNTOWN HOSTEL ●

*Rådhuspladsen*

VESTER VOLDGADE

FARVERGADE

LØNGANGSTRÆDE

RADISSON COLLECTION ROYAL HOTEL, COPENHAGEN
ℹ️

VESTERBROGADE

★ COPENHAGEN CITY HALL

H.C. ANDERSENS BLVD

STORMGADE

NATIONAL MUSEUM OF DENMARK ★

VESTER VOLDGADE

VESTERBROGADE

*TIVOLI GARDENS* ✦

● NIMB HOTEL

COPENHAGEN CENTRAL STATION

BERNSTORFFSGADE

LETZ SUSHI

*NY CARLSBERG GLYPTOTEK* ✿

TIETGENSGADE

VED GLYPTOTEKET

NIELS BROCKS GADE

STOLTENBERGGADE

CABINN CITY ●

HAMBROSGADE

COACH DEPARTURE AREA ■

BERNSTORFFSGADE

MITCHELLSGADE

KALVEBOD BRYGGE

CARSTEN NIEBUHRS GADE

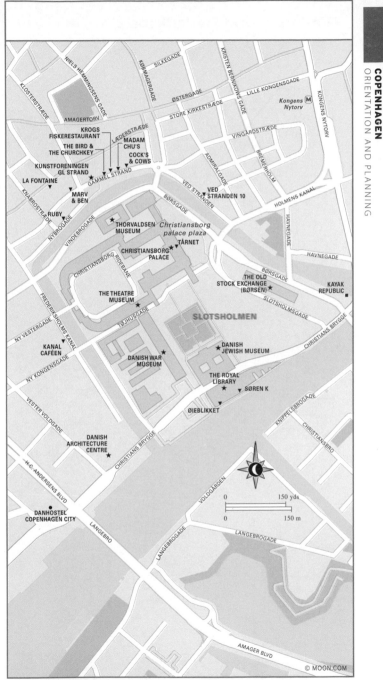

# Vesterbro and Frederiksberg

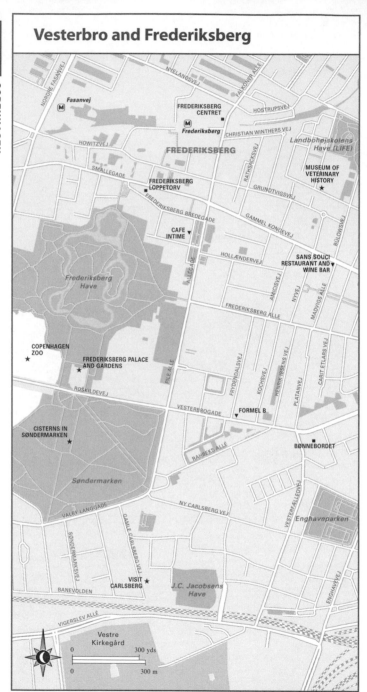

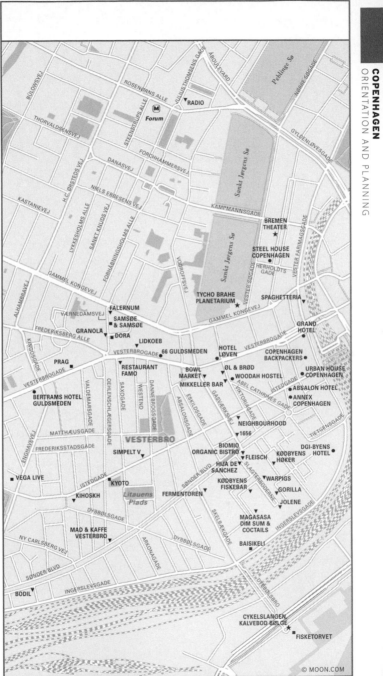

BØLOWSVEJ

ROSENØRNS ALLE

JULIUS THOMSENS GADE

ÅBOULEVARD

Peblinge Sø

HOBRØSGADE

GYLDENLØVESGADE

THORVALDSENSVEJ

STEENSTRUPS ALLE

RADIO

M Forum

FORCHHAMMERSVEJ

DANASVEJ

H.C. ØRSTEDSVEJ

NIELS EBBESENS VEJ

KAMPMANNSGADE

KASTANIEVEJ

LYKKESHOLMS ALLE

SANKT KNUDS VEJ

FORBLÆNINGSHOLMS ALLE

Sankt Jørgens Sø

VODROFFSVEJ

BREMEN THEATER ★

STEEL HOUSE COPENHAGEN ★

HERHOLDTS GADE

VESTER FARIMAGSGADE

VESTERSØGADE

ALHAMBRAVEJ

GAMMEL KONGEVEJ

Sankt Jørgens Sø

TYCHO BRAHE PLANETARIUM ★

SPAGHETTERIA

KINGOSGADE

FALERNUM

VÆRNEDAMSVEJ

SAMSØE & SAMSØE

GAMMEL KONGEVEJ

GRAND HOTEL

FREDERIKSBERG ALLE

GRANOLA

DORA

LIDKOEB

VESTERBROGADE

66 GULDSMEDEN

HOTEL LØVEN

VESTERBROGADE

COPENHAGEN BACKPACKERS

PRAG

VESTERBROGADE

RESTAURANT FAMO

BOWL MARKET ▼

ØL & BRØD

WOODAH HOSTEL

ISTEDGADE

URBAN HOUSE COPENHAGEN

VALDEMARSGADE

OEHLENSCHLÆGERSGADE

SAXOGADE

WESTEND

DANNEBROGSGADE

MIKKELLER BAR

ABEL CATHRINES GADE

GASVÆRKSVEJ

ABSALON HOTEL

ANNEX COPENHAGEN

BERTRAMS HOTEL GULDSMEDEN

VIKTORIAGADE

ENGHAVEVEJ

MATTHÆUSGADE

ESKILDSGADE

ABSALONSGADE

NEIGHBOURHOOD

TIETGENSGADE

FREDERIKSSTADSGADE

1656 ▼

**VESTERBRO**

SIMPELT V ▼

BIOMIO

ORGANIC BISTRO ▼

FLEISCH ▼

KØDBYENS HØKER

DGI-BYENS HOTEL

VEGA LIVE ▼

ISTEDGADE

KYOTO ▼

SØNDER BLVD

HIJA DE SANCHEZ

KØDBYENS FISKEBAR

SLAGTERBODERNE

WARPIGS

GORILLA

KIHOSKH ▼

*Litauens Plads*

FERMENTEREN ▼

JOLENE

DYBBØLSGADE

SKELBÆKGADE

INGERSLEVSGADE

MAD & KAFFE VESTERBRO ▼

NY CARLSBERG VEJ

ARKONAGADE

DYBBØLSGADE

MAGASASA DIM SUM & COCTAILS

BAISIKELI ●

SØNDER BLVD

INGERSLEVSGADE

NY DYBBØLSBRO

BODIL ▼

CYKELSLANGEN KALVEBOD BØLGE ★

FISKETORVET ●

© MOON.COM

# Nørrebro

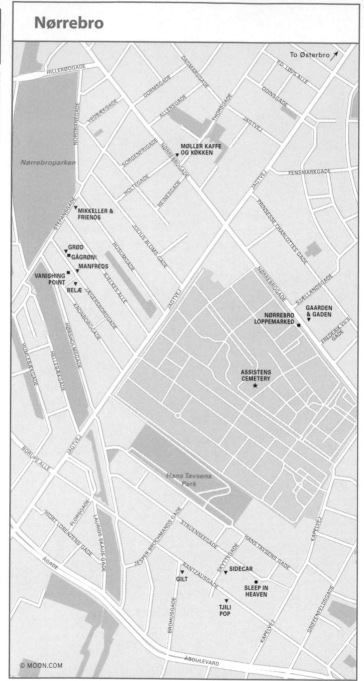

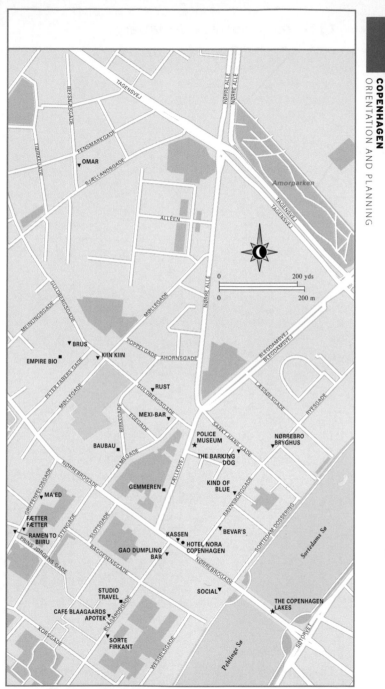

# Christianshavn and Amager

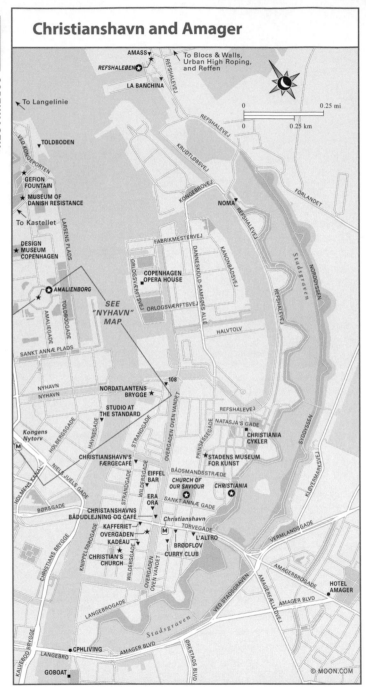

AMASS

REFSHALEØEN

LA BANCHINA

To Blocs & Walls,
Urban High Roping,
and Reffen

REFSHALEVEJ

To Langelinie

TOLDBODEN

KRUDTLØBSVEJ

KONGEBROVEJ

FØRLANDET

NOMA

VED KONGEPORTEN

★ GEFION
FOUNTAIN

★ MUSEUM OF
DANISH RESISTANCE

To Kastellet

DESIGN
MUSEUM
COPENHAGEN

LARSENS PLADS

FABRIKMESTERVEJ

DANNESKIOLD-SAMSØES ALLE

KANONBÅDSVEJ

ORLOGSVÆRFTSVEJ

COPENHAGEN
OPERA HOUSE

Stadsgraven

NORDDYSSEN

★ AMALIENBORG

TOLDBODGADE

AMALIEGADE

SEE
"NYHAVN"
MAP

ORLOGSVÆRFTSVEJ

HALVTOLV

SANKT ANNÆ PLADS

NYHAVN
NYHAVN

108

NORDATLANTENS
BRYGGE ★

OVERGADEN OVEN VANDET

REFSHALEVEJ

NATASJA'S GADE

★ CHRISTIANIA
CYKLER

HOLBERGSGADE

STUDIO AT
THE STANDARD

HAVNEGADE

STRANDGADE

PRINSESSEGADE

STIDYSSEN

Kongens
Nytorv

M

CHRISTIANSHAVN'S
FÆRGECAFE ▼

EIFFEL
BAR ▼

★ STADENS MUSEUM
FOR KUNST

NIELS JUELS GADE

WILDERSGADE

BÅDSMANDSSTRÆDE

CHURCH OF
OUR SAVIOUR
✪

CHRISTIANIA
✪

HOLMENS KANAL

ERA
ORA ▼

SANKT ANNÆ GADE

BØRSGADE

STRANDGADE

CHRISTIANSHAVNS
BÅDUDLEJNING OG CAFÉ

KAFFERIET ★

OVERGADEN
KADEAU ▼

Christianshavn
TORVEGADE

M

L'ALTRO

KNIPPELSBROGADE

CHRISTIANS
CHURCH ★

BRØDFLOV
CURRY CLUB

VERMLANDSGADE

CHRISTIANS BRYGGE

WILDERSGADE

OVERGADEN
OVEN VANDET

AMAGERBROGADE

KLØVERMARKSVEJ

LANGEBROGADE

VED STADSGRAVEN

AMAGERALLÉVEJ

HOTEL
AMAGER

AMAGER BLVD

KALVEBOD BRYGGE

LANGEBRO

● CPHLIVING

AMAGER BLVD

ØRESTADS BLVD

Stadsgraven

■ GOBOAT

© MOON.COM

N

0        0.25 mi

0        0.25 km

which has reached a level of high post-industrial aesthetic and is home to a range of excellent places to eat, drink, and stay out late.

Continuing west you will find the **Carlsberg District,** where the original brewery of the international lager monolith was built in 1847. The area is characterized by the handsome, red brick 19th-century buildings, many of which have been restored. Look out for the giant twin elephant statues at the Elephant Gate and Tower.

Crossing Vesterbro to the north on Valdemarsgade or Enghavevej connects to middle-class Frederiksberg, a serene neighborhood that begins with the regal **Frederiksberg Palace and Gardens,** where you can enjoy a summer boat ride on the canals.

## NØRREBRO AND ØSTERBRO

A long walk north through Frederiksberg on the main streets of Allegade and Falkoner Alle takes you directly to Nørrebro's **Assistens Cemetery,** the final resting place of Hans Christian Andersen and Søren Kierkegaard, among others. The clay-colored wall of the northern flank of the cemetery from one side of Nørrebrogade, which is the main street through the district, leads back to Nørreport and the Inner City via the popular Queen Louise's Bridge (Dronning Louises Bro). **Nørrebrogade** is the beating heart of urban Nørrebro, with a cluster of eating and nightlife options around Stefansgade, Griffenfeldsgade, and Ravnsborggade. Further north, the Superkilen Park and Red Square are public outdoors areas. These areas, often socioeconomically marginalized but a magnet for diversity, are a culturally important

face of Copenhagen and provide context to the polished grandeur of Slotsholmen and Amalienborg.

Head northeast on Jagtvej, and you'll be between Nørrebro and middle-class Østerbro, which is marked by **Fælled Park** and **Telia Parken,** the home stadium of Denmark's national football (soccer) team. Østerbrogade runs almost directly north-south, leading back to the Trianglen junction and *søerne*—the Lakes—which separate Østerbro and Nørrebro from the Inner City. In the opposite direction, Østerbrogade heads north toward outlying districts and daytrip destinations north of the city.

## CHRISTIANSHAVN AND AMAGER

Slotsholmen connects via the Knippelsbro bridge to Christianshavn, a highly historic harbor area where cobbled streets, canals, and townhouses have to a great degree retained their 17th-century layout. Christianshavn is itself a series of artificial islands connected by canals, with Zealand on its west side and Amager to the east and south. Heading north from Christianshavn on Prinsessegade will take you to the entrance to **Christiania.** You can't miss the gate, which is on the far side of the heavily graffitied walls of Gallopperiet—an art center and café located within the enclave. Christiania is a subversive, part-autonomous haven, which started as a hippie squat in the 1970s. It is now a run-by-consensus community that often comes under the microscope of the Danish state and law enforcement. While Christiania is part of Christianshavn, geographically, they are considered two different neighborhoods.

## WHERE TO STAY IF...

### IT'S YOUR FIRST TIME IN COPENHAGEN

Staying closely to **Nyhavn** or **Kongens Nytorv** will ensure Copenhagen's iconic sights, harbor, nightlife, and a rich choice of shopping and entertainment options are right outside your door.

### YOU WANT TO SURROUND YOURSELF WITH DANISH DESIGN

Stay close to the **harbor** in the area south of the central station where the **Inner City merges with Vesterbro**. Here, you'll be close to the Danish Architecture Center in the blocky new BLOX building, the Royal Library, aka the Black Diamond—one of the most handsome buildings in the city—and the central shopping area with its plethora of top-end interior design and furniture flagship outlets.

### YOU'RE SEEKING *HYGGE*

**Christianshavn**, a 500-year-old island district of quaint bridges, canals, and historical buildings, has plenty of cafés, lakes, and parks for you to feel the cozy vibe all year round. The nearby Christiania, an anarchist alternative living enclave, has a form of *hygge* all of its own, which is embodied in alternative cafés and artsy surroundings.

### YOUR DAY BEGINS AT 5PM

The **Istedgade** and **Meatpacking District** areas of **Vesterbro** are lively at all hours. Once a rough-handed industrial area with a reputation for crime and drugs, Istedgade retains its hard edge but has been transformed by the gentrification of its immediate surroundings. The Meatpacking District's heady mix of international-class craft beers, concept restaurants, and thumping nightclubs attract crowds of attractive, cool, young people from Copenhagen and the world.

### YOU WANT TO FEEL LIKE A COPENHAGENER

**Amager,** the large island to the south of Copenhagen proper, has a district which is administratively part of the city. It takes no time to reach by bicycle or Metro. Lacking in cultural attractions, it makes up for this with a wealth of nature—always a hit with Danes—and a salt-of-the-earth city atmosphere.

### YOU WANT TO GO BACK TO ANOTHER ERA

Pick a spot in the **Inner City** close to **Slotsholmen**, the island district that is home to Christiansborg, the former royal palace and seat of parliament. A wealth of museums abounds in this area, and Amalienborg Palace is only a short distance to the north.

---

At the far northern end of Christianshavn, is Refshaleøen, a promontory and industrial area that is quickly being populated with gourmet restaurants, activity centers, and a not-to-be-missed street food market. Though road connections make Refshaleøen feel like an extension of Christianshavn, it is actually part of Amager, a larger island to the east and south of Christianshavn. Amager has an urban sprawl but offers no shortage of cafés, restaurants, and shopping along the main drag of Amagerbrogade, while the Islands Brygge area on the Amager side of the harbor, has a large park area and swimming facilities and becomes a magnet for sunbathing Copenhageners in the summer. Amager is also home to Copenhagen's largest nature reserve, Amager Nature Park. The northern section of this reserve, Amager Fælled, is just to the east of Islands Brygge.

## KASTELLET AND LANGELINIE

Kastellet and Langelinie are possibly as familiar to visitors as to

Copenhageners, given that these areas are somewhat removed from residential neighborhoods or the bustling commercial districts. Heading north from Nyhavn along the harborfront will bring you to the grassy, former military base known as Kastellet, and eventually to the statue of Hans Christian Andersen's Little Mermaid, which sits near the entrance of the Langelinie pier and promenade. Blink and you'll miss her.

# PLANNING YOUR TIME

Copenhagen is the center of Danish politics and culture and like other capital cities requires an extended stay to be seen from a perspective nearing that of permanent residents. However, given its relatively small size, three or four well-planned days can be enough to gain insight into and understanding of its layout, diversity, and history. Spend a day wandering the crowded central shopping districts of the Inner City and the royal and parliamentary quarters around Amalienborg and Christiansborg, respectively. Then spend a second day in quaint Christianshavn and its alter ego enclave Christiania, followed by one to two leisurely days immersing yourself in local life in the less touristy but no less international neighborhoods of Vesterbro and Nørrebro, and you'll have a good idea of what Copenhagen is about. Extra days added to this basic itinerary provide the opportunity to visit some of the city's impressive array of museums, including the National Gallery of Denmark, Ny Carlsberg Glyptotek, and the David Collection, or to wander around natural areas such as Amager Fælled and Amager Strandpark in the south.

## SIGHTSEEING PASSES
### Parkmuseerne

Parkmuseerne (The Park Museums) is a collective term for six attractions in the vicinity of King's Garden: the David Collection, Hirschsprung Collection, Rosenborg Castle, the National Gallery of Denmark, the Natural History Museum of Denmark, and Cinematheque.

A single ticket, the Parkmuseerne ticket, can be purchased giving access to all six attractions. It costs 195kr, a substantial saving on the individual costs of visiting the museums, and is valid for an entire year, during which each of the museums can be visited once. It can be bought at any of the participating museums. At the David Collection, where entrance is free, ticket holders are entitled to a 10 percent discount in the bookstore. The ticket provides admission to one film screening at Cinematheque, which is part of the Danish Film Institute.

### Copenhagen Card

The Copenhagen Card (https://copenhagencard.com) is a prepaid card that provides admission to 86 attractions in the city as well as travel on buses, S-trains, and the Metro throughout the capital region. It also offers discounts at selected restaurants, bars, and sightseeing tours. Full details of these can be found on the Copenhagen Card website and app. Prices depend on the length of validity of the card and range €54-121 for adults for periods of 24-120 hours. It can provide value for money, and it's also a convenient way to access public transport. However, many of the attractions it covers may be closed on the day you visit, particularly if that day is a Monday, and if you want to walk or cycle around town at a leisurely pace you may not visit enough sights to cover your costs. Overall, it's more suitable for those who prefer carefully planned, busy trips to a slower, more flexible program.

# Itinerary Ideas

## COPENHAGEN ON DAY ONE

This itinerary takes in the splendor of the Royal Quarter as well as some sight-seeing big-hitters.

**1** Start your day the Danish way with a coffee to go and dense cinnamon *kanelsnurre* from the **Meyers Bageri** branch at Store Kongensgade in the Royal Quarter near Amalienborg.

**2** Five minutes' walk from the bakery, take in the full scope of royal Danish history at **Amalienborg** with a wander through the chambers of royal monarchs past, gardens, and gala halls.

**3** A short walk from Amalienborg is **Nyhavn**, manna for Instagrammers with its photogenic pastel-colored houses, and extensive selection of quay-side restaurants and cafés, some of which are housed on boats.

**4** Stop in for a New Nordic lunch and coffee at **Apollo Bar**.

**5** After lunch, take a leisurely walk along the historic **waterfront**, taking in the quayside of Inderhavnsbroen, which is a bicycle and pedestrian bridge. Have a peek at a survivor from Nyhavn's brusquer past—the tattoo parlor in the basement of Nyhavn 17, **Tattoo Ole**—even if you don't want to get inked (though, of course, you can if you want—they take walk-ins).

**6** Cross Kongens Nytorv (King's New Square) and head directly for the **Round Tower**, a 42-meter-high (138 ft), 17th-century tower smack in the middle of modern Copenhagen. The swirling, snail-like stone path to the top is unlike anything else in European period architecture. Enjoy the view and don't run on the way down.

**7** After descending from the Round Tower, catch your breath and people watch on one of the benches in the leisurely, regal **Kongens Have (King's Garden)**.

**8** Walk to **Kastellet** (the Citadel), a well-preserved example of a European medieval star fortress. Walk around the raised rampart, which provides views across the harbor and the surrounding historic buildings.

**9**   On the far side of the citadel, get your camera ready and be quick: the **Little Mermaid** sits discreetly by the water at the beginning of the Langelinie promenade.

**10 Restaurant Palægade** is a fine option to round off a day of classic Copenhagen sights: The Danish-inspired dishes served in a rustic setting are worth a little splurge.

**11**   Finish the day with a drink at legendary jazz bar **La Fontaine,** where live concerts take place every Friday, Saturday, and Sunday.

## COPENHAGEN ON DAY TWO

Get familiar with the Copenhagen built by the industrious King Christian IV, including the charming Christianshavn and autonomous Christiania. Nearby, Refshaleøen, a purely industrial dockyard until recently, is quickly becoming a destination not to miss.

**1**   Start with coffee and croissant at **Kafferiet** on the corner of Torvegade, the main road through Christianshavn. Seat yourself at the window and watch the morning traffic of bicycling parents with their kids in trailers, suited officials on their way to ministry buildings, and international students heading to the library.

**2**   Head southeast on **Torvegade** to the **canals**, where you can take an easy walk among the winding streets, many of which are cobbled and connected by arched stone bridges. This area is quiet and picturesque with sailboats moored alongside the paths and plenty of nooks to explore.

**3**   Visit the baroque **Church of Our Saviour**. The real treat is climbing (almost) to the top of the 90-meter-tall (295 ft.) spire, where the handrail and footsteps taper into nothing, and you are left with a vertigo-inducing—but spectacular—panorama over the rooftops of Christianshavn. It gets busy on summer afternoons, so it's better to come in the morning during peak season.

**4**   For lunch, enjoy a selection of herring and salmon *smørrebrød* at the more than 150-year-old **Christianshavns Færgecafé**, with its black lettering and easy-to-find location on the corner of one of Christianshavn's cobbled bridges. If you're feeling brave, you can wash down lunch with a glass of the breathtakingly strong Danish herbal liqueur schnapps.

**5**   Walk along Prinsessegade to the main entrance of the alternative enclave of **Christiania** and stop for a coffee at **Café Nemoland**.

**6**   Cross the bridge to **Dyssen** and walk along the quiet riverside pathways flanked by the unique houses of improvised architecture.

# Copenhagen Itineraries

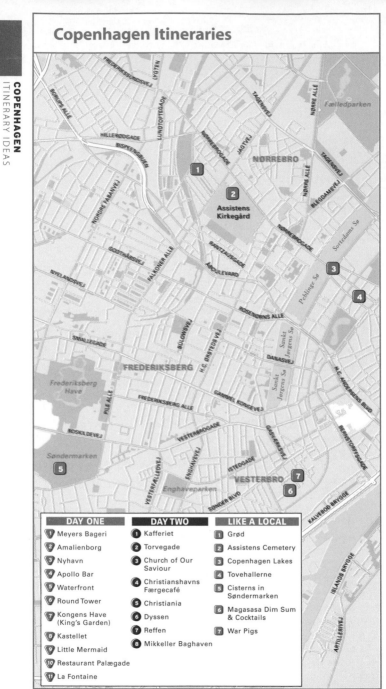

| DAY ONE | DAY TWO | LIKE A LOCAL |
|---------|---------|--------------|
| 1 Meyers Bageri | 1 Kafferiet | 1 Grød |
| 2 Amalienborg | 2 Torvegade | 2 Assistens Cemetery |
| 3 Nyhavn | 3 Church of Our Saviour | 3 Copenhagen Lakes |
| 4 Apollo Bar | 4 Christianshavns Færgecafé | 4 Tovehallerne |
| 5 Waterfront | 5 Christiania | 5 Cisterns in Søndermarken |
| 6 Round Tower | 6 Dyssen | 6 Magasasa Dim Sum & Cocktails |
| 7 Kongens Have (King's Garden) | 7 Reffen | 7 War Pigs |
| 8 Kastellet | 8 Mikkeller Baghaven | |
| 9 Little Mermaid | | |
| 10 Restaurant Palægade | | |
| 11 La Fontaine | | |

**7** Continue north to Refshaleøen, and visit the new street market **Reffen** for dinner. The pulled chicken burger and fries at Miss Mums and the African spicy potatoes and sausages at Hot Batata are recommended but the choice is huge.

**8** Stay around and end the night with a craft beer or a few at **Mikkeller Baghaven**.

## COPENHAGEN LIKE A LOCAL

Vesterbro, Frederiksberg, and Nørrebro are arguably the real Copenhagen. These primarily residential neighborhoods are crying out to be explored, either by bicycle or on foot, combined with bus, Metro, or taxi hops. Highlights include the Meatpacking District, the graves of Søren Kierkegaard and Hans Christian Andersen at Assistens Cemetery, and Frederiksberg Palace, not to mention a variety of nightlife options.

**1** Start your day in Nørrebro at porridge specialist **Grød**. Its memorable selection of oats and other healthy, breakfasty delights should give you a good constitution for the day ahead.

**2** Head to the **Assistens Cemetery** and join the locals for a morning stroll around the gravestones. See if you can spot the resting places of some of Denmark's most famous people: Kierkegaard, Andersen, physicist Niels Bohr, poet Michael Strunge, and singer Natasja.

**3** From Assistens, walk along the lively Nørrebrogade in the direction of Inner City to Queen Louise's Bridge (Dronning Louises Bro) for a stroll around the **Copenhagen Lakes** and a little bit of people watching from a bench. If you need a pick-me-up, check out one of the coffee vendors.

**4** Cross Queen Louise's Bridge and venture into the Inner City for lunch at **Torvehallerne**, an indoor food market where more than 60 different food stalls are good for everything from seafood to cheese, pastries to smoked meats, wraps to freshly ground coffee.

**5** Walk about 4km (2.5 mi) southwest of Queen Louise's Bridge (or to save time, take bus 6A from Nørreport) to the **Cisterns in Søndermarken,** an underground labyrinth originally built to secure water supply to the city that is now the setting for art exhibitions and other events.

**6** When you're hungry, head east into Vesterbro (you can jump back on the 6A in the opposite direction) along Vesterbrogade before turning right and continuing south, crossing the rough-and-ready Istedgade before eventually arriving at the Meatpacking District (Kødbyen), the embodiment of modern Copenhagen cool, for dinner at **Magasasa Dim Sum & Cocktails**.

**7** Continue your evening with a few pints at nearby brewpub **WarPigs**.

# Sights

Copenhagen's sightseeing opportunities span the classical (Amalienborg Palace) to the modern (Nikolaj, Copenhagen Contemporary Art Center), panoramic views from church towers to floating city tours on harbor taxis. Some of Denmark's most highly regarded exports are well represented—design and architecture, for example—and can be explored throughout Copenhagen's buildings, museums, and city landscape. The majority of the sights are found in the Inner City area, but there are several gems further afield—the old Carlsberg district, Frederiksberg Palace, and the Cisterns, to name a few. The Inner City is primed for exploration on two wheels, but it is also compact enough that you can cover a lot of ground on foot.

## NØRREPORT AND AROUND

The central area around Nørreport boasts a throng of cultural delights, including the underrated gem of the David Collection as well as museums connected to the park area around Kongens Have. The gardens and lawns are a great place to go for a walk along tree-lined paths while taking in the impressive red-bricked splendor of Rosenborg Castle. The Round Tower is a short walk away along Købmagergade. Everything is easy to get to; Nørreport is the primary internal transport hub for the city.

### CHURCH OF OUR LADY (Vor Frue Kirke)

*Nørregade 8; tel. 33 15 10 78; www.domkirken.dk; daily 8am-5pm; free; bus 2A, 9A Stormbroen (Nationalmuseet)*

The Church of Our Lady is Copenhagen's cathedral and has been the central place of worship in the city since the 13th century. The modern church was built in the middle of the spacious Frue Plads (Square of Our Lady) in the 1810s and 1820s, designed by neo-Classicist architect C. F. Hansen, as evidenced by the contrast between the Greek-style columns that almost seem grafted onto the otherwise boxy edifice. Inside, sculptures depict Jesus Christ and his Apostles. The church has seen much of Copenhagen's history. A small museum recounts this (11am-4pm Mon.-Thurs. and noon-4pm Sat.-Sun.). The funeral of Søren Kierkegaard, the grandfather of Danish intellectualism, took place at the church. More recently, Crown Prince Frederik married Australian Mary Donaldson here in 2004.

### ✪ THE ROUND TOWER (Rundetårn)

*Købmagergade 52A; tel. 33 73 03 73; www.rundetaarn.dk; daily 10am-8pm; adults 25kr, children 5kr; bus 5C 9A, 14, 66 Nørreport, S-Train B, C Nørreport; Metro Nørreport*

"I can't control this song / it sticks with me / and goes round and round and round and round with you," indie singer and Copenhagen native Katinka sings in one of the catchier Danish tunes of recent years. She was singing about a breakup, not a 17th-century stone observatory tower. But Katinka's words make for a calming backdrop to the dizzying climb up the cobbled, coiled ascent of the Round

Tower, one of Copenhagen's essential sights. The 42-meter-high (138 ft.) tower rises above the rooftops yet appears out of nowhere in the middle of the Inner City's high streets. Its swirling, snail-like stone path to the top is 209 meters (686 ft.) in length, twisting through seven and a half circles. It was built in the 1630s by master constructor King Christian IV as part of the Trinitatis Church at a time when a library and astronomical observatory were desired for Copenhagen University students. In modern times, the tower is used as a quirky location for temporary art exhibitions—check the website to see what might be on exhibit during your visit—but the primary reason for visiting is the unique climb to the top and spectacular view over Copenhagen city.

## NIKOLAJ, COPENHAGEN CONTEMPORARY ART CENTER
### (Nikolaj Kunsthal)

*Nikolaj Plads 10; tel. 33 18 17 80; www. nikolajkunsthal.dk; Tues.-Fri. noon-6pm, Sat.-Sun. 11am-5pm; adults 70kr, students 50kr, under 17 free; bus 1A (Holmens Kirke (Holmens Kanal), 9A, 2A Christiansborg (Vindebrogade)*

"I'm not a church," reads the sign outside Nikolaj, Copenhagen Contemporary Art Center, found in the former Church of St. Nicholas which originates from the 13th century. The historical surroundings sit in contrast with the art center now housed by the building. Nikolaj Kunsthal is a venue for contemporary and experimental art; visitors sometimes even become part of the installations, which are rotated regularly. Anohni, Haroon Mirza, and Tommy Støckel all had exhibitions at the

aerial view of the Round Tower in the city center

museum in 2018, reflecting the mix of styles—visual art, sculpture, and design—a visitor might come across, as well as the combination of Danish and international art.

## KING'S GARDEN
### (Kongens Have)

*Øster Voldgade 4; tel. 33 95 42 00; https:// slks.dk/slotte-ejendomme-og-haver; advisory opening times summer, 7am-10pm, winter 7am-5pm; free; bus 5A, 6A, 14, 40, 42, 43 Nørreport, Metro Nørreport*

Opened to the public at the beginning of the 1700s, the King's Garden is one of the most popular parks in Copenhagen and forms a large, green space near the crossroads of the Inner City and Nørrebro. Its long, straight pathways that crisscross linden boulevards and enclaves adorned with statues and benches make it a great spot for picnicking in summer or a quieting, contemplative winter walk. Nearby Rosenborg Palace further adds to the scenery and gracious feel of the surroundings, where families, students, and professionals alike can be found taking a break on a typical afternoon, along with the many visitors on their way to and from the many landmarks and sights in the vicinity. It is lined with an abundance of refreshment stops and is a short walk from Nørreport Station.

## ✪ THE DAVID COLLECTION
### (Davids Samling)

*Kronprinsessegade 30; tel. 33 73 49 49; www.davidmus.dk; Tues.-Sun. 10am-5pm, Wed. until 9pm; free; bus 1A (Store Kongensgade/Bredgade), 26 (Sølvgade), Metro Nørreport, Kongens Nytorv*

The plush, polished former home of Christian Ludvig David houses the largest collection of Islamic art in Scandinavia. David, a prominent lawyer and art collector in the first half of the 20th century, legally protected his collection and made it open to the public in 1945. The beautiful artifacts have been gathered from across the Islamic world—from Morocco to Indonesia—and span the 8th-19th centuries, which means that local cultural influences on Islamic art can be appreciated. The extensive museum also includes 18th and 19th century European art and a collection of early modern Danish art, including both paintings and sculptures, with a considerable collection of works by famous 19th-century Copenhagen artist Vilhelm Hammershøi. However, my favorite part of the museum remains the beautiful Islamic art. With its ornate calligraphy and alternative ways of depicting perspective compared to European art from corresponding periods, as well as the surprise of Islamic works from China, Sufis, and dervishes, the entire exhibit is a pleasure. The captivating presentation in backlit, darkened rooms further serves to make this museum highly recommendable. Tours lasting around one hour can be arranged for the price of 650kr for a maximum 12 people and are recommended; the guides are helpful and highly knowledgeable. Book at least two days in advance but ideally before that, by calling the museum or emailing m.korsholm@davidmus.dk.

## WORKER'S MUSEUM
### (Arbejdermuseet)

*Rømersgade 22; tel. 33 93 25 75; www. arbejdermuseet.dk; daily 10am-4pm, Wed. until 7pm; over 25 75kr, 18-25 55kr, under 18 free; bus 5C Nørre Farimagsgade (Frederiksborggade), Metro, S-Train Nørreport*

Strong labor movements course through the veins of Danish society,

Amalienborg

and the Worker's Museum is a glimpse into this history. Much of the museum is dedicated to the 1950s and the life and home of the Sørensen family, a normal family that moved to Copenhagen in the late 19th century. Period goods available to the Danish working classes, such as bitter wartime-style coffee (using substitute) and cakes can be sampled in the museum's Coffee Bar, giving you a real taste of Copenhagen in the 1950s.

## ✪ AMALIENBORG

*Amalienborg Slotsplads 5; tel. 33 15 32 86; www.kongernessamling.dk/amalienborg; Jan.-Apr. & Nov.-Dec. 11am-4pm; May-June, Sept.-Oct.: 10am-4pm; June-Sept.: 10am-5pm; adults 95kr, students 65kr, under 17 free; bus 1A, 20E (Bredgade and Store Kongensgade), 26 (Dronningens Tværgade), 350S (Kongens Nytorv)*

Royal Danish history is on full display at Amalienborg, the official home of the royal family. As with Denmark's popular royals, the palace is an accessible example of old European monarchy. The chambers of royal monarchs past, gardens, and gala halls can be visited. Don't miss the changing of the guard each day at noon (the Royal Guards actually march through town from their barracks at Rosenborg Castle, finishing at Amalienborg for the changeover). Actually formed of four palaces, two of which are open to the public, permanent exhibitions cover the history of the Danish monarchy and everyday life of royalty, and the exquisite furniture of rococo palace rooms is also open to view. Tours of the regular exhibitions and of some special exhibitions are available for groups, including inside the museum and Christian VII's Palace as well as small guided city walks in the Royal Quarter. Tours last about one hour and must be booked at least two weeks in advance by calling 33 18 60 55 on Tues.-Fri. between 10am and noon.

## ROSENBORG CASTLE

*Øster Voldgade 4A; tel. 33 15 32 86; www.kongernessamling.dk; Nov.-Apr. 10am-3pm;*

One of the most rewarding ways to spend a day in Copenhagen is to leave the Inner City behind and visit areas that don't conform to stereotypes about Scandinavia. Copenhagen is far from a homogeneous city, and diversity is one of its strengths. Nowhere is this more explicit than in Nørrebro—sometimes dubbed "Nørrebronx" by locals—a large, urban area with many new immigrants, refugees, second- and third-generation minority ethnic Danes, international students, and Bohemian types who are attracted by the unpretentious and multicultural makeup of this part of Copenhagen.

The Middle Eastern influence on Nørrebro is impossible to miss. Shop signs have Arabic translations, travel agents advertise fares to Beirut and Istanbul, and shisha cafés abound. If you look closely enough, you'll find food that is a faithful replica of what you might be served down a side street in Damascus or Jerusalem.

It's worth hunting for a Lebanese bakery called **Ali Bageri** for a taste of the *manakish*—a flat-baked dough topped with oily *za'atar* (a spice blend), cheese, or ground meat—among other authentic snacks (page 116).

**Sorte Firkant** (Blågårdsgade 29 A-E; tel. 50 20 22 69), a Middle Eastern-style bar started in 2017 by refugees from Syria, currently serves food only on Saturdays, but if your timing is right, it's more than worth the effort to visit. Indulge in hummus, soujouk, kibbeh, labneh, fatteh, and all the other staples of the east Mediterranean cuisine (page 117).

Nørrebro is not the only part of Copenhagen that's home to Middle Eastern culture. The **David Collection** is a quite remarkable museum of Islamic art housed in the plush, polished former home of benefactor Christian Ludvig David, a prominent lawyer and art collector in the first half of the 20th century (page 53).

---

*Apr.-June 10am-4pm; June-Sept. 9am-6pm; adults 110kr, students 75kr, under 17 free; combined ticket with Amalienborg 155kr; bus 5A, 6A, 14, 40, 42, 43 Nørreport, Metro Nørreport*

The red brick turrets and elegant spires of Christian IV's Dutch Renaisssance castle, Rosenborg, stand out splendidly in the middle of Copenhagen. Built in the early 1600s and a royal residence until 1710, the castle overlooks the King's Garden (Kongens Have), a serene green space with crisscrossing paths and alleys of linden trees. Rosenborg Castle houses four centuries of royal treasures, regalia, and the Crown Jewels, the Crown Regalia, the Crown of the Absolutist Kings, and the Queens' Crown, all of which are on display in the Treasury. There's plenty more for those fascinated by royal history, pomp, and ceremony too—coronation thrones, silver life-sized lions, and immaculately preserved monarchs' chambers as well as the personal stories of past rulers of the Kingdom. Guided tours of Rosenborg, taking around an hour, are available, and all tours finish in the Treasury. Price: Mon.-Fri. 800kr plus admission fee, Sat.-Sun. 900kr plus admission fee. Book at least two weeks ahead by emailing booking@kosa.dk or by calling 33 18 60 55 Tues.-Fri. between 10am-noon.

# GREATER INNER CITY

## TOP EXPERIENCE

### ✪ TIVOLI GARDENS

*Vesterbrogade 3; tel. 33 15 10 01; www. tivoli.dk; Mar.-Sept., mid-Oct.-early Nov., mid-Nov.-Dec. 31: Mon.-Thurs. 11am-11pm; Fri.-Sun. 11am-midnight; adults & over 8 100kr, children 3-7 50kr, under 3 free; bus Tivoli v. Hovedbanegåden (Central Station); S-Train: Hovedbanegåden (Central Station)*

Tivoli Gardens at night

The iconic 19th-century amusement park Tivoli Gardens celebrated its 175th anniversary in 2018, and it remains among Denmark's most popular attractions, with tourists and locals alike.

Founder Georg Carstensen opened Tivoli Gardens on August 15, 1843, with the permission of King Frederik VIII. Hans Christian Andersen visited the new park in its opening season and is said to have drawn inspiration for his description of the emperor's garden in his fairy tale "The Nightingale." Some of Tivoli's most iconic buildings were built during its early decades and still survive, including the open-air Pantomime Theater, the pagoda-like Japanese Tower, now home to an Asian restaurant, and the Nimb, built in the "Moorish style" to house a restaurant and today a boutique, five-star hotel.

Unique in its location in front of Copenhagen Central Station, Tivoli's four roller coasters and dozens of other rides catering to all ages can be seen peeking out over its walls like naughty children from the moment you arrive in the city. The 103-year-old original wooden roller coaster known simply as the *Rutschebane* is still going strong, while spectacular new rides such as the 60 mph (100 kph) Vertigo also offer more modern thrills. The latter was voted Europe's Best Ride in 2014. Other amusements include arcades and an aquarium, and there are ongoing theater performances and concerts.

The amusement park is particularly magical at Christmas. Decorated trees, the woodland smell of fir chips spread around the grounds, and the aroma of traditional Danish Christmas treats like roasted almonds, strong mulled wine known as *glögg*, and small donuts called *æbleskiver* all help to give Tivoli an unmistakable festive feeling. Meanwhile, the Tivoli Concert Hall has regular performances of *The Nutcracker*. But even at other times of the year, magical lights are part of Tivoli's heritage: regular displays culminate in a huge fireworks festival during the Christmas opening.

An entire afternoon and evening can comfortably be spent inside the park. The perfect way to end your day at the fairgrounds is by dancing with your loved one while a live band plays swing stanzas. You won't go hungry either: Tivoli counts many chain and fast food restaurants among its concessions. Popular Copenhagen sushi brand Letz has an outlet here, but if you prefer fish and chips or Danish *frikadeller* (meatballs), you can have that too.

## NATIONAL MUSEUM OF DENMARK (Nationalmuseet)

*Prince's Mansion, Ny Vestergade 10; tel. 33 13 44 11; https://natmus.dk; Tues.-Sun. 10am-5pm; Victorian Home, Mon.-Fri. 10am-4pm; adults 85kr, under 18 free, joint ticket for 1 adult + 1 child 75kr; bus 1A, 2A, 9A (Stormbroen, Nationalmuseet)*

The imposing National Museum contains a wealth of exhibits that cover Denmark from the Stone Age through the Vikings and up to 20th century: 14,000 years of history. Look out for the "Egtved Girl," a Bronze Age Dane whose preserved remains were discovered in a bog in Jutland in 1921. She can be found neatly enclosed in a glass case in the ancient Denmark section. Other highlights include the Trundholm sun chariot, which is a 1,400-year-old gilded statue of a horse on spoked wheels pulling a disc that originates from the Nordic Bronze Age. It's thought to be evidence of astronomic knowledge. There is also a medieval runestone that was found in Greenland.

There are eight main exhibitions in all, encompassing Danish prehistory, the Middle Ages, and the Renaissance; royal coins and medals, stories from Danish colonies, an ethnographic collection, and a children's museum, as well as a collection of classical and near eastern antiquities, where some of the exhibits come from digs carried out by Danish archaeologists. In additions to these, there are temporary exhibitions that change regularly.

The Prince's Mansion has been home to Denmark's National Museum since 1853 and was most recently renovated in 2008. It could be argued that the style of the exhibitions is not the most modern in Copenhagen, although perhaps it doesn't need to be. Its two floors are easy to navigate.

The fully furnished and preserved Victorian-era merchant's apartment, located close to the National Museum, can be visited on Saturday from June to September at 2pm (ticket 95 kr) as an add-on to the main museum. Ask at the information desk for tickets.

## ✪ NY CARLSBERG GLYPTOTEK

*Dantes Plads 7; tel. 33 41 81 41; www. glyptoteket.com; Tues.-Sun. 11am-6pm; Thurs. 11am-10pm; adults 115kr, under 27 85kr; under 1 free; Tues. free (special exhibitions 60kr); bus 1A, 2A, 9A Glyptoteket (Tietgensgade)*

Brewer Carl Jacobsen—yes, of Carlsberg fame—had a penchant

National Museum of Denmark

for art and history. The philanthropist and art collector founded Ny Carlsberg Glyptotek in 1897, and it has grown over the decades into a beautiful exhibition of historical artifacts. Today, the sumptuous collection will get art lovers drooling from the moment they pass the resplendent columns and arches of the museum's entrance.

Ancient Greece, Rome, and Egypt are among the classical cultures that can be enjoyed in a stroll through the marble halls of the Glyptotek, with exhibits up to 3,500 years old. Greek and Roman sculptures abound; Egyptian exhibits include sculptures and architecture from the time of pharoahs, including Ramesses II and Tutankhamun.

These classical exhibitions sit alongside modern collections from the Danish "Golden Age" and French paintings by, for example, Matisse, Cézanne, and Monet, as well as the largest collection of Rodin sculptures outside of France. Other artists represented include Picasso and Van Gogh.

Incidentally, the "Ny" (Danish for "new") in the museum's name dates back to a feud between Jacobsen and his father, who for a time, ran rival Carlsberg breweries named New Carlsberg and Old Carlsberg, which later merged.

## NATIONAL GALLERY OF DENMARK
### (Statens Museum for Kunst)

*Sølvgade 48-50; tel. 33 74 84 94; www.smk. dk; Tues.-Sun. 11am-5pm, Wed. until 8pm; adults 110kr, adult with child 90kr, under 30 85kr, under 18 free; bus 5C, 6A, 11A, 14, 26 Nørreport; Metro Nørreport; S-Train Nørreport, Østerport*

The National Gallery of Denmark—financed by the state—has Danish and foreign art collections dating up to 700 years old. It includes special as well as permanent exhibitions, the latter including the Renaissance and the Danish Golden Age, 20th-century French art, and around 2,500 cast statues. The art exhibition includes more than 260,000 Scandinavian and international paintings, including the world's largest collections by Danish masters Christen Købke and Vilhelm Hammershøi. Rembrandt, Cranach, and Mantegna can be listed among a weighty European section. Look out, too, for Abraham Bloemaert's *Venus and Adonis*, as well as Mantegna's *Christ as the Suffering Redeemer*. This is all best enjoyed at a relaxed pace over the course of an afternoon. It's included in the Park Museums group ticket.

## COPENHAGEN CITY HALL (Rådhuset)

*Rådhuspladsen 1; tel. 33 66 25 86; www. kk.dk/artikel/rundvisninger-paa-raadhuset; guided tours in English Mon.-Fri. 1pm, Sat. 10am; tower tours Mon.-Fri. 11am, 2pm, Sat. noon; guided tours 50kr tower tours 30kr; bus 2A, 5C, 9A Rådhuspladsen*

The big, square, red brick building on City Hall Square is, of course, Copenhagen City Hall. It's not the most beautiful or spectacular city center piece—it doesn't have the aesthetics of Milan's Duomo or Brussels' Grand-Place, but it is nonetheless an interesting cornerstone of modern Copenhagen. It was built in the late 1890s in National Romantic style and is still an important center of civic administration. Guided tours, which take around 45 minutes, take place on weekdays; it is not necessary to book in advance. The top of the 105-meter-high (345 ft.) tower can also be visited on a separate tour, taking visitors to a part of the building not otherwise open to the public.

## KUNSTFORENINGEN GL STRAND

*Gammel Strand 48; tel. 33 36 02 60; www. glstrand.dk; Tues.-Sun. 11am-5pm, Wed. 11am-8pm; adults 75kr, students & seniors 65kr, under 16 free; bus 1A, 2A, 6A, 15, 26, 29 Kongens Nytorv; Metro Kongens Nytorv*

A leading destination for modern and contemporary art in the city, GL Strand is located in one of the elegant canalside houses close to Christiansborg. With no permanent exhibition, the association-run gallery seeks to promote the work of up-and-coming Danish artists. It also shows arthouse films in its in-house cinema. The gallery was reopened by David Lynch in 2010 after extensive renovation.

## MEDICAL MUSEION

*Bredgade 62; tel. 35 32 38 00; www. museion.ku.dk; Tues.-Fri. 10am-4pm, Sat.-Sun. noon-4pm; adults 75kr, students, under 16, seniors 50kr; bus 1A Fredericiagade (Bredgade)*

One of seven museums attached to the city's university, the Medical Museion is located in the former Royal Academy of Surgeons, where thousands of Danish medical students have sharpened their dissection skills over the years. Walk through its Roman columns and imposing black double doors to reach the exhibits and artifacts on medical history, including skulls and skeletons, instruments, and medicines. The total permanent and rotating exhibition space is around 1,000 square meters (10,764 sq. ft.).

## DANISH ARCHITECTURE CENTER

*BLOX, Bryghuspladsen 10; tel. 32 57 19 30; https://dac.dk; daily 10am-6pm, Thurs. until 9pm; adults 110kr, students 85kr, under 18 free; bus 1A, 2A or 9A (Stormgade) 66 (Det Kongelige Bibliotek/Royal Danish Library)*

Located in the striking new BLOX building on the quayfront between Slotsholmen and Vesterbro, the Danish Architecture Center is a showcase for architectural design in Denmark and internationally. Danish design history is exhibited through a series of sound, film, and furniture scenographies, which provide some context to Denmark's global reputation as a design superstar. New design trends and innvoations are also on show, while recent rotating exhibitions have taken in such topics as the design of the Danish home and photography of urban space. The center, which has permanent and rotating exhibitions, also offers various guided tours (during the summer) to some of the city's notable architectural achievements. In the winter (or if you're shy), you can download an app (in Danish) from the museum's website and create your own private tour.

## THE MARBLE CHURCH (Frederik's Church)

*Frederiksgade 4; tel. 33 91 27 06; www. marmorkirken.dk; church, Mon.-Thurs., Sat. 10am-5pm, Fri. and Sun. noon-5pm; dome, July 15-Aug. 31 daily 1pm; rest of year, Sat. & Sun. 1pm.; admission to dome, adults 35kr, under 18 20kr (cash only); bus 1A Amalienborg (Bredgade), 26 Dronningens Tværgade*

The green dome of the Church of Frederik, more commonly known as the Marble Church, is something of an outlier. Built after the time of spire enthusiast Christian IV, the Marble

Frederik's Church, also known as the
Marble Church

One of several museums encompassed by the University of Copenhagen and part of the museum district Parkmuseerne located around King's Garden, the geological natural history museum includes extensive collections of minerals, fossils, petrology, and meteorites and has existed since the late 18th century. It has a strong focus on education and a recently opened permanent exhibition on the history of the solar system.

## BOTANICAL GARDENS

*Øster Farimagsgade 2B; tel. 35 32 22 22; http://botanik.snm.ku.dk; garden, Apr.-Sept. 8:30am-6pm, Oct.-Mar. 8:30am-4pm; Palm House, Apr.-Sept. 10am-5pm, Oct.-Mar. 10am-3pm; free except for Palm House and Butterfly House (adults 60kr, children 3-16 40kr); bus 5A, 6A, 14, 40, 42, 43 Nørreport, Metro Nørreport*

Attached to the Natural History Museum and the university, the Botanical Gardens contain Denmark's biggest collection of plants, along with preserved mushrooms, herbs, herbal gardens, various seed collections, and plenty more for those of a green-fingered disposition. It also has 27 greenhouses, most notably the old Palm House from 1874. Guided tours can be arranged by writing to rundvisning@snm.ku.dk. Covering a 10-hectare (25-acre) area, it includes an outdoor café (www. botaniskhavescafe.com) and gift shop and can be accessed via the Geological Museum. A rhododendron garden, alpine plant area, observatory hill, and butterfly house surround a central lake.

Church was designed in the rococo style during the mid-18th century and was an attempt to bring a character to the area around Amalienborg that would distinguish it from Christianshavn and Slotsholmen. It took a while for those ambitions to come to fruition: the church suffered from budget cuts and stood as a ruin for nearly 150 years before being completed in 1894—in limestone, rather than the originally intended marble. Finally, the rising dome of the church could provide the dramatic backdrop to Amalienborg seen today. Inside, the ceiling of the dome is decorated with stunning frescoes depicting the 12 Apostles while also reflecting the 12 columns that support the curved structure.

## NATURAL HISTORY MUSEUM OF DENMARK (Geological Museum)

*Øster Voldgade 5-7; tel. 35 32 22 22; http:// geologi.snm.ku.dk; Tues.-Sun. 10am-5pm; adults 95kr, children 3-16 50kr (ticket gives free access to Zoological Museum); bus 6A, 26 Geologisk Museum, Metro Nørreport*

## HIRSCHSPRUNG COLLECTION

*Stockholmsgade 20; tel. 35 42 03 36; www. hirschsprung.dk; Wed.-Sun. 11am-4pm;*

*adults 85kr, under 18 free; included in
Parmuseerne group ticket; bus 6A, 14,
42, Sølvtorvet; Metro Nørreport; S-train
Nørreport, Østerport*

At the eastern end of the Inner City, the Hirschsprung Collection is Copenhagen's go-to gallery for 19th- and early 20th-century Danish art, taking in the "Danish Golden Age" of productivity and the school of artists who were based in the town of Skagen on the northern tip of Jutland during the 1800s.

TOP EXPERIENCE

### THE COPENHAGEN LAKES

*Dronning Louises Bro or Peblinge Dossering;
free; bus 2A, 66 Peblinge Dossering
(Åboulevard)*

If the King's Garden is the green lung of central Copenhagen, the Lakes are without doubt the blue version. Flanking the northern edge of the Inner City and connecting the three 'bros—Vesterbro, Nørrebro, and Østerbro—the lakes form a natural atrium that joins the various districts. In summer, the lakeside paths hum with life as Copenhageners come out to jog, picnic, or people-watch on a bench while passing the time of day. In winter, seagulls land on the frozen surfaces. Paddle boats can be rented from Kaffesalonen close to the Dronning Louises Bro/Nørrebrogade connection (Peblinge Dossering 6; tel. 35 35 12 19; http://kaffesalonen.com/ waterbike-rental; daily 10am-8:30pm; from 100kr for 30mins).

## SLOTSHOLMEN
### CHRISTIANSBORG PALACE

*Prins Jørgens Gård 1; tel. 33 13 44 11; http://
kongeligeslotte.dk; Royal Reception Rooms,
daily 9am-5pm May-Sept., Tues.-Sun.
10am-5pm Oct.-Apr.; Royal Kitchen &
the Ruins, daily 10am-5pm (closed Mon.*

Christiansborg Palace

*Oct.-Apr.); Royal Stables, daily 1:30pm-4pm*
*(closed Mon. Oct.-Apr.); Palace Chapel,*
*Sundays & Easter holidays plus 10am-5pm;*
*all four attractions adults 150kr, students*
*125kr, under 18 free; Royal Reception Rooms,*
*adults 90kr, students 80kr, under 18 free;*
*Royal Kitchens, Ruins, Royal Stables adults*
*150kr, students 125kr, under 18 free; bus 1A,*
*2A, 26, 40, 66 Stormbroen, Nationalmuseet*
*(Vindebrogade)*

Fans of royal splendor should not miss the tapestries, splendid tiled floors, and frescoed passages of Christiansborg Palace. Though the palace, located on the island of Slotsholmen, is primarily known as the seat of Parliament, it is also used by the royal family for various functions of high ceremony, including state visits, funerals, and the proclaiming of monarchs. A combination ticket is the best of the entry options and includes an optional guided tour.

The **Royal Reception Rooms** are where Queen Margrethe II receives visting dignitaries, and during state visits the thrones (no longer used, but relics from preconstitutional times) can be seen in a lavishly decorated chamber of marble and silk, while the stunning 10-meter-high (33 ft.), 40-meter-long (131 ft.) Great Hall, with its magnificent chandeliers and tapestries, can accommodate up to 400 guests for royal galas. In the **royal kitchen**, which has been restored to the furnishings and equipment (including a huge range of copperware) of wartime king Christian X, visitors can follow preparations for the banquets of the 1930s—specifically the King's Silver Jubilee in 1937. Christiansborg Palace is built on 800-year-old **ruins** of a castle, and some of the remains of these buildings still exist and can be visited. Here, you can learn about the brutal past of battles against pirates

whose heads were put on stakes, or about the political prisoners of the blue tower, the other structure with ruins under Christiansborg. The **royal stables**, which have been home to the royal family's horses since the 1700s, are surviving buildings from the Baroque palace of Christian VI. The horse-drawn coaches at Queen Margrethe's New Year levees—the gold leaf-coated Golden State Coach— is housed in the stables area.

## THE ROYAL LIBRARY
## (Det Kongelige Bibliotek)

*Black Diamond, Søren Kierkegaards Plads*
*1; tel. 33 47 47 47; www.kb.dk; Mon.-Fri.*
*8am-9pm; Sat. 9am-7pm; Black Diamond*
*free, check ticket prices for individual*
*events; library tours 60kr, under 18 free;*
*bus 66, Det Kongelige Bibliotek (Christians*
*Brygge)*

Denmark's national library is commonly known as the Black Diamond due to the glimmering dark architecture of the modern part of the complex, which juts out toward Copenhagen Harbor, forming one of the most characteristic features of the waterfront. Public guided tours of the library take place on Saturdays at 3pm, and private tours can also be arranged (contact library for details). Exhibitions, concerts, and other events regularly take place at the Diamond, which also houses a café and restaurant.

## THORVALDSEN MUSEUM

*Bertel Thorvaldsens Plads 2; tel. 33*
*32 15 32; www.thorvaldsensmuseum.*
*dk; Thurs.-Sun. 10am-5pm; adults 70kr,*
*students 50kr, seniors & under 18 free;*
*bus 9A, 2A Stormbroen, Nationalmuseet*
*(Vindebrogade)*

Another of Slotsholmen's cultural-historical treasures, the Thorvaldsen

Thorvaldsen Museum, Slotsholmen

Museum houses the work of Neoclassicist early 19th-century sculptor Bertel Thorvaldsen, who was born to an Icelandic family in Copenhagen and spent much of his adult life in Italy. The stately façade of the museum, which bears a passing resemblance to Berlin's Brandenburg Gate, gives a good first impression of the classical splendor within, including Thorvaldsen's personal collection of Greek and Roman sculptures as well as his own works. A free audio guide is available.

## DANISH JEWISH MUSEUM

*Proviantpassagen 6; tel. 33 11 22 18; http:// jewmus.dk; Sept.-May, Tues.-Fri. 1pm-4pm, Sat.-Sun. noon-5pm; June-Aug., Tues.-Sun. 10am-5pm; adults 60kr, students & seniors 50kr, under 18 free; bus 9A, 2A Børsen (Børsgade)*

Denmark was occupied by Germany throughout the Second World War, and Danes of older generations often proudly recall the efforts made by the country's citizens and small but significant resistance movement in helping Jewish Danes escape to neutral Sweden. The story is thoroughly documented at the Danish Jewish Museum, which presents Jewish life in Denmark over a 400-year period.

## THE THEATRE MUSEUM

*Christiansborg Ridebane 18; tel. 33 11 51 76; www.teatermuseet.dk; Tues.-Sun. noon-4pm; adults 40kr, students & seniors 30kr, half price with Christiansborg Palace combo ticket; bus 1A, 9A Stormbroen, Nationalmuseet (Vindebrogade); 66 Det Kongelige Bibliotek (Christians Brygge)*

The Theatre Museum provides a thespian component to the cultural history packed onto the tiny island of Slotsholmen. The former Royal Theatre of 1767 is the setting here for a presentation of historical and modern Danish theater. Costumes, set designs, set drawings, and photos —and a dramatic real-life story of *lèse-majesté*— await within.

## THE OLD STOCK EXCHANGE (Børsen)

*Børsgade 1; tel. 33 74 60 00; www. borsbygningen.dk; not open to the public; bus 9A, 2A Børsen (Børsgade)*

In a sea of spires around Slotsholmen and Christianshavn, one of the most striking is the tightly twisted tin of the Old Stock Exchange—its thin tower set on the blue of the weathered copper. Built in the Dutch Renaissance style by King Christian IV, the current copper roof was not actually added until the 19th century. The building itself is not open to the public, so you'll have to make do with walking around it, visualizing Renaissance Copenhagen.

## DANISH WAR MUSEUM (Krigsmuseet)

*Tøjhusgade 3; tel. 33 13 44 11; https:// natmus.dk; Tues.-Sun. 10am-7pm; adults 75kr, 1 child + 1 adult 60kr, under 18 free;*

the Old Stock Exchange (Børsen)

bus 9A, 2A Børsen (Børsgade); 1A, 2A, 11A, 14, 14, 26 and 40 the Royal Library (Det Kongelige Bibliotek)

It's not known as a nation of warfare, but Denmark has been involved in scores of armed engagements over the last five centuries, including skirmishes with its Scandinavian neighbors, the 1864 defeat to the German Confederation, and participation in the American-led coalition in Afghanistan. Specializing in both the history of military conflicts and war technology, the Danish War Museum is housed in one of King Christian IV's robust works on Slotsholmen.

## DANISH MUSEUM OF ART & DESIGN
### (Designmuseum Danmark)

*Bredgade 68; tel. 33 18 56 56; https:// designmuseum.dk; Tues., Thurs.-Sun. 10am-6pm, Wed. 10am-9pm; adults 115kr, seniors 80kr, under 26 free; bus 1A Fredericiagade (Bredgade)*

Arne Jacobsen, Bjarke Ingels, Jørn Utzon . . . Denmark is famed for its design and not without reason. The country's heritage of design and architecture is beautifully showcased at the (unsurprisingly) well-arranged Designmuseum Danmark. International creative and industrial design are also on display. You can purchase your very own piece of Danish design in the museum's gift shop. There are both permanent and rotating exhibitions at this extensive design museum, with the former category taking in Danish chair design and porcelain and the country's 20th-century design history. With a library and archives alongside the exhibitions, the museum is a key center of knowledge for the discipline.

## NYHAVN
### KUNSTHAL CHARLOTTENBORG

*Nyhavn 2; tel. 33 74 46 39; https:// kunsthalcharlottenborg.dk; Tues.-Fri. noon-8pm; Sat.-Sun. 11am-5pm; adults 75kr, students 50kr, under 16 free; bus 1A, 15, 19, 26 (Kongens Nytorv), Metro Kongens Nytorv*

Like an oasis of calm in the middle of popular Nyhavn, exhibition space Kunsthal Charlottenborg can be found almost magically. You slip away from the bustling harbor and suddenly find yourself in a calming stone courtyard at the entrance to a stately old building. In addition to its international contemporary art exhibitions, the building contains a cinema, a bookshop, a bar, and a restaurant.

## VESTERBRO AND FREDERIKSBERG

### MUSEUM OF VETERINARY HISTORY

*Søndre Sti 4, Bülowsvej 17; tel. 21 94 91 26; https://ivh.ku.dk/om-instituttet/ veterinaerhistorisk_museum; no fixed opening hours: call ahead to arrange tour; 50kr per person for group tours; bus 2A Det Biovidenskabelige Fakultet (Rolighedsvej), 9A Bülowsvej (Gammel Kongevej)*

The University of Copenhagen's Museum of Veterinary History is a niche attraction a little off the beaten track. What started life as a collection of disease-formed horse bones has now expanded to a wide range of artifacts, horse shoes, and instruments from the animal healthcare practice that date from the war period all the way back to Viking times.

### TYCHO BRAHE PLANETARIUM

*Absalonsgade 12; tel. 33 12 12 24; www. planetariet.dk; Mon. noon-7:10pm, Tues.-Thurs. 9:30am-7:10pm, Fri.-Sat. 10:30am-8:30pm, Sun. 10:30am-7:10pm; movies, adults 160kr, students 128kr, children 99kr; bus 9A, 31 Det Ny Teater (Gammel Kongevej), S-Train Vesterport*

An active and interactive space and astronomy center suitable for a family outing, the Tycho Brahe Planetarium's pride and joy is its dome theater, equipped with 1,000-square-meter (3,290 sq. ft.) screen and flight seats that show digital and IMAX films about space, the sea, or the jungle (but always space—every showing begins with a short space journey). English narration is available through the purchase of headphones for 20kr at the ticket desk. Movie tickets also provide access to the center's permanent astronomy exhibition.

### CYKELSLANGEN

*Dybbølsbro, Kalvebod Brygge; free; S-Train Dybbølsbro*

The "Bicycle Snake" is a bicycle bridge connecting Vesterbro and Amager via the Fisketorvet shopping mall. It opened in 2014 and is now one of the most recognizable features of the harbor area. If you've rented a bicycle during your stay, it's well worth pedaling by and seeing the city from a unique, two-wheeled vantage point. Part of the Bicycle Snake is accessible only if you're on two wheels, but other bridges nearby allow pedestrians to cross the harbor at the same points (and view the bridge). Starting at Dybbølsbro, the bridge winds its way for more than 200 meters (656 ft.) and is up to 7 meters (23 ft.) above the harbor at its highest point, before connecting to the older Bryggebro—which includes a pedestrian lane—to complete the journey across to Islands Brygge on Amager.

### FREDERIKSBERG PALACE AND GARDENS

*Roskildevej 28 A; tel. 72 81 77 71; www. frederiksbergslot-frbslot.dk; Palace, guided tours last Sat. of month 11am, 1pm; Gardens open 6am and close between 5pm and 11pm, depending on season; voluntary 50kr donation for guided tour of palace, free access to gardens; bus 6A Zoologisk Have (Roskildevej)*

# DANISH DESIGN

Danish Design is an umbrella term given to the **functionalist** style of design and architecture that emerged in Denmark in the **mid-20th century** and has since become one of the country's most famed exports. Known for its clean, straight edges, timeless styles, simplicity, and high quality in both architecture and design, the movement sprang out of the **German Bauhaus school** and went on to form an identity entirely of its own.

It's not just broad stylistic themes that make design and Denmark so synonymous with each other. Particular pieces such as the egg chair or the PH lamp, or buildings like the Sydney Opera House or the Radisson Collection Hotel, are instantly evocative.

The **minimalist motif,** which is one of the hallmarks of Danish design, was born out of necessity. In the 1950s (as well as before World War II), materials were low in both supply and quality. Out of that was born a simplistic and functional style.

## FAMOUS NAMES

A range of Danish designers have achieved international recognition through their work since the middle of the 20th century. These include **Jørn Utzon**, the architect of Sydney's Opera House; furniture designer **Hans J. Wegner** and interior design master **Finn Juhl**; and modern architect **Bjarke Ingels**, founder of the Bjarke Ingels Group, which drew up building designs for Manhattan's VIA 57 West, the M/S Maritime Museum in Helsingør, and the VM Houses and Amager Resource Center in Copenhagen. Meanwhile, fashion designers such as **Stine Goya** and **Mads Nørgaard** are highly visible in the boutiques and clothing stores of the Inner City.

## ARNE JACOBSEN

The godfather of Danish design is Arne Jacobsen, who will forever be synonymous with the iconic **"ant"** and **"egg" chair** designs. His **Series 7 chair** is remarkable, not least for its use in the famous 1963 photo of Christine Keeler by Lewis Morley. Jacobsen's cutlery, including left-handed and right-handed spoons, features in Stanley Kubrick's 1968 sci-fi classic *2001: A Space Odyssey.*

Jacobsen is no less prominent in architecture. Internationally, he designed the Royal Danish Embassy in London and Landskrona Sports-Hall in Sweden, but his legacy is most prominent in Denmark. In and around Copenhagen, the **Bellevue Theatre** and **pier at Klampenborg, Skovshoved Petrol Station,** and **Radisson Collection Hotel** are particularly notable, while buildings such as **Stellings Hus**, on the corner of the Gammeltorv square in the Inner City, are more subtle examples of Jacobsen's contribution to the city landscape.

## AROUND TOWN

The Danish capital's modern urban space has been directly altered and influenced by the country's design and architectural tradition. Today, square, blocky, modern buildings tessellate and make use of their space without shooting far into the sky like skyscrapers in other cities. **BLOX**, the new building on the harbor that is home to the **Danish Architecture Center**, is a fitting example, but these buildings can be found all over the city, particularly in the **Ørestad** area of Amager and along the **harborfront** and parts of the **Inner City**. Just look up and around you, and you're likely to see at least one structure that draws on the legacy of Jacobsen and his peers. To get a taste of Danish design under one roof, visit the **Danish Museum of Art & Design.**

Frederiksberg Palace, a former royal summer residence, looks grandly across the broad green Frederiksberg gardens, a perfect place for a summer picnic or a winter walk. Winding paths and babbling lakes (rowing boat tours available) adorn the gardens, while monthly guided tours offer a chance to see inside the palace. The northern end of the gardens adjoins Copenhagen Zoo. A broad, elongated palace in the Baroque style, the three-story H-shaped building was completed in 1709.

## COPENHAGEN ZOO

*Roskildevej 32; tel. 72 20 02 00; www.zoo. dk/da; winter 10am-4pm; summer 9am-6pm; exceptions apply, see website; adults 180kr (195kr in July and Aug.); 3-11 100kr; under 3 free; bus 6A Zoologisk Have (Roskildevej)*

Tigers, hippos, capybara, chimps, tarantulas, polar bears, lemur, not to mention a host of Nordic animals—more than 250 species in all—Copenhagen's zoo has enough to rival similar animal attractions in other major cities. The 11-hectare (27-acre) zoo has partnerships with a number of conservationist organizations. It is currently undergoing some fairly major redevelopment, with the former Elephant House with its Greek-style columns knocked down to be replaced by a brand-new panda enclosure. China has agreed to loan two of its endangered bears to Copenhagen from April 2019.

## CISTERNS IN SØNDERMARKEN

*Søndermarken; tel. 30 73 80 32; www. cisternerne.dk; Apr. 15-Nov. 30, Tues., Wed. 11am-6pm, Thurs. 11am-8pm, Fri.-Sun. 11am-6pm; adults 70kr, students & seniors 50kr, under 18 free; 6A Zoologisk Have (Roskildevej)*

You can find the entrance to the underground Cisterns between two glass pyramids opposite Frederiksberg Palace. They were originally built to secure a water supply to the city after a cholera outbreak in the 1850s. In modern Copenhagen, they are the setting for art exhibitions in a mix of genres and other events that take advantage of the unique architecture and very un-Scandinavian climate—humidity is almost 100 percent. Regardless

of what's on, the watery underground chambers are a great value for exploration. It's also a good place to visit on a hot day because the underground chambers retain a cool temperature.

## VISIT CARLSBERG

*Gamle Carlsberg Vej 11; tel. 33 27 13 98; www.visitcarlsberg.dk; daily May-Sept. 10am-6pm, Tues.-Sun. Oct.-Apr. 10am-5pm; adults 100kr, students & under 17 70kr, under 5 free; beer tasting 80kr; guided history tour 60kr; bus 1A Enghavevej; 8A, 26 Kammasvej.*

Craft beer is all the rage in Denmark these days, but that doesn't mean the heritage of Carlsberg as one of the country's biggest exports and products has been, or should be, forgotten. Located in the brewery's handsome old brick warehouses, the Visit Carlsberg experience includes horsedrawn carriage tours, tasting sessions (Carlsberg is not just lager), a museum tour detailing the history and story of the brand, and the biggest collection of beer bottles you'll ever see. A free shuttle bus leaves hourly from Vesterbrogade 6 (near Copenhagen Central station) between 11am and 4pm.

# NØRREBRO AND ØSTERBRO

## ASSISTENS CEMETERY

*Kapelvej 4; tel. 35 37 19 17; http://assistens. dk/kirkegarden; daily Apr.-Sept. 7am-10pm, daily Oct.-Mar. 7am-7pm; free, themed guided tours from 50kr (often in Danish), check website for program or call ahead; bus 5C Sjællandsgade (Nørrebrogade)*

Assistens is not the only cemetery in the world to be a tourist attraction, but it is perhaps unique in being considered a genuinely pleasant place, and many Copenhageners take advantage of the green space in a busy part of the city for a morning jog, an afternoon stroll, or a picnic among the

Assistens Cemetery

gravestones. The calm, green areas and creaking, reassuring presence of the old trees are one reason for this. Some of Denmark's most famous sons and daughters, including philosopher Søren Kierkegaard, physicist Niels Bohr, and fairy tale author Hans Christian Andersen, are buried here.

## SUPERKILEN PARK AND RED SQUARE

*Nørrebrogade 208; free; bus 5C*
*Nørrebrohallen (Nørrebrogade)*

A strip of Nørrebro that is a former train track converted into an urban park area, Superkilen covers a 750-meter (2,460 ft.) stretch of the outer part of the neighborhood to the north of Nørrebrogade and close to a similarly long green area stretching back toward the western corner of Assistens Cemetery. Designed with the collaboration of Bjarke Ingels's prestigious BIG architecture company, the concreted Superkilen has an incongruous international aesthetic, with multicolored paving, a large red star at the top

of a pole, and various skateboarding jumps, bicycle paths, and rock climbing frames. Superkilen consists of three areas: the Red, Black, and Green squares, which have primary functions as an activity area, city square, and park, respectively. The rolling concrete of the park is traversed by white lane markers, while neon signs display both a red star and a green crescent. Intended to promote a sense of community in one of Copenhagen's more marginalized areas, its internationality and diversity sets out to reflect the demographic of the area. It can be used as a park and place of exercise.

## POLICE MUSEUM (Politimuseet)

*Fælledvej 20; tel. 40 32 58 88; www.*
*politimuseum.dk; Tues., Thurs., & Sun.*
*11am-4pm; adults 40kr, under 18 free; bus 5C*
*Ravnsborggade (Nørrebrogade)*

The Police Museum in the heart of Nørrebro tells the story of Copenhagen's law enforcement through permanent exhibitions on the history of the police force in the Danish capital—expect uniforms, mugshots, and police bikes—as well as exhibitions on famous events in history, such as the riots of 1993 or the double murder on Peter Bangs Vej that shocked post-war Copenhagen in 1948.

## DEN FRIE UDSTILLING

*Oslo Plads 1; tel. 33 12 28 03; http://denfrie. dk; Tues.-Sun. 12-6pm, Thurs. until 9pm; adults 70kr, students 50kr, under 12 free; bus 1A, 15 Østerport, S-Train Østerport*

The artist-owned, current issue-focused Den Frie Center of Contemporary Art has around 10 different Danish and international contemporary art exhibitions annually, tackling current affairs and societal considerations. The association based art museum has existed in various iterations and locations since 1891. Guided tours of the exhibitions, as well as to the architecture of its historic home on Oslo Plads, are available. Ring ahead for details.

## NATURAL HISTORY MUSEUM OF DENMARK
### (Zoological Museum)

*Universitetsparken 15; tel. 35 32 22 22; https://zoologi.snm.ku.dk; Tues.-Sun. 10am-4pm; adults 95kr, 3-16 50kr, ticket gives free access to Geological Museum; bus 8A, 42 Universitetsparken*

With extensive permanent exhibitions on Darwin and evolution, wildlife in Denmark more than 20,000 years ago, and Arctic climate zones, the strong educational focus of the Zoological Museum means that the exhibits are presented in a neat and easy-to-follow order. Look out for "Misty," a 17-meter-long (56 ft.) diplodocus skeleton, in a zoology, botany, and geology section that also includes Hans Christian Andersen's snail collection.

The Zoological Museum comes under the State National History Museum umbrella and after-hours guided tours for kids and adults are available.

# CHRISTIANSHAVN AND AMAGER

One of Copenhagen's oldest districts and named for the king, Christian IV, who built much of what still stands in the area today, Christianshavn is essential Copenhagen. It combines charming canals and spires with everyday to and fro, as cyclists charge toward Knippelsbro on their way to work and people grab coffees and pastries at the bakeries around Christianshavn Square. Meanwhile, the hippie squat-turned-alternative enclave of Christiania is quite unlike anywhere else in Europe.

**TOP** EXPERIENCE

## ✪ CHURCH OF OUR SAVIOUR

*Sankt Annæ Gade 29; tel. 32 54 68 83; www.vorfrelserskirke.dk; May-Sept., Mon.-Sat. 10am-7pm, Sun. 10:30am-7pm; last week of Feb.-Apr. & Oct.-Dec. 15: Mon.-Sat. 10am-4pm, Sun. and public holidays 10:30am-4pm; church free; spire, adults 50kr, children free; bus 9A, 2A Christianshavn St. (Torvegade), Metro Christianshavn St.*

The gilded spire of the baroque Church of Our Saviour rises quite splendidly above the low rooftops of Christianshavn, showcasing the flair of King Christian IV.

Legend has it that Laurids de Thurah, the designer of the 17th-century spiral spire threw himself from its top after realizing it had been "twirled" counterclockwise. This is no more than a myth, however. He actually died in his bed, seven years after

Church of Our Saviour in Christianshavn

## ☉ REFSHALEØEN

*Refshaleøen; http://refshaleoen.dk; bus 9A*
*(Refshalevej)*

Gray concrete, the clang of steel on steel and the clash of waves against the quayside: recreation is being welded onto a large former industrial area on the eastern limits of Copenhagen. Refshaleøen is set to emerge in the coming years as Copenhagen's new must-see destination.

An important element in this development is **Copenhagen Street Food**. After four years on nearby Paper Island, the large—and highly popular—indoor street food market reopened as **Reffen** (Refshalevej 151, tel. 32 54 32 21, https://reffen.dk) on a 10,000-square-meter (33,000 sq. ft.) plot here in May 2018. Crowds of Copenhageners and visitors make the relatively long bicycle trip out to the converted shipping containers that are lined up in diagonal rows as far as the eye can see. Vendors sell world food, including Indian, Mexican, Greek, and plenty of others. Benches are laid out on a wide swath of open space between the containers and the edge of the harbor. Kastellet and Langelinie can be seen across the water.

Refshaleøen is still in touch with its roots as an industrial area, once far from tourist attractions. Boathouses, crumbling factories, and neglected plots of land shared the space with workshops and **Blocs & Walls** climbing club, along with the newly built home of famous gourmet restaurant **Noma**. Danish craft beer icon Mikkeller has opened a large bar, **Mikkeller Baghaven** and gourmet restaurant **Amass** also calls the island home. **La Banchina**, with its jetty seating area, is a good spot to view the sunset over the sea while drinking a glass of wine. Refshaleøen also

its completion. What's more, the counterclockwise twirl is considered to be correct—theoretical defenders of the spire would have held the railing with their left hand and their weapon with the right.

The church can be visited year-round for free. Its sober, red bricks and Baroque style, not to mention its size—the 36 meters (118 ft.) to the ceiling rafters dwarfs other places of worship in Denmark—are worth taking the time to stop by. But the real treat is climbing the spire, where a view from 90 meters (295 ft.) above Copenhagen can be enjoyed. There are 400 steps to the top, of which the last 150 are actually on the outside of the spire, so you get a full 360-degree panorama as you go up. Be warned: the outside section is not for those who are averse to heights. You'll likely have a little more elbow room here than at the more popular, but significantly stumpier, 42-meter-high (138 ft.) Round Tower (Rundetårn). It does get busy on summer afternoons, though, so it's better to come in the morning during peak season.

seems to have confirmed its position as one of, if not *the*, places to be seen in Copenhagen by joining fashionable Nørrebro and Vesterbro as a location for the annual hedonistic summer festival Distortion.

In addition to by bus, Refshaleøen can be reached by boat through sightseeing operator Stromma (www.stromma.dk/kobenhavn), which brings tourists directly to Refshaleøen from the Inner City, with a drop off at the Halvandet Beach Bar.

## ✪ CHRISTIANIA

*Prinsessegade; tel. 32 95 65 07; www.christiania.org; guided tours Sat. & Sun. 3pm; 50kr; bus 9A Bodenhoffs Plads (Prinsessegade), Metro Christianshavn St.*

"You are now leaving the EU," a sign above the entrance to Christiania used to read. The sign disappeared at some point in the late 2000s, but it epitomized the anti-establishment thought that was the essence of its founding and which still exists today.

In the late 1960s, Denmark's military began to leave the Bådsmandsstræde barracks in Christianshavn with no plans for the future of the buildings at the site. In 1971 the first "Christianites" broke in and before long, the new "Freetown" of Christiania was declared, its first residents a group of hippies, artists, homeless people, and drug addicts united by their desire to live on principles of freedom, creativity, and community. The buildings were turned into homes, and weekly meetings were held to decide how the community should be run. To this day, the flat hierarchy still forms the basis on which its residents administer the enclave.

The occupation of the former military buildings was illegal from the outset, and throughout its history, relations between Christiania and

the police have been fraught, often with aggressive and violent confrontations between the two. The famous Pusher Street Market, which openly sells marijuana and related products, is one source of the tension, with spells of tough clampdowns alternating with calmer periods.

In 1989, the government passed a law that legalized Christiania, but in 2004 lawmakers passed a bill seeking to normalize and redevelop the area, including tearing down buildings that did not comply with construction standards and a much stricter approach to the cannabis trade. Nevertheless, this unusual enclave has persisted as a semi-independent part of the city. Around 900 people live there today, and it is not a part of the city that just anyone can move into: waiting lists are years long, and hopefuls must be genuinely engaged with the community in order to be accepted.

Thousands of tourists visit annually, and Christiania generally welcomes visitors: the cafés, market, and shops are open to anyone who passes by. The atmosphere here is unlike anything you would come across anywhere else and is certainly unique for Copenhagen, with its highly liberal, accepting, and free outlook underpinned by a sense of rebellion that never feels far from the surface. It's safe to visit, but there are a couple of things you should bear in mind.

Photography is generally not allowed around the Pusher Street area, and anyone taking pictures could find themselves being confronted and asked to delete them. There are normally signs in both Danish and English, making it clear which parts Christianites don't want photographed, but when in doubt, resist the temptation to take out your camera or your phone. Police raids do occur, sometimes very regularly, and confrontations between the two sides can be aggressive, although they will never target outsiders. However, anyone buying from the illicit hash trade is breaking the law and does so at their own risk. It is worth checking local news reports, such as the English-language publications *The Local Denmark* (http://thelocal.dk) and *Copenhagen Post* (http://cphpost. dk), for any warnings not to visit. You should also be prepared for the chance of passively inhaling very "pungent," smoky clouds in some of the cafés and outdoor areas.

A **guided tour** (www.christiania. org) is available for tourists, led by a "native" Christianite who presents the residents' side of the story and shows visitors around the "free state," which at 84 acres is larger than you might expect. Because the tour is run by Christianites, it's respectful of the space and not at all exploitative. The tour meets at the main entrance to Christiania on Prinsessegade.

### Dyssen at Christiania

*Prinsessegade; www.christiania.org; free; bus 9A Bodenhoffs Plads (Prinsessegade), Metro Christianshavn St. for access via Christiania or bus 2A Christmas Møllers Plads (Torvegade), Metro Christianshavn for access via Christmas Møllers Plads*

The "unknown" Christiania, Dyssen— literally "cairn," but a name with its origins in slang—is a long strip of land on the opposite side of the Stadsgraven lake, the crescent-shaped body of water that separates Christianshavn and Christiania from Amager. Not part of the former barracks, which the original squatters occupied to found

Dyssen at Christiania

Christiania in the 1970s, the 2km (1mi) stretch of land now has a variety of unusually designed houses built by Christianites. It's a remarkably quiet green area where you can stroll and listen to the birds sing. The northern end of Dyssen brings you nicely onto Refshaleøen.

### Stadens Museum for Kunst

*Loppebygningen, Sydområdet 4 A, 2.tv, Christiania; tel. 22 24 09 08; www. gallopperiet.dk; Tues.-Sun. 2pm-7pm; free; bus 9A Bodenhoffs Plads (Prinsessegade), Metro Christianshavn St.*

Riffing the Danish name for the National Gallery ("Staden" instead of "Staten" means the gallery belongs to Christiania, rather than the Danish state), this gallery provides space for local artists to displays their works. Exhibitions change regularly and new ones often appear at short notice, so phone or check on the website to see what's on. It's located on the second floor of a former barrack building separating Christiania from Christianshavn.

## OVERGADEN

*Overgaden Neden Vandet 17; tel. 32 57 72 73; https://overgaden.org; Tues.-Fri. 1pm-5pm, Sat.-Sun. 11am-5pm; free; bus 2A, 9A Knippelsbro (Torvegade)*

This welcoming, non-profit gallery has a splendid setting in one of the elegant tall houses on the Christianshavn canal. Besides having up to 10 exhibitions of new contemporary art annually, its two floors regularly play host to varying events, talks, and performances.

## CHRISTIAN'S CHURCH
### (Christians Kirke)

*Strandgade 1; tel. 32 54 15 76; www. christianskirke.dk; Tues.-Fri. 10am-4pm, church services Sun. 10am; free; bus 2A, 9A Knippelsbro (Torvegade)*

It's not as spectacular as the nearby Church of Our Saviour, but the 18th-century Christian's Church has its own unique charm and is located on an atmospheric square set back from Christianshavn's busier areas. The 19th century pastor and philosopher N. F. S. Grundtvig was a hugely important figure in Denmark's cultural history, leading evening song at the church in the 1830s. It is now regularly used for concerts, which are often free and are listed on the church's website.

## NORTH ATLANTIC HOUSE
### (Nordatlantens Brygge)

*Strandgade 91; tel. 32 83 37 00; www. nordatlantens.dk/en/home; Mon.-Fri. 10am-5pm, Sat.-Sun. noon-5pm; adults 40kr, seniors 30kr, students 20kr, under 12 free; bus 2A, 9A Knippelsbro (Torvegade)*

Nordatlantens Brygge showcases the culture of the northern Nordic nations of Iceland, Greenland, and the Faroe Islands through its exhibitions, while also acting as a venue for performances, dance, music, films, lectures, and anything else related to the region (Iceland's 2018 World Cup football matches were shown here).

## KASTELLET AND LANGELINIE
### KASTELLET (THE CITADEL)

*Gl. Hovedvagt, Kastellet 1; tel. 72 84 00 00; www.kastellet.dk; free; bus 1A Esplanaden (Grønningen), S-train Østerport*

One of the best-preserved examples of a medieval star fortress in Europe, the Citadel—Kastellet in Danish—is actually still used by the military, which occupies some of its buildings. Much of the Citadel, which forms a pentagram surrounded on all sides by water, is open to the public, and its grassy ramparts make for a pleasant walk with great views of the surrounding area including the barracks, the harbor and the city. Sights include a former powder house, a church, a prison, and a windmill.

### THE LITTLE MERMAID

*Langelinie; www.mermaidsculpture.dk; free; bus 1A Esplanaden (Grønningen), S-train Østerport*

The Little Mermaid

Kastellet

It likely needs little introduction, but Copenhagen icon the Little Mermaid, which was inspired by Hans Christian Andersen's fairy tale, is easy to miss. The diminutive bronze statue is tucked away up on Langelinie. Instantly recognizable from thousands of Copenhagen stock images, the real thing can feel a bit anticlimactic, but viewing it can easily be fitted into a walk in the Kastellet area. If you want your photo with the Mermaid, arrive early in the day or be prepared to wait your turn. To find the statue, continue to the end of Amaliegade past Amalienborg Palace, then walk past the Gefion Fountain onto the Langelinie promenade. Follow the path through a small park—the harbor will be spread to your right, and Kastellet will be on the left. After around 200 yards you will spot the statue—it is below the main walkway of the promenade on a plinth placed on some rocks that can be stepped onto for photo opportunites.

## MUSEUM OF DANISH RESISTANCE

*Churchillparken 6; tel. 41 20 62 91;*
*https://en.natmus.dk; currently closed; 1A*
*Esplanaden (Grønningen)*

Unfortunately closed since 2013 due to a serious fire, the Museum of Danish Resistance is scheduled to reopen in late 2019. Its return will be welcome, given its role, along with the Danish-Jewish Museum, in maintaining a record of everyday life during the Nazi Occupation of 1940-1945.

## GEFION FOUNTAIN

*Churchillparken; 1A Esplanaden*
*(Grønningen)*

The monumental Gefion Fountain is a relatively overlooked sculpture by Danish naturalist Anders Bundgaard, at the southern end of Kastellet near the harbor. It depicts a group of animals being driven onward by Norse goddess Gefjon, who, according to legend, ploughed the island of Zealand out of the sea between Sweden and the rest of Denmark. While many hurry

Gefion Fountain

past the fountain or take another route on their way to see the Little Mermaid, the Gefion Fountain—which is for ornamental purposes only—is no less admirable.

# Recreation

Primed for exploration by two wheels or on the gentle waters of the harbor, recreational options in Copenhagen make use of two very Danish transportation forms, sailing and cycling. Copenhageners are very outdoorsy for city dwellers and those not running or biking can exercise by joining climbing clubs of the urban or traditional variety. Take care if sailing or kayaking in Copenhagen Harbor—maritime traffic can be hectic during the summer months.

## PARKS
### Amager Strandpark

*Amager Strand Promenaden 1; tel. 26 30 24 82; www.amager-strand.dk; Metro Amager Strand St.*

A 4.5km (almost 3-mile) stretch of beach with 60 hectares (148 acres) of park and an artificial island, Amager Strandpark is a beautiful spot on the east coast of Amager. On a clear evening you can watch the twinkling of car headlights crossing the Øresund Bridge from Sweden, see aircraft taking off from Copenhagen Airport, spot the silhouettes of the turbines of the Middelgrunden wind farm, and make out the coast of Malmö in the distance. If it's a full moon, the light glistens off

Amager Strandpark, looking toward the Øresund Bridge

the lagoon between the beach and the rest of Amager. By day, runners make use of the paths, and there is a "city beach" area with a promenade, courts for ballgames, and parking. The area is best during the summer, but it's also romantic in the winter if you want to brave the cold.

### Amager Fælled

*Artillerivej, Amager; www.kk.dk/artikel/ amager-fælled; Metro Islands Brygge*

Amager Fælled is a beautiful area of grassy bush, wooded paths, and reeds that glow orange when the unimpeded low sun shines through them for hours during the long summer sunsets. The common is a (currently) 233-hectare (575-acre) national park covering a large expanse of western Amager between Islands Brygge, the Field's shopping mall, and the distinctive Bellacentret conference center. Most of the area has been left to grow wild, with various nature types and terrain, including open and dense thicket, marsh, grasslands, lakes, and meadow. There are lanes and paths suitable for bicycling, and various species of wild animal and bird can be spotted, including species such as the Eurasian bittern, a wader, and the western marsh harrier, a bird

of prey—both are rare elsewhere in Denmark.

# BICYCLING

With almost 350km (217 miles) of bicycle lanes, Copenhagen is one of the least daunting cities in the world to hop on two wheels as a neophyte. The first thing you'll probably want to do is try out the two winding, fast bicycle-only bridges: the **Cykelslangen**, which connects Vesterbro to Amager, and **Inderhavnsbroen** between Nyhavn and Christianshavn.

"**Super bike lanes**" (supercykelstier, http://supercykelstier.dk) are a coherent network of "fast" bicycle connections with easy-to-follow set routes that take you in and around the city. The routes are planned to go as smoothly and with as few stops as possible with better comfort—for example, there are bicycle-height rails and foot rests to make waiting at traffic lights that much easier. The paths are well maintained, and there are pumps and other service spots located regularly along them. The **Cykelplanen app**, available via the **Supercykelstier website**, shows you the routes and helps you plan a two-wheeled journey on both the regular and express paths.

### Bike Copenhagen with Mike

*Sankt Peders Stræde 47; tel. 26 39 56 88; http://bikecopenhagenwithmike.dk; daily except Tues. at 10am and/or 2:30pm, fewer tours offered in winter; tours 300kr; bus 5C (Jarmers Plads (Nørre Voldgade)*

These enthusiastically delivered tours by the eponymous Mike take visitors around central Copenhagen on a three-and-a-half hour all-weather tour that covers a lot of ground, ticking off many of the sights and filling

# STROLLING

Going out for a walk is a big deal in Copenhagen. In no other city have I found simply going for a walk to be such a popular and everyday in-and-of-itself activity. I don't mean walking for the sake of going to the shops or the train station or to get to work, but just walking, because it's pleasant to do so. That reflects the many spacious and green or waterside spots scattered across the city where you can go out and stretch your legs. The following are some favorite places to stroll:

- **Copenhagen Lakes**, the lengthy rectangular bodies of water between the Inner City and outer neighborhoods, are surrounded by pathways, where people walk on the gravel paths and feed the ducks or use the pavement and road bridges for a better vantage point (page 61).

- **Frederiksberg Gardens** are a quaint, romantic English-style landscape garden with delicate bridges and boats, overlooked by the Baroque Frederiksberg Palace (page 65).

- The **Botanical Gardens** and adjacent **King's Garden** are popular and relaxing spots, full of tree-lined avenues, statues, and history in the busy Inner City (page 60 and 53).

- In Nørrebro, **Assistens Cemetery** is also a popular spot for locals to go for a walk, and you can combine it with the fun and perhaps a little weird diversion of hunting for the graves of historical figures—there are signs directing you to the most famous ones (page 67).

- Christiania's **Dyssen** is a short walk of around 2.4 kilometers (1.5 miles) in total that takes you from Christianshavn along a quiet path overhung by trees, past rickety houses and old stone barns, coming out at the southern end of Refshaleøen (page 72).

- The island of **Amager** is a great place to get outside with two bracing options. **Amager Strandpark**—a long stretch of human-made beach with a promenade, lagoons, jetties, and views of Malmö—is blustery in the winter and exhiliratingly hip and family-friendly in the summer, and it's always refreshing. The large **Amager Fælled** nature reserve is a brambly mass of marshland and field where birdwatchers and hikers could happily spend an entire day (page 75 and 76).

up cyclists with local history, knowledge, and stories. You'll need to be able to bicycle in traffic.

## Green Bike Tours

*Gothersgade 148; tel. 24 85 10 07; www. greenbiketours.dk; tours on Thurs. 10am-1pm & Sat. 2pm-5pm; 300kr per tour plus bicycle rental; bus 5C (Nørre Farimagsgade (Frederiksborggade)*

In the words of Green Bike Tours, "Discover and experience a capital that plans to be carbon neutral by 2025." Green Bike offers, well, green, sustainability-focused, two-wheeled tours around the city, which means you'll get to see places like bike bridges, green architecture, and city planning and wind technology, or even visit organic eateries, depending on the tour you take (check ahead for availability). A shorter walking version of the tour is also offered. The young, eco-friendly guides are passionate about both the planet and their bicycles.

### Christiania Cykler

*Mælkevejen 83A; tel. 70 70 76 80; www. christianiacykler.dk; Mon.-Fri. 9am-5pm, Sat. 11am-3pm; bus 2A, 9A Christianshavns St., Metro Christianshavn*

The classic Christiania three-wheeled cargo cycles, commonly seen with one or more children in the front being ferried around Copenhagen by a parent, can be rented at Christiania Cykler in Christiania itself, for 450kr for a day, with 150kr per day for additional days. If you want to splurge, they can be purchased in various models and sizes. A new bike will set you back at least 10,000kr.

## KAYAKING AND BOATING

### Kayak Republic

*Børskaj 12; tel. 22 88 49 89; https:// kayakrepublic.dk; kayaks available Apr.-May noon-6pm, June-Aug. 10am-9pm, Sept 10am-7pm, tours daily at 10am during opening months; kayak rental from 125kr (certified), 175kr (noncertified), tours 395kr per person; bus 2A (Knippelsbro/ Christianshavn St.), Metro Christianshavn St.*

Paddle it out and see Copenhagen's harbor and canals from a true sea-level perspective with Kayak Republic, which offers guided kayak tours as well as free-sailing kayak rental. Single and double kayaks are available, as are sea kayaks. An IPP 2 or BCU 2 certificate and ID must be presented to rent the latter. You can refuel at the attached restaurant and bar, Kayak Bar, once you've done paddling for the day.

### GoBoat

*Islands Brygge 10; tel. 40 26 10 25; http:// goboat.dk; 9:30am-sunset; 1 hour 449kr per boat, reduced rates for additional hours; bus 5C, 12 (Langebro)*

The cheapest and easiest way to be on a boat of your own on Copenhagen harbor. Go Boats are easy-to-use motorized boats with a capacity of up to eight and a little table where you can enjoy a picnic or even a glass of champagne with your crewmates. Boats can be operated by anyone over the age of 18 and no prior experience is required. Book ahead during the summer.

## TOURS

### Stromma

*Nyhavn, various hop on/hop off points around the city; tel. 32 96 30 00; www. stromma.dk/kobenhavn; boat tours from 85kr, bus tours from 175kr; Metro Kongens Nytorv*

Stromma is one of the largest tour groups operating in the city and offers a range of bus and boat tours, including a classic one-hour boat trip with a guide as well as hop-on, hop-off services. In May 2018, Stromma became the first canal tour operator to bring tourists directly to the Reffen food market at Refshaleøen from the Inner City. Various combinations are available, as is a snail's pace trailer train, which takes visitors around the central sights. Audio guides are included in ticket prices.

### Urban Adventures

*Reventlowsgade 7; tel. 20 82 52 87; www. urbanadventures.com; Mon.-Sat. 3pm; 500kr; bus/Metro/S-train Copenhagen Central Station*

Urban Adventures, an international tour company that specializes in alternative and sustainable city tours, offers a "Vice and Vesterbro" tour in Vesterbro, which is now a trendy district for the upwardly mobile but once was a marginalized area with social problems including prostitution and high levels of drug addiction. The tour aims to educate about this part of the area's history and does not leave out the negative side of gentrification. Over-18s only.

### Nordic Noir Tours

*Vesterport Station; http://nordicnoirtours. com; Sat. 4pm; from 200kr depending on number of participants; bus/S-Train Vesterport*

*The Bridge, The Killing, Borgen*— the locations of the dark drama of Nordic Noir are the subject of Nordic Noir Tours, which specializes in walks inspired by the atmospheric Scandinoir of these shows, which have been among Denmark's most popular cultural exports in recent years. Advanced reservations are necessary, and inquiries are by email only. Check ahead (you will receive a response the same day) as to whether tours are on and how many people have signed up: if there are fewer than six people, the cost per person increases. Tours at other times than the regular Saturday 4pm can be arranged. A monthly tour is also offered in Malmö.

## ADVENTURE SPORTS
### Blocs & Walls

*Refshalevej 163D; tel. 32 57 25 00; www. blocs-walls.dk; Mon.-Fri. 10am-11pm, Sat. 10am-8pm, Sun. 10am-10pm; beginner courses including equipment rental 350kr per person, day passes 65kr children, 130kr adults plus equipment rental; bus 9A Refshaleøen (Refshalevej)*

Copenhagen climbing center Blocs & Walls offers professional and accessible outdoor and indoor facilities on Refshaleøen for climbing enthusiasts or those who want to try scaling the heights for the first time. The club's name is a nod to B&W, a former Refshaleøen shipyard.

### Urban High Roping

*Refshalevej 177; tel. 51 20 77 03; https:// urbanrangercamp.dk; Thur.-Sun. 10am-4pm; 395kr per person for highroping, other packages available; bus 9A Refshaleøen (Refshalevej)*

Not for the fainthearted or those with aversions to heights, Urban High Roping is a ropes course high above the floors of the old S2 shipyard hall— 50 meters (164 ft.)above, in fact, making it the highest ropes course of its kind in the world. With 28 different activities on four individual tracks of varying difficulty and a zip line down to the bottom once you're done, you'll see Refshaleøen's shipping containers from an entirely new and quite possibly terrifying perspective.

## SPECTATOR SPORTS
### Parken Stadium

*Per Henrik Lings Allé 2; tel. 35 43 31 31; www. parken.dk; bus 1A, 3A, 14 (Trianglen)*

Denmark's national team soccer stadium Telia Parken is also the home of FC Copenhagen (locally known as FCK), the country's most well-known and wealthiest soccer team that competes most seasons in the UEFA Champions League or Europa League. The stadium also often hosts major concerts with the likes of Beyoncé, Jay-Z, and Coldplay having played there in the past. Tickets for big events such as these, as well as national team and Champions League matches, are generally snapped up quickly, but Danish league matches are easier to attend. Tickets are sold via FC Copenhagen's website: https:// billet.fck.dk. Tours of the stadium are sometimes available during school holidays but are normally in Danish, though English-language private tours can be arranged.

# Theater and Performing Arts

Copenhagen is not lacking in the fine arts department, with the architectural marvel that is the quayside Opera House, the Old Stage at Det Kongelige Teater (the Royal Theater), and state broadcaster DR's concert hall backed up by a strong supporting cast of smaller venues.

## ARTS AND CULTURE

### THE ROYAL THEATER
(Det Kongelige Teater)

The Royal Theater (Det Kongelige Teater) is now an umbrella name used for three different cultural institutions in Copenhagen: Gamle Scene, Operaen, and Skuespilhuset.

### The Old Stage
(Gamle Scene)

*Kongens Nytorv; tel. 33 69 69 69; https:// kglteater.dk; from 100kr; Metro Kongens Nytorv*

The stately Gamle Scene is the oldest Royal Theater building. It opened in 1874 and was designed by Vilhelm Dahlerup, the architect responsible for a number of other classical Copenhagen landmarks, including the Ny Carlsberg Glyptotek, Hotel D'Angleterre, and Dronning Louises Bro. It is an elegant mix of alcoves, archways, and sculptures. Originally built for theater, opera, and ballet, it is now primarily home to the the Royal Danish Ballet. Check the website for details of ballets and ticket availability. English-language theater tours are sometimes available. The season runs from August to June.

### Royal Danish Playhouse
(Skuespilhuset)

*Sankt Annæ Pl. 36; tel. 33 69 69 69; https://kglteater.dk; from 40kr, occasional free events; bus 66 Sankt Annæ Plads, Skuespilhuset (Sankt Annæ Plads), Metro Kongens Nytorv*

The 750-million kroner harborside theater Skuespilhuset opened in 2008 with a production of the most famous play ever to be set in Denmark, *Hamlet*. The building can't be missed—with clean, low-slung square lines, and glass facades almost overhanging the harbor. It was designed specifically to optimize theater production, with ballet and opera given their own, separate Royal Theater homes. With an ensemble of 20 actors, contemporary, modern, and classical plays all appear on the theater's program. English subtitles are occasionally available for some productions.

### Copenhagen Opera House
(Operaen)

*Ekvipagemestervej 10; tel. 33 69 69 69; https://kglteater.dk; from 80kr; bus 9A Fabrikmestervej (Danneskiold-Samsøes Allé)*

Dramatically complementing the Playhouse from its setting on the Christianshavn side of the harbor, the Opera House is one of the visual highlights of the entire city. Completed in 2004, its neofuturist style incorporates a large, curved glass and metal grid front, a limestone exterior, and small canals that make you feel as though you're on an island. Inside, large spherical chandeliers designed by Icelandic artist Olafur Eliasson illuminate the marble floors; the patterns and reflections change depending on

Copenhagen Opera House

the viewing angle. The cavernous interiors and Eliasson globes are almost as dramatic as the opera itself. Concerts and operas alike can be enjoyed here.

## TIVOLI CONCERT HALL

*Tietgensgade 30; tel. 33 15 10 01; www.tivoli. dk; from 185kr including Tivoli Gardens; bus/S-train Copenhagen Central Station*

The concert hall at Tivoli Gardens is a charming place to take in an evening show. It's set in the middle of the old-fashioned fairground's flowery gardens, lights, fountains, and restaurants. Orchestra, ballet, opera, and Danish folk favorites regularly appear at the venue, which is open during Tivoli's normal operating seasons.

## THE ROYAL LIBRARY
### (Det Kongelige Bibliotek)

*Black Diamond, Søren Kierkegaards Plads 1; tel. 33 47 47 47; www.kb.dk; Mon.-Fri. 8am-9pm, Sat. 9am-7pm; free entry to Black Diamond, check ticket prices for individual events; Exhibitions from 60kr, students 30kr or free with Copenhagen card, concerts from 100kr; bus 66, Det Kongelige Bibliotek (Christians Brygge)*

The Royal Library has regular exhibitions and guest lectures that are commonly international and therefore given in English. Topics can vary from literary and cultural to art and philosophy. Classical and jazz concerts also take place in the library's Dronningesalen (Queen's Hall), which has a capacity of up to 600 people.

## BREMEN THEATER

*Nyropsgade 39-4; tel. 30 32 40 90, http:// brementeater.dk; from 200kr; bus 2A, 66 Vester Farimagsgade (Gyldenløvesgade)*

Billing itself as an alternative to traditional theaters, Bremen is host to stand-up comedy and a fair selection of concerts. These categories include both domestic and international acts, notably U.S. comedians and European bands as well as the significant Danish contingent. The fall 2018 program included Damien Jurado, T. J. Miller, and The Tallest Man on Earth.

## LIVE MUSIC

### Jazzhus Montmartre

*Store Regnegade 19A; tel. 70 20 20 96;*
*www.jazzhusmontmartre.dk; from 270kr,*
*tables must be booked in advance; bus/*
*Metro/S-train: Nørreport*

Historic jazz club Jazz Montmartre has hosted concerts at the same Copenhagen venue since 1959 and enjoyed a heyday in the 1970s when a number of top internationals artists spent time in the Danish capital. It was restored and reopened in 2010 and regularly hosts concerts with up-and-coming and estabished acts.

### Vega Live

*Enghavevej 40; tel. 33 25 70 11; https://vega.*
*dk; from 225kr; bus 3A Tove Ditlevsens Plads*
*(Enghavevej)*

Vega's concert halls have a strong program of mainly indie acts with some other musical genres also represented—you maybe be lucky enough to catch one of your favorite bands visiting during your stay. The venue consists of two concert rooms: Store (Large) Vega, which has a capacity of 1,500 standing guests or 900 seated; and Lille (Little) Vega, with 500 standing or 160 seated spots. In addition to the music stages, smaller concerts as well as events such as poetry slams and quizzes take place in an attached bar, Ideal Bar.

### DR Koncerthuset

*Ørestads Blvd. 13; tel. 35 20 62 62; https://*
*drkoncerthuset.dk; from 90kr; Metro DR*
*Byen*

DR Koncert Hall, the super modern concert venue in "DR City," the Amager District that is home to the national broadcaster, stands out in an already clean, futuristic-looking area around the DR Byen Metro Station. Big band, swing, and the Danish National Girls' Choir are regular features on a wide-ranging program. With a total surface of 25,000 square meters (270,000 sq. ft.), the complex includes an 1,800-person capacity concert hall as well as three recording studios with varying acoustics.

### Royal Arena

*Hannemanns Allé 18-20; tel. 32 46 04 60;*
*www.royalarena.dk; from 300kr; Metro*
*Ørestad St.*

Catering to the biggest names—Justin Timberlake, U2, Elton John, and 50 Cent are among those who played in 2018—the 16,000-capacity Royal Arena is located a 20-minute Metro ride from central Copenhagen in south Amager. It occasionally also hosts sporting events and was home to the Ice Hockey World Cup in 2018.

### Amager Bio

*Øresundsvej 6; tel. 32 86 08 80; https://*
*amagerbio.dk; from 125kr; bus 5C*
*Amagerbrogade (Øresundsvej), Metro*
*Amagerbro St.*

The prolific Amager Bio is one of Copenhagen's most well-visited venues with around 200 concerts yearly and a capacity of 1,000 in its converted cinema theater. A wide range of established stars and hopefuls from Denmark and abroad play a span of genres including rock, indie, pop, blues, metal, and jazz.

## CINEMA

### Grand Teatret

*Mikkel Bryggers Gade 8; tel. 33 15 16*
*11; https://grandteatret.dk; from 70kr;*
*bus 2A Stormbroen, Nationalmuseet*
*(Vindebrogade), 12 Rådhuspladsen*
*(Vesterbrogade)*

Grand Teatret is not a theater at all, but an independent art house cinema that has existed in architect Anton Rosen's handsome building since 1913. Look out for festivals and other cultural events.

### Empire Bio

*Guldbergsgade 29; tel. 35 36 00 36; www.empirebio.dk; from 75kr; bus 5C Kapelvej (Nørrebrogade)*

In the heart of Nørrebro in a former locomotive workshop and later car dealership, Empire Bio is a good spot to take in a Hollywood flick if you want a more local feel than one of the mulitplexes scattered around town.

### Cinematheque

*Gothersgade 55; tel. 33 74 34 00, www.dfi.dk/en/english/cinematheque-and-archives; 80kr; bus 2A, 66 Vester Farimagsgade (Gyldenløvesgade)*

Cinematheque is a traditional art-house cinema that shows more than 70 films monthly, many of which are in English or have English subtitles. A café and bookstore are attached. On the first floor, there is an impressive library of film literature and an archive of posters.

# Festivals and Events

Festival peak season in Copenhagen is unsurprisingly during the summer, when (theoretically) warmer weather brings people out in large numbers to enjoy the late nights and outdoor events. Distortion, a raw ode to hedonism that turns the city upside down for five days in June, is probably the most notable, but perhaps also the most controversial festival since those who are not partying themselves often lament the morning-after condition of their local neighborhoods.

### Copenhagen Jazz Festival

*Various locations; tel. 33 93 20 13; http://jazz.dk/copenhagen-jazz-festival-2018/forside; July; many concerts free*

A nine-day festival sprawling across the Inner City, Vesterbro, Frederiksberg, and beyond, Copenhagen Jazz Festival is one of the most well regarded of its kind in Europe. Jazz springs up in parks, city squares, on street corners, and in bars and concert venues all over the city

during the first half of July. It's hard to miss it. A public transport "event ticket," which is valid for 12 hours, can be bought for 30 kroner (or 60 kroner if you are traveling outside the city) to enable easier bus, Metro, and train access to the various events.

### Distortion

*Various locations in Nørrebro, Vesterbro, Refshaleøen; www.cphdistortion.dk; May/June; full pass 550kr; pass for main street parties 130kr*

Young Copenhageners come out in droves to attend the decadent street festival Distortion at the end of May/beginning of June. With a focus on electronic and dance music, Distortion is very much a street party (mostly chaotic outside partying). Its buzz is infectious, although local residents are often driven to distraction by a lack of sleep and post-partying streets that resemble a scene from *28 Days Later*. Distortion takes its "festival" tag seriously: if you don't have a place to crash in Copenhagen during the festivities, there is a campground set up on Refshaleøen during the event.

## CPH:DOX

*Various locations, primarily Kunsthal Charlottenborg, Nyhavn 2; tel. 33 93 07 34; https://cphdox.dk; Mar.; individual screenings from approx. 60kr; bus/Metro Kongens Nytorv*

CPH:DOX—Copenhagen International Documentary Film Festival—is one of the largest of its kind in the world. Founded in 2003, more than 110,000 people attended in 2018. The festival lasts for almost two weeks and, in addition to documentary screenings, includes audiovisual concerts, panel debates, exhibitions, and regional film events.

## Copenhagen Pride

*Regnbuepladsen; http://copenhagenpride. dk; Aug.; free; bus 12 Rådhuspladsen (Vesterbrogade)*

Pride is becoming a bigger event in Copenhagen, with the Danish capital set to host two major LGBTQ events in 2021—EuroGames and WorldPride. Copenhagen Pride is the city's annual weeklong pride festival and takes place at Regnbuepladsen (Rainbow Square, renamed in 2014) adjacent to Rådhuspladsen (City Hall Square). A human rights program and entertainment at the square take place throughout the week before the Pride march, which since 2011 has proceeded through Frederiksberg and Vesterbro.

## VinterJazz

*Various locations; tel. 33 93 20 13; http:// jazz.dk/vinterjazz-2018/om-festivalen; February; many concerts free*

The winter edition of Copenhagen Jazz Festival is actually a nationwide event and includes a large quantity of small and large jazz concerts and happenings in Copenhagen—enough to keep you moving in the height of the winter cold.

## St. John's Eve (Sankthansaften)

Midsummer is celebrated in Denmark, as it is in a number of other northern European countries, by lighting a bonfire. The Danish interpretation of this is Sankthansaften (St. John's Eve). Held on June 23, the evening before midsummer, and in keeping with Nordic tradition, Danes typically set up a large bonfire and top it with a witch figure. After speeches and singing, the bonfire is lit, and the figure goes up in flames before the festivities continue long into the bright evening.

Despite its modern incarnation as a pleasant family summer evening, the St. John's tradition in Denmark has a very gruesome history. As many as 1,000 women and men convicted of witchcraft are thought to have been burned alive in the country during the 16th and 17th centuries. The practice, which has its origins in Pagan rituals, was once said to ward off witches and trolls who gathered under the midsummer night.

In Copenhagen, the celebration can be seen in several places. These include Frederiksberg Gardens and Amager Strandpark, with the former, on the expansive lawn in front of the palace, one of the largest gatherings of its kind in the city.

Due to Denmark's climate, Sankthansaften can often end up a wet or chilly affair, so be sure to dress appropriately if staying out late. This was far from the case in 2018, however, when a freakishly hot, dry summer caused bonfires to be banned across the country because the risk of wildfire was so great.

# Shopping

Denmark is famous for its minimalist design, most prominently that of iconic architect Arne Jacobsen, whose most famous works include the "ant" chair and the classic wristwatch. Although these would make wonderful Danish souvenirs, they don't come cheap. Shops such as Pilgrim and Panduro offer a less expensive way to try out a bit of Danish design.

Famous clothing brands include Han Kjøbenhavn, WoodWood, Samsøe & Samsøe, and Won Hundred, often showcasing Danes' preference for pared-down, black outfits, but there are plenty of places to find vintage styles too.

Souvenir shops dotted around central Copenhagen offer Viking-horned hats, wooden soldiers holding Danish flags, and Little Mermaid miniatures.

## SHOPPING DISTRICTS
### Strøget and Købmagergade

Strøget, in the area around Nørreport, is the closest to a "main shopping street" Copenhagen has to offer, and as such offers an array of chain stores, electronics, sports, and fast food outlets. At its eastern end around Amagertorv, there are **flagship design and department stores**, including famous Danish names such as **Hay** and **Illum.** Nearby, **Magasin Du Nord,** just off Kongens Nytorv square, is perhaps the most recognizable store in the country.

Købmagergade, which bisects Strøget, is similarly commercial, with

shop windows, Inner City

## LGBTQ+ COPENHAGEN

Denmark was the first country to recognize same-sex partnerships in 1989. Same-sex marriage in church was made legal in 2012. In 2017, the country unilaterally declassified transgenderism as a mental illness, something the World Health Organization has yet to do. Copenhagen's Pride event is growing by the year and reached an estimated 40,000 participants in 2018. The government, a coalition of conservative parties, appointed a commissioner for LGBT issues in 2018 and announced an action plan to promote equality.

Denmark and Copenhagen can claim to be at the forefront of equality now, but the 1960s saw some resistance to what was, for its time, a liberal approach to LGBTQ+ issues, with a police commissioner who encouraged officers to step in if two men were seen dancing together in public. By the time this policy was axed in 1973, the sexual revolution was truly underway in Denmark's capital.

People interested in LGBTQ+ nightlife and events while visiting Copenhagen won't be short of options, including:

- The many LGBTQ+-friendly bars in the **Inner City,** particularly around the **Kattesundet**, **Lars Bjørns Stræde,** and **Studiestræde** streets, just a block from City Hall Square (Rådhuspladsen)

- **My Fair Ladies,** a musical-themed cocktail bar with table service (page 126)

- **Centralhjørnet,** the city's oldest gay bar (page 126)

Copenhagen will host two major LGBT events in 2021: **WorldPride**, a 10-day festival of parades and cultural activities; and **EuroGames**, an LGBT sporting event organized by the European Gay and Lesbian Sport Federation. For further recommendations or information about LGBTQ+ events, contact or drop by the **Copenhagen Pride** office (H. C. Andersens Boulevard 27; tel. 31 50 24 68; http://copenhagenpride.dk).

a number of **fashion outlets** concentrated at its eastern end near the Gammel Mønt street. All of these areas are also well stocked with **kitschy souvenir shops**, reflecting the city center location.

It's worthwhile to wander away from the two main streets in this area, too—adjacent and parallel streets, including Læderstræde, **Fiolstræde,** and **Kronprinsensgade,** can be calmer alternatives offering up **jewelry, fashion,** and **design** and no shortage of **cafés** should you need a pit stop.

### Larsbjørnsstræde

To the north of Strøget in the area sometimes referred to as the "Latin Quarter," Larsbjørnsstræde is known for **avant-garde** and **designer fashion boutiques** as well as stylish **vintage clothing stores** (expect to pay something between thrift store and boutique prices).

### Værnedamsvej and Istedgade

Tucked between Vesterbro and Frederiksberg, Værnedamsvej has **French cafés, teashops,** a **chocolaterie,** and enough **boutiques** for a little window shopping. If you want to extend your shopping session in Vesterbro, head further south across Vesterbrogade to Istedgade, where you will find **independent fashion** and **home wares** mixed in with **tattooists, cafés, second-hand shops,** and **liquor stores.**

## Amagerbrogade

No-frills Amagerbrogade, which begins across the bridge from Christianshavn and stretches deep into Copenhagen's island district, could become a little frillier in coming years with a renewal project tidying up the sidewalks and making the area gradually more pedestrian-friendly. Its northern end has **thrift stores** mixed in with **antique, bric-a-brac,** and **second-hand bookshops,** before a long stretch more dominated by **chain outlets,** including at the **Amager Center shopping mall** just off the main street, close to Amagerbro Metro station. A couple of miles along, south of Englandsvej and Peder Lykkes vej, is a small cluster of independent **vintage clothing** shops, independent **bookstores,** and small **furniture** and **design** specialists.

## Ravnsborggade

In Nørrebro, the Ravnsborggade area reflects the alternative style of the neighborhood, with a number of **thrift stores** and **vintage** or **antique** shops. Adjacent **Nørrebrogade,** Nørrebro's main thoroughfare, has independent **grocery stores, electronic outlets,** and **supermarkets.**

## Jægersborggade

Further into Nørrebro, Jægersborggade also has a good smattering of independent shops, including **thrift** and **clothing stores, gifts, home wares,** and at least one **tattoo artist**.

# NØRREPORT AND AROUND

The area around Nørreport is the essential destination for Copenhagen shopping, with the main brands on Strøget and Købmagergade, boutiques, department stores, and small independent specialist and second-hand shops all densely packed into a small area.

## CLOTHING AND ACCESSORIES
### Storm

*Store Regnegade 1; tel. 33 93 00 14; www. stormfashion.dk; Mon.-Thurs. 11am-5:30pm, Fri. 11am-7pm, Sat. 10am-4pm; bus, Metro Kongens Nytorv*

Storm is a lifestyle and brand-focused fashion store that also sells books, magazines, and games. Pick up brand-name fashion such as trainers from Puma or Nike, Kangol hats, and Timex watches as well as lifestyle magazines such as *Monocle* or *Wallpaper*—all with in-store exhibitions, smart displays, and smartly dressed staff.

### NN07

*Gammel Mønt 7; tel. 38 41 11 41; www.nn07. com; Mon.-Thurs. 10am-pm, Fri. 10am-7pm, Sat. 10am-5pm, Sun. noon-4pm; bus, Metro Kongens Nytorv*

Priding itself on equality—"NN" stands for "no nationality"—this independent men's fashion brand draws from its passion for international travel and food culture. The style is casual, contemporary, and simple, with a focus on high quality.

### Baum und Pferdgarten

*Vognmagergade 2; tel. 35 30 10 90; www. baumundpferdgarten.com; Mon.-Fri. 10am-6pm, Sat. 10am-4pm; bus, Metro Kongens Nytorv*

Created in 1999 by designers Rikke Baumgarten and Helle Hestehave ("Hestehave" literally means "Garden Horse"—a translation of the latter's surname), this women's fashion brand plays on colors and prints, helping it to stand out from the popular darker tone favored in the clothing choices of many Danes.

## Han Kjøbenhavn

*Vognmagergade 7; tel. 52 15 35 07; www. hankjobenhavn.com; Mon.-Fri. 11am-6pm, Sat. 10am-5pm; bus, Metro Kongens Nytorv*

This unique brand combines fashion with short filmmaking, with the results used to present their collection of Scandinavian, workwear-inspired men's fashion. It started out as an eyewear brand, and spectacle frames remain an important part of its market. The Copenhagen flagship store is itself a spectacle in the clean lines and optimal lighting of Danish design.

## Wood Wood

*Grønnegade 1; tel. 35 35 62 64; www. woodwood.dk; Mon.-Fri. 10:30am-6pm, Fri. 10.30am-7pm, Sat. 10.30am-5pm, Sun. noon-4pm; bus, Metro Kongens Nytorv*

A popular choice with the Copenhagen hipster set, Wood Wood is a contemporary fashion brand now with stores in Aarhus and Berlin. The men's and women's clothing mixes high-end fashion, sportswear, and street style influences but tries to keep things grounded, as is reflected in the simple, clean designs of the store's interior.

## Stine Goya

*Gothersgade 58; tel. 32 17 10 00; www. stinegoya.com; Mon.-Fri. 11am-6pm, Sat. 11am-4pm; bus, Metro Kongens Nytorv*

Stine Goya is an ideal spot to find elegant Danish-designed women's clothes to take home. Designer Stine Goya, whose name is carried by the store, began her fashion career in 2006 and is known for a detailed, high quality, colorful range—something of a break from Danes' penchant for black. Goya's designs have achieved international acclaim, including that

of world-famous Danish supermodel Helena Christensen. The store itself is as chic as the products, with stucco coving, pastel colors, and brass railings that make for a strikingly handsome setting.

## Mads Nørgaard

*Amagertorv 13-15; tel. 33 12 24 28; www. madsnorgaard.dk; Mon.-Thurs. 10am-6pm, Fri. 10am-7pm, Sat. 10am-5pm; bus, Metro Kongens Nytorv*

A Danish fashion designer with a sense of classical looks for men and women, Mads Nørgaard's signature striped designs will have you blending in with style-conscious Danes who will instantly recognize the brand. Inside the store, the colorful, tight spaces are often busy with browsers dropping in from busy Amagertorv.

## & Other Stories

*Amagertorv 29; tel. 36 97 88 19; www. stories.com/en_dkk/index.html; Mon.-Fri. 10am-7pm, Sat. 10am-6pm, Sun. noon-6pm; bus, Metro Kongens Nytorv*

& Other Stories, H&M's less-well known but better-quality sister company, won a Danish retail prize for women's fashion in 2017 for its store on Amagertorv. The ranges are colorful and staff are helpful in a personal but not overbearing way. In addition to clothes, accessories such as jewelry, sunglasses, and even pencils and notebooks are on sale at the central Copenhagen branch. The narrow, high-ceilinged store normally hums with shoppers. It's located at one of the busiest pedestrian points in the city.

## Liafi Studio

*Studiestræde 18 st tv; tel. 21 69 20 61; http:// liafistudio.com; Mon.-Thurs. 11am-5:30pm, Fri. 11am-6pm, Sat. 11am-5:30pm, Sun.*

noon-4pm; Bus 5C Larslejsstræde (Nørre Voldgade)

Liafi is a concept store selling used, premium items, with sports brands such as Nike and Kappa often prominent alongside Acne, Luis Vuitton, and Commes de Garcons. Jackets, shoes, accessories, sweats, and pants are all on sale in the store, which is a handsome affair with a blue workshop-style flooring and interior brickwork. Although this is technically a second-hand shop, don't expect to pick up any bargains—it's pricey.

### Time's Up Vintage

*Krystalgade 4; tel. 33 32 39 30; www.timesupshop.com; Mon.-Thurs. 11am-6pm, Fri. 11am-7pm, Sat. 10am-5pm; bus, Metro Nørreport*

This glamorous selection of vintage designer labels including YSL, Gucci, Versace, Chanel, and Valentino is located on the exclusive Krystalgade, a cobbled street that is home to several high-end boutiques. It's a small, wooden-floored shop with wares arranged in open closets, on glass-topped tables, and on racks, the prices are not low, but the quality and cut of the fabric is always high.

### Georg Jensen

*Amagertorv 4; tel. 33 11 40 80; www.georgjensen.com; Mon.-Sat. 10am-6pm, Sun. 11am-4pm; bus, Metro Kongens Nytorv*

Founded in 1904 in Copenhagen by silversmith Georg Jensen, the Amagertorv store is the home of what is possibly Denmark's most famous jewelry brand. Its products—which include housewares, accessories, and cutlery as well as jewelry—are characterized by clean, sleek, graceful lines. There may be a feeling of exclusivity, given the high prices of most of the products—the cheapest items just scrape under 300 kroner. Head upstairs for vintage design and a view of Amagertorv.

### Wasteland

*Studiestræde 19; tel. 33 32 54 05; www.shopwasteland.com; Mon.-Thurs. 10:30am-6pm, Fri. 10:30am-7pm, Sat. 10:30am-5pm, Sun. noon-4pm; bus 14 Mozarts Plads, Metro Nørreport*

At Wasteland, pop music—often from a radio station in London—hums in the background, and the staff, many of whom have British or Irish accents themselves, are effortlessly cool and stylish. Despite this, there's a distinctly American feel to the clothing, which is hardly surprising given Wasteland's Californian origins. The high-quality vintage selection is a little more expensive than second-hand clothing elsewhere. Located just off the main shopping district near Nørreport.

## INTERIOR DESIGN

### Stilleben

*Niels Hemmingsensgade 3; tel. 33 91 11 31; www.stilleben.dk; Mon.-Fri. 10pm-6pm, Sat. 10am-5pm; bus, Metro Kongens Nytorv*

This is a fabulous collection of color-rich ceramics and glass, jewelry, glitter socks, fabric bags, kitchen gear, and artsy prints. Everything on sale at Stilleben was chosen for its uniqueness—many of the products are "one of a kind." Designs from around the world are included, but Danish design does not take a back seat. Named by *Forbes* magazine as one of Copenhagen's top five design stores, its thoughtfully arranged shelves and framed artwork gives you a taste for bringing the clean Scandinavian style to your own home.

## GUBI Store

*Møntergade 19; tel. 53 61 63 68; www.gubi. dk; Mon.-Fri. 10am-6pm, Sun. 10am-4pm; bus, Metro Kongens Nytorv*

Luxurious design store with innovative, aesthetic chairs, lamps, and furniture showing prominent influence from the Arne Jacobsen functionalist school. It's spread across 400 square meters (4,300 sq. ft.) in a classic Copenhagen building from 1916 with a spiral staircase and precision-picked articles and ornaments.

## Vipp Concept Store

*Ny Østergade 34; tel. 45 88 88 15; www. vipp.com; Mon.-Fri. 11am-6pm; bus, Metro Kongens Nytorv*

*At vippe* is a Danish verb meaning something similar to "flip" or to quickly turn over an object. Vipp's kitchen and bathroom modules are characterized by ergonomic lids that flip open—not least the instantly recognizable kitchen trash can. The company has also branched into designing forest shelters. The resulting 150 square meters (1,600 sq ft) concept store is similar to a niche furniture showroom.

## Royal Copenhagen Flagship Store

*Amagertorv 6; tel. 33 13 71 81; www. royalcopenhagen.dk; Mon.-Fri. 10am-7pm, Sat. 10am-6pm, Sun. 11am-4pm; bus, Metro Kongens Nytorv*

At Royal Copenhagen, both you and your wallet can be regal for a while. The brand is a Danish classic and its products are to be found in many a Danish home. The iconic fine, white crockery is instantly recognizable, but be prepared to shell out, even for a small piece, if you want to treat yourself. The flagship outlet is in a stunning 1616 three-story Renaissance building on Amagertorv and has been a Royal Copenhagen store since 1911. It exudes the delicate manners of fine china and a tradition of fine craftsmanship.

## ART
## Posterland

*Gothersgade 45; tel. 33 11 28 21; www. posterland.dk; Mon.-Thurs. 9:30am-6pm, Fri. 9:30am-7pm, Sat. 9:30am-6pm; bus, Metro Kongens Nytorv*

A plethora of posters fill the space, including art prints, films, nature, maps, and vintage advertisements for Tuborg and other quintessential Danish companies. The extensive Posterland is located near King's Garden, a short step from the mainstream shops along Strøget. If you are worried a poster might get crushed in your luggage, the postcard versions also make great mementos. While away an hour or two among the crowded racks as you flip through travel, art, and advertising prints from throughout the years.

## Kortkartellet

*Niels Hemmingsens Gade 6; tel. 53 65 01 22; www.kortkartellet.dk; Wed.-Fri. 10am-6pm, Sat. 10am-5pm; bus, Metro Kongens Nytorv*

Kortkartellet—"The Map Cartel"—is an art print and poster store that revolves around the concept of using maps as the basis for art, but there is a broad range of designs, with plants and letters among other prominent themes. The idea makes for a great souvenir or gift. You can also buy smaller items such as cards, mugs, and magnets.

## SOUVENIRS
## Hay House

*Østergade 61; tel. 42 82 08 20; www.hay.dk; Mon.-Fri. 10am-6pm, Sat. 10am-5pm; bus, Metro Kongens Nytorv*

A charming shop set on several floors with a terrific view of the main Strøget shopping thoroughfare and the Stork Fountain—a popular gathering place for hippies in the 1960s. Hay is bursting with modern, sleek Danish design and is highly popular with locals. The store itself resembles an upper-class Copenhagen home with a staircase acting as its main entrance. The travel notebook and fabric carrier bags are affordable but no less classy, potential souvenirs.

### Copenhagen Souvenir & Design

*Østergade 11; tel. 33 36 27 43; http://copenhagensouvenir.com; Mon.-Thurs. 10am-6pm, Fri. 10am-7pm, Sat. 10am-4pm; bus, Metro Kongens Nytorv*

Carlsberg hats, Viking magnets, Little Mermaid plates, "clap hats" (baseball caps with two hands on the peak that can be made to clap are popular among Danish soccer fans) . . . and not to mention umbrellas. You will probably find all the quintessential souvenirs and tourist fare you will need here, although there are many similar shops scattered all over the Inner City, should you miss this particular one.

### DEPARTMENT STORES
### Illum

*Østergade 52; tel. 33 14 40 02; www.ilum.dk; daily 10am-8pm; bus, Metro Kongens Nytorv*

Illum is a luxurious Danish department store with an impressive layout and attractive displays. It's located at the central Amagertorv square, and stocks all the major Danish and international cosmetics, interior design, and clothing brands and plenty more. The store's top floor has an extensive food court and outside balcony with a fantastic view of the buskers and passers-by below, as well as an eye-level sight of the characteristic Copenhagen spires.

### Magasin du Nord

*Kongens Nytorv 13; tel. 33 11 44 33; www.magasin.dk; daily 10am-8pm; bus, Metro Kongens Nytorv*

The historic department store Magasin du Nord started out as a draper's shop in the mid-nineteenth century. It now has branches across Denmark, and the store at the impressive French Renaissance Revival style building at Kongens Nytorv, built on the site of the earlier Hotel du Nord, boasts seven floors of fashion, home design, furnishings, beauty supplies and toiletries, books, toys, kitchenware, and groceries, not to mention a large delicatessen. A personal shopper can be arranged by calling in advance.

## GREATER INNER CITY

The end of the Inner City close to Rådhuspladsen (City Hall Square) has many chain and tourist-oriented stores as well as a few gems, including Politikens Boghal, paradise for bookworms.

### Klassik

*Bredgade 3; tel. 33 33 90 60; www.klassik. dk; Mon.-Fri. 11am-6pm, Sat. 10am-4pm; Metro Nørreport*

Located on sulubrious Bredgade, Klassik is in equal parts history lesson and furniture store, but it's more than just a secondhand shop. The range of restored furniture is a journey into the classics of Danish design, and the staff know their stuff too. The calming store resembles an extended version of an incredibly tasteful 20th-century home with its arrangements of dining and coffee tables, lighting, ornaments, and bookcases.

### Politikens Boghal

*Rådhuspladsen 37; tel. 30 67 28 06; https://
politikensforlag.dk/politikens-boghal/c-9;
Mon.-Thurs. 9am-7pm, Wed.-Fri. 9am-8pm
Sat. 10am-6pm, Sun. 11am-6pm; bus 5C
Rådhuspladsen (H. C. Andersens Boulevard)*

Politikens Boghal is home territory for Politiken, one of Denmark's major news media and publishers. It's easy to find signed (usually Danish) books or even spot a famous Nordic author. The store also regularly hosts literary or cultural events and has excellent coffee in its in-house café. A large case spanning the entire back wall comprises a comprehensive selection of books in English.

## NYHAVN

### Tattoo Ole

*Nyhavn 17; tel. 33 15 90 86; https://
tattoo-ole.dk; Tues.-Sat. noon-8pm, other
times by appointment; bus, Metro Kongens
Nytorv*

The tattoo parlor in the basement of Nyhavn 17 is a throwback to days when the area was far from the tourist attraction it is today. The locale has had a tattoo artist since 1884, making it the world's oldest tattoo parlor. If you're feeling brave enough to get inked in Nyhavn, you still can—for now: the owner of the building reportedly wants to convert the location into extra space for the restaurant that occupies the other floors. Reservations are not strictly necessary but recommended to avoid disappointment, and the friendly tattoo artists are generally happy to talk to walk-ins about their options.

## VESTERBRO AND FREDERIKSBERG

Vesterbro, once known only for crime, poverty, and drug addiction, has been redeveloped and gentrified. Its former industrial area is now one of the trendiest bar and restaurant districts in the entire country, and the Værnedamsvej shopping street, the "Little Paris" of Copenhagen, is a cluster of cozy cafés and shops. It still retains enough of its edge to ensure its history remains part of the present, however.

## CLOTHING AND ACCESSORIES

### Samsøe & Samsøe

*Værnedamsvej 12; tel. 35 28 51 02; www.
samsoe.com; Mon.-Thurs. 10am-6pm, Fri.
10am-7pm, Sat. 10am-5pm, Sun. 11am-4pm;
bus 9A Værnedamsvej (Gammel Kongevej)*

Founded by brothers Klaus and Preben Samsøe in a small Copenhagen shop in 1993, the Samsøe & Samsøe brand is near-synonymous with formal men's clothing in Denmark, although the company is also known for women's fashion. The style is also classically Danish, with simple lines and colors. The Værnedamsvej branch is small and cozy, in keeping with local surroundings.

### Dora

*Værnedamsvej 6; tel. 32 21 33 57; www.
shopdora.dk; Mon.-Fri. 10am-6pm, Sat.
10am-5pm, Sun. 10am-4pm; bus 9A
Værnedamsvej (Gammel Kongevej)*

A home goods store with a cluttered aesthetic and a street corner setting, Dora touts accessories, iron-on prints for jackets, housewares, Christmas decorations, jewelry, and more.

### Prag

*Vesterbrogade 98A; tel. 33 79 00 50 www.
pragcopenhagen.com; Mon.-Fri. 10am-6pm,
Sat. 10am-5pm, Sun. noon-5pm; bus
Vesterbrogade (Enghavevej), 9A
Værnedamsvej (Gammel Kongevej)*

Prag is a busy secondhand clothing store with well-selected accessories that range from sunglasses, hair bands, and jewelry to tights and denim jackets. Frilly dresses, 1980s power designs, and summer frocks can all be found in this trove of pre-worn style, as can leather shoes, plaid shirts, and moleskin slacks. You can also buy a fabric bag with the store's logo with which to carry away your haul—reuse the bag for extra Copenhagener street cred.

### Kyoto

*Istedgade 95; tel. 33 31 66 36; www.kyoto. dk; Mon.-Thurs. 10am-6pm, Fri. 10am-7pm, Sat. 10am-5pm; bus 9A Værnedamsvej (Gammel Kongevej)*

On raw Istedgade close to the Meatpacking District, staff and customers look like the original models of the clothes at Kyoto, which is a designer store for men and women located in the heart of Vesterbro on Istedgade. There's an emphasis on known brands and simple styles for casual wear.

## INTERIOR DESIGN
### Bønnebordet

*Vesterbrogade 137; tel. 24 24 73 62; http:// boennebord.dk; Mon.-Fri. 10am-5:30pm, Sat. 10am-2pm; bus 6A Platanvej (Vesterbrogade).*

A shop entirely devoted to the "Bean Table," a coffee table in the shape of, you guessed it, a bean—a very recognizable design by Dane Karsten Lauritzen in 1995 for an art exhibition and now a staple in the country's living rooms. "I know (the table) is at the home of an oil sheikh in his luxury apartment in Paris as well as at the places of many students in Vesterbro," Lauritzen once said. You can build your own bean table, choosing between 15 models, five sizes, and two heights, at the showroom in Vesterbro

or online. Note the tables take around four weeks to make—it is not possible to purchase "off the peg."

## FLEA MARKETS
### Frederiksberg Loppetorv

*Frederiksberg Bredegade 13; tel. 38 21 42 20; www.frederiksberg.dk/loppetorv; Sat. 7am-3pm; bus 8A Frederiksberg Rådhus(Allegade)*

You'll need to arrive at Frederiksberg Loppetorv early on Saturday to look for undervalued antiques. It's upmarket for a flea market, which is possibly a knock-on effect of Frederiksberg's affluence. The 90 or more stalls offer most things you might hope to find—Danish design desk lamps, metal teapots, plastic sunglasses, crystal decanters, toy cars, LPs, shoes, shirts, and so on. One of the biggest and busiest flea markets in the city, though it closes during the winter months, usually November through February, though exact dates are variable.

## MALLS
### Fisketorvet

*Kalvebod Brygge 59; tel. 33 36 64 00; www. fisketorvet.dk; daily 10am-8pm; bus 34, S-train Fisketorvet (Dybbølsbro)*

Shopping mall Fisketorvet, which is quite close to Copenhagen Central Station, has a classic range of Scandinavian chain stores, including H&M, Zara, and Matas. The mall is well-frequented by families who use its restaurants—some chains include Lélé (Asian), Gorms (pizza), and McDonald's. A cinema complex is also housed in the center.

### Frederiksberg Centret

*Falkoner Allé 21; tel. 38 16 03 40; https:// frbc-shopping.dk; Mon.-Fri. 10am-7pm, Sat.-Sun. 10am-5pm; Metro Frederiksberg St.*

Frederiksberg Center, in upmarket

Frederiksberg, has a strong reputation as one of the city's leading malls and houses mainly chain stores, encompassing a supermarket, optometrist, jeweler, health food, clothing, shoes, interior design, and sports. Its atmosphere is calm and child-friendly, reflecting the neighborhood it calls home. It is served directly by the Copenhagen Metro.

# NØRREBRO AND ØSTERBRO

While more about colorful streetlife and nightlife than shopping, Nørrebro has its share of vintage clothing shops, where you might find the kind of bargain that would be unlikely in the Inner City.

## CLOTHING AND ACCESSORIES
### Studio Travel

*Blågårdsgade 14; tel. 26 84 12 60; https://
studio-travel.com; Mon.-Sat. 11am-6pm; bus
5C Ravnsborggade (Nørrebrogade)*

A vintage clothing store in which items are handpicked at Italian flea markets, Studio Travel's quiet, whitewashed boutique is an oasis of Nørrebro calm. With both men's and women's ranges.

### Rán Rosanna

*Nordre Frihavnsgade 60; tel. 35 55 16 61;
www.instagram.com/ranrosanna; Mon.-Fri.
11am-5:30pm, Sat. 10am-2pm; bus 3A
Hobrogade (Nordre Frihavnsgade), 1A
Trianglen (Østerbrogade)*

Rán Rosanna in Østerbro is one of Copenhagen's oldest vintage clothing stores and also one of its best regarded, catering to the young family demographic of the area with its hip, diverse clothing for women and kids and a reputation for friendly service.

### Gemmeren

*Fælledvej 9; tel. 22 56 53 34; www.
noedhjaelp.dk/genbrug; Mon.-Fri. noon-6pm;
bus 5C Ravnsborggade (Nørrebrogade)*

Cheap but stylish, alternative Danish secondhand threads are abundant at the charmingly messy Gemmeren, where books (normally in Danish, but you might be lucky) are also sold. Staff are always decked out in clothes from the shop. It's also a charity shop, rather than a vintage store (although its target market overlaps), so you can expect to find a bit of everything.

### BauBau

*Birkegade 3; tel. 40 86 29 37; www.
baubaushop.com; Mon.-Fri. 11am-6pm, Sat.
11am-4pm; bus 5C Elmegade (Nørrebrogade)*

The "revived apparel" at BauBau has a 1980s feel, including coats, jackets, shoes, bags, sweatshirts, and vests—even the walls look like distressed denim. Brands such as Gucci and Lanvin and plenty of sportswear add to the high fashion feel. It's ostensibly a menswear store, but there are also plenty of female customers attracted to the well-kept vintage and handmade interior products. Shopping here feels like an upcycling experience in itself: closely packed racks hang from old bicycle inner tubes, and shelves are formed from driftwood.

## INTERIOR DESIGN
### Normann Copenhagen

*Østerbrogade 70; tel. 35 27 05 40; www.
normann-copenhagen.com; Mon.-Fri.
11am-5:30pm, Sat. 10am-3pm; bus 1A, 3A
Trianglen*

Normann Copenhagen was named by the *New York Times* as one of 12 shopping treasures in Europe in 2014. The sprawling design store is located in a former cinema and sells sculptural lighting and innovative home accessories—even the dust-pans and brushes have effortless style. Highlights include a steel corridor, crisscrossing ceiling lamps, and a room colored entirely in pink.

## Paustian

*Kalkbrænderiløbskaj 2; tel. 39 16 65 65;*
*www.paustian.com; Mon.-Fri. 11am-6pm, Sat.*
*10am-4pm; S-train Nordhavn*

Paustian is located on the Nordhavn waterfront in a spectacular building designed by Jørn Utzon (and later extended by Utzon's son), the Danish architect who designed the Sydney Opera House. The columns of Paustian house evoke a mixture of a forest, an airport, and a Greek temple, and wares include classic chair designs, flip-lid trash cans, Louis Poulsen lamps, home accessories, mirrors, shelves, and cupboards.

## ART

### Vanishing Point

*Jægersborggade 45; tel. 25 13 47 55; www.*
*vanishing-point.dk; Mon.-Wed. 11am-5:30pm,*
*Thurs. 11am-3pm, Fri.-Sat. 11am-4pm, Sun.*
*11am-3pm; bus 5C Stefansgade, 66 Jagtvej*
*(Borups Allé)*

A studio as well as a craft shop in Nørrebro's atmospheric Jægersborggade, Vanishing Point sells arts and crafts made by in-house or local artists or work it has acquired through collaborations with international nongovernmental organizations (NGOs). These include jewelry, hand-knitted quilts, ceramics, and art prints.

### Gågrøn!

*Jægersborggade 48; tel. 40 18 07 72; www.*
*gagron.dk; Mon.-Thurs. 11am-5:30pm,*
*Fri.-Sat. 11am-4pm; bus 5C Stefansgade, 66*
*Jagtvej (Borups Allé)*

The 100 percent sustainable Gågrøn (GoGreen) on atmospheric Jægersborggade sells housewares made entirely from recycled, upcycled, or eco-friendly materials, so you won't feel frivolous about buying souvenirs. Products include bamboo kitchen utensils, organic cotton towels, and chemical-free water bottles. The small store is also well stocked with environmental enthusiam from the guests and staff.

## FLEA MARKETS

### Nørrebro Loppemarked

*Nørrebrogade; tel. 32 69 39 48; www.*
*berling-samlerting.dk; Sat. 8am-3pm*
*Apr.-Oct.; bus 5C Nørrebrogade*

Saturdays in the summer season see a giant flea market running the length of Assistens Cemetery. Arriving early is encouraged for the kind of bargains you won't find in the profit-savvy vintage stores: books, LPs, electronics, and antiques. The flea market is located on a sidewalk, so be prepared for a lack of elbow room, especially in good weather.

# CHRISTIANSHAVN AND AMAGER

Christianshavn is not known for its shopping options, although the occasional vintage clothing shop has been known to spring up in the area in the past. Over on Amager, the main street Amagerbrogade caters to most daily needs while a little further out is Field's, a hulking out-of-town mall.

### Field's

*Arne Jacobsens Allé 12; tel. 70 20 85*
*05; https://fields.steenstrom.dk; daily*
*10am-8pm; bus 33 Ørestad St. (Ørestads*
*Boulevard), Metro Ørestad St.*

Field's, the largest shopping mall in Scandinavia, is filled with 140 stores, including an complete Magasin department store. The mall also boasts an entire floor dedicated to leisure, with restaurants, cafés, a fun golf course and play areas for kids, and a lounge furnished with Arne Jacobsen furniture. If you're driving, you'll probably be okay for parking—there are 3,000 spaces.

# Dining

Copenhagen has 15 Michelin-starred restaurants as of February 2018, including the three-starred Geranium. That makes it the most-starred city in the Nordic region. But the culinary experience is not just about exclusive or fine dining. Street food, food markets, and ethnic restaurants in Refshaleøen, the Inner City and Nørrebro, respectively, contribute to a rich variety, while the Meatpacking District (Kødbyen) in Vesterbro is a world-class destination, as evidenced by the internationally reknowned chefs that work in its restaurants.

## NØRREPORT AND AROUND

### DANISH AND NEW NORDIC
Schønnemann

*Hauser Plads 16; tel. 33 12 07 85; www. restaurantschonnemann.dk; Mon.-Sat. 11:30am-5pm, from 69kr-169kr, three-course set menu 259kr; bus, Metro, S-train Nørreport*

It doesn't get much more Danish than Schønnemann, a classic lunch restaurant where *smørrebrød* and schnapps are de rigeur. Crisp, white tablecloths and polite service accompany the traditional fish and meat dishes, such as the grandmother's kitchen-evoking *tarteletter*, a small, open-topped pie with a creamy gravy, meat, and veg filling.

### Café Halvvejen

*Krystalgade 11; tel. 33 11 91 12; www. cafehalvvejen.dk; Mon.-Thurs. 11am-2am, Fri.-Sat. 11am-3am; kitchen, Mon.-Sat. noon-3pm; lunch from 59kr-175kr; bus, Metro, S-train Nørreport*

Café Halvvejen is a lunch restaurant (the kitchen closes at 3pm) that is also a pub. The menu consists primarily of what Danes call *rugbrødsmadder*—rye bread with toppings piled on, commonly meat or fish-based (there's not much wiggle room for vegans here). The atmosphere is earthy, the lighting low, and darkly paneled walls adorned with decades-old framed posters and portraits. The food will give you enough ballast to wash down with an afternoon beer.

### Aamanns 1921

*Niels Hemmingsens Gade 19-21; tel. 20 80 52 04; https://aamanns.dk/aamanns-1921; lunch Mon.-Sat. 11:30am-4:30pm (last order 3pm), Sun. 11:30am-5pm (last order 3:30pm), dinner Tues.-Sat. 6pm-midnight (last order 9:30pm); lunch: smørrebrød from 95-155kr, dinner: set four-course menu 390kr; bus, Metro, S-train Nørreport*

Aamanns 1921, which opened in September 2017, serves high-quality, up-to-date versions of Danish *smørrebrød*, made with fresh, seasonal ingredients. The knowledgeable table staff are happy to present the dishes. Chef Adam Aamann was interviewed by the *New York Times*, where he was praised for his attention to such detail as the choice of scented soaps in the restrooms. Courses include cured halibut with oysters and vegetables, fish *frikadeller* (meatballs) with red cabbage, and wild duck with beetroot, blackcurrant, and duck sauce.

## Restaurant Palægade

*Palægade 8; tel. 70 82 82 88; https:// palaegade.dk/frontpage; daily 11:30am-4pm, Mon.-Sat. 6pm-midnight; entrées from 125-175kr; Metro Kongens Nytorv*

Palægade is intimate with atmospheric lighting and lovingly prepared and presented *smørrebrød*. The restaurant's young team stress their passion for traditional Danish food. Dishes include roasted turbot, white veal with cabbage and mushrooms, and a beef wellington for two (which should be pre-ordered).

## Restaurant Koefoed

*Landgreven 3; tel. 56 48 22 24; www. restaurant-koefoed.dk; Tues.-Sat. noon-3pm, 5:30pm-10pm; smørrebrød from 95-175kr, tasting menu 495kr; bus 26 St. Kongensgade (Dronningens Tværgade), Metro Kongens Nytorv*

With both à la carte and a choice of set tasting menus, Restaurant Koefoed applies the New Nordic concept of delicate taste and fresh ingredients to Danish staples like *smørrebrød* and *tarteletter*. Menu elements take in smoked eel, steak tartare, guinea fowl, Tuscan kale, truffle, and caviar, with an extensive wine cellar specializing in Bordeaux. Attentive service in cozy but minimalistic and unpretentious surroundings.

## Rebel

*Store Kongensgade 52; tel. 33 32 32 09; www.restaurantrebel.dk; Tues.-Sat. 5:30pm-midnight (kitchen until 10pm); menu with four dishes plus wine 825kr, entrées and other single dishes from 100kr; bus 1A Amalienborg (Bredgade)*

A foodie's favorite, Rebel is a highly rated fine dining, New Nordic restaurant with extensive tasting menus for those who want to "challenge their taste buds." The "Rebellious Evening" menu, which includes a glass of bubbly and seven wines (1,475kr per person), is the ultimate experience—you'll need to set aside several hours. Dishes include braised octopus, duroc pork belly, caviar, and Norwegian lobster, while Rebel is particularly known for a signature steak tartare. Reservation necessary. The interior is handsome with black-framed mirrors, black furniture, and a menu written on blackboards; a bustling, cozy vibe.

## BREAKFAST AND DINERS

### Restaurant Sult

*Vognmagergade 8 B; tel. 33 74 34 00; www. dfi.dk; Tues.-Sun. breakfast 9am-11:30am, lunch 11:30am-4pm, dinner 5pm-10pm; café 9am-10pm; snacks/tapas 55kr; entrées from 95-115kr; Metro Kongens Nytorv*

Located inside the Danish Film Institute's buildings opposite Kongens Have, the 300-seater Sult—named after a seminal 1960s Danish film by director Henning Carlsen—is both a café and a restaurant. In the former, organic Danish style, breakfasts are on offer, while the latter has an excellent organic brunch (including, but far from limited to, eggs, rye bread, bacon, salmon, and fruit) with vegetarian and vegan options on weekends. There are a lot of tables, and they are close to each other, so there's no shortage of human interaction.

### Greasy Spoon Diner

*Studiestræde 14; tel. 20 15 14 84; www.greasyspoon.dk; Mon.-Thurs.*

Danish café culture, which takes on a specific character of its own in the capital, reflects both continental European influence and the colder climate of the north. At cafés, Danes can commonly be seen outside, shivering under blankets, sitting at sidewalk tables at times of the year when the weather is far too chilly to be exposed to the elements. It's understandable—the winters are long, and people long to get outside and re-create the Italian al fresco feeling. In fact, cafés are at their best in Denmark during the winter, when you can hunker down at a table with a good **Americano** or **latte** or, in December, a mug of *glögg*—the cinnamon-flavored mulled wine synonymous with Christmas—and a *wienerbrød.* In contrast to the stop-go nature of Italian espresso culture, Danes like to **linger** at cafés, spending an hour or three catching up with a friend or even alone, getting some work done or reading a book.

Copenhagen itself has every type of café imaginable, from **small independent roasteries** to **large chains** to **pastry and bread specialists**. Some cafés are **daytime-oriented** while others have **beer** on tap or bottled microbrews, play increasingly upbeat music as the day goes on and finish up becoming out-and-out **bars** as night falls. Others still are lined by wall-to-wall bookshelves and have a distinctly professorial air. The choice is yours.

*10:30am-9:30pm; Fri.-Sat.*
*10:30am-10:30pm; Sun. 9:30am-9:30pm;*
*breakfast 75-110kr; bus 14 Krystalgade*
*(Nørregade)*

This well-located and wallet-friendly diner is what it says it is. If you've spent too much time indulging at the nearby bars the night before, then you'll find it very welcoming. Traditional English breakfasts—not always easy to find in rye bread and oats-happy Denmark—accompany hefty burgers on the menu, which also includes the classic Danish *bøfsandwich* (beef sandwich) with its messy brown sauce topping. The establishment does not seem to suffer from overcrowding, allowing for a relaxed, easy diner feel.

## CAFÉS AND BAKERIES
### La Glace

*Skoubogade 3; tel. 33 14 46 46; www.laglace.dk; Mon.-Fri. 8:30am-6pm, Sat. 9am-6pm; Sun. 10am-6pm; cakes from 62kr per slice, confections 1 piece 277kr, 5 pieces 110kr; bus 14 Mozartsplads*

There is often a long line outside La Glace, supplier of the finest cakes in Denmark. It was founded in 1870 and retains the air and elegance of a Victorian confectioner. The prices can feel steep, but this is hardly an ordinary slice of cake with coffee—the whipped cream is fluffy, and the sponge cake melts in your mouth. Seating is available in keeping with the 19th-century tearoom feel.

### Democratic Coffee

*Krystalgade 15; tel. 40 19 62 37; Mon.-Fri. 8am-4pm; Sat.-Sun. 9am-4pm; Metro Nørreport*

The bakery is popular among students, located inside the university library opposite the synagogue on Krystalgade, and famed for its almond croissants and excellent single origin light-roasted coffee. Baked goods are prepared on the premises—the croissants are so popular that they sell out regularly by noon. There's seating and window space, so you can get work done or simply people watch.

### Meyers Bageri

*Store Kongensgade 46; tel. 25 10 75 79; www.meyersmad.dk; Mon.-Fri. 7pm-6pm, Sat.-Sun. 7pm-4pm; coffee from 25kr, pastries from 20kr; Metro Kongens Nytorv*

Meyers Bageri is a chain of bakeries

with outlets across Copenhagen—the brand, started by chef Claus Meyer, has existed for 25 years (although the first bakeries were not opened until 2010). The branch at Store Kongensgade 46 is a great place to start the day with a croissant or, if you're feeling sweet-toothed, a dense cinnamon *kanel-snurre*. There's a busy and friendly morning vibe that can sometimes evoke local shops from days gone by as regular customers call in to pick up their preferred loaf of rye.

## SEAFOOD
### Musling
*Linnésgade 14; tel. 34 10 56 56; www. musling.net; Tues.-Thurs. noon-midnight; Fri.-Sat. noon-1am (kitchen until 10pm); entrées 105-145kr, four-course menu from 500kr; Metro Nørreport*

This moules frites and oysters specialist offers ambience with its open kitchen. As well as moules, other main dishes include lobster, steamed cod, and sirloin, and side orders range from kimchi to French fries. There's a casual atmosphere, with bar seating as well as white linen tables.

### Fishmarket
*Hovedvagtsgade 2; tel. 88 16 99 99; www. fishmarket.dk; Mon.-Thurs. 11am-11pm, Fri.-Sat. 11am-1am, Sun. 11am-11pm (kitchen until Mon.-Sat. 10:30pm, Sun. 9:30pm); entrées 95-145kr; Metro Kongens Nytorv*

Fishmarket is a French fish bistro with a Mediteranean-style menu—but no less delicious rye bread for it—featuring fresh fish sourced from local suppliers. The menu includes lobster, mussels, and ribeye steak. The restaurant interior is somewhat reminiscent of an old-fashioned train carriage, with wooden and upholstered bench seats and racks to place overcoats. Book in advance.

## BURGERS
### Jagger
*Købmagergade 43; http://jagger.dk; daily 11am-9pm; burgers 50kr-90kr; Metro Nørreport*

Now a stable part of Copenhagen's fast food scene, Jagger, which also has branches in Vesterbro, Nørrebro, Frederiksberg, and Amager, offers a better quality bite to the larger chains. This is reflected in its slightly higher prices. It retains the simple and un-fussy vibe of a diner with its high stools and bright lighting. Pulled pork burgers, cheesburgers, and chicken burgers accompanied by fries can be washed down with chocolate or vanilla milkshakes.

### Gasoline Grill
*Landgreven 10; www.gasolinegrill.com; daily 11am until sold out; burgers from 75kr; Metro Nørreport*

A juicy, fast food burger joint in a converted gas station, offering up sat-isfying, greasy, filling burgers to grab on the go. Including a regular burger cheeseburger, veggie burger, and lim-ited outside seating. There's a sec-ond location at Niels Hemmingsens Gade 20.

## EUROPEAN
### Brace
*Teglgårdstræde 8A; tel. 28 88 20 01; www.restaurantbrace.dk; Tues.-Sat. 5:30pm-midnight, lunch Fri.-Sat. noon-3:30pm; à la carte mains 105-220kr, tasting menu from 515-775kr excluding wine pairings; bus 6A Larslejsstræde (Nørre Voldgade)*

Brace offers Italian food with a Scandinavian twist. The Northern Italian chefs have chosen to infuse well-established Italian recipes with the more experimental approach of the New Nordic kitchen. Results

# RYE BREAD AND *SMØRREBRØD*

While Denmark is well known for its cakes, nothing could be more quintessentially Danish than rye bread—the dark, dense bread which forms the ballast of most Danes' everyday diet. There are various types. My personal favorite is the pumpkin seed-infused *græskarrugbrød*. The taste and density can take a little getting used to, but once initiated, you'll see why rye is often the first thing Danes say they miss when traveling abroad.

And, of course, rye serves as the basis for *smørrebrød*, the classic Danish open-faced sandwich. Don't leave Copenhagen without eating one (or two or three).

## WHERE TO EAT *SMØRREBRØD* IN COPENHAGEN

- **Aamanns 1921** and **Aamanns Etablissement** both serve high-quality, updated versions of *smørrebrød* made with fresh, seasonal ingredients (page 96 and 103).

- Savor a traditional meal of *smørrebrød* and schnapps at the atmospheric **Christianshavns Færgecafé** set in Christianshavn's cobbled streets (page 120).

- Enjoy a cold brew with your artisanal *smørrebrød*—perhaps potato with crispy bacon and chives or curried herring with apple and cress—at **Øl & Brød**, which literally means "beer and bread" (page 109).

- For a change of pace from the more traditional offerings, try some meatier *smørrebrød* at **Fleisch** (page 109).

include Arctic trout carpaccio with oyster sauce, steamed beetroot with goat ricotta, and ravioli with chestnut and mushrooms. It's best experienced slowly while sitting on stylish bluegray bench seats under the tastefully calm ceiling lamps.

## Ché Fè

*Borgergade 17A; tel. 33 11 17 21; www. chefe.dk; Mon.-Thurs. 6pm-9pm, Fri.-Sat. 6pm-10pm; three-course menu 435kr; bus 26 St. Kongensgade (Dronningens Tværgade)*

The traditional Italian food is based on organic ingredients and is often sourced from Italy. An organic wine list includes 70 from Tuscany and Piedmont. The menu rotates seasonally—past items include spiced clams, jaw of veal, baked cod, and tiramisú. Dishes are always presented in detail. It's located in a smart, brick building on the corner of Borgergade, close to Amalienborg Palace and the Marble Church.

## Marchal

*Hotel D'Angleterre, Kongens Nytorv 34;*
*tel. 33 12 00 94; www.dangleterre.com;*
*lunch daily noon-4:30pm, dinner Sun.-Mon.*
*6pm-10pm, Fri.-Sat. 6pm-11pm; signature*
*dishes 450-700kr; Metro Kongens Nytorv*

Marchal offers a French fine dining experience for the purists at the famous D'Angleterre Hotel on Kongens Nytorv. It was awarded a Michelin star in 2017, so reserve ahead. Dishes include lobster, chateaubriand, turbot in turbotiere, venison with dried beets, and fried duck with liver.

## Kong Hans Kælder

*Vingårdstræde 6; tel. 33 11 68 68; www.*
*konghans.dk; signature five-course menu*
*1,700kr, entrées 425-605kr; Metro Kongens*
*Nytorv*

Kong Hans Kælder opened in 1976 in one of Copenhagen's oldest cellars on Vingårdstræde, and it was given a Michelin star in 2018. This is one of the city's most-expensive restaurants with formal service and gourmet French food. Mains include Danish black lobster, salt-baked turbot, and salted mallard. Reserve ahead.

## ASIAN
### The Market Asian Kitchen & Bar

*Kristen Bernikows Gade 9-11; tel. 70 70 24*
*35; www.themarketcph.dk/asian; Sun.-Wed.*
*11:30am-midnight (kitchen until 10pm),*
*Thurs.-Sat. 11:30am-1am (kitchen 10:30pm);*
*entrées 95-135kr; Metro Kongens Nytorv*

This is an Asian fusion restaurant with everything from Japanese to Thai cuisine and an extensive wine list in a trendy setting. Asian cocktails can also be tasted at the bar, which stays open until late. Starters include sashimi and tempura vegetables; mains include Korean-style

pork belly and Wagyu fillet. It's in close proximity to a number of bars, which provides ample opportunity for an after-dinner cocktail.

## Wokshop Cantina TakeAway

*Ny Adelgade 6; tel. 33 91 61 21; http://*
*wokshop.dk; Mon.-Sat. noon-9pm; woks/*
*curries 75-145kr; Metro Kongens Nytorv*

With good portions at a central location near Kongens Nytorv, Wokshop Cantina is an ideal option for a Thai green curry during a break from shopping. There's a busy atmosphere with both takeaway and serving in the basement restaurant area.

## Royal Garden

*Dronningens Tværgade 30; tel. 33 15 16 07;*
*www.royalgarden.dk; Tues.-Sun. noon-11pm*
*(kitchen 10pm); entrées from 55kr; bus 26 St.*
*Kongensgade (Dronningens Tværgade)*

Royal Garden is a delicious, busy, high-value dim sum specialist right in the center of town.

## LATIN AMERICAN
### Llama

*Lille Kongensgade 14; tel. 89 92 66 87;*
*www.llamarestaurant.dk; Sun.-Thurs.*
*6pm-12:30am; Fri.-Sat. 6pm-2am; small*
*dishes from 60kr, tasting menu 395kr; Metro*
*Nørreport*

Latin American fusion restaurant Llama's menu combines the cuisines of Peru, Argentina, Bolivia, Ecuador, and Chile, as well as some Central American countries, in its range of ceviches, tacos, and beef dishes, not to mention the fiery range of spirits: pisco, mezcal, tequila, and more. Don't be put off by the colorful beaded skulls (!): the décor is lively with patterned tiles adorning the walls and floor.

## DANISH CAKES

Cakes are a key part of Danish culture—meeting for coffee and cake or bringing cakes to work to celebrate birthdays and other events are part of Danish everyday life. Just don't ask for a Danish pastry, as that could mean anything. The baked product known as a "Danish" in the United States or the United Kingdom is commonly referred to as a *wienerbrød*—literally, Vienna bread. So there are plenty of other delicious options for the sweet tooth. These include *hindbærsnitter,* the Danish version of Alexandertorte; chocolate-covered marshmallow treats with waffle and marzipan bases known as *flødeboller;* and **cinnamon rolls** (*kanelsnegle,* which translates literally to "cinnamon snails").

### ORGANIC, VEGETARIAN, AND VEGAN
#### SimpleRaw

*Gråbrødretorv 9; tel. 35 35 30 05; www. simpleraw.dk; Mon.-Sat. 10am-10pm, Sun. 10am-9pm; snacks from 25kr, sandwiches from 80kr, salads from 90kr, brunch menu 135kr; Metro Kongens Nytorv*

SimpleRaw uses food sourced directly from the wild and features a menu entirely free of sugar, gluten, and milk products (although milk is available in coffee, should you wish to make a small exception). It's a spacious and light restaurant that is big on friendly service and not least healthy food. Both the brunch menu and warm burger are recommended, washed down with a vitamin bomb of a fresh juice.

#### 42Raw

*Pilestræde 32; tel. 32 12 32 10; www.42raw. com; Mon.-Fri. 8am-8pm, Sat.-Sun. 9am-6pm; salads from 79kr, breakfast bowls from 89kr; Metro Kongens Nytorv*

This small, intimate raw food eatery on a narrow Inner City street is gluten free, lactose free, and 100 percent plant-based. The cakes are tasty and the interior welcoming, if busier and a lot smaller, with a more cluttered style than competitor SimpleRaw. Truffle burger, avocado salad, sweet potato fries, and acai bowls are among the offerings.

### FOOD HALL
#### Torvehallerne

*Frederiksborggade 21; tel. 70 10 60 70; https://torvehallernekbh.dk; Mon.-Thurs. 10am-7pm, Fri. 10am-8pm, Sun. 11am-5pm; dishes from 50kr, cakes from 30kr, coffee from 30kr; Metro Nørreport*

Gathering everything that is great about Danish food culture under one broad roof right next to Nørreport station, Torvehallerne's more than 60 different food stalls are good for everything from seafood to cheese, pastries to smoked meats, wraps to freshly ground coffee. Its twin glass halls are home to dozens of stands of artisan food, which you can take with you or enjoy while perched on a bar seat. Some of the most popular outlets among Copenhageners include **Grød** (tel. 50 59 82 15; https://groed.

various breads on display in the market of Torvehallerne

com; bowls from 45kr), a paradigm changer for porridge with its selection of oats including berry, liquorice, and nut-based toppings; **Hallernes Smørrebrød** (tel. 60 70 47 80; http://hallernes.dk; *smørrebrød* from 52kr), a premium open-sandwich bar where you can wash down your salmon or potato rye bread with a schnapps; and an outlet of **Hija de Sanchez** (tel. 53 73 95 10; www.hijadesanchez.dk), the Meatpacking District taco joint that is a market leader for Mexican food in Copenhagen. You can also stop by to window shop the myriad fish and meat markets and grab a coffee: specialist **Coffee Collective** (tel. 60 15 15 25; https://coffeecollective.dk) has a stand; beans are sourced directly from farmers.

# GREATER INNER CITY
## DANISH AND NEW NORDIC
### Studio at the Standard

*Havnegade 44; tel. 72 14 88 08; http://thestandardcph.dk/en/studio; Tues.-Wed. 6:30pm-midnight, Thurs.-Fri. noon-3pm, 6:30pm-midnight, Sat. 6:30pm-midnight; five-serving lunch 700kr, twelve-serving dinner 1,300kr excluding wine; Metro Kongens Nytorv*

One of 16 Copenhagen restaurants to be awarded Michelin stars, Studio's open kitchen bar serves dishes such as razor clam, grilled heart, scallop ceviche, and sheep's yogurt with lime and bergamot. The emphasis is on fine dining that doesn't require an entire evening. Defining itself as Nordic cuisine touched by the South American roots of head chef Damian Quintana and with a view across the harbor toward Christianshavn, this high-end option has been praised for its atmosphere and romantic setting.

### Aamanns Etablissement

*Øster Farimagsgade 12; tel. 20 80 52 02; https://aamanns.dk/etablissement; lunch noon-4pm (last order 3pm), dinner Wed.-Sat. 6pm-11pm (last order 9pm); smørrebrød 75-125kr, lunch platter for two 315kr, dinner small dishes 75-120kr, set menu 285kr per person; bus 14 Webersgade (Øster Farimagsgade)*

As a sister restaurant to Aamanns 1921, Aamanns Etablissement has high-quality, up-to-date, and meticulously presented versions of Danish *smørrebrød*, made with fresh, seasonal ingredients. *Smørrebrød* with Icelandic salmon or baked celery grace the lunch menu, with prawn cocktails, fried fish, and tartare in the evening. The place is bright and friendly with stencils of plants and fish decorating the walls. It's closed for most of July for summer holidays. A deli and takeaway are available next door (tel. , 20 80 5201; https://aamanns.dk/deli).

### Kokkeriet

*Kronprinsessegade 64; tel. 33 15 27 77; https://kokkeriet.dk; Mon.-Sat. 6pm-1am; nine-course tasting menu 900kr excluding wine, smaller menus available Mon.-Thurs.; bus 26 Kronprinsessegade (Sølvgade)*

Service-minded Michelin-starred Kokkeriet's innovative New Nordic dishes include turbot, tongue, beetroot, poussin, and scallop—a nine- or twelve-dish tasting menu is available, so you will not leave your fine dining experience feeling hungry. Simple, clean lines and spacious tables offer a friendly approach.

### Marv & Ben

*Snaregade 4; tel. 33 91 01 91; www.marvogben.dk; Mon.-Thurs. 5:30pm-1am (kitchen closes 10pm), Fri.-Sat. 5:30pm-1am (kitchen closes 11pm); four-course menu*

400kr, 800kr with wine pairings; bus 12
Stormgade (H.C. Andersens Boulevard)

In a small room on a quiet side street with a window to the kitchen, New Nordic Marv & Ben uses only locally produced ingredients, a high proportion of which are organic. The fish is caught close to the Danish coast, and the meat is also sourced close to home. Head chef David Andersen was trained at the Hotel d'Angleterre and has also worked for high-profile, Michelin-starred restaurant Kadeau, a fact reflected by the delicate taste combinations on the menu, which include scallop and fermented cucumber, grilled plums, and mallard. Marv & Ben is significantly more budget-friendly than Michelin-starred options.

### Restaurant Mes

Jarmers Plads 1; tel. 25 36 51 81;
www.restaurant-mes.dk; Mon.-Sat.
5:30pm-midnight; five-course set menu
350kr; bus 5C Jarmers Plads (Vester
Voldgade)

The five-dish tasting menu at Restaurant Mes features egg yolk with pearl barley, veal brisket, and cucumber with scallops and cream cheese. It can be coupled with a wine tasting menu for about the same cost and is a great way to taste a range of Nordic-based dishes as life hums by on busy Jarmers Plads outside.

### Kanal Caféen

Frederiksholms Kanal 18; tel. 33 11 57
70; www.kanalcafeen.dk; Mon.-Fri.
11:30am-5pm, Sat. 11:30am-3pm; smørrebrød
66-109kr; bus 2A, 9A Stormbroen,
Nationalmuseet (Vindebrogade)

The busy, historic Kanal Caféen's walls are adorned with an eclectic mix of pictures of local sites, maritime scenes, characters from popular television series, and commemorative plates; the low ceiling is a sturdy set of beams. In the summer, outside seating is available on a moored barge opposite the restaurant. The entire classic range of Danish smørrebrød is here: herring, red cabbage, roast pork, fried onion, and the bitter remoulade dressing. There are also lunch platters with traditional fare such as the frikadeller meatballs and fish fillets, pâté, and cheese. Open for lunch only.

### AOC

Dronningens Tværgade 2; tel. 33 11 11
45; http://restaurantaoc.dk; Tues.-Sat.
6:30pm-12:30am (kitchen closes 9pm); set
menu 1,700-2,000kr excluding wine; bus 1A
Amalienborg (Bredgade)

Situated in a vaulted 17th-century cellar close to Amalienborg, innovative New Nordic AOC is one of only three restaurants in Copenhagen that have two Michelin stars or more (Kadeau is also two-starred, while Geranium has three). Menu samples include mackerel with vendace roe and butternut squash, baked onion with caviar, and quail flowers with roasted potato skin. It's normally closed for most of July due to holiday.

## BREAKFAST AND DINERS

### Din Nye Ven

Skt. Peders Stræde 34 A; tel. 42 42 50 68;
www.dinnyeven.dk; Mon. 10am-midnight,
Tues.-Wed. 8am-midnight, Thurs.-Fri.
8am-2am, Sat. 10am-2am; breakfast dishes
from 28kr; Bus 5C Jarmers Plads (Nørre
Voldgade)

In homely surroundings on a city center side street, early opener Din Nye Ven (which translates to "Your New Friend") offers up a range of filling Danish-style breakfast plates including eggs, bacon, and, of course, toasted rye bread. Organic and vegetarian breakfast options are also available, as well as yogurt and oats—and ice cream. The menu changes throughout the day, with lunch and evening-friendly options intoduced, and there is a decent range of Danish beers if your visit takes place in the evening.

## SEAFOOD
### Letz Sushi

*Store Kongensgade 44; tel. 53 78 67 35; http://letzsushi.dk; daily 11:30am-10pm; starters from 35kr, sashimi dishes from 65kr, platters from 125kr; bus 26 St. Kongensgade (Dronningens Tværgade), Metro Kongens Nytorv*

Having become synonymous with quality sushi in Copenhagen since opening its first restaurant in 2003, Letz has a string of sushi outlets across the city. The fish is freshly sourced, the menu broad, and the service quick while the prices are competitive with the growing number of challengers. There's fast service with takeaway also available and simple, unpretentious surroundings.

### Krogs Fiskerestaurant

*Gammel Strand 38; tel. 33 15 89 15; https://krogs.dk/velkommen; Mon.-Sat. 11:30am-3pm, 5:30pm-10pm; entrées from 145kr, three-course menu 375kr; bus 2A Christiansborg (Vindebrogade)*

Krogs Fiskerestaurant's prime location near Højbro Plads and its view of Christiansborg Palace (unfortunately curtailed by some rather imposing construction hoardings at the time of writing) are no small part of the selling pitch. The restaurant is also handsome on the inside, with an elegant traditional design and some highly rated seafood platters. An extensive wine list accompanies a small but thoroughly prepared cocktail menu. The table and bar staff also deserve a

mention for their attention to detail and welcoming approach.

## BURGERS
### Cock's & Cows

*Gammel Strand 34 (and other locations); tel. 69 69 60 00; https://cocksandcows. dk; Sun.-Thurs. 11:30am-9:30pm, Fri.-Sat. 11:30am-10:30pm; burgers 89-139kr; bus 2A Christiansborg (Vindebrogade)*

With a string of restaurant-slash-cocktail-bars across Copenhagen, bustling Cock's & Cows (the rogue apostrophe in the name remains a mystery) is a solid option for a hearty mix-and-match burger—vegetarian options available. Various side orders and extras can be added—I particularly like the chili mayo, while there are also aioli, tarragon, and mustard alternatives. There is also an extensive cocktail list, including the vodka, orange, and cranberry juice combo Cock's on the Beach. Grammar fans, look away now.

## TAKEAWAY
### Shawarma Grill House

*Frederiksberggade 36; tel. 33 12 63 23; http://shawarmagrillhouse.dk; Sat.-Wed. 11am-1am, Thurs. 11am-3am, Fri.-Sat. 11am-6am; shawarma sandwich from 45kr; Metro Nørreport/Kongens Nytorv*

The first Lebanese restaurant to open on the central Strøget shopping thoroughfare back in 1980, Shawarma Grill House retains its reputation as one of the best kebab places outside of Nørrebro. It's popular with daytime visitors as well as late-night guests, the signature meal is still the juicy, tender lamb shawarma kebab, but a range of other Middle Eastern staples, including hummus, shish kebabs, and vegetarian options including falafel are also solid takeaway options.

## EUROPEAN

### Vespa

*St. Kongensgade 90; tel. 33 11 37 00; https://
cofoco.dk/restauranter/vespa; Mon.-Thurs.
6pm-midnight (kitchen 9:30pm), Fri.-Sat.
6pm-midnight (kitchen 10pm); four-course
set menu 275kr; bus 1A Fredericiagade
(Bredgade)*

Italian Vespa is an Osteria-style restaurant set in one of the older parts of Copenhagen's Inner City, a stone's throw from the steeped dome of Frederik's Church. It's almost shabby-chic in style with its mismatching chairs, good value meals, and simple approach. Antipasti, primo, and secondi dishes include octopus, pumpkin risotto, and porchetta with hazelnuts.

### Brace

*Teglgårdstræde 8A; tel. 28 88 20
01; www.restaurantbrace.dk; lunch
Fri.-Sat. noon-3:30pm, dinner Tues.-Sat.
5:30pm-midnight, kitchen closes 9:30pm;
tasting menu with five snacks and four
servings 515kr; bus 5C Larslejsstræde (Nørre
Voldgade)*

The beautiful and inventive presentation of Brace's fusion dishes will have you reaching for your smartphone faster than you can say "Instagram." As Nordic as it is Italian, the restaurant's head chef and co-founder Nicola Fanetti likes to use wild and farmland ingredients from both Denmark and his homeland. Current offerings include beef tartare, raw langoustine, risotto, and monkfish served with ramson blossom. It's closed during winter and summer breaks in late January and July.

### Clou

*Øster Farimagsgade 8; tel. 91 92 72
30; www.restaurant-clou.dk; Wed.-Sat.
6am-midnight; 20-serving set menu 1,600kr*

*excluding wine; Bus 14 Webersgade (Øster
Farimagsgade)*

After moving to new premises on Øster Farimagsgade in 2017, Michelin-starred Clou's French fine dining is now nestled in an intimate setting with capacity for no more than 20 guests. Head chef Jonathan K. Berntsen and assistant head chef Martin G. Sørensen present courses in person. It's praised for its wine pairings. Advanced reservations are necessary. Examples of courses include salted yogurt and anchovy, lobster and coffee bisque, and foie gras and raspberry.

## SLOTSHOLMEN

### Tårnet

*Christiansborg Slotsplads; tel. 27 90 30 61;
www.taarnet.dk/restauranten; Tues.-Sat.
11:30am-11pm; Sun. 11:30am-5:30pm;
smørrebrød 95-125 kr, cake 60kr, evening
set menus 425-575kr; bus 2A, 9A Børsen
(Børsgade)*

There's no doubting what's unique about Tårnet—the restaurant in the tower at Christiansborg—the seat of the Danish Parliament. The restaurant, operated by Bojesen, which also has a restaurant in the Copenhagen Opera, is a high-class version of classic Danish food such as salmon or potato *smørrebrød*, high tea (or coffee) with cake and cod, steak or artichoke-based set evening menus. There are separate lunch, afternoon tea, and dinner menus. Book in advance. Combine a meal here with sightseeing at Slotsholmen, if you want to spend a little extra on lunch.

### Søren K

*Søren Kierkegaards Plads 1; tel. 33 47 49
49; www.soerenk.dk; Lunch: Mon.-Sat.
11:30am-2pm; dinner Mon.-Sat. 6pm-9pm;
smørrebrød 85-90kr, small dishes 115kr*

(three dishes 300kr); bus 66 Det Kongelige Bibliotek (Christians Brygge)

Inside the Black Diamond, also known as the Royal Library, Søren K boasts unfettered views across the harbor from Slotsholmen. The ground floor location next to the building's glass fronting is capable of provoking thought in the spirit of Denmark's most famous philosopher, Kierkegaard, for whom the restaurant is named. Separate lunch and evening menus rely heavy on locally sourced fish and vegetables. Small dishes, including creamed barley, cod browned in butter, and fried cauliflower with Hollandaise can be combined—around three corresponds to a main evening meal. Also on the ground floor is the Black Diamond's café, **Øieblikket,** where you can get a slighty-pricier-than-normal coffee with harbor views and people-watching.

### Kayak Bar

*Børskaj 12; tel. 22 88 49 89; http://kayakbar. dk; Sun.-Thurs. 11am-midnight, Fri.-Sat. 11m-2am; sides from 45kr, mains 85-145kr; bus 2A Knippelsbro/Christianshavn St., Metro Christianshavn St.*

Kayak Bar offers a range of café standards including moules frites, Greek salads, and burgers. The bar and restaurant are attached to the kayak rental and tour operator Kayak Republic, which provides a lively harborside weekend vibe when the weather is suitable for sitting outside.

# NYHAVN

Nyhavn has the highest concentration of tourists of anywhere in Copenhagen or indeed the whole of Denmark, and the extensive rows of restaurants and cafés in the historic quayfront buildings and moored boats cater well to the demand, meaning you are unlikely to struggle with finding somewhere to eat, even at busier times. Some of the less generic options in this incredibly picturesque and correspondingly popular area include an innovative pizza restaurant and takeaway, a lunch buffet at an art and cultural center, and a down-to-earth, multipurpose eatery.

### Gorm's

*Nyhavn 14; tel. 60 40 12 02; www. gormspizza.dk/restauranter/nyhavn; Sun.-Thurs. noon-10:30pm, Fri.-Sat. noon-11:30pm, kitchen closes 1 hour before closing; pizzas 120-140kr; Metro Kongens Nyhavn*

Inexpensive, fast food pizzas are easy to come by almost anywhere in Copenhagen, but Gorm's, which now has several branches in the city having been founded in 2008, steps up the game to what it classes as "gourmet" pizza in a restaurant setting for about double the price of the common variety. Its signature location on Nyhavn offers pizzas with lamb and truffles as well as a lot of recognizable favorites. Gluten-free options are available.

### Union Kitchen

*Store Strandstræde 21; tel. 33 14 54 88; www.theunionkitchen.dk; Mon.-Thurs. 7:30am-11pm, Fri. 7:30am-midnight, Sat. 8am-midnight, Sun. 8am-11pm; brunch plate 169kr, breakfast dishes from 69kr; Metro Kongens Nyhavn*

If you find yourself craving American-style scrambled eggs, bacon, and coffee while in Copenhagen, Union Kitchen should hit the spot with its broad menu of full plates as well as some lighter options such as salads, oats, and a filled croissant. The evening menu (available from 5pm) consists of small dishes with roots in various international cuisines designed

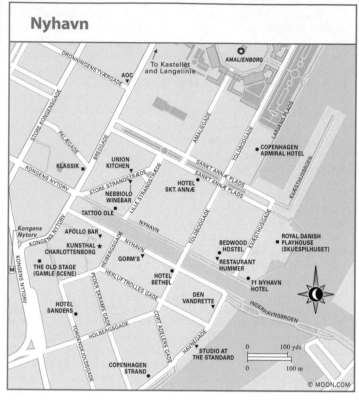

# Nyhavn

to complement each other. Many of these are "balls," variations on the meatball concept including pork balls, beef balls, chicken Thai balls, falafel balls, and several other types of balls. There's a bustling coffee shop feel, and it gets particularly busy on weekends.

## Apollo Bar

*Nyhavn 2; tel. 60 53 44 14; http://apollobar. dk; cantine open Tues.-Fri. noon-2pm, bar Tues. 8am-5pm, Wed.-Fri., 8am-midnight, Sat. 10am-midnight, Sun. 10am-5pm; mains 85kr, students 45kr; Metro Kongens Nyhavn*

Apollo Bar, which is part of Nyhavn's art and cultural center Kunsthal Charlottenborg, offers a less-expensive and healthy vegetarian lunch at its canteen on weekdays (except

Mondays) as well as à la carte meals from its bar, which is open until late. The canteen menu changes daily but expect couscous, beans, roasted cauliflower, broccoli, and other such hearty goods. It's a good and wallet-friendly, as well as usually less-crowded, alternative to the many tourist-focused eateries around Nyhavn. Note the student discount: almost half price for the canteen vegetarian lunch.

## Restaurant Hummer

*Nyhavn 63A; tel. 33 33 03 39; www. restauranthummer.dk; daily noon-11pm; four-course menu 375kr; Metro Kongens Nyhavn*

A lobster and seafood specialist ("hummer" in Danish means lobster, rather than a type of military vehicle), Restaurant Hummer looks over the iconic sights of Nyhavn. Whole or half lobsters, poached or grilled, can be chosen from the à la carte list, as can moules frites, halibut ceviche, and lemon sole meuniere. There's plenty of atmosphere, with the location providing a good stream of guests. The blue-tiled floors and buoys displayed on the walls give a captain's cabin feel to the décor.

# VESTERBRO AND FREDERIKSBERG
## DANISH AND NEW NORDIC
### Øl & Brød

*Viktoriagade 6; tel. 33 31 44 22; www.ologbrod.dk; Thurs. noon-10pm, kitchen noon-4pm and 6pm-8:30pm, Fri.-Sat. noon-11pm, kitchen noon-4pm and 6pm-9:30pm, Sun. noon-10pm, kitchen noon-4pm and 6pm-8:30pm; lunch, five smørrebrød 300kr; dinner, three-course menu 400kr; bus, S-train Copenhagen Central Station*

Øl & Brød, which means "beer & bread," is a restaurant project opened by the Mikkeller brewery in 2014, a *smørrebrød*'s throw from the original Mikkeller Bar in Vesterbro. Serving high-quality, artisanal open sandwiches—curried herring with apple and cress, salmon with salted cucumber, potato with crispy bacon and chives—the menu varies according to the season and is matched to the beer selection, while there is also a wide range of Danish and foreign aquavit and schnapps. Busy and cozy. Book in advance.

### Formel B

*Vesterbrogade 182, Frederiksberg; tel. 33 25 10 66; https://formelb.dk; Mon.-Thurs. 5:30pm-midnight, Fri.-Sat. 5:30pm-1am; à la carte entrées 140kr, tasting menu 1,250kr; bus 6A Platanvej (Vesterbrogade)*

This romantic, Michelin-starred restaurant in Frederiksberg features 20 small, beautifully presented dishes that are regularly rotated according to season. Emphasis is not only on high-end dining but also on interior design, with handsome fittings, warm lighting, and the kitchen visible through a large interior window on the ground floor. Known for its informal atmosphere.

### Bodil

*Sønder Boulevard 105; tel. 55 55 23 00; https://timos.dk//restaurant-bodil; Mon.-Wed. 5pm-11pm (kitchen 9pm), Thurs.-Sat. 5pm-11:45 pm (kitchen 9:30pm); four-course menu 350kr; bus 1A Knud Lavards Gade (Ingerslevsgade)*

High value, down-to-earth Bodil is a great place to try New Nordic, internationally influenced food (scallop, beef tartare, and beetroot with coffee and buckwheat) without breaking the bank. Situated in an unassuming Vesterbro residential building, the interior also has a welcoming, simple vibe with tables close enough to be intimate but not intrusive and hanging wine bottles providing the décor.

### Fleisch

*Slagterboderne 7; tel. 61 68 14 19; www.fleisch.dk; Sun.-Thurs. 11:30am-midnight, Fri.-Sat. 11:30am-1am, kitchen lunch daily 11:30am-3pm, dinner Sun.-Thurs. 5:30pm-9:30pm, Fri.-Sat. 5:30pm-10:30pm; lunch smørrebrød 85-145kr, tasting menu with main course 395kr, à la carte entres from 95-145kr; bus 10 Gasværksvej (Istedgade)*

One of the most recognizable names in the Meatpacking District, Fleisch pays tribute to the legacy of the area with its interior design—not least the silver bull's head behind the bar—and its working in-house butchers shop and hanging meat hooks. Meat is front and center: braised ox jaw, cured sirloin steak, and smoked seabass are among the main courses. The bar even serves bacon-infused cocktails.

## BREAKFAST AND DINERS
### Mad & Kaffe Vesterbro

*Sønder Boulevard 68 (other locations in Amager and Frederiksberg); tel. 32 17 70 44; www.madogkaffe.dk; daily 8:30am-8pm; breakfast from 89kr; bus 14 Saxogade (Istedgade)*

At Mad & Kaffe ("Food and Coffee") you will be provided with a slip of paper and a pencil, Ikea-like, on which to cross off the options you would like to make up your breakfast. These include salad, dairy, bread, meat, fish, and pastry components, and you can choose between three and seven, depending on your appetite and budget. My favorites are the avocado in chili oil, the organic sourdough rye bread, the thin, crispy Danish bacon, and the smoked salmon. It's a recommended option for a flexible breakfast or brunch—you may find yourself waiting a short while to be seated on weekends.

### Granola

*Værnedamsvej 5; tel. 31 31 15 36; www. granola.dk; Mon.-Wed. 7:30am-11pm, Thurs.-Fri. 7:30am-midnight, Sat. 9am-midnight, Sun. 9am-5pm; croissant 25kr, breakfast/brunch platter 145kr, entrées from 75kr; bus 9A Værnedamsvej (Gammel Kongevej), 26 Værnedamsvej (Frederiksberg Allé)*

The blueberry pancakes are often a morning favorite, and breakfast and brunch café Granola is open from early until evening, when popular meals (moules frites, steak frites,

mushroom risotto, and others) take over, as does a lively evening vibe in Parisian-style surroundings. Outside seating is available and well worth making use of in decent weather, so you can take in Værnedamsvej's stylish comings and goings. Gets busy in the morning.

### Bowl Market

*Gasværksvej 3; tel. 24 82 60 90; www. instagram.com/bowlmarketcph; daily 7:30am-6pm; signature oatmeal dishes from 50kr; Bus 6A Vesterbros Torv (Vesterbrogade)*

It's hard to find a healthier start to the day than the almost entirely vegan and organic, gluten-free oatmeal, porridges, acai-based smoothie bowls, soups, and baked goods at Bowl Market Copenhagen, with the added bonus of coffee from the Coffee Collective. Toppings include apples, caramel, coconut flakes, walnuts, blueberries, and peanut butter. Sit inside and by the window.

## SEAFOOD
### Kødbyens Fiskebar

*Flæsketorvet 100; tel. 32 15 56 56; http://fiskebaren.dk; Mon.-Thurs. 5:30pm-midnight, Fri.-Sat. 11:30am-2am, Sun. 11:30am-midnight, kitchen open daily 6pm-11pm, plus Fri.-Sun. 11:30am-3pm; mains 110-435kr; bus 10 Gasværksvej (Istedgade)*

Kødbyens Fiskebar, a Bib Gourmand winner opened in 2009, specializes in clasically prepared oysters and shellfish, but you can also get fish and chips. The setup is informal, with meals served at the bar or sofas as well as at tables, the white-tiled walls in keeping with the raw aesthetic of the Meatpacking District. Most of the fish and seafood is caught in Danish waterways and sourced from suppliers with an eye on sustainability. Book ahead and expect to have plenty of company.

## TAKEAWAY
### Kødbyens Høker

*Slagtehusgade 7A; tel. 25 12 72 02; http:// koedbyenshoeker.dk; Mon.-Thurs..9am-3pm, Fri. 9am-10pm, Sat. 10am-10pm, Sun. 10am-3pm; burger 55kr, breakfast roll 32kr; bus 10 Gasværksvej (Istedgade)*

Grab a salty, meaty sandwich, including the classic roast pork *flæskestegssandwich*, *frikadelle* (meatball), and bacon, eggs and honey all enclosed in fresh bread at this hole-in-the-wall bakery. You can also try a filtered coffee for the astonishingly low price of 10 kroner.

## EUROPEAN
### Spaghetteria

*Vester Farimagsgade 2; tel. 33 22 60 60; www.spaghetteria.dk; Sun.-Thurs. 6pm-midnight, Fri.-Sat. 6pm-2am; menu (5-6 antipasti plus main) 340kr; bus, S-train Copenhagen Central Station*

Don't be fooled by the concrete setting. It's a classicly Italian place with a menu consisting of several antipasti and one or two mains, which changes constantly, depending on the season and available produce imported from Italy. Spaghetteria opened in 2016 by chefs Morten Kaltoft and Emil Alsbo. Wine is served from the restaurant's own Piemont vineyard.

### Restaurant FAMO

*Saxogade 3; tel. 33 23 22 50; www.famo. dk; daily 5:30pm-10pm; four-course menu 350kr, entrées 145kr; bus 6A Frederiksberg Allé (Vesterbrogade)*

Opened in 2005, Famo has ploughed on as the New Nordic wave has taken over Copenhagen. It's an affordable family restaurant that uses Italian ingredients. The menu changes daily but always includes a primo of pasta, risotto, or similar and a main course with meat and seasonal vegetables (vegetarian options also available).

### Falernum

*Værnedamsvej 16; tel. 33 22 30 89; www. falernum.dk; Sun.-Thurs. noon-midnight (kitchen closes 10pm), Fri.-Sat. noon-2am (kitchen closes 11pm); wines from 75kr glass, lunch mains 85-135kr, tasting menu 375kr; bus 9A, 71 Værnedamsvej (Gammel Kongevej), 26 Værnedamsvej (Frederiksberg Allé)*

Trendy, informal Falernum is an intimate and lively wine bar—the casually dressed bartenders are highly knowledgeable—as well as a restaurant. Personalized wine tastings for up to 10 people can be arranged. Snacks, a tasting menu, and tapas-style dishes, such as cauliflower soup with poached egg and croutons; hake with cider-pickled apple and mustard; and langoustine with leek and pearl onion, are influenced by Mediterranean, French, and Danish cuisine.

### Sans Souci Restaurant and Wine bar

*Madvigs Allé 15; tel. 33 21 74 63; www.sanssouci.dk; Mon.-Sat. lunch 11:30am-3:30pm, dinner 5:30pm-9:30pm, wine bar until midnight; lunch smørrebrød 88-148kr, dinner entrées 120-195kr; bus 9A Bülowsvej (Gammel Kongevej)*

Historic Sans Souci has called its elegant rooms in Frederiksberg home since 1902. The current menu includes luxurious *smørrebrød* during lunch hours—bacon and caramelized onions; beef tartare with beetroot, horseradish, and capers; and smoked salmon with scrambled eggs and chives—and a selection of classic Danish and French bistro dishes such as beef bourgignon in the evening.

## HYGGE: MORE THAN JUST A COZY PLACE

"Some words are simply little cultural bombs," Danish linguist Carsten Levisen said in an interview with online newspaper *forskning.no* in February 2018. "They say something about the way we perceive the world. Words that your whole world revolves around."

In 2017, the *Oxford English Dictionary* added the Danish word *hygge* to its lexicon. How did such an unpronounceable, untranslatable Danish word make it into the English dictionary? A BBC article in 2015 is thought to have been the start of a surge of interest in the concept, with a string of lifestyle articles and at least a dozen English-language books with the word *hygge* in their titles starting to be published.

Danes will often say that the closest English synonym for *hygge* is "cozy." Danish publisher Gyldendal's Danish-English dictionary translates the adjective form of the word, which can also be used as a noun or verb, as "cozy," "comfortable," "pleasant," and "homelike," among other things. But a closer explanation of the concept is actually, and more simply, "having a nice time."

*Hygge* is associated with pleasant activities such as drinking a cup of tea by the fireplace or sitting down to eat with friends around a candlelit table. But the word is used in a wide range of other situations, too. Danes can often be heard saying, for example, "'It was *hyggeligt* to meet you" after bumping into an old acquaintance. Playing an informal game of soccer can be described as "Doing it for the sake of the *hygge*." Tasteful background music is *hyggemusik*. There are many ways of creating this elusive feeling of well-being, but the search for it is a near-subconscious part of everyday Danish life.

### HOW IS IT PRONOUNCED?

Somewhat ironically, *hygge* is far from easy to pronounce. The Danish "y" vowel does

---

Brasserie-style décor with white cloths and candles.

## MEDITERRANEAN
### Gorilla

*Flæsketorvet 63; tel. 33 33 83 30; http:// restaurantgorilla.dk/forside; Mon.-Thurs. 5:30pm-midnight (kitchen 10pm), Fri.-Sat. 5:30pm-2am (kitchen 11pm); 10-serving tasting menu 395kr, dishes 55-155kr, varying sizes; bus 10 Gasværksvej (Istedgade)*

More than just an alpha-male eatery, hip restaurant and bar Gorilla has shareable snacks and fish, pasta, and meat-based and primarily Mediterranean-style dishes of various sizes, as well as a tasting menu (but there are plenty of other influences). Dishes range from salted scallops with green tomato and wasabi mayo through falafel, cucumber, and feta, to pumpkin ravioli with dried pork and ricotta. In a large, open-plan space with seating for up to 200 guests, and an unpretentious atmosphere, the restaurant is a former meatpacking warehouse: white tiles still adorn the walls. Reservations are required at peak times.

## ASIAN
### Magasasa Dim Sum & Cocktails

*Flæsketorvet 54-56; tel. 33 23 80 89; http:// magasasa.dk/dim-sum-cocktails; Sun.-Thurs. 11am-11pm (kitchen closes at 10pm), Fri.-Sat. 11am-midnight (kitchen closes at 10:30pm); dim sum 40-58kr, noodle soup 68-85kr; bus 10 Gasværksvej (Istedgade)*

Tucked away in one of the quieter parts of the Meatpacking District but close enough for the area's energy to still be felt in its own atmosphere, Magasasa Dim Sum & Cocktails is something of a hidden gem, given its high value and delicious combination of dumplings and drinks. The classic *siu mai* with not exist in English, and the short "e" on the end of the word is also uncommon. While Americans and Brits can be forgiven for pronouncing *hygge* as they read it ("higgy"), the pronunciation "hoo-gah" or "hue-guh" is also a little inaccurate.

Approximate pronunciation for the Danish "y" is the "u," as in "put" (try saying it with your jaw slightly tighter), and the "e" is roughly the vowel sound in the French article "le." The "h" and the double "g" are, thankfully, pronounced as you might expect. H-y-gg-e.

**PLACES TO FIND *HYGGE***

Just as there's no definitive way of translating the word, there is also no one specific way of finding *hygge*. It is far more a state of mind than something embodied by a particular place. Nevertheless, here are some good places to start looking for it:

- At a café such as **Paludan Bog & Café** (Fiolstræde 12; tel. 33 15 06 75; www. paludan-cafe.dk), where the walls are lined with books, the coffee is inexpensive, and the atmosphere is relaxed.

- At a rowdy pub such as Christianshavn's **Eiffel Bar** (Wildersgade 58; tel. 32 57 70 92, http://eiffelbar.dk).

- **At Café Ægir** (Ægirsgade 16, tel. 35 83 10 02) in Nørrebro, a classic "brown bodega" with a punky twist and a promise you will "come happy and leave happy."

- Taking a Saturday morning stroll along a quiet pathway such as the unusual **Dyssen in Christiania**.

---

pork, shrimp, and shiitake mushroom, and *cha siu bao* buns with roasted barbecue pork are personal favorites, and the chili sour cocktail prepared with bourbon and fresh red chili has the perfect amount of kick.

## LATIN AMERICAN
### Hija de Sanchez

*Slagterboderne 8; tel. 53 73 95 10; www. hijadesanchez.dk; Mon.-Thurs. noon-8pm, Fri.-Sat. noon-10pm, Sun. 11am-6pm; individual small tacos from 37kr; bus 10 Gasværksvej (Istedgade)*

Started by Mexican-American chef and Chicago native Rosio Sanchéz, the Meatpacking District's diminutive Hija de Sanchez is arguably the best Mexican restaurant in Copenhagen. Inside it feels more Veracruz than Vesterbro, as Latin American jazz jangles in the background and the chefs prepare pork carnitas, huevos rancheros, and the many types of tacos on the rotating menu. You can sit at one of the small tables inside the restaurant or benches outside, though space is limited—takeaway is a viable option. The restaurant also has a booth at the Torvehallerne food square.

## ORGANIC, VEGETARIAN, AND VEGAN
### Neighbourhood

*Istedgade 27; tel. 32 12 22 12; www. neighbourhood.dk; Mon.-Wed. 5pm-11pm, Thurs. 5pm-midnight, Fri. 5pm-1am, Sat. 10am-1am, Sun. 10am-11pm; pizzas 145kr; bus 10 Gasværksvej (Istedgade)*

Organic pizza restaurant-slash-lounge bar Neighbourhood is based in a former butcher's shop in what was once the heart of Vesterbro's red light district. Stay for a cocktail after you've finished your pizza—the thin sourdough crust eclectically topped with the pancetta and apples, potato brie, roast pumpkin or chili salami, will not overfill you. Salads also available; no reservations necessary.

## Radio

*Julius Thomsens Gade 12; tel. 25 10 27 33; http://restaurantradio.dk; Tue.-Sat. 5:30pm-midnight, Fri.-Sat. lunch noon-3pm; three-course menu 350kr, weekend lunch dishes 115kr; Metro Forum St.*

Close to the Copenhagen Lakes and Forum Metro station, the organic, New Nordic Radio takes its name from the former broadcasting house in which it is located. Organic ingredients—apple, parsnip, quince, mushrooms—come from land cultivated just outside Copenhagen. Advance reservation required. Co-owned by veteran chef and entrepreneur Claus Meyer. Stylish and intimate with a reputation for good service.

## BOB—Biomio Organic Bistro

*Halmtorvet 19; tel. 33 31 20 00; http:// bobbistro.dk/en/home; Mon.-Sat. noon-10pm, Sun. noon-9pm; lunch 85-160kr, dinner mains 160-210kr 85kr; bus 10 Gasværksvej (Istedgade)*

One of most iconic sights of the Meatpacking District is the neon glowing "BOSCH" sign that marks the beginning of the fashionable nightlife zone. Behind the panoramic windows of the Bosch building is organic bistro BioMio, now more commonly known as "BOB." Everything here is organic down to the cocktails and the salt. Dishes include fish ("catch of the day") with cabbage, berries, and mustard sauce; pumpkin with mustard and beans, and an artisan burger. In addition to its fully organic status, BOB boasts collaborations focusing on sustainability, social responsibility, and upcycling. A landmark.

# NØRREBRO AND ØSTERBRO
## DANISH AND NEW NORDIC
### ✪ Geranium

*Per Henrik Lings Allé 4; tel. 69 96 00 20; www.geranium.dk; Wed.-Sat. noon-4pm, 6:30pm-midnight; sixteen-course tasting menu 2,500kr excluding wine pairings; bus 1A Gustav Adolfs Gade (Østerbrogade)*

Second arguably only to Noma as the most prestigious restaurant in the city and currently the only holder of three Michelin stars, Geranium's reputation speaks of creative, innovative dishes that are flawlessly executed works of art. The wine list is a tome and an attraction in its own right but requires an extraordinary budget. It's located high up inside Parken, the national soccer stadium, with views of treetops, rooftops, and the Øresund. Booking ahead—up to 90 days in advance—is normally the only way to get a table (an online reservation system is available on Geranium's website). Expect unmatched hospitality and flavors that catch you unaware; the menu changes seasonally.

### Guldkroen 11

*Fredensgade 11A; tel. 31 31 04 04; www. guldkroen.dk; Wed.-Sat. 5:30pm-midnight, Sun. 5:30pm-10pm, kitchen closes 9pm; entrées from 115kr; bus 42 Rigshospitalet Syd (Tagensvej)*

Danish-Turkish owner Umut Ra Sakarya's Guldkroen 11 is as Danish as you can get, lovingly making traditional dishes such as roast pork, *tarteletter*, potatoes, and gravy "without sparing any butter or cream." The brown interior, flowery wall paper, folk music, and walls adorned by deer antlers are all part of the concept: this is Danishness turned up to the max. With a two-hour "free bar" offer of all you can drink for two hours for 275

### THE "PANT" RECYCLING SYSTEM

Denmark's "pant" system means that, every time you buy certain drinks in cans or bottles, you are also paying for the packaging. If that sounds like an unwanted extra cost, fear not: the surcharge, or deposit, is paid back to consumers when bottles are returned via specialized machines, which are located at most supermarkets. Shoppers feed bottles and cans (as well as plastic crates for beer bottles) into the machines, which tally up the amount of money due to be returned. A ticket is then issued, and the amount can be refunded for cash or spent in the supermarket. Alternatively, "pant" money can be donated to charity by pressing a button (usually green or blue) on the machine instead of requesting credit to be returned.

If you have a bottle or can in your hand but don't want to carry it and can't find a supermarket, don't just throw it in a bin: many trash cans around the city have special can-sized collars attached to the outside, where the cans and bottles can be left to be picked up by someone else. This is often to the benefit of underprivileged or homeless people who commonly use the system to make a bit of extra money by collecting these and returning them to pant machines. It's not uncommon to see people waiting by the machines with huge sacks of "pant" early in the morning, particularly in the summer or after events in the city during which people have been drinking outside. So it's not just the environment you'll be helping out by leaving your drink cans on the outside of the trash can.

kroner, late evenings can, and do, occasionally get spirited.

## BREAKFAST AND DINERS

### Grød

*Jægersborggade 50; tel. 50 58 55 79; http://groed.com; Mon.-Fri. 7:30am-9pm, Sat.-Sun. 9am-9pm; oatmeal 45-75kr; bus 5A Stefansgade (Nørrebrogade,. also Vesterbrogade 105b (tel. 32 15 35 35)*

A game changer for porridge with its selection of oats, including delicious berry, liquorice, and nut-based toppings and other healthy, breakfasty delights, Grød also serves a risotto, which more than holds its own later in the day. With a stand at the Torvehallerne food market, there is ample seating space despite the busy "walk-in-and-on-the-way-to-work" concept.

### Møller Kaffe og Køkken

*Nørrebrogade 160; tel. 31 50 51 00; www. moellerkbh.dk; daily 9am-3pm; coffee from 28kr, breakfast dishes from 22kr; bus 5C Stefansgade (Nørrebrogade)*

This brunch spot on Nørrebrogade, popular with local students, is one of the growing number of cafés that allows guests to build their own breakfasts by choosing from a list of components—egg, bacon, bread, waffles, sausage, and salad. The concept is particularly well implemented here with tasty, fresh food and wallet-friendly prices by Copenhagen standards. Cash is not accepted, so bring your credit or debit card. You might have to wait a while to be seated at peak times.

### Sidecar

*Skyttegade 5; tel. 20 99 97 27; www. sidecarnoerrebro.dk; Mon. 8am-4pm, Tues., Wed. 8am-10:30pm, Thurs. 8am-midnight, Fri. 8am-12:30pm, Sat. 9am-12:30 am, Sun. 9:30am-10:30pm, kitchen closes Tues.-Sun. 9pm, Mon. 3pm; yogurt with fruit and granola 40kr, all-day breakfast plates 149-165kr, Asian street food dishes from 45kr; bus 12 Skyttegade (Rantzausgade)*

A breakfast and brunch café that also houses Asian streetfood venture

Maobao (http://maobao.dk) in the evening, Sidecar Nørrebro has gained recognition as one of the city's best cafés. This is a breakfast place with "all the good stuff," in Sidecar's own words. Scrambled eggs, sausages, bacon, granola, pancakes, and rye bread. A vegetarian version with a generaous portion of avocado is also available. There is a positive, welcoming energy, but like many brunch spots it gets busy on weekends.

### Fætter Fætter

*Griffenfeldsgade 17; tel. 88 13 21 20; http://faetter-faetter.dk; Tues.-Wed. 5pm-11pm, Thurs. 5pm-midnight, Fri.-Sat. 11am-midnight, Sun. 11am-8pm; toasted sandwiches from 40-95kr; Bus 5C Elmegade (Nørrebrogade)*

"Welcome! We are a toast bar, not a restaurant," Fætter Fætter proclaims to make sure there are no misunderstandings about its laid-back style. There are plenty of stools to perch on, and there is outside seating during the summer. These are no ordinary toasts. Offerings include rocket pesto and grilled Danish cheese (given the name "Cheesus Christ" on the menu), pastrami, Russian dressing and Emmenthal, and flambéed Bechamel and Parmesan. There is also a selection of coffee, wine, and beer, albeit a disappointing lack of tea from a break-fasting point of view. No reservations necessary, of course.

## CAFÉS AND BAKERIES
### Social

*Peblinge Dossering 4; tel. 53 70 00 53; www. facebook.com/Socialcoffeecopenhagen; Mon.-Thurs. 9am-8pm, Fri. 8am-8pm, Sat. 9am-8pm, Sun. 10am-8pm; coffee from 20kr, breakfast bowls 65-75kr, salads, sandwiches 89kr; bus 5C Ravnsborggade (Nørrebrogade)*

Fresh salads and waffles complement oats, acai bowls, pastries, snacks, and more at the bohemian Social, a cozy nook with hanging plants, cushions, and bookshelves. Close to Dronning Louises Bro, where Nørrebro connects to the Inner City, this highly rated café won newspaper *Berlingske*'s award for best café in Copenhagen in 2017.

### Bevar's

*Ravnsborggade 10B; tel. 50 59 09 93; www.bevars.dk; Mon. 9am-11pm, Tue.-Wed. 9am-midnight, Thurs. 9am-2am, Fri. 9am-3am, Sat. 10am-3am, Sun. 10am-10pm; breakfast dishes 45-115kr; warm dishes 85-145kr; bus 3A, 5C Elmegade (Nørrebrogade)*

All-day Bevar's, located on popular Ravnsborggade, has everything from freshly brewed coffee and freshly baked bread in the morning, *smørre-brød* in the afternoon, and sultry jazz concerts and lively bar scenes at night. The restaurant prides itself on diversity and has a comfortable feel with its shabby tables and chairs, bookshelves, and homemade food, which ranges from bread with jam and cheese or yogurt with muesli in the morning to egg, potato, or salmon *smørrebrød* to a dish or soup of the day in the evening.

### Ali Bageri

*Heimdalsgade 39; tel. 32 57 63 42; http:// alibageri.dk; daily 8am-6pm; manakish from 20kr; bus 6A Haraldsgade (Tagensvej)*

Difficult-to-find Ali Bageri is not visible from the street: the only hint of its presence is a small metal sign on the sidewalk by the entrance to the back-yard, in which it is located next to a mosque. A scruffy, busy little shop, the quality of the food belies first impressions. The *manakish*—a flat-baked dough topped with oily *za'atar* (thyme), cheese, or ground meat—is its staple, as it would be at a typical Middle Eastern bakery, but there are plenty of other delicious, authentic snacks available, including the garlicky yogurt *fattah*; *msabaha*, a dish made from chickpeas and sesame oil; and the ubiquitous hummus. This Lebanese bakery is a perspective of the daily lives of many working-class people of immigrant backgrounds who live in Copenhagen. A second, larger branch at Nørrebrogade 211 has the same basic plastic seating and quick service with less of the charm of the original but is easier to find.

## EUROPEAN
### Terra Organic Urban Trattoria

*Ryesgade 65A; tel. 28 59 64 17; https://www. ilmattarello.dk/; Tues.-Thurs. 11am-11pm, Fri. 11am-11:45pm, Sat. 11am-11:30pm; entrées from 95kr, three-course set menu 375kr excluding wine; bus 42 Rigshospitalet Syd (Tagensvej)*

Tèrra, an organic trattoria and wine bar in Østerbro, offers Italian food with a Nordic twist: small dishes, organic wines, and a signature cocktails list. Intended as an homage to the "terra madre" but with inspiration from Nordic life, in the words of co-founder Lucia De Luca. This is perhaps reflected in the pared-back, tasteful décor (metal chairs, bare brick walls, and low-hanging bulbs emitting warm light), and friendly approach of the owners. Beef tartare or organic beetroot starters can be followed with freshly made, organic pasta with anchovies and and butter or oxtail stew (vegetarian options also available). Closed in the second half of July for summer vacation.

### Bæst

*Guldbergsgade 29; tel. 35 35 04 63; https://baest.dk; daily 5pm-10:30pm, lunch Thurs.-Sun. noon-3pm; pizzas 85-135kr; bus 5C Kapelvej (Nørrebrogade)*

Featured on Netflix's *Ugly Delicious*, Bæst has claims to being Copenhagen's most famed—and best—pizza restaurant. Its organic meats, fresh mozzarella, and woodfired cooking all give the claim considerable substance. There are tables with chairs and stools in the ample restaurant area, which also boasts a poster of Barack Obama drinking an Americano.

## ETHIOPIAN
### Ma'ed

*Griffenfeldsgade 7; tel. 31 84 24 53; www. maed.dk; daily 11am-11pm; mains from 99kr; bus 5C Elmegade (Nørrebrogade)*

A few yards from Nørrebrogade, Ma'ed Ethiopian Restaurant offers up round, metal platters of spicy food that must be eaten without cutlery by picking it up with Ethiopian *injera* bread instead (the bread is made from teff flour and thereby gluten-free). The décor is monotone, the food far from it, while service is extraordinarily friendly and welcoming, with English used as the main working language, possibly due to the multinational staff. Dishes include traditional spicy meat, garlic, butter, and vegetable platters including *kitfo*, *misto*, *qey wat*, and *bayinat* meat.

## MIDDLE EASTERN
### Sorte Firkant

*Blågårdsgade 29; tel. 50 20 22 69, www. sortefirkant.org; Tues.-Thurs. 3pm-midnight, Fri.-Sat. 2pm-1am, limited (mainly summer) opening Sun.-Mon.; mezzé: full meal around 200kr excluding drinks; bus 5C Ravnsborggade (Nørrebrogade)*

Sorte Firkant currently serves food only on Saturdays (call ahead to check serving hours, which vary), but if your timing is right, it's more than worth the effort. The restaurant opened in 2017 and is operated by refugees from Syria. There is a separate bar serving cocktails and beers the rest of the week. The place has a genuine, Middle Eastern feel: you can go to the bar and informally chat with the staff—who are of varied nationalities—in an uninhibited way that is difficult to find in a Danish context. The Saturday menu is a classic Levant *mezzé*: hummus, soujouk, kibbeh, labneh, fitteh, and all the other staples of the eastern Mediterranean table. Call to check availability and book a table. Lebanese or Syrian Tarab or Oud-style concerts, as well as cultural events such as film screenings or poetry readings also take place here. You can almost hear the waves crashing against the warm sea outside or the high-pitched whine of Beirut's traffic.

### Omar

*Refsnæsgade 32; tel. 27 51 52 57; www.restaurantomar.dk; Mon.-Sat. noon-midnight, kitchen closes Mon.-Thurs. 9:30pm, Fri.-Sat. 10:30pm; entrées 75-85kr, mains 155-190kr; bus 6A Nørre Campus (Tagensvej)*

Low-key *hygge* is the vibe at Omar, which emerged in 2017 from the refurbished café Wascator (the characteristic blue- and black-tiled façade remains). It's loosely defined as a "no rules" kitchen but with everything from Middle Eastern to South American to Mediterranean influences, as well as plenty of passion present on the menu. There are barbecue-style duck hearts, roasted cabbage with pea puree and hazelnuts, lamb brochettes with jalapeños, and more.

## ASIAN
### Kiin Kiin

*Guldbergsgade 21; tel. 35 35 75 55; www.kiin.dk; Mon.-Sat. theater menu 5:30pm-7:30pm, regular menu 6pm-midnight, latest reservation 10:30pm; theater menu 495kr excluding wine, regular menu 975kr excluding wine; bus 5C Kapelvej (Nørrebrogade)*

The only Asian restaurant in Copenhagen to have a Michelin star, Kiin Kiin also offers a relatively inexpensive way to access fine dining, through its Theater menu, which consists of snacks and appetizers followed by a four-course menu that is only served early in the evening. The meal is designed to be finished by 7:30pm, and there is also a regular menu with seven courses and appetizers. A Thai restaurant unlike any other—including in Thailand itself—changes seasonally, with past and present dishes, including a green curry risotto with lobster, eggplant peas, and thai basil; dumplings with pork and pumpkin pickle; and fried foie gras with plum-wine sauce and ginger. It can be busy, so reserve in advance.

### GAO Dumpling Bar

*Blågårdsgade 3; tel. 34 12 46 26; www.gaodumpling.com; Mon.-Sat. noon-10pm, Sun. noon-8pm; dumplings 55kr for six pieces; bus 5C Ravnsborggade (Nørrebrogade)*

Copenhagen's oldest dumpling bar puts a flash of Chinese color into the sober surroundings of the Danish interior design. The straightforward selection, including spinach, cabbage, chicken, and mushroom dumplings, can be topped up with sides such as bok choy, noodles with carrot and cucumber in nut sauce, and deep-fried tofu.

### Ramen to Biiru

*Griffenfeldsgade 28; tel. 50 53 02 22; http://*
*ramentobiiru.dk/norrebro; Mon.-Thurs.*
*noon-9pm, Fri.-Sat. noon-11pm, Sun.*
*noon-8pm; ramen 100-120kr; bus 5C*
*Elmegade (Nørrebrogade)*

Tokyo noodle bar meets Copenhagen craft beer at nearby Ramen to Bíiru, where no reservations are necessary (or possible). Food is ordered in the same way you might proceed in a Japanese noodle bar—by inserting money into a machine, choosing your dish, pressing a button, and then taking a ticket to the counter to receive your food. Several spicy, meaty, and vegetarian options are available, but you might have to sit elbow-to-elbow with other patrons. The spicy miso is a favorite—wash it down with a Mikkeller beer.

## ORGANIC, VEGETARIAN, AND VEGAN

### Relæ

*Jægersborggade 41; tel. 36 96 66 09; www.*
*restaurant-relae.dk; dinner Tues.-Sat.*
*5pm-midnight, lunch Fri.-Sat. noon-3pm;*
*tasting menu 475-895kr excluding wine; bus*
*12 Jagtvej (Borups Allé)*

A Michelin-starred restaurant that succeeds in being 90 percent organic as well as relatively affordable, Relæ, located on the popular Jægersborggade street, has earned rave reviews, not least for its sourdough bread. Cutlery stored in drawers under the tables adds a quirky feature to the dining room. Dishes are dependent on the season, with many ingredients plucked the same day they are presented. Example elements include cured mackerel, zucchini with basil and pistachio sauce, and lamb with shaved radish, vinegar, and yogurt. Booking ahead is recommended.

### Manfreds

*Jægersborggade 40; tel. 36 96 65 93;*
*http://manfreds.dk; daily noon-3:30pm,*
*5pm-10pm; tasting menu 285kr excluding*
*wine, small dishes 50-105kr; bus 8A*
*Jægersborggade (Jagtvej)*

Manfreds claims to be "probably the world's only veggie-focused restaurant famous for its raw meat" due to its tartare, which was inherited from big-sister restaurant (and Michelin-starred) Relæ, just across the street. It is also certified as being between 90 and 100 percent organic and focuses on natural wines, raw ingredients, and rustic-style small dishes (2-3 dishes per person recommended)—steamed Danish mussels; celeriac, radishes and capers; and beef tartare with cress and rye bread, to name but a few. There are also plenty of vegetarian choices at affordable prices. It's a great budget-friendly, high-quality restaurant option.

# CHRISTIANSHAVN AND AMAGER

## DANISH AND NEW NORDIC

### Noma

*Refshalevej 96; tel. 32 96 32 97; http://noma.*
*dk; Tues.-Sat. 5pm-midnight; tasting menus*
*from 2,250kr not including wine pairings,*
*student discouts available; bus 9A Lynetten*
*(Refshalevej)*

Chef René Redzepi's Noma is Denmark's most famous restaurant. Guests from all over the world travel to Copenhagen for no other reason than to dine here. After reopening in a converted naval bunker near Christiania in 2018 (its first round of bookings sold out in hours), Noma changed the way it defines its seasons, now dividing the calender into three distinct parts, ripping up the menu, and starting again at the end of each. Seafood season runs from January to

June 1, before vegetable season takes over for the summer and September, with the year being closed out by game and forest season from October through December. Securing a reservation is notoriously difficult and should be made as far in advance as possible through Noma's website. A cancellation policy applies. The new restaurant is set in a peaceful area between Christiania and Refshaleøen with lakes on two sides and a garden area where some of its wild ingredients grow.

## Færgecafé

*Strandgade 50; tel. 32 54 46 24; https:// faergecafeen.dk; lunch Mon.-Sat. 11:30am-3:30pm, dinner (June to Sept.) Mon.-Thurs. 5:30pm-9:30pm, Fri.-Sat. 5:30pm-10pm, (Oct. to May) Mon.-Thurs. 5:30pm-9pm, Fri.-Sat. 5:30pm-10pm, Sun. 11:30am-9pm (kitchen closes 8pm); lunch from 72kr, smørrebrød from 82kr, dinner mains 189-235kr; bus 2A, 9A, Christianshavns Torv, Metro Christianshavns St.*

The archetypically Danish Christianshavns Færgecafé is unmissable in the midst of Christianshavn's cobbled streets and arched bridges, its rich orange exterior and bold letters proudly proclaim its presence as a busy provider of victuals in an area once frequented by people used to plying their trade at sea. Herring and *smørrebrød* are the order of the day, as is the homemade "skipper's schnapps," if you're feeling brave. In the evening, you will find schnitzel, a "captain's steak" with bearnaise, and duck with red cabbage among the main course options.

## Kadeau

*Wildersgade 10B; tel. 33 25 22 23; www.kadeau.dk; dinner, Tues.-Sat. 6:30pm-midnight, lunch, Sat. noon-4pm; 14-serving tasting menu 1,950kr excluding wine; bus 2A, 9A, Christianshavns Torv, Metro Christianshavns St.*

Cultivated and foraged natural ingredients from the Baltic Sea island of Bornholm are the mainstay of intimate, minimalistic two-starred Michelin restaurant Kadeau. That means seafood, berries, herbs, and fermented infusions delicately poised together in immaculately presented dishes, giving head chef and cofounder Nicolai Nørregaard's restaurant one of the very best reputations of all Copenhagen's Michelin dining experiences. Christianshavn is in full charm mode here, with the bright, simply decorated restaurant found on an ancient side street, with wooden frames still showing on some of the houses and vines creeping up the walls of the buildings.

## 108

*Strandgade 108; tel. 32 96 32 92; https://108.dk; daily 5pm-midnight; eight-serving tasting menu 1,150kr excluding wine; bus 9A Bodenhoffs Plads (Prinsessegade)*

New Nordic Michelin restaurant, sometimes referred to as "Noma's little sister," opened in 2016 by chef Kristian Baumann, who was only 28 at the time. Reservations are advised, but limited walk-in tables are also available. The à la carte menu consists of small dishes such as raw lamb with pickles, brown beech mushrooms with smoked egg yolk sauce, or grilled quail with beetroot. Located in a corner building across the harbor from Nyhavn via the pedestrian Inderhavnsbroen bridge, the inside of the restaurant has a stripped-down look with bare concrete pillars and brick walls.

## La Banchina

*Refshalevej 141A; tel. 31 26 65 61; www.labanchina.dk; May-Sept Mon.-Fri. 8am-11pm, Sat.-Sun. 9am-midnight; winter, café Mon.-Fri. 8am-6pm, Sat.-Sun. 9am-4pm, restaurant Thurs.-Sun. 6pm-midnight; summer dishes from 95kr, winter four-course menu 400kr; bus 9A Refshaleøen (Refshalevej)*

La Banchina is a great Italian-inspired Nordic summer natural wine and gastro option at Refshaleøen, as well as a year-round café. The restaurant, housed in a converted, blue-washed wooden hut that was once a waiting room for ferry passengers, has a jetty seating area that can be used to view the sunset over the sea while enjoying a fresh seafood or vegetarian dish. In the winter months, the concept changes to an indoor gourmet dining experience. Inside, there is seating only for 16, and it is particularly popular among trendy Refshaleøen visitors, so restaurant reservations are recommended during the summer but less necessary in the winter season.

## BREAKFAST AND DINERS
### Wulff & Konstali

*Lergravsvej 57; tel. 32 54 81 81; http://wogk. dk; Mon.-Fri. 7am-7pm, Sat.-Sun. 8am-6pm; brunch 129kr for five selected components; bus 77 Lergravsvej (Strandlodsvej), Metro Lergravsparken*

Light, airy, and near the beach at Amager Strandpark, Wulff & Konstali is an ideal spot for breakfast or lunch. Pick and mix your own breakfast and brunch from the selection of 22 different components including croissant, eggs, avocado, grape, melon, organic cheese, smoked salmon, fresh bread straight from the on-site bakery.... I could continue. It's a busy spot, particularly on weekends or when the weather's good. There's seating along a bench table and at stools facing the window, and it also functions well as a café, deli, and takeaway that serves sandwiches, *smørrebrød*, and salads.

## CAFÉS AND BAKERIES
### Brødflov

*Torvegade 50 (and other locations); tel. 31 60 83 98; www.broedflov.dk; Mon.-Fri. 7am-7pm, Sat.-Sun. 7am-6pm; pastries from 25kr; bus 2A, 9A, Christianshavns Torv, Metro Christianshavns St.*

This premium bakery uses entirely organic ingredients and bakes all its bread from sourdough rather than using yeast. The result is bread with deep taste and texture—the granola bread is particularly good and the rye bread is as good as in Copenhagen. Sandwiches, *smørrebrød*, and a mouthwatering selection of cakes are also available, and you can grab a coffee to go or sit at one of the café seats by the window and observe busy Christianshavn Square. Brødflov also has branches in Frederiksberg and in Tivoli's food hall.

### Kafferiet

*Wildersgade 26; tel. 20 20 85 77; http://kafferiet.dk; Mon.-Fri. 7am-6pm, Sat.-Sun. 7am-9pm; coffee from 25kr, pastries from 25kr; bus 2A, 9A, Christianshavns Torv, Metro Christianshavns St.*

On the corner of Torvegade, the main road through Christianshavn, Kafferiet is a cozy nook on the corner where the coffee is good, the service friendly, and you can get a pastry, sit near a window, and watch the world go by for a bit.

## EUROPEAN
### Era Ora

*Overgaden Neden Vandet 33B; tel. 32 54 06 93; www.era-ora.dk; Mon.-Sat. lunch noon-4pm (kitchen closes at 2pm), dinner*

6:30pm-midnight (kitchen closes at 10pm); lunch menu two courses 498kr excluding wine, dinner menu 980-1280kr excluding wine; bus 2A, 9A, Christianshavns Torv, Metro Christianshavns St.

Era Ora is one of Copenhagen's oldest Italian restaurants and was first given a Michelin star in 1997. Housed in an 18th-century building by the canal in Christianshavn, chandeliers hang from the high ceilings of its modern-looking rooms. Dishes such as ravioli with fennel and chestnuts, sturgeon with chard, and duck with black grapes and chicory are among those you can expect to enjoy.

### L'Altro

Torvegade 62; tel. 32 54 54 06; http://laltro. dk; Mon.-Sat. 5:30pm-midnight; four-course set menu 395kr; bus 2A, 9A, Christianshavns Torv, Metro Christianshavns St.

This Italian restaurant sells wonderful, homemade Umbrian and Tuscan cuisine in a homely two-floor (tip: it's a little brighter upstairs) near the noisy Christianshavn-Amager crossing. Examples of dishes include risotto with broccoli, ravioli with beetroot and ricotta, and a mackerel, yogurt, and chives starter, but changes can be made to the menu, depending on season and available fresh produce.

## ASIAN
### Curry Club

Dronningensgade 46; tel. 28 73 43 46, www. curryclub.dk; Tues.-Sun. 4pm-10pm; curries from 99kr-115kr; bus 2A, 9A, Christianshavns Torv, Metro Christianshavns St.

An unassuming but colorful Indian restaurant and takeaway just off Christianshavns Torv, Curry Club was opened in March 2017 by two curry-mad brothers who will gladly spend 10 minutes explaining minute details of the various traditional Indian dishes. Meals can be eaten on the low-key benches inside the brightly lit restaurant or taken away. The restaurant is beginning to be noticed, but it has been a hidden favorite of Christianshavn locals in a city where Indian food is often overlooked. I recommend the Achari Murghi, a strong chicken dish with chili pickles, and Palak Gosht, a spinach curry made using Irish lamb. Vegan and vegetarian dishes are also available.

## ORGANIC, VEGETARIAN, AND VEGAN
### Amass

Refshalevej 153; tel. 43 58 43 30; https:// amassrestaurant.com; dinner Wed.-Sat. 6pm-midnight, last seating 9:15pm, lunch Fri.-Sat. noon-3:30pm, 1ast seating 1pm; tasting menu 695-1,095kr excluding wine; bus 9A Refshaleøen (Refshalevej)

Organic Amass sources a large proportion of its ingredients from its own garden, which has more than 80 varieties of leafy vegetables, berries, herbs, and flowers that appear daily on the menu. The menu changes seasonally and in line with what's available. The restaurant itself oozes industrial chic in keeping with its Reshaleøen setting.

## FOOD MARKET
### Reffen

Refshalevej 151; tel. 32 54 32 21; https:// reffen.dk; Mon.-Sat. 11am-8pm, Sun. noon-6pm, weekends only Oct.-Mar.; small plate from 40kr, mains from 70kr; bus 9A (Refshaleøen)

Reffen, a huge new open-air food market opened in May 2018, quickly established itself as a primary attraction as the warm early summer months got underway, with crowds of Copenhageners and visitors making the relatively long bicycle trip out to the old industrial harbor, where converted shipping containers are lined up in diagonal rows as far as the eye can see. World food including Indian, Mexican, Greek, and plenty of others are sold from within their corrugated steel walls. Benches are laid out on a wide, dusty open space between the containers and the edge of the harbor. **Blue Taco** (www.bluetaco.dk) serves colorful Mexican snacks; **Crispy Pig** makes roast pork burgers with crisp, salty crackling still on the meat; and **Satay Copenhagen** has spicy chicken and beef satay skewers, Malaysian style; there are more than 50 restaurants, bars, and other creative start-ups in all.

## KASTELLET AND LANGELINIE

This area consists of a seafront promenade extending north from the royal area of the Inner City and a former medieval citadel-turned-barracks, so there are few residences (or residents). If you find yourself here for sightseeing purposes—the famous Little Mermaid statue is just off the Langelinie shore—then walking back toward Nyhavn along parallel streets Borgergade, Store Kongensgade, and Bredgade will bring you to the closest

restaurants, and there are plenty of excellent options here.

### Toldboden

*Nordre Toldbod 24; tel. 33 93 07 60; http:// toldboden.com; Mon.-Fri. 10am-9pm, Sat.-Sun. 9:30am-9pm, opening times subject to seasonal variation; mains from 110kr, brunch 225kr; bus 1A Esplanaden (Grønningen)*

Set in the former ferry terminal at Copenhagen Harbor with a view of Refshaleøen and the Opera House, Toldboden has a decidedly maritime feel, but there's more than seaworthy nostalgia to this grill bar. The restaurant's long opening hours include breakfast (Mon.-Fri. 10am-noon), weekend brunch (Sat.-Sun. 9:30am-3pm), and grilled meat and vegetable buffets (Thurs.-Sun. from 5:30pm). Regular events (sometimes including free welcome drinks) are held with details posted on Toldboden's Facebook page. Watch for the classic cars that are parked outside the restaurant on Tuesday evenings. Food is good quality pub fare—think burgers, Caesar salad, soup of the day, and a continental breakfast—and prices are slightly above average, which may be related to the lack of competitors in the close vicinity and the visitors attracted by the nearby Little Mermaid.

# Bars and Nightlife

Copenhagen has a wealth of nightlife and drinking options, with a range of tastes catered to and high quality close by wherever in the city you find yourself. However, drinking in Denmark is expensive compared to almost every other country in the world.

For example, in Copenhagen, a **draft beer** on tap will set you back between 45 and 80 kr, depending on whether you're drinking a Carlsberg or the latest Mikkeller IPA (although there are less-expensive craft beers); **cocktails** range from 85-120kr; a decent glass of wine will cost at least 60-70 kr, stretching up to more than 200 kr for a Barolo or Grand Cru. However, cover charges are relatively rare: when you do come across them, the price is rarely more than 50 kr.

There are savings to be had if you look in the right places. A number of late-opening bars have happy hours in the early part of the evening, when cocktails, for example, can be half or two-thirds of regular prices: check social media accounts and websites, where these are often advertised. Visit a bodega where a bottle of Carlsberg or Tuborg can be had for as little as 25kr. These rough-and-tumble pubs also sell bottom-shelf schnapps (from 20kr) and mixed drinks (from 25-60kr). The latter are often served in plastic cups or scratched tumblers and are hardly cocktail bar standard. Not that they claim to be—the experience here is more about the drinking and atmosphere than the taste.

# NØRREPORT AND AROUND

Copenhagen hums with life in the evening hours around the Inner City, as people head into town on foot and by bicycle. The possibilities for a night on the town have few limits, and one bar can quickly be swapped for another, depending on the vibe of the evening. Some of the bars along Gothersgade are rather unimaginative and best avoided, while others are worth seeking out. The area around Nørreport offers a variety of bars—everything from quiet wine tasting to boisterous pubs and lively dance floors.

### The Living Room

*Larsbjørnsstræde 17; tel. 33 32 66 10; www. facebook.com/thelivingroomdk; Mon.-Thurs. 9am-11pm, Fri. 9am-2am, Sun. 10am-7pm;*

*bus 5C, 6A Jarmers Plads (Nørre Voldgade), Metro, S-train Nørreport.*

A chilled-out and popular café during the day, coffee is swapped for (relatively) less-expensive cocktails as evening kicks in at the Living Room. With a hearth and comfy sofas on the lower floor, it can be a great way to shelter from the aching cold of the winter season. Upstairs seating has a decent view of the busy central streets, ideal for people watching over a margarita or mocha. Busy all round on Friday and Saturday.

### 1105

*Kristen Bernikows Gade 4; tel. 33 93 11 05; http://cocktailkompagniet.dk; Wed.-Thurs. 7pm-2am, Fri. 4pm-2am, Sat. 6pm-2am; Metro Kongens Nytorv*

Several of the bartenders at 1105 have won awards for their bartending skills, including for specialities such as the gin, mange tout, and lime Snap Fever, and frozen raspberry, gin, and schnapps Cucumber Yum Yum. The smartly dressed, thirty-something guests look no less distinguished. This is a high-quality cocktail bar that is particularly busy around midnight on weekends.

### Bo-Bi Bar

*Klareboderne 14; tel. 33 12 55 43; Mon.-Sat. noon-2am, Sun. 2pm-2am; Metro Kongens Nytorv*

Reportedly founded by a sailor during the First World War, smoky Bo-Bi Bar retains the old-fashioned, rather than consciously retro, feel of a harborside drinking establishment. Known for being a place where artists and writers once convened, this down-to-earth bodega is attractive to literary types for just that reason. Note, smoking is permitted inside.

### The Jane

*Gråbrødretorv 8; tel. 61 69 21 64; www.*
*thejane.dk; Thurs. 8pm-late, Fri. 4pm-late,*
*Sat. 8pm-late; Metro Kongens Nytorv*

There's a distinctly Mad Men feel to cocktail bar the Jane, one of a number of tourist-friendly options around the Gråbrødretorv plaza, close to the Round Tower, and central shopping streets. Its small rooms, dimmed lights, and bookcases insinuate secret doorways, and space is made for a dance floor as the hours tick away into the night.

# GREATER INNER CITY

## WINE

### Bibendum

*Nansensgade 45; tel. 33 33 07 74; https://*
*bibendum.dk; Mon.-Sat. 4pm-midnight; bus,*
*Metro Nørreport*

One of Copenhagen's oldest wine bars by its own estimations, diminutive Bibendum, with its candlelit tables and blackboard menus ("Wine is the answer…what was the question?") has a calming vibe and an enormous wine list. There's a rotating selection of organic, bio, and sparkling wines as well as reds and white to cater to all preferences, with Spanish and French-inspired snacks on hand.

### Ved Stranden 10

*Ved Stranden 10; tel. 35 42 40 40; www.*
*vedstranden10.dk; Mon.-Sat. noon-10pm;*
*Metro Kongens Nytorv*

Located in a listed building that dates back to the time of Hans Christian Andersen and Søren Kierkegaard and directly facing Christiansborg Palace, there's certainly a sense of history about Ved Stranden 10. An extensive wine list from all over the world, including a good selection of natural wines, no shortage of space, and knowledgeable staff to guide you

through it. In summer, you can sit outside and take in the canalside view.

## COCKTAILS

### Ruby

*Nybrogade 10; tel. 33 93 12 03; https://rby.*
*dk; Mon.-Sat. 4pm-2am, Sun. 6pm-2am; bus*
*1A, 2A, 9A Stormbroen, Nationalmuseet*
*(Vindebrogade)*

Close to the harbor at Nybrogade, cocktail bar Ruby has plenty of elbow room and large, comfy chairs for you to sink into while you enjoy a cocktail. The bartenders, who are cocktail enthusiasts as well as being well informed, are versed in the customs and traditions of their trade—enough to give Ruby a placing of 34 in the 2015 edition of "The World's 50 Best Bars" (www.worlds50bestbars.com). The music is not turned up too high, in keeping with Ruby's broad appeal. Keep your ears peeled when you visit the lavatory, though: Eddie Murphy stand-up classic "Raw" plays on loop through WC speakers for your enjoyment.

### The Bird & The Churchkey

*Gammel Strand 44; tel. 60 12 23 18;*
*www.thebird.dk; Mon.-Wed. 4pm-1am,*
*Thurs. 4pm-2am, Fri.-Sat. 4pm-4am, Sun.*
*2pm-10pm; Metro Kongens Nytorv*

Gin and tonic and beer specialist The Bird & The Churchkey has more than 20 variations of the former and 50 of the latter (there are actually 102 different gins alone). On the atmospheric Gammel Strand (once current renovation work on the canalside is complete), the tiled floors and self-styled "East London" atmosphere make for a buoyant, noisy experience, and you certainly won't go thirsty. Cocktails start from 60kr and average out at around 100kr for a good quality

G&T, a not-unreasonable price by Copenhagen terms.

## Madam Chu's

*Gammel strand 40; tel. 69 69 20 24; www. madamchu.dk; Wed.-Sat. 6pm-late; Bus 1A, 2A, 9A Christiansborg (Vindebrogade)*

Old Shanghai-inspired Madam Chu's, with its curtains, dark walls, red lamps, and Chinese motifs, is a themed variation on the extensive choice of cocktail bars near Gammel Strand and stays open well into the night. Look out for happy hour specials (often before 8pm): normal prices hover around 100kr for a cocktail.

## BODEGAS
### Bankeråt

*Ahlefeldtsgade 27; tel. 33 93 69 88; www. bankeraat.dk; Mon.-Tues. 9:30am-11pm, Wed.-Fri. 9:30am-midnight, Sat. 10:30am-midnight, Sun. 10:30am-6pm; bus 37 Ahlenfeldtsgade (Nørre Farimagsgade)*

Bankeråt almost has the appearance of an old-fashioned "brown bodega" (pub) with its deep-red-painted walls and various stuffed animal heads adorning the walls, but the hanging fairy lights and other assorted knickknacks add a touch of the surreal. There's a good selection of local and foreign craft beers from 49kr; Carlsberg, Tuborg, and coffee is a little cheaper. Brunch and a range of café meals are also available.

## DANCE/LIVE MUSIC
### La Fontaine

*Kompagnistræde 11; tel. 33 11 60 98; www. lafontaine.dk; Mon.-Sun. 8pm-5am; bus 1A, 2A, 9A Stormbroen, Nationalmuseet (Vindebrogade).*

Lady Gaga once showed up unannounced to play an improvised concert at La Fontaine, reportedly just because she liked it. She's not the only one. Crowded and a bit rough around the edges with a slightly older crowd, this longstanding jazz bar is a Copenhagen classic. When Gaga's not around, live concerts take place every Friday, Saturday, and Sunday from 9pm until 1am.

## LGBTQ+
### Centralhjørnet

*Kattesundet 18; tel. 33 11 85 49; www. centralhjornet.dk; Sun.-Wed. noon-2am, Thurs. noon-3am, Fri.-Sat. noon-4am; bus 2A, 5C, 9A, Copenhagen Central Station*

The self-titled "world's oldest gay bar" may well live up to that claim, and it is certainly Copenhagen's first: rumor has it that in the 1920s the army ordered conscripts not to go there, such was its reputation. In its modern form, there's a welcoming and low-key atmosphere during the day and regular events at night, such as live music and drag shows. Flamboyant decorations mark Easter and Christmas (hundreds of multicolored, glitter-painted outsize eggs hang from the ceiling or a forest of Christmas baubles in the same place). The gin and tonics are decent, and beers and cocktails are also on the menu. Smoking is allowed inside, adding to the sense of a throw-back to a previous era provided by the brown fittings and old-fashioned pint mugs with glass handles.

### My Fair Ladies

*Mikkel Bryggers Gade 11; tel. 60 52 24 36; www.myfairladies.dk; Sun.-Thurs. noon-3am, Fri.-Sat. noon-9am; bus 14 Strøget (Nytorv), 12, 14 Rådhuspladsen (H. C. Andersens Boulevard)*

Copenhagen's only musical-themed LGBTQ+ bar has a distinctive color theme—the cushions and stools as well as the walls are all pink. Hollywood versions of musicals play on the multiple screens, as the bartenders mix cocktails into the night. It's open late every day of the week and has karaoke every Wednesday. Happy hour until 6pm daily.

## NYHAVN
### Nebbiolo Winebar

*Store Strandstræde 18; tel. 60 10 11 09; http://nebbiolo-winebar.com; Mon.-Thurs. 3pm-midnight, Fri.-Sat. 3pm-2am, Sun. 3pm-midnight; bus 66 Sankt Annæ Plads, Skuespilhuset (Sankt Annæ Plads), Metro Kongens Nyhavn*

There are vintage Italian scenes on its walls, boxes of wine on the floor, and cured ham hanging from the ceiling. Wine specialists at Nebbiolo always have a large number of open bottles from throughout the Mediterranean, which are sold by the glass (75-125kr). Complimentary antipasti tapas are served with the wine: if you get a taste for a meal, a full plate can be purchased. It's a nice breather from Nyhavn's busy crowds, though it's still crowded on weekends.

### Den Vandrette

*Havnegade 53A; tel. 72 14 82 28; www. denvandrette.dk; Tues.-Fri. 2pm-11pm, Sat. 1pm-11pm, Sun. 1pm-9pm; Metro Kongens Nytorv*

Den Vandrette is just around the corner from Nyhavn and overlooks the water, which allows you to avoid much of the area's foot traffic. With sketches of fish and bottles of wine on its façade, Den Vandrette ("The Horizontal") was one of Denmark's first importers of natural wines. Wines are featured from 10 French regions along with Spain, Portugal, Italy, Germany, and the New World. Tapas-style side dishes complement the wines.

## VESTERBRO AND FREDERIKSBERG
### COCKTAILS
### Lidkoeb

*Vesterbrogade 72B; tel. 33 11 20 10; www. lidkoeb.dk; Sun.-Tues. 8pm-2am, Wed.-Sat. 4pm-2am; bus 6A, 9A Frederiksberg Allé (Vesterbrogade)*

The high-end cocktail bar has leather sofas and stark, whitewashed walls. It's from the people who brought you the Inner City favorite Ruby. The bartenders wear leather aprons, and there's always plenty of room: Lidkoeb is in a three-story building that was once a pharmacy. A dedicated whisky bar on the top floor opens every Friday and Saturday.

### 1656

*Gasværksvej 33; tel. 20 47 27 47; http:// cocktailkompagniet.dk; Mon.-Wed. 6pm-1am, Thurs.-Sat. 6pm-2am, Sun. 6pm-1am; bus 10, 14 Gasværksvej (Istedgade)*

Yards from the Meatpacking District but hidden from obvious view (keep looking if you don't see it at first), the speakeasy-style 1656, with its wooden panels and dark upholstery, has a huge cocktail menu. The sofas are comfy, and the vibe intimate with dimmed lights and lively conversation. Try the 3-Star Daiquiri, named for the artisanal rum used to make it.

### BEER
### Mikkeller Bar

*Viktoriagade 8; tel. 33 31 04 15; http:// mikkeller.dk; Sun.-Wed. 1pm-1am, Thurs.-Fri. 1pm-2am, Sat. noon-2am; bus Copenhagen Central Station*

Mikkeller's bar on Vesterbro has a classical minimalistic look, all white walls and straight lines, with simple wooden seats and squeaky clean floors. There are 20 taps—in time-honored Mikkeller style—which are dedicated to the brewery's own concoctions as well as to beers from around the world. The bartenders will help you to choose and ply you with tasters to help you decide on your tipple. The menu rotates regularly, so the service is likely to be useful each time you go back.

## Fermentoren

*Halmtorvet 29C; tel. 23 98 86 77; http:// fermentoren.com; Mon.-Wed. 3pm-midnight, Thurs. 2pm-1am, Fri.-Sat. 2pm-2am, Sun. 4pm-midnight; bus 1A Dybbølsbro St. (Ingerslevsgade)*

This craft beer pub has stouts, IPA, trippels, and more from microbreweries from across Denmark and beyond, and the selection is rotated regularly, so you're probably find something new every time you visit. An outside terrace makes for a nice city spot to sit and enjoy a cold brew in the summer time.

## WarPigs

*Flæsketorvet 25; tel. 43 48 48 48; http:// warpigs.dk; Mon.-Thurs. 11:30am-midnight, Fri.-Sat. 11am-2am, Sun. 11am-11pm (kitchen closes 10pm); bus 10 Gasværksvej (Istedgade)*

In spacious, stark, industrial surroundings with a strong, musky smell from its giant meat smokers, this Floyds and Mikkeller collaboration brewpub takes the Meatpacking District to heart. Go to the bar and order a chocolate stout and wait while it is poured from the bonehandle taps. The menu is in the style of a Texas barbecue with ribs, pork, "slaw, mac 'n' cheese, and pecan pie (steaks from 45kr and sides from 30kr).

## Kihoskh

*Sønder Blvd. 53; tel. 33 31 11 98; www. kihoskh.dk; Sun.-Thurs. 7am-1am, Fri.-Sat.*

*7am-2am; bus Copenhagen Central Station, S-train Dybbølsbro St.*

It looks like a normal liquor store or a Berlin *Spätie* from the outside, but Kihoskh is a venerable beer paradise with its cellar of new releases and rarities as well as broad range of Danish craft beers. You can bag your purchases (bring your own bag) and take them home, but there is also outside seating, and it is perfectly acceptable to enjoy them on the spot, reinforcing the Berlin vibe. This is naturally more advisable during the summer.

## Simpelt V

*Istedgade 96; tel. 69 69 20 25; www. simpeltv.dk; Mon.-Tues. 6pm-2am, Wed. 6pm-3am, Thurs. 6pm-4am, Fri.-Sat. 3pm-5am, Sun. 5pm-2am; bus 10, 14 Saxogade (Istedgade)*

The grungy late opener Simpelt V on Istedgade serves inexpensive beers and schnapps to the light of candles wedged into old Jack Daniels bottles. Guns 'n' Roses, Sex Pistols, and Led Zeppelin provide inspiration for both the décor and the playlist. Smoking inside is permitted—be prepared for a lot of smoke.

## LGBTQ+
### Jolene

*Flæsketorvet 81-85; tel. 35 85 29 45; www.jolene.dk; Thurs. 8pm-3am, Fri.-Sat. 7pm-4am; no cover; bus 10 Gasværksvej (Istedgade)*

One of the first bars to open in the Meatpacking District in 2008, underground electronic music is still a big part of Jolene's identity. The slogan "This Is Not A F*cking Cocktail Bar" is painted in large letters behind the bar, and the drinks menu supports that claim. Beer, shots, and simple mixers are what you'll get at this weathered nightclub, along with

## MIKKELLER: HOW A MATH TEACHER'S MICROBREW CHANGED COPENHAGEN BEER CULTURE

Back in 2006, Mikkel Borg Bjergsø was a Copenhagen-based math teacher with a passion for beer and running. Today, Mikkeller (http://mikkeller.dk), the microbrewery he started in his kitchen, exports beer to more than 50 countries and has bars in a long list of international cities, including New York, Bangkok, Tokyo, Berlin, Singapore, Barcelona, Seoul, and San Francisco. Scores of new brews are developed every year—Bjergsø is reported to retain close control of recipes—and a visit to one of the company's many locations around the city is a certain way to find something unique. The brand has a total—at the last count—of 16 establishments, including its bottle shops and restaurant collaborations, in Copenhagen alone.

The lightning-fast growth of the brand has not been without its challenges. One well-documented story is the rift between Bjergsø and his twin brother, Jeppe Jarnit-Bjergsø, who in the early days sold Mikkeller's beers from the now-closed Ølbutikken shop in Vesterbro. Jeppe Jarnit-Bjergsø later founded the nomadic brewery Evil Twin, which, like Mikkeller, enjoys a high level of international recognition among beer lovers and experts.

Despite the meteoric growth and aggressive expansion of the brand, it has retained the look and feel of a small, independent microbrewery—no two locations are the same. Highlights in Copenhagen include:

- **WarPigs:** a collaboration with American brewery 3 Floyds in the Meatpacking District (page 128)

- **Mikkeller Bar:** designed by bureau Femmes Regionales and voted bar of the year by Danish newspaper *Politiken* in 2012 (page 127)

- **La Neta:** a Mexican taqueria-inspired, brightly lit establishment with a characteristic tiled façade on Nørrebrogade (Nørrebrogade 29; tel. 31 12 01 05; Sun.-Wed. noon-10pm, Thurs. noon-midnight, Fri.-Sat. noon-2am)

  These, though, are far from the only options.

---

an exuberant crowd, disco balls, and neon signs. The DJs occasionally give way to rock bands, and there are monthly LGBTQ+ nights as well as other events that are listed on the Jolene Facebook page.

### Café Intime

*Allegade 25; tel. 38 34 19 58; www. cafeintime.dk; daily 4pm-2am; bus 8A Frederiksberg Rådhus (Allegade)*

Leafy Frederiksberg is home to Café Intime, an LGBT+-friendly café, jazz bar, and hangout that is busy most nights. You can't miss the name lit in bright bulbs over the door, nor the eclectic and somewhat old-school cabaret feel. Smoking is permitted inside.

## NØRREBRO AND ØSTERBRO

### COCKTAILS

#### Mexi-Bar

*Elmegade 27; tel. 35 37 77 66; http:// mexibar.com; Mon.-Tue 7pm-1am, Wed.-Thurs. 7pm-2am Fri. 3pm-3am, Sat. 7pm-3am; bus 3A Skt. Hans Torv (Blegdamsvej)*

On the corner of Sankt Hans Torv, Mexi Bar's student-friendly prices, with cocktails from as little as 49kr, make it a popular spot for hip, young locals—and often also a crowded one due to its diminutive size. Arrive in good time. The "Passion Splash," a fresh, sweet mix of vodka, creme de menthe, and passion fruit, is recommended.

## TOP EXPERIENCE

# ✪ NIGHTLIFE IN VESTERBRO AND NØRREBRO

Looking for a good night out on the town in Copenhagen? Look no further than **Vesterbro and Nørrebro**. The highlight of nightlife in Copenhagen is arguably **Vesterbro's Meatpacking District** (Kødbyen to the locals), which in recent years has developed into an inventive and diverse district that exudes urban chic while exploring its industrial past: many of the bars and restaurants have a white-tiled, metallic aesthetic that chimes with the cool sense of style of the customers. On summer weekends, the area buzzes with people sitting, standing, and dancing in and outside of the many bars, clubs, and restaurants, with wide asphalted spaces ample for impromptu partying.

Elsewhere in Vesterbro, **Istedgade**, is a gritty area that is far more welcoming now than in the days when its name was intrinsically linked to drugs, crime, and poverty. It has become a vibrant spot with bars, *bodegas* (the small, rowdy, publike bars with tobacco-stained walls and cheap schnapps to go with grizzled locals), and restaurants; **Viktoriagade** and **Vesterbrogade** are also good areas to seek out.

The scene in **Nørrebro** is equally lively, particularly in the areas around **Ravnsborggade, Stefansgade, Elmegade, Jægersborggade,** and **Sankt Hans Torv** where the people are as diverse as the bars, which vary from Middle-Eastern-style cafés to dive bars to craft beer pubs.

### The Barking Dog

*Sankt Hans Gade 19; tel. 35 36 16 00; www. thebarkingdog.dk; Sun.-Mon. 6pm-midnight, Tues.-Thurs. 6pm-1am, Fri.-Sat. 6pm-2am; bus 3A Skt. Hans Torv (Blegdamsvej)*

In a basement on pleasant plaza Sankt Hans Torv, the Barking Dog is a "cocktail pub" with a broad selection of cocktails, beers, and liquors as well as a relaxed Copenhagener atmosphere. The checkered floor, cacti, and skull paraphernalia are part of its character, as are the creative cocktail names (such as "Space Daiquiri," "Tree Hugger" and "Christian J. Collins").

### Gilt

*Rantzausgade 39; tel. 27 26 80 70; https:// gilt.dk; Tues.-Thurs. 6pm-midnight, Fri.-Sat. 6pm-2am; bus 66 Skyttegade (Rantzausgade)*

Opened in 2003 in Nørrebro well before the area was rich in cocktail bars and craft beer pubs, GILT has moved with the times and remains popular, serving cocktails inspired by the Nordic lands: an olive vermouth, cognac with sage or gin with beetroot, and pear cider and liquorice, to name just a handful of the seasonal offerings. Inside, it is decorated in soft grays and browns, in keeping with the relaxed, welcoming style for which it is known.

### BEER
### Brus

*Guldbergsgade 29; tel. 75 22 22 00; https://tapperietbrus.dk; Mon.-Thurs.. 3pm-midnight, Fri.-Sat. noon-3am, Sun. noon-midnight; Bus 5C Kapelvej (Nørrebrogade)*

In an old iron foundry and locomotive factory, smart brewpub Brus has a rotating on-tap selection of more than 30 microbrews by owning brewery To Øl, a Danish brand that has gained worldwide recognition. The helpful bartenders offer tasting samples before you make your choice. Grab a savory snack and settle down—there's plenty of space inside and out.

## Mikkeller & Friends

*Stefansgade 35; tel. 35 83 10 20; http://*
*mikkeller.dk/location/mikkeller-friends;*
*Sun.-Wed. 2pm-midnight, Thurs.-Fri.*
*2pm-2am, Sat. noon-2am; bus 5C*
*Stefansgade (Nørrebrogade)*

Mikkeller and Friends on Stefansgade offers a great chance to see the world-famous Copenhagen craft beer brand on its home turf: in a converted cellar in Nørrebro. Although the company actually started in Vesterbro, the Stefansgade bar manages to encapsulate the diverse Mikkeller styles and bars across Copenhagen, distilling them in one place. Beers on tap are rotated.

## Nørrebro Bryghus

*Ryesgade 3; tel. 35 30 05 30; www.*
*noerrebrobryghus.dk; Mon.-Thurs.*
*noon-11pm, Fri.-Sat. noon-1am, Sun.*
*noon-10pm; bus 3A Skt. Hans Torv*
*(Blegdamsvej)*

One of the original players in the microbrewing trend that has taken Copenhagen by storm in recent years, Nørrebro Bryghus calls the large brickwork premises close to the lakes home, where, as well as tasting different beers at the spacious bar, you can grab lunch or a bite of New Nordic-style dinner at the in-house restaurant.

## WINE
### Gaarden & Gaden

*Nørrebrogade 88; tel. 55 55 08 80; http://*
*gaaga.dk; Tues.-Thurs. 10am-midnight,*
*Fri.-Sat. 10am-2am, Sun. 10am-midnight;*
*bus 5C*

You can spot Gaarden & Gaden by the large neon locksmith sign at the corner of the block. This bar holds the keys to a relaxing evening, with its range of natural wines (more than 300!). Though it's much more than a restaurant, the daytime and evening menus will not leave you feeling hungry—these include eggs benedict on the weekends (115kr, until 3:30pm), and anchovies and squid (each 75kr) as well as larger plates in the evening. Gets busy in the evenings on Fridays and Saturdays, when it can be harder to find a table.

## BODEGAS
### Cafe Ægir

*Ægirsgade 16; tel. 35 83 10 02; Sun.-Wed.*
*10am-midnight, Thurs.-Sat. 10am-2am; bus*
*5C Stefansgade (Nørrebrogade)*

A raw pub or "brown bodega" in the heart of Nørrebro, Café Ægir is a *værtshus*, the nearest thing Denmark has to a local boozer. It won't hit your wallet too hard, and you might meet a character or two along the way. You can play billiards (more popular than pool as a bar game in Denmark) and will probably hear 4 Non Blondes at some point in the evening, although there's often live music too.

## CAFÉ BARS
### Tjili Pop

*Rantzausgade 28; tel. 35 35 90 20;*
*Mon.-Tues. 10am-midnight, Wed. 10am-1am,*
*Thurs. 10am-2am, Fri.-Sat. 10am-3am,*
*Sun. 10am-midnight; bus 12, 66 Skyttegade*
*(Rantzausgade)*

Tjili Pop is a café-bar hybrid with good vibes in shabby chic surroundings that gave it, along with a number of its 2000s contemporaries, the popular label "Berliner-cool." But Tjili Pop has more than just a little bit of a kindred spirit with the German capital's artsy side, with its graffiti'ed exterior, secondhand furniture, and a "distressed" interior doing as much to re-create the Kreuzberg style as a good selection of German beers. The "Berliner-cool" feel remains in place whether you come for a morning coffee, attend one of the regular small concerts, or just want to grab a pilsner.

### Café Blaagaards Apotek

*Blågårdsgade 20; tel. 35 37 24 42; www.*
*kroteket.dk; Mon.-Sat. noon-2am, Sun.*
*noon-10pm; bus 3A Prins Jørgens Gade*
*(Stengade)*

All types come to gather at Café Blaagaards Apotek, a non-profit café that plays host to live music and cultural and social events. Concerts four times a week—usually jazz—are always free and are listed on the bar's website. There are also jazz jamming sessions, open mic events, and a gallery with new artwork every month. The bar itself is a former pharmacy, hence the name, and what was once a medicine counter is now the bar.

## DANCE AND LIVE MUSIC
### Rust

*Guldbergsgade 8; tel. 35 24 52 00; www.*
*rust.dk; Fri.-Sat. 8:30pm-5am; bus 3A Skt.*
*Hans Torv (Blegdamsvej). Cover charge 80kr*

Rust is named after Mathias Rust, who famously landed his light aircraft on Moscow's Red Square in a daring Cold War-era protest stunt. The venue has served as a home for Copenhagen's musical underground since the 1990s and has played host to concerts by MØ and Rufus Wainwright in recent years. Check the website for upcoming events. On Fridays and Saturdays it becomes a raucous, multilevel nightclub with a young crowd spilling drinks on the dance floor and international DJs playing electro and hip-hop.

### Kassen

*Nørrebrogade 18B; tel. 42 57 22 00;*
*http://kassen.dk; Wed.-Thurs. 8pm-3am,*
*Fri. 4pm-4am, Sat. 8pm-4am; bus 5C*
*Ravnsborggade (Nørrebrogade)*

"It's hip to be square" is the motto of former café-turned-bar Kassen (the name translates to "the Box" or "the Cube"). Its mirrored disco ball hangs over a sticky dance floor. Prices can be kept low, particularly if you arrive before 10pm on the weekend and take advantage of the two-for-one happy hour (cocktails normally cost around 80-85kr here), filling up with a Ginger Collins or an espresso martini.

### Kind of Blue

*Ravnsborggade 17; tel. 26 35 10 56; http://*
*kindofblue.dk; Mon.-Wed. 4pm-midnight,*
*Thurs.-Sat. 4pm-2am; bus 5C Ravnsborggade*
*(Nørrebrogade)*

There's a chilled-out jazz vibe at Kind of Blue, which is named after a Miles Davis album and has a color scheme in keeping with the name as well as comfortable seats and cushions and a cello and piano for decorative purposes. There's a decent selection of craft beers as well as cocktails. The music—from Bob Dylan and Lou Reed as well as jazz—is kept to a soft volume, conducive to conversation. It's not hard to spot a first date or two taking place around the tables. Hop in for a breather from surrounding Ravnsborggade.

# CHRISTIANSHAVN AND AMAGER
## BEER
### Mikeller Baghaven

*Refshalevej 169B, tel. 70 27 02 96; http://*
*mikkellerbaghaven.dk; Mon.-Thurs.*
*1pm-10pm, Fri.-Sat. 1pm-midnight, Sun.*
*1pm-10pm; bus 9A Refshaleøen (Refshalevej)*

Mikkeller's new bar adjacent to the Reffen street food market on Refshaleøen oozes with the aura of a brand and a concept that knows when it's on home turf. Outside, Trabants and other 1960s cars double as flower beds. Inside the bar, a converted former shipbuilder's workshop, beers are aged in oaked vessels while a dozen or more craft brews rotate on tap. There's seating and standing space inside and out.

## Ingolfs Kaffebar

*Ingolfs Allé 3; tel. 32 59 95 96; www.*
*ingolfskaffebar.dk; Mon.-Tues. 9am-10pm,*
*Wed. 9am-11pm, Thu-Fri. 9am-midnight, Sat.*
*10am-midnight, Sun. 10am-9pm; bus 5C*
*Smyrnavej (Amagerbrogade)*

A quirky, creative interior design influenced by 1950s U.S. diners and breakfast and brunch options, as well as a good range of beers are the focus here. Ingolfs, hidden on a side street far into the depths of Amager, is a hit with many students attending KUA, the University of Copenhagen's southern facility where a number of arts and humanities disciplines are taught. In the summer, there's a beer garden of sorts, as the yard behind the restaurant is opened and guests flock to its picnic area.

## BODEGAS
### Eiffel Bar

*Wildersgade 58; tel. 32 57 70 92; http://*
*eiffelbar.dk; daily 9am-3am; bus 2A,*
*9A Knippelsbro (Torvegade), metro*
*Christianhavn St.*

As the name suggests, Eiffel Bar has taken the French capital's trademark and run with it. Inside, a veritable Little Paris awaits, decorated with charming vintage photos of the city, mostly the Eiffel Tower itself, the silhouette of which also appears on the bar's own-label pilsners (which will set you back the wallet-friendly price of 30kr). The bar service is incredibly friendly and welcoming—very few pubs in the city can boast better. The clientele is a mixture of grizzled regulars and young students, indie music plays loudly from the sound system. A great example of a Copenhagen bodega and well worth a visit.

## CAFÉS
### Christanshavns Bådudlejning og Café

*Overgaden Neden Vandet 29; tel. 32 96 53*
*53; http://baadudlejningen.dk; Mon.-Thurs.*
*10am-10pm, Fri.-Sat. 10am-midnight, Sun.*
*10am-10pm, reduced opening during winter;*
*bus 9A, 2A, Christianshavns Torv, Metro*
*Christianshavn St.*

A nice spot to sit in the sunshine with a cold beer or white wine, Christianshavns Bådudlejning and Café draws crowds to its decking right by the Christiania canal throughout the summer months. The seafood-based café fare can be handy if you get peckish, but the location and atmosphere are the main draws here.

## DANCE/LIVE MUSIC
### Halvandet Beach Bar

*Refshalevej 325; tel. 70 27 02 96; https://*
*halvandet.dk; Wed. 3pm-9pm, Thurs.*
*3pm-10pm, Fri. noon-11pm, Sat. 11am-11pm,*
*Sun. 11am-8pm; bus 9A Refshaleøen*
*(Refshalevej)*

As with much of the nightlife on Refshaleøen, Halvandet Beach Bar is located in a former industrial works: in this case, the former Burmeister and Wain shipyard. These days, the location is used to host summer-like parties, with deck chairs and a harborside bar ready for when the weather's bright. Concerts and festival events, including the Copenhagen Jazz Festival, often take place at the beach bar—check the program on Halvandet's website.

# Accommodations

Accommodations in Copenhagen are not cheap, and even budget selections can feel steep in comparison with other Western European countries, although they are about on a par with Norway and Sweden. Chain hotels are also dominant, including international brands such as Scandic and Radisson as well as smaller Scandinavian companies such as Cabinn. Hostels are relatively few, and their quality and style vary, but there are some excellent options to be found. Booking ahead is a necessity in the peak months for these budget options.

## NØRREPORT AND AROUND

Nørreport is slightly less hotel-heavy than the areas of the Inner City and Vesterbro that shoulder Copenhagen Central Station, but there are still plenty of options. Heading toward Kongens Nytorv and the historic, deluxe Hotel d'Angleterre, things get a little on the exclusive side, but there are also less-expensive beds in this area.

### UNDER 500KR
### ✪ Generator Hostel

*Adelgade 5-7; tel. 78 77 54 00; https://
generatorhostels.com/destinations/
copenhagen; shared room from 195kr,
private room from 600kr; Metro Kongens
Nytorv, 177 rooms*

My pick of the options for sociable, low-budget backpackers is Generator. It can be found on a slightly seedy-looking street a few footfalls from nightlife action along Gothersgade. Don't be put off by the harsh lighting and spacey house music in the stairwell—once you're inside, there's a well-trodden sense of comfort. This sprawling five-story accommodation can hold up to 692 guests. It's organized into 44 dorms (of either six or eight beds) and 133 private rooms. A giant common room and bar area is home to foosball, air hockey, a big screen for watching sports, and a long bar that serves food and often hosts live music, pub quizzes, or other forms of party games. Walking tours, bicycle and helmet rental (from 100 kroner for six hours), laundry service, and towel rental can all be arranged at reception, where you'll find helpful, informal staff that somehow manages to bring the feel of a small, intimate hostel to this expansive facility. The high traffic of people can leave the communal toilet facilities looking worse for wear by the end of the day, but use of these can easily be avoided as there is a toilet and bathroom in every dorm and private room.

### 500-1,000KR
### Hotel Jørgensen

*Rømersgade 11; tel. 33 13 81 86; www.
hoteljoergensen.dk; shared room from 150kr,
private room from 650kr; Metro Nørreport,
6 rooms*

On Israels Plads at the northern end of the Inner City/Nørreport area close to Rosenborg Castle and Kongens Have, Hotel Jørgensen is a more earthy—and less expensive—offering than much of its central Copenhagen competition. It's split into hotel and hostel sections: breakfast is included only for hotel bookings, while hostel users must pay an extra fee for bed linen. Rooms are basic with flat screen televisions and

## BEST ACCOMMODATIONS

✪ **GENERATOR HOSTEL:** A behemoth of a hostel teeming with amenities, things to do, and people to meet. It's located at the very center of town (page 134).

✪ **HOTEL SKT. ANNÆ:** Once a secretive, illegal port hideout for smugglers, the Skt. Annæ is now an airy and comfortable hotel near Nyhavn and Amalienborg. Its rooms are a mix of clean white and aquatic blue shades with designer armchairs and marble coffee tables (page 138).

✪ **HOTEL SANDERS:** Close to the Royal Theater, Nyhavn and Amalienborg, this gorgeous new top-end option is an evocative, luxuriant blend of handsome design and good service (page 139).

✪ **66 GULDSMEDEN:** Located on the main thoroughfare in fashionable Vesterbro, this colorful, family- and pet-friendly hotel has the added benefit of certified sustainability. It was awarded the Green Globe standard for its environmental practices (page 140).

✪ **CPH LIVING:** A converted barge on the Islands Brygge harborside with shipping containers as rooms, underfloor heating, and a spectular floating view (page 143).

sinks, while some of the hotel rooms have en-suite bathrooms.

### WakeUp Copenhagen

*Borgergade 9; tel. 44 80 00 00; www. wakeupcopenhagen.com; double occupancy room high season from 400kr; bus 5C Polititorvet (Carstern Niebuhrs Gade), Metro Kongens Nytorv (Borgergade);,498 rooms*

The budget, compact hotel option, WakeUp, has small rooms, which are rather podlike with the rounded bed corners and shower cubicles, and a bright and airy lobby. An extra charge of 90kr is applicable for breakfast. Small, clean, basic, and well organized. A second WakeUp can be found at Carsten Niebuhrs Gade 11, close to Copenhagen Central Station.

### 1,000-2,000KR
### Hotel Skt. Petri

*Krystalgade 22; tel. 33 45 91 00; www. sktpetri.com; double occupancy room high season from 2,150kr; bus 14 Mozarts Plads, Metro Nørreport; 288 rooms*

The central Hotel Skt. Petri has modern interior design in a variety of colors, a mazy lobby floor motif, and a rooftop terrace that looks great in nice weather. Facilities include a gym with sauna and steam bath. Breakfast is not included but can be added for 140kr. Located on central Krystalgade five minutes' walk from Nørreport station, many of the rooms on upper floors boast rooftop views over the city or of Copenhagen University.

### OVER 2,000KR
### Hotel d'Angleterre

*Kongens Nytorv 34; tel. 33 12 00 95; www. dangleterre.com; double occupancy room*

*high season 6,950kr; Metro Kongens Nytorv;*
*92 rooms*

The concierges in top hats and tails tell you what to expect the moment you walk into the five-star, 250-year-old Hotel d'Angleterre, one of the most famous hotels in Copenhagen. The elegant building looks out over Kongens Nytorv and its central location, minutes from the Round Tower, Nyhavn, and Amalienborg, makes this an ideal base for exploring the Inner City—if you have the budget for it. The plush, roomy suites have thick drapes, Bang and Olufsen televisions, and marble bathrooms. Facilities include a spa, swimming pool, Michelin-starred restaurant, and afternoon tea that, as if to make its decadence absolutely clear, adds a serving of sparkling wine to the traditional tea and cakes.

# GREATER INNER CITY

## UNDER 500KR

### Danhostel Copenhagen City

*H. C. Andersens Boulevard 50; tel. 33 11 85*
*85; https://danhostelcopenhagencity.dk/*
*da; shared room from 195kr, private room*
*from 600kr; bus 5C Otto Mønsteds Plads*
*(Rysensteensgade); 192 rooms*

A hostel with a view to rival anything else in the city, the towering 16-floor Danhostel near the Langebro Bridge is a great option for budget travelers. It belongs to the YHA scheme and, like many Hostelling International accommodations, can lack the sense of life and spontaneity found at more independent hostels. That said, the design and cleanliness here are first class—and then there's that view. Breakfast, sandwiches, snacks, and lunch packs are all available, although the buffet breakfast can be a bit of a squeeze.

## Copenhagen Downtown Hostel

*Vandkunsten 5; tel. 70 23 21 10; www.*
*copenhagendowntown.com; shared room*
*from 260kr, private room from 460kr;*
*bus 9A, 2A Stormbroen, Nationalmuseet*
*(Vindebrogade); 88 rooms*

This is a solid backpackers' hostel with various sized dorms of six-, eight-, and 10-bed mixed dorms and four-person female dorms. Private rooms can be reserved for up to 10 people. Both en-suite and shared bathrooms are available in both the dorms and private rooms. Centrally located between City Hall, the National Museum and Christiansborg, Copenhagen Downtown Hostel has a social atmosphere that revolves around its bar, along with other facilities including a foosball table, darts, and board games, while regular social events are arranged by staff. Bed linen, Wi-Fi, and even a yoga lesson are included, and guests can use the kitchen to make their own meals.

## 500-1,000KR

### Cabinn City

*Mitchellsgade 14; tel. 33 46 16 16; www.*
*cabinn.com/en/hotel/cabinn-city-hotel;*
*double occupancy room high season from*
*840kr; bus, S-train Copenhagen Central*
*Station, bus 5C Politorvet; 352 rooms*

This low-cost option, part of the Cabinn chain, which has hotels in most major Scandinavian cities, is conveniently located near the rail station. Despite the high capacity, with 352 rooms and 1,020 beds, advance booking is necessary for the standard and economy rooms. Free Wi-Fi is available in every room. Breakfast buffet can be opted in on booking. Rooms have a clean design—many double rooms are bunk beds in keeping with the "cabin" space-saving concept.

## 1,000-2,000KR

### Ibsens Hotel

*Vendersgade 23; tel. 33 45 77 44; www.arthurhotels.dk/ibsens-hotel; double occupancy room high season from 1,100kr; bus 5C Nørre Farimagsgade (Frederiksborggade); 118 rooms*

Adjoining the Hotel Kong Arthur in a charming 19th-century building, the lower-priced Ibsens Hotel shares the advantage of proximity to the lakes and Dronning Louises Bro, as well as to all the amenities of the Inner City. Compact, comfortable rooms have a quiet feel despite proximity to busy city streets and are tastefully furnished with modern-style fixtures. Breakfast can be added to booking.

### Hotel Kong Arthur

*Nørre Søgade 11; tel. 33 11 12 12; www.arthurhotels.dk; double occupancy room at high season from 1,270kr; Metro Nørreport; 155 rooms*

Looking out over the lakes, the elegant white façade of the Hotel Kong Arthur is a welcoming first impression for newcomers to Copenhagen. Amenities include spa rooms, a running club, and a gym, while fair trade and ecology are also a focus. The rooms are beautifully furnished in different syles of modern décor.

## OVER 2,000KR

### Nimb Hotel

*Bernstorffsgade 5; tel. 88 70 00 00; www.nimb.dk; double occupancy room high season from 2,800kr; bus, S-train, rail Copenhagen Central Station; 38 rooms*

In the iconic 1909 Middle Eastern-imitation building—arches, domes, and all—overlooking Tivoli Gardens, the boutique Nimb Hotel has spectacular history, view, and location, minutes from the central station and the heart of Inner City shopping, eating,

and bars. Its high ceilings, chandeliers, and plush carpets do the glamour no harm at all. Services include a rooftop terrace with pool and cocktail bar as well as a small gym. The smart, modern interior designs reflect the hotel's exterior look, with arched windows and intricately patterned quilts. Receives consistently positive feedback from guests.

### Radisson Collection Royal Hotel, Copenhagen

*Hammerichsgade 1; tel. 33 42 60 00; www.radissoncollection.com/en/royalhotel-copenhagen; double occupancy room high season from 2,800kr; bus, S-train, rail Copenhagen Central Station; 261 rooms*

Plush, five-star top-ender, the Radisson Collection Royal Hotel has the distinction of being designed by famous Danish architect Arne Jacobsen: room 606 has been preserved as a showpiece of Jacobsen's original modernist style from the 1960 build: ant chairs, grey-blue minimalism, and wood panels. The rest of the rooms are smart and modern, while the architect's influence remains present, with reupholstered Jacobsen chairs providing ambience throughout. The big, rectangular, blocky building still splits opinion as much as it did in the 1960s. Located near the central station, Tivoli, and Rådhuspladsen, its 260 luxury rooms have great views of the city, including from 20th-floor gourmet restaurant Alberto K.

## NYHAVN

### UNDER 500KR

### Bedwood Hostel

*Nyhavn 63; tel. 61 42 61 46; http://bedwood.dk; shared room from 229kr, private double room from 1,089kr; Metro Kongens Nytorv; 6 rooms*

Unlike other warehouses-turned-accommodation around Nyhavn, Bedwood Hostel is the only truly budget option. It retains much of the charm of its more lavish peers, though, with its hand-built wooden bunk beds made to match the jagged beams of the building. A 24-hour reception and plenty of common areas for socializing including a garden that is open until midnight on weekends ensure a sociable feel, and there is also a kitchen for guests' use. Laundry services and a communal kitchen are available, as is a breakfast buffet (55kr). Dorms range from six to twelve bunks and there are two private double rooms.

71 Nyhavn Hotel

### 500-1,000KR
#### Hotel Bethel Sømandshjem

*Nyhavn 22; tel. 33 13 03 70; www. hotel-bethel.dk; double occupancy room high season from 995kr; Metro Kongens Nytorv; 30 rooms*

Distinguishable from its red brick finish and corner tower, Hotel Bethel was once a seamen's home. Down to earth and with a buffet breakfast included in the price. Rooms, which have private bathrooms, are basic and clean and can suffer from outside noise, particularly on the courtyard-facing side. This is balanced by an outstanding location that overlooks Nyhavn, which punches well above its budget weight. Corner rooms with views are available.

### 1,000-2,000KR
#### 71 Nyhavn Hotel

*Nyhavn 71; tel. 33 43 62 00; www.71nyhavnhotel.com; double occupancy room high season from 1,024kr; Metro Kongens Nytorv; 130 rooms*

The hotel is situated in a prime spot on the corner overlooking Inderhavnsbroen and Christianshavn to the south and not least the masts and rooftops of iconic Nyhavn right outside the door. Rooms are affordable, and prices can be kept low by deselecting the buffet breakfast. There are 130 rooms in two converted former warehouses that have been given a modern finish, with sturdy, dark beams providing a bit of maritime atmosphere.

#### ✪ Hotel Skt. Annæ

*Sankt Annæ Plads 18; tel. 33 96 20 00; https://hotelsktannae.dk; double occupancy room high season from 1,141kr; bus 66 Nyhavnsbroen (Holbergsgade), Metro Kongens Nytorv; 147 rooms*

The former Hotel Neptune, which put up smugglers in the 19th century, is today the boutique Hotel Skt. Annæ, and there is little trace of its disreputable past. Features an airy gardenlike atrium. Some rooms have air conditioning—not a given, even in expensive hotels in Copenhagen given the cold climate, but nevertheless something that can greatly enhance your stay when the summer heats up. Located on a relatively quiet, grassy square, very close to both Nyhavn and Amalienborg. The smart lobby has comfy armchairs, marble coffee tables, and durable wooden flooring, and rooms are comfortable and easy on the eye in light shades of gray and blue. Breakfast not included in basic price bracket.

## Copenhagen Strand

*Havnegade 37; tel. 33 48 99 00; www. copenhagenstrand.dk; double occupancy room high season from 1,994kr; bus 1A Holmens Kirke (Holmens Kanal), 9A, 2A Børsen (Børsgade); 174 rooms*

Newly renovated three-star Copenhagen Strand has marine-blue rooms and a prime harbor location minutes from Nyhavn as well as Kongens Nytorv. Breakfast not included. Nordic design and clean lines characterize the rooms, some of which have balconies and views over the water. Manages to maintain a quiet air despite proximity to popular areas.

## OVER 2,000KR
### ✪ Hotel Sanders

*Tordenskjoldsgade 15; tel. 46 40 00 40; https://hotelsanders.com; double occupancy room high season from 2,610kr; bus 66 Tordenskjoldsgade (Holbergsgade), Metro Kongens Nytorv; 54 rooms*

Located on a quiet, cobbled street just behind the Royal Danish Theater (Det Kongelige Teater) at Kongens Nytorv, Hotel Sanders opened in 2017 in the former Opera Hotel, where owner Alexander Kølpin, a former Royal Danish Ballet dancer, stayed on a number of occasions while performing at the Royal Theater during his career. The lobby, packed with designer sofas, rugs, and warm lighting, sets the tone for the tasteful design of the pinewood furniture in the rooms, which have nice throwback touches including old-fashioned analogue alarm clocks with bells outside their round casings and replicas of pulse dial telephones. À la carte breakfast included.

## Copenhagen Admiral Hotel

*Toldbodgade 24-28; tel. 33 74 14 14; https://admiralhotel.dk; double occupancy room high season from 2,125kr; bus 1A Amalienborg (Bredgade), 66 Sankt Annæ Plads, Skuespilhuset (Sankt Annæ Plads); 366 rooms*

An impressively renovated former warehouse and customs office on the waterfront is home to Copenhagen Admiral Hotel, which retains some signs of its previous guises in the form of wooden beams and brickwork. Its location is an ideal base for sightseeing around Nyhavn and Kastellet as well as the rest of the Inner City. Copenhagen Opera sits directly across the harbor. Some of the hotel's rooms have terrific views over the water. Its large size means it is less intimate than competitors, but the staff is friendly and the rooms are modern and spacious.

# VESTERBRO AND FREDERIKSBERG

Hotels in the gentrified Vesterbro area are generally what most would consider walking distance from both Copenhagen Central Station and the long-distance bus terminal on Ingerslevsgade, making them convenient if you are arriving at these terminals or plan to venture outside of Copenhagen during your stay. With the notable exception of Tivoli, the historical attractions are further away than from Inner City accommodation, but staying among the buzzing Vesterbro life, with its hip shops and pulsating nightlife, is a worthy trade-off.

## UNDER 500KR
### Copenhagen Backpackers

*Reventlowsgade 10A; tel. 30 14 40 14; http://copenhagen-backpackers.dk; shared*

*room from 209kr; bus, S-train Copenhagen*
*Central Station; 4 dorm rooms*

This modern, well-equipped back-packers' hostel close to the Central Station has competitive prices for dorms. Although one room can have as many as 18 beds (others have 6 or 8 beds), there are dividers on each bunk to give guests extra privacy. With only 38 beds total, there's a more personal feel than at some of the larger hostels in the city. A breakfast buffet (55kr) is prepared for guests every morning with freshly baked bread, and there is also a small bar.

## Steel House Copenhagen

*Herholdtsgade 6; tel. 80 30 30 45; www.*
*steelhousecopenhagen.com; shared room*
*from 125kr, private room from 600kr; S-train*
*Vesterport St.; 253 rooms*

Although it bills itself as a "luxury hostel," the 253-room Steel House Copenhagen is, at the time of writing, the least expensive place to stay in Copenhagen that isn't a couch. A stylish, metallic look—the building used to house the Danish Union of Metalworkers—belies the low rates, and there are also facilities more commonly associated with starred hotels: a gym, a pool, and even a cinema; as well as a communal kitchen, a café and bar (with particularly comfortable armchairs). Great location within walking distance of four neighborhoods: Vesterbro, Fredriksberg, Nørrebro, and Inner City.

## Urban House Copenhagen

*Colbjørnsensgade 5-11; tel. 33 23 29 29;*
*https://urbanhouse.me; shared room from*
*281kr, private room from 1,331kr; bus, S-train*
*Copenhagen Central Station; 228 rooms*

A hotel/hostel hybrid, Urban House lives up to its name, not just through its location on the Vesterbro side of the Central Station: individual graffiti-style artwork in the rooms puts a touch of the street on the otherwise neat and tidy facilities. Live music on Wednesdays is one of a range of social events in the bar, where a cold breakfast (75kr) is served in the morning and burgers and salads (from 70kr) in the afternoon and evening. Other features include laundry, a library, a pool room, a lounge, and a quiet "hangover room."

## Woodah Hostel

*Abel Cathrines Gade 1-3; tel. 23 90 55 63;*
*http://woodah-hostel.com; shared room*
*from 250kr; bus, S-train Copenhagen*
*Central Station, bus 10 Gasværksvej*
*(Istedgade); 3 rooms*

This small, eco-conscious inde-pendent hostel is located near the Meatpacking District and Central Station. Its 22 beds are all custom made, and the breakfast buffet is organic—and included in the price. There are daily yoga classes for 25kr (book the night before), and you can also purchase yoga paraphernalia in the café. The décor is homey, warm, and calm—don't be surprised if you spot a Buddha statue or two.

## 500-1,000KR

### ✪ 66 Guldsmeden

*Vesterbrogade 66; tel. 33 22 15 00; https://*
*guldsmedenhotels.com; double occupancy*
*room high season from 995kr; bus 6A*
*Vesterbros Torv (Vesterbrogade); 74 rooms*

66 Guldsmeden on lively Vesterbrogade is a 15-minute walk from the Central Station and has some competitive rates and a colorful courtyard and patio, along with four-poster beds in every room. Breakfast can be added when booking or paid for separately. Rooms contain rustic wooden furniture and art made by the owner's

father-in-law. Service emphasizes family friendliness and approachability, with children and pets made to feel like they belong. The balconies and fireplace in the restaurant, which is lit in winter, indicate the keenness to initiate a feeling of *hygge* among guests. Industry certifications hang on the walls for the hotel's focus in sustainability as well as for using more than 90 percent organic produce in its restaurant. It's owned by the same group as the nearby, larger Axel Guldsmeden (Colbjørnsensgade 14; tel. 33 31 32 66; 202 rooms) and smaller Bertrams, which have a similar sustainable focus.

### Hotel Løven

*Vesterbrogade 30; tel. 33 79 67 20; http:// en.loevenhotel.dk; double occupancy room high season from 699kr; bus 6A Vesterbros Torv (Vesterbrogade); 49 rooms*

In a building that has been a hotel since the 1840s, Hotel Løven is a good, low-budget option with a handy location in the center of Vesterbro, with fairly basic but clean, recently renovated rooms. Guests will benefit from staying at a convenient location for Central Station. A shared kitchen for guest use is located on the first floor.

### Annex Copenhagen

*Helgolandsgade 15; tel. 33 31 43 44; www. annexcopenhagen.dk; double occupancy room high season from 935kr; bus, S-train Copenhagen Central Station; 81 rooms*

Small, basic rooms are decorated in a range of funky colors and with the option of adding the buffet breakfast at adjoining Absalon Hotel (the two hotels share an entrance). Rooms are available with both private and shared bathrooms. In a side street at the seedier end of Istedgade near the Central Station, with a young and friendly vibe.

## 1,000-2,000KR
### DGI-byens Hotel

*Tietgensgade 65; tel. 33 29 80 70; www. dgi-byen.com/hotels/dgi-byens_hotel; double occupancy room high season from 1,118kr; bus, S-train Copenhagen Central Station; 104 rooms*

The hotel is part of the DGI-Byen sports and leisure complex and rooms are within view of the station and across the road from the coach terminal. Rooms are simple and functional and come with breakfast and access to pool and fitness areas, which are included, as well as a free game in the bowling alley. Can suffer from noise, with busy traffic areas servicing the nearby bus and rail termini.

### Absalon Hotel

*Helgolandsgade 15; tel. 33 24 22 11; www. absalon-hotel.dk; double occupancy room high season from 1,125kr; bus, S-train Copenhagen Central Station; 161 rooms*

The Absalon has a great location if you want to explore Vesterbro, with the Istedgade, Meatpacking District, and Halmtorvet areas right outside the door, although the former can give a rough-and-tumble first impression on first arrival via the nearby central rail station. The plush rooms have three different color schemes. Breakfast is included. Rooms have splashes of bright, stripy, or flowery color.

### Grand Hotel

*Vesterbrogade 9; tel. 33 27 69 00; www. grandhotel.dk; double occupancy room high season from 1,625kr; bus, S-train Copenhagen Central Station; 161 rooms*

In an area of high hotel density on Vesterbrogade close to the central station, the classic Grand Hotel, built in 1892, stands out with its ornate façade and historical vibe. Rooms are showing signs of age—the style is a little dated—but are bright and clean. Breakfast buffet included.

### Bertrams Hotel Guldsmeden

*Vesterbrogade 107; tel. 70 20 81 07; https:// guldsmedenhotels.com/bertrams; double occupancy room high season from 1,780kr; bus 6A Enghavevej (Vesterbrogade); 47 rooms*

Bertrams is the smallest of the Guldsmeden group's five boutique hotels in Copenhagen and aims for an intimate atmosphere where guests and staff can chat over a coffee in the lounge garden. The company has a Green Globe sustainability certificate, which means it has a continued commitment to improving green energy use; as well as a Danish Ministry of Food and Agriculture certificate for using at least 90 percent organic products. Four-poster beds in a number of the comfy, modern rooms are an enjoyable touch.

### OVER 2,000KR
### Tivoli Hotel & Congress Center

*Arni Magnussons Gade 2; tel. 44 87 00 00; www.tivolihotel.com; double occupancy room high season from 2,195kr; S-train Dybbølsbro St.; 679 rooms*

Removed slightly from the hustle and bustle around the Central Station, there is a serious side to Tivoli Hotel & Congress Center, which is as much a place for business travelers as for tourists. Nevertheless, standards are high, and there is no shortage of facilities. A swimming pool and several restaurants are housed within the hotel building.

## NØRREBRO AND ØSTERBRO

Staying in either rough-and-ready, hipster Nørrebro or middle-class Østerbro is sure to give you a different perspective on Copenhagen, simply by virtue of being away from the traditional visitor surroundings of the Inner City. As such, second-time visitors might appreciate switching their base here, but newcomers should not be put off either. Neither neighborhood is far from the central attractions, particularly if you are handy on two wheels or happy to make a few short journeys on public transportation, or if you want to walk around the pleasant Lakes, which are located between these two areas and the Inner City.

### UNDER 500KR
### Sleep in Heaven

*Struenseegade 7; tel. 35 35 46 48; www.sleepinheaven.com; shared room from 160kr, private room from 700kr; bus 12, 66 Griffenfeldsgade (Rantzausgade); 22 rooms*

Not far from Nørrebrogade, Sleep in Heaven is a sound choice for backpackers who want to stay somewhere other than Vesterbro or Nyhavn. With a lively atmosphere, large communal spaces and daily happy hour, the concept is designed to provide a social atmosphere, typical for backpackers' hostels, which can be taken out into Nørrebro's nightlife. Basic metal bunk beds and small private rooms with linen included but no communal guest kitchen. Book ahead in peak season. Maximum guest age limit for dorm beds is 35; for private rooms it's 45.

### A&O Copenhagen Nørrebro

*Tagensvej 135-137; tel. 32 72 53 21; www.aohostels.com/en/copenhagen/kobenhavn-norrebro; shared room from 160kr, private room from 520kr; bus 6A Bispebjerg Torv (Tagensvej); 270 rooms*

Budget hotel and hostel A&O Copenhagen takes you into the vibrant heart of Nørrebro. Housed in a big brick-and-glass building, all rooms are equipped with bathroom facilities, and there is a spacious reception/lounge area. Linen is included only with hotel bookings. Breakfast can be added separately, and a guest kitchen is available. The communal areas, including the guest kitchen, can become crowded, but the rooms have a simple, quiet feel.

## 500-1,000KR
### Hotel Nora Copenhagen

*Nørrebrogade 18B; tel. 35 37 20 21; www. hotelnora.dk; double occupancy room high season from 1,000kr; bus 5C Ravnsborggade (Nørrebrogade); 42 rooms*

This comfortable and clean budget option is housed in an extravagant building on busy Nørrebrogade at the "city" end, within walking distance of Dronning Louises Bro and the Inner City and with great views from the rooftop. Breakfast is included. The light rooms come with free tea and coffee; noise can sometimes be heard from the street below.

## 1,000-2,000KR
### Hotel Østerport

*Oslo Plads 5; tel. 70 12 46 46; www. hotelosterport.dk; double occupancy room high season from 1,400kr; S-train Østerport; 170 rooms*

With its clean and tidy design, Hotel Østerport is a convenient place to stay in quieter Østerbro and is next to the S-train station (light sleepers take note) at Østerport, where there's a nice view overlooking the tracks. This also means you can get back into the Inner City easily. Breakfast included with all direct bookings. Rooms are very smart and clean-looking, with soft, low lighting, designer chairs, and olive-green or eggshell monochrome walls.

# CHRISTIANSHAVN AND AMAGER

Less hotel-heavy than the Inner City, the Christianshavn area is a great place to base yourself if you want to see Copenhagen at its most photogenic while staying within a short distance of the Inner City's big attractions and shopping. Working-class Amager will give a feel of everyday life away from the city's showpiece areas and has a beach and a national park. Although there are fewer hotel options here, CPH Living, located on the Islands Brygge area of Amager on the harbor facing Copenhagen, is one of my accommodation top picks.

## UNDER 500KR
### Danhostel Copenhagen Amager

*Vejlands Allé 200; tel. 32 52 29 08; https:// danhostelcopenhagen.dk; shared room from 200kr, private room from 420 kr; bus 34 Vandrerhjem (Vejlands Allé); 156 rooms*

Far, far from town in the Amager Fælled nature reserve, it's well worth making the effort to stay at Danhostel's family-friendly Amager hostel if you want some fresh air and a break from the noise of the city. Its 96 en-suite rooms and 60 dorms with two to five beds and shared bathrooms accommodate up to 540 guests. Bus 34 stops at the door, making your journey from town as simple as possible (it takes about 30 minutes from Central Station). Clean, modern rooms and a buffet breakfast are 75kr (40kr for children). There's plenty of space to stretch your legs both inside and out.

## 1,000-2,000KR
### ✪ CPH Living

*Langebrogade 1A; tel. 61 60 85 46; www. cphliving.com; double occupancy room high season from 1,380kr; bus 5C Klaksvigsgade (Amager Boulevard); 12 rooms*

You might feel like you're being rocked to sleep at CPH Living, and that's because you actually will be. Denmark's first floating hotel, converted from a former barge is anchored by the Langebro bridge and is walking distance from Christianshavn—and a skip to shore from Islands Brygge. All 12 of the hotel's double rooms offer dramatic harbor and city views through broad windows and French balconies, while the heated wooden floors and portholes give a simultaneously Scandinavian and maritime feel to things. Television, Wi-Fi access and hair dryers are included in each room, while a rooftop terrace enables guests to sit on "deck" and enjoy the floating vantage point. A cold-cut breakfast buffet is included.

### AC Hotel Bella Sky Copenhagen

*Center Blvd. 5; tel. 32 47 30 00; http://acbellaskycopenhagen.dk; double occupancy room high season from 1,695kr; bus 250S Bella Center, Metro Ørestad; 811 rooms*

Four-star designer accommodation AC Hotel Bella Sky is located adjacent to the Bella Convention and Congress Center on the outer limits of the urban part of Amager, in two tilting wedges that tower so far above the surrounding landscape they look like just-landed alien spacecraft. The 76.5-meter (250 ft.) height of the buildings was limited by their close proximity to Copenhagen Airport. Its premium rooms and facilities are popular with visiting conference delegates. Floor-to-ceiling windows ensure you make the most of the elevated vantage point. The location is not ideal, however, if you want to drop in and out of your room between excursions into the city—expect a public transport (bus or Metro) journey of around 30 minutes each way.

### OVER 2,000KR
### STAY Copenhagen

*Islands Brygge 79A; tel. 72 44 44 34; http://staycopenhagen.dk; apartments from 1,960kr; bus 250S Drechselsgade (Artillerivej); 172 apartments*

STAY Copenhagen is a complex of spacious, private vacation studio apartments on Islands Brygge looking back toward Copenhagen. The apartments, which can accommodate a maximum of either six or eight guests are designed by the Danish interior company Hay, with a clear focus on Scandinavian minimalism. Kitchens come fully equipped (and there are also washing machines and dryers), but there's a restaurant on site if you don't feel like cooking. Other facilities include a rooftop terrace and fitness room.

# Tours and Tourist Information

## COPENHAGEN VISITOR SERVICE

*Vesterbrogade 4; tel. 70 22 24 42; visitorservice@kk.dk; daily 9am-4pm, open until later depending on season)*

Copenhagen Visitor Service is a good first port of call if you need assistance on arriving in the city (or at any other time later). You can pick up maps and brochures and buy the **Copenhagen card** that enables you the use of the urban transport network (although normal tickets are just as easy to purchase in stations). Current events listings can also be browsed on touch screens via the **digital Copenhagen Visitor Guide**. You can also hashtag your social media posts from around the city and try to get them posted onto the interactive SoMe wall. **Free Wi-Fi** is available.

In addition to the main Copenhagen Visitor Service Office on Vesterbrogade near the central station, there are **eight authorized information spots** around the city where someone will be on hand to help with directions and advice. These are: Copenhagen City Hall, Tivoli Gardens, the National Gallery of Denmark, the Illum Department Store on Amagertorv, the National Museum, and the Frederiksberg Center mall, all of which have listings elsewhere in this book; plus the library in the Nordvest neighborhood (Rentemestervej 76; tel. 82 20 54 30), which is located north of Nørrebro, and Enigma Museum of Post, Tele and Communication (Øster Allé 1; tel. 33 41 09 00; www.enigma. dk), which is closed for renovation until 2019.

# Getting There

**Copenhagen Airport** (or Kastrup) is the largest airport in the Nordic region and the third-busiest in northern Europe, with almost 30 million passengers passing through annually. That means **direct flights** are available from almost anywhere in **Europe** as well as many **Asian** and **North American cities**.

**Trains** arrive regularly from **Sweden**—Malmö is a commuter town for many working in Copenhagen—while there are also regular services from **Germany** via southern Denmark or Jutland. A recent spate of competition between **bus operators** seems to have settled with three main companies now offering relatively inexpensive fares within Denmark and to international destinations.

For travel within Copenhagen and between Danish cities, the essential resource is **Rejseplanen.dk**, which can be accessed via their website or app (an English-language version is available). Part-owned by local travel authorities, Rejseplanen suggests the fastest and easiest routes between destinations, combining bus, Metro, S-train, harbor bus, and regional train connections, and tells you how much it will cost.

The **Rejsekort**, an electronic ticket system, is an easy way to source tickets for journeys within Copenhagen and all around Denmark.

## BY AIR

International flights arrive at **Copenhagen Airport**, also known colloquially as Kastrup after the suburb of Amager that neighbors the airport (Kastrup, the suburb, has its own separate Metro stop—make sure you don't get off there when traveling back to the airport). In October 2017, EU rules were amended so that all passengers traveling on routes crossing Schengen countries must now have their passports checked.

Copenhagen Airport is the busiest airport in Scandinavia. **Scandinavian Airlines** (SAS) (www.

flysas.com) operates services from a number of U.S. and Asian cities, including New York, Boston, Chicago, San Francisco, Beijing, Tokyo, and Hong Kong. Ryanair (www.ryanair.com), Norwegian (www.norwegian.com), and to a lesser extent Easyjet (www.easyjet.com) all operate low-budget services to Copenhagen from much of Europe, making Copenhagen quite accessible from a number of cities via a nonstop, relatively inexpensive flight.

## GETTING TO THE CITY CENTER
### Metro and Train

The easiest way to reach the city center from the airport is with the Metro, the underground rail system that has a station attached to the airport and is on an elevated track for much of the journey, providing nice views of Amager. There is no direct connection to the Copenhagen Central Station at the time of writing (but a brand new line, currently under construction, is scheduled to open in 2019, including a Central Station stop), so change to an S-Train at Nørreport station to get here. The journey from the airport to Nørreport takes 15 minutes, and trains run around the clock: departing every few minutes during the day and every 15-20 minutes at night.

You can also take a train directly from Copenhagen Airport to Copenhagen Central Station. These leave approximately every 10 minutes and take around 20 minutes. They are not S-trains, and they leave near the main arrivals area. The signs are easy to follow in order to find them.

Tickets for the train or Metro can be purchased from machines in the terminal (36 kroner), or you can check in using a Rejsekort if you have one, spending 20kr of prepaid credit.

### Bus

A number of bus lines travel between the airport and the city. Although these take longer than the Metro or train, they can be useful if your destination is close to one of the lines (check location of bus stops on https://dinoffentligetransport.dk). Lines 35 and 36 leave from outside Terminal 3. The former is the most frequent, leaving every 20 minutes during the day, while line 36 departs twice an hour. However, both require a change of bus to line 5C to get to central Copenhagen. For line 35, change at Vejlands Allé (Amagerbrogade); for line 36, change at Bredager Torv (Kastruplundgade). Tickets can be purchased from the driver using cash, and you can check in with a prepaid Rejsekort. Expect around 45 minutes for the bus journey into town.

In general, it's of no benefit to take the bus unless you are going somewhere very close to the route of lines 35 or 36. Use Rejseplanen.dk or the dinoffentligetransport.dk official timetable website, which publishes complete bus timetables, to check routes.

### Taxi

Taxis are normally easy to pick up from the rank outside Terminal 3. You should be able to pay by credit card, and tips are not customary. The fare will likely be 300kr or more, depending on traffic and your destination within the city. Unless it's rush hour, you should be at your accommodation within 20-30 minutes. Rush hours—8-9am and 4-5pm on weekdays, 3-4pm on Friday—can cause delays but are usually less severe than in major U.S. cities.

## Car

The airport's **Car Rental Center** is located a short distance from the terminal entrances. Free terminal buses leave every 10 minutes from both Terminal 2 and Terminal 3. The center is open from 6am-11pm. **Avis** (www. avis.dk; tel. 70 24 77 02), **Europcar** (www.europcar.dk; tel. 32 50 30 90), **Budget** (www.budget.dk; tel. 32 52 39 00), **Sixt** (www.sixt.dk; tel. 32 46 29 43), **Hertz** (www.hertzdk.dk; tel. 33 17 90 30) and **Enterprise** (www. enterprise.com; tel. 70 21 23 50) all have offices here.

# BY CAR

Coming by car from either mainland Europe via Germany or from Sweden via the Øresund Bridge remains straightforward, though complications have been added in recent years. Denmark is part of the European Union's Schengen area, which allows passport-free travel between member countries—in theory. At the beginning of 2016, the government implemented "emergency" border controls on the southern borders with Germany, as did Sweden on its border with Denmark via the Øresund Bridge. Two and a half years on, at the time of writing, the border controls remain in place. This means being stopped on the border for a spot check is likely: always have your passport with you.

From **Malmö** to Copenhagen via E20 (Øresund Bridge) is 42km (26mi) and takes 45 minutes by car. Note that the **bridge toll** (52 euros for cars for a single journey, 47 euros for advance payments) can be reduced by purchasing a **BroPas** annual subscription (42 euros). This reduces prices enough to make it worth purchasing, if you are planning a return journey across the

bridge. Passes and tickets can be purchased via www.oresundsbron.com.

From **Møn** in the south, take the **E47** for 128km (80mi) (1 hour 45 minutes) to get to Copenhagen. Taking the E47 from **Helsingør** and **Humlebæk** (where the Louisiana MoMA is located) up north will also lead you to Copenhagen. The trip from Helsingør is 45km (28mi) (55 minutes), and the trip from Humlebæk is 39km (24mi) (45 minutes).

From **Roskilde** to Copenhagen, the drive via route 21 is 34km (21mi) and takes 45 minutes. It only takes 35 minutes to drive from **Klampenborg**, where Bakken is located, to Copenhagen (13km, 8mi,, via route 152), and **Dragør** is a short 25-minute car drive away, via route 221 (14km, 9mi).

# BY TRAIN

**Copenhagen Central Station** (Hovedbanegården, often abbreviated to Hovedbanen; Bernstorffsgade 16–22), at the western end of the Inner City on the boundary with Vesterbro, is linked to the European network via Stockholm to the north and Amsterdam, Hamburg, and Berlin to the south. International tickets can be booked via Denmark's state rail operator **DSB** (www.dsb.dk; tel. 70 13 14 18). If you are planning an extended trip around Denmark or further afield by rail, it is advisable to look into the two main European rail passes, **Eurail** (www.eurail.com) for non-Europeans and **Interrail** (interrail.eu) for European citizens. Both are particularly useful for travelers under 25.

Travel times and fares to Copenhagen from:

- **Stege, Møn**: Two hours via bus 660R Stege-Vordingborg, train

Vordingborg-Copenhagen, 116kr, hourly departures

- **Helsingør**: 45 minutes, 65kr, departures every 20 minutes
- **Humlebæk** (Louisiana Museum of Modern Art): 35 minutes, 53.50kr, departures every 20 minutes
- **Roskilde**: 25-30 minutes, 48kr, departures every 5-10 minutes
- **Dragør**: 40 minutes via bus 350S Dragør-Tårnby, train Tårnby-Copenhagen, 36kr, every 10 minutes
- **Klampenborg**: 18-20 minutes, 48kr, every 10 minutes (the S-Train also services Klampenborg)

## BY BUS

German company **Flixbus** (www.flixbus.com) operates international bus services into Denmark from both Sweden and Germany, with departures every two to three hours from Malmö (6-11 euros, 1 hour 15 minutes). **Gråhundbus** (http://graahundbus.dk) has three arrivals daily serving the Copenhagen-Malmö route, at 120kr return; this is a less-expensive albeit less-convenient option than the train. Buses leave and depart from the rather underwhelming **terminal**, which is in fact no more than a road side with a series of bus stands, at **Ingerslevsgade**. The nearest public transport stop is **Copenhagen Central Station**.

## BY BOAT

**DFDS** (www.dfdsseaways.dk) operates overnight boats to Copenhagen from Oslo, for which inexpensive tickets can usually be procured in advance. Cabin prices range between 1,000kr and 2,500kr; from two-person economy cabins to five-person cabins with sea views, or you can travel with a car for from 495kr per person, with a standard cabin included in the price. There's a restaurant and tax-free shop on board. Overnight voyages depart daily and take 16 hours 30 minutes. Ferries arrive at the DFDS terminal at Dampfærgevej 30 in Østerbro, close to the Langelinie pier.

# Getting Around

## BY PUBLIC TRANSIT

Copenhagen's public transportation system is comprehensive, consisting of **bus** and **Metro** systems as well as an over-ground network known as the **S-tog (S-train)**. The **Rejseplanen app**, which is available in English, is a must-have for instant planning of journeys that combine all of the networks. In addition to Rejseplanen, official site **Din Offentlig Transport (DOT)** (https://dinoffentligetransport.dk) is a good resource for updated public transport information and timetables.

Instances of petty and violent crime, including against tourists, do occur in Copenhagen as in any large city, but there are no specific reasons to avoid public transportation in any part of the city or at any time due to safety considerations.

### TICKETS AND PASSES
#### Rejsekort

For those planning to use public transport in Copenhagen for more than a couple of days, the Rejsekort is a must-have time- and stress-saving alternative (if not money-saving, once the cost of the card is taken into account) to repeat purchases of single tickets. The prepay Rejsekort is Denmark's equivalent of an Oyster Card in London or a New York City Metro Card, but it can be used universally across the country. It can be ordered via Rejsekort. dk at the cost of 50kr (plus 25kr credit) or bought straight from a machine at Metro and rail stations for 80kr (plus 100kr credit). The same machines (look out for their neon blue cladding) can be used to top up credit on the cards. Alternatively, single tickets can be bought in Metro and S-train stations and from bus drivers. Generally, if you have time, the best approach is to pre-order a Rejsekort before traveling to Copenhagen.

The Rejsekort is valid for use on the city buses, Metro, S-train, and Harbor Bus (as well as regional trains). Journeys using any (or a combination of) these within the three-zone Copenhagen metropolitan area cost as little as 15kr with the Rejsekort, as opposed to 24kr purchased directly from drivers. Remember to check in and out on the card readers at station platforms or inside buses to validate your journey.

When using the Rejsekort, you must "check in" by holding the card over the sensor inside the bus or on the train platform at the beginning of your journey—the check-in points, with their front-facing domed sensors, are easy to spot. "Check out" from the separate "check out" sensor (there's a red sign on the sensor with the words "Check ud") when you are at or about to reach your destination. If you connect to a different bus/train, you should not check out, but must "re-check in" to the second bus or train after switching. You then check out

for the entire journey when you reach your destination.

If you change buses or between transport forms during the journey, you must check in again every time you change, but do not check out until you reach your final destination or you will be charged double.

### City Pass

Alternatively, you can travel on a City Pass, which can be valid for 24 hours (adults 80kr, children 40kr), 48 hours (adults 150kr, children 75kr), 72 hours (adults 200kr, children 100kr), or 120 hours (adults 300kr, children 150kr). These are available on the DOT website and app or from station machines or counters.

## METRO

The Copenhagen Metro, which currently consists of only two networks, opened in 2002 and does not—at the time of writing—serve Copenhagen Central Station. It is, nevertheless, very useful, linking the airport with Nørreport—a key hub within the city—and connects the Amager, Christianshavn, Inner City, and Frederiksberg neighborhoods.

There are currently two lines, both of which serve the route from Vanløse in the northwest of the city, traveling east and south through Frederiksberg, Nørreport, Kongens Nytorv, and Christianshavn, before splitting and continuing on Amager as two separate lines. Line M2 terminates at the airport and also stops at Amagerbro and the Amager Strand beach and lagoon area; M1 has stations at Islands Brygge and Vestamager, from where you can access the Amager Fælled national park and Amager Nature Center.

Open 24 hours, trains on both

lines run every 2-4 minutes at peak times, 3-6 minutes during the day, and every 15-20 minutes at night (but every 7-8 minutes during the night on weekends). Travel times are good: a journey from the airport to Nørreport in the center of the city, for example, takes 15 minutes, while the journey from Nørreport to Christianshavn is a short 3-minute trip.

Two new lines, adding 24 new stations including at Copenhagen Central and in the Nørrebro district, will be opened in 2019 and 2020. The first of these, the M3 City Circle Line (Cityringen), is scheduled for completion in the summer of 2019 and will significantly extend the reach of the Metro. It will add a north-south span and bring Metro stations to a host of important neighborhoods, transport hubs, and sites of interest, including Copenhagen Central Station, City Hall Square (Rådhuspladsen), Nørrebro, Trianglen (Østerbro), Østerport Station, and Frederik's Church (the Marble Church).

An M4 line connecting harbors in the north and south of the city is also under construction with scheduled opening in 2020. There has been talk of extending the Metro further in the long term—perhaps, even, as far as Malmö, which would make it the world's first international metropolitan train.

## TRAIN

The S-train (S-tog) is an extensive urban and suburban rail consisting of seven lines and 85 stations, serving the Greater Copenhagen area, with the exception of Amager and Christianshavn. It connects Copenhagen Central Station with Nørreport, from where there are S-train connections to stations in all of the other neighborhoods mentioned in this chapter, as well as Jægersborg, Klampenborg and Hellerup north of Copenhagen. S-trains pass through the Central Station and depart regularly throughout the day 5am-12:30am—there is a train every 10 minutes until the evening, and every 20 minutes until around midnight. All-night services with 30-minute departures run on some lines on weekends.

## BUS

Buses can be used to get almost anywhere and are generally reliable. Primary routes have an "A" in their route number, with the exception of the 5C, an iconic (and often maligned) route that crosses the city. This route was in fact called 5A until 2017, when it got a makeover, new $CO_2$-neutral vehicles, and a new identity. The "A" routes (and the 5C) run 24 hours a day, while other routes close between around 1am and 5am, replaced by lesser-spotted night buses (only a handful of departures nightly).

## BOAT

Havnebussen (The Harbor Bus) is a great way to see Copenhagen from the harbor without taking an expensive tour, but the boats also act as an efficient means of transportation. For the price of a normal bus ticket you can connect the harbor pool at Teglholmen in the south with Refshaleøen in the north by traveling between stops at the Royal Library (Det Kongelige Bibliotek), Knippelsbro (at Slotsholmen and Christianshavn), Nyhavn, and the Opera. There are normally two departures hourly 7am-7pm—the timetable is available at https://dinoffentligetransport.dk and is also plugged into the Rejseplanen app. The harbor buses are distinctive, squat yellow vessels—although these are set to become obsolete as newer, greener models are phased in during the coming years.

## ON FOOT

Copenhagen is largely pedestrian-friendly and rewarding to walk around, although some of the cobblestones can leave your ankles feeling sore if you're not used to them. The Inner City and Christianshavn have this kind of paving. Streets in the city center, shopping, and residential districts have spacious sidewalks with plenty of room to push a stroller or baby carriage. There are few pedestrian streets outside of Strøget.

Almost all roads in Copenhagen and the rest of Denmark have designated bicycle lanes. This means there are two curbs: one between the sidewalk and the bicycle lane, and one between the bicycle lane and the road. Don't mistake the bicycle lane for the sidewalk and dawdle or walk in it—you are likely to be on the end of some irritated invective from a passing cyclist and risk causing a serious accident. Similarly, look carefully when stepping off buses into a bicycle lane, which you have to cross to get to the sidewalk: cyclists are not obliged to slow down for you (although they will if they see you, of course).

When crossing roads at pedestrian crossings, you'll notice that the locals tend to wait patiently for the green man to flash before crossing, even when there's no traffic. Jaywalking is against traffic laws, and breaking these can land you with a fine. When crossing, keep an eye out for right-turning vehicles. Motorists are allowed to turn right on green-lighted pedestrian crossings if they are clear.

Danish drivers can have an impatient bent and will sometimes hurry to make their turn just before or after you cross the street, which can be unsettling.

## BY BIKE

Copenhagen's flat terrain and broad bicycle paths make it ideal for exploration on two wheels. From the Inner City, all outer districts are within a 15- to 30-minute bike ride, depending on your fitness level: Copenhagen's flatness makes things as painless as possible if you're not accustomed to this form of transport. Be careful of the heavy traffic when bicycling in the city center. The busy, multilane roads within central Copenhagen are usually fine to travel by bike—you'll see plenty of others doing so—but there are areas in the Inner City, particularly around Kongens Nytorv, Gothersgade, and Nørreport Station, where you might feel a little exposed, particularly during rush hours (8am-9am and 4pm-5pm on weekdays, 3pm-4pm Friday).

### BIKE RENTAL

Many **hostels** and **hotels** operate their own **bike rental** services, but there are countless other options.

bikes parked next to the Nørreport train station

These include (relatively) inexpensive secondhand bikes from nonprofit Baisikeli (Ingerslevsgade 80; *tel.* 26 70 02 29; www.baisikeli.dk; from 80kr for a full day's rental, discounts for longer periods). The more commercial Copenhagen Bicycles (Nyhavn 44; tel. 33 93 04 04; http://copenhagenbicycles.dk) offers rental from 90kr per day. Or you can rent a genuine Christiania cargo bike with Christiania Rent a Bike (Fabriksområdet 91; tel. 32 95 45 20; www.christianiacykler.dk/12/Rentabike) from 450kr for the first day and 150kr for each subsequent day.

Also available—and easy to find in their docking stations spread around the city—are the white Bycykler city bikes (Vesterbrogade 4B; *tel.* 89 88 39 10; www.bycyklen.dk), which come equipped with GPS and require you to set up an account and enter payment details, which can be done in the bikes' integrated tablets. They cost a basic rate of 30kr per hour so are best suited for shorter trips within the city.

Donkey Republic (www.donkey.bike) is a Europe-wide app that allows you to find, unlock, and rent a bicycle using an app and is highly visible in Copenhagen.

## TOURS

If you want to do the cycling with navigation provided, Green Bike Tours (Gothersgade 148; tel. 24 85 10 07; www.greenbiketours.dk) and Bike Copenhagen with Mike (Sankt Peders Stræde 47; tel. 26 39 56 88; http://bikecopenhagenwithmike.dk) are among numerous tour operators. Bicycle rental is included in the price with the Bike with Mike tours; with Green Bike, you can bring your own or add bicycle rental to your package.

## RULES

Bicycles can be carried for free on S-trains with the exception of Nørreport at peak hours (weekdays from 7am-8:30am and 3:30pm-5pm); and on the Metro for an additional fee of 13kr, again excluding peak times (weekdays from 7am-9am and 3:30pm-5:30pm). Purchase bike tickets at stations. They cannot be brought on buses.

Bicycle helmets are not required by law and surprisingly few Danes wear them, although bike rentals will provide them. I strongly recommend taking the option for your own safety: accidents can and do happen, regardless of the city's excellent bicycle lanes.

The bike paths, normally broad enough for two bicycles, are available on the vast majority of roads through the city. They are usually marked by a curb, clearly distinguishing them from the road and sidewalk on each side. Where there is no curb, for instance, when a bicycle path crosses a road junction, there will be clear markings painted on the road.

On the relatively few streets where there are no bicycle lanes, make sure you keep to the righthand side and rejoin the bicycle path once it reappears on a later street.

## BIKE PARKING

Bikes can be parked on most sidewalks, and you will see long rows of them lined up with their front wheels jammed into the metal bike stands provided by the city. You don't have to use a stand if you can't find one, but some shops and businesses place "no bicycle parking" signs on walls and in windows. Bicycles are usually secured using a locking device that fits to the back wheel, consisting of a metal bar that clicks into place between the spokes, preventing the wheel from turning, and requiring a key to unlock. An alternative method is the old-fashioned chain lock. Some people use both: bicycle theft is, unfortunately, all too common. If you're leaving a bicycle parked overnight, strength in numbers is a good idea: try to leave it in a stand with other bikes rather than conspicuously on its own.

## BY CAR

Although bicycling is as much an ingrained part of the Danish mindset as a convenient form of transportation, Copenhagen is quite suitable for exploring by car if you are traveling between neighborhoods. Within individual neighborhoods, distances are generally too short to warrant the use of a car.

All parts of the city are easy to reach by car, and parking is usually possible, even if it can take patience to find a spot in popular areas. All cars in Denmark display a parking disc, which looks like an analogue clock, on the inside of the windshield. This must be set at the time you leave your car if you are parking in an area that does not have a parking charge. If there is a time limit for parking, it will be displayed on a signpost on the street or parking lot: hence, the need to display the time you arrive. Failure to set your parking disc or parking illegally can result in your vehicle being issued with a ticket or booted ("clamped"). Many private parking lots have their own payment and ticketing systems, some of which don't use the parking discs—be sure to check the system in place at your chosen parking lot.

## BY TAXI

Taxis are a reliable and easy way to get from point A to point B. They come at a premium: the baseline price is 55kr, and the meter (taxis use meters as standard) moves quickly: a five-minute journey within the city center on a weekday will cost in excess of 100kr, and rates are likely to go up at night, during weekends, and on public holidays, depending on the taxi company.

It is possible to hail cabs on the street. Look out for a green "FRI" ("vacant") sign in the window or a lit *taxa* or taxi sign on the car. Taxi stations are located around the city, including at the Central Station and outside the airport terminal. Almost all taxis accept credit cards, but check with the driver to be certain. Be sure to only use officially marked taxis. Uber no longer operates in Denmark. It withdrew from the country in 2017, following regulation that was introduced favoring traditional taxi businesses.

Taxi companies operating in Copenhagen include DanTaxi (tel. 48 48 48 48), 4x27 (tel. 27 27 27 27), and Taxa 4x35 (tel. 35 35 35 35), the latter of which has an app that can be used to book journeys. The taxi.eu app, which connects taxi services in several European countries, can also be used to book cabs in Copenhagen.

# NORTH OF COPENHAGEN

## Nature and nostalgia are plenti-

ful, and there's an engaging mix of working-class entertainment, earthy history, bracing outdoors, and upmarket real estate in the areas north of Copenhagen.

Bakken is the most famous attraction in the area and one of the world's oldest amusement parks. Its history traces back to a mythical event in the 16th century, when a spring was found in the forest. The area later became a draw for Copenhagen gentry and, later, carnival rides and roller coasters. The amusement park lies

# HIGHLIGHTS

✪ **DYREHAVSBAKKEN:** More commonly known as "Bakken," this amusement park makes serious attempts to outdo Tivoli Gardens in the retro amusement park stakes (page 157).

✪ **JÆGERSBORG DYREHAVE:** An embracing expanse of protected Danish open space sprinkled with ancient trees, historic buildings, and wild animals that is crying out to be explored (page 160).

✪ **FRILANDSMUSEET:** Ride a horsedrawn cart into Denmark's rural past at this out-of-town, outdoorsy museum (page 165).

within the Jægersborg animal park, a 10-square-kilometer (3.8 sq mi) wild area with a Baroque hunting lodge in the middle and hundreds of deer roaming the grounds. Head to the coast and you'll find a sandy beach and surrounding affluent streets which are stamped with the timeless imprint of architectural icon Arne Jacobsen, while further inland, one of the largest open-air museums anywhere will transport you back through industrialization to Denmark's roots as a rural, agricultural society. Straddling the city and the countryside, Copenhagen's northern suburbs allow you room to breathe. Perhaps that's why so many Copenhageners as well as visitors find themselves drawn to this part of the city.

## ORIENTATION

Klampenborg and Kongens Lyngby, the two primary areas covered in this chapter, are both part of the greater Copenhagen metropolitan area and are located around 10km (6.2 mi) north of the city, the former to the east on the coast, and the latter inland to the west. From Copenhagen, the journey to each is between 20 and 40 minutes by car or rail, depending on the time of day and your precise destination. Travel between the two takes around 35-50 minutes by public transportation (sometimes it's faster to travel back to Copenhagen to change bus or train) or 20 minutes by car.

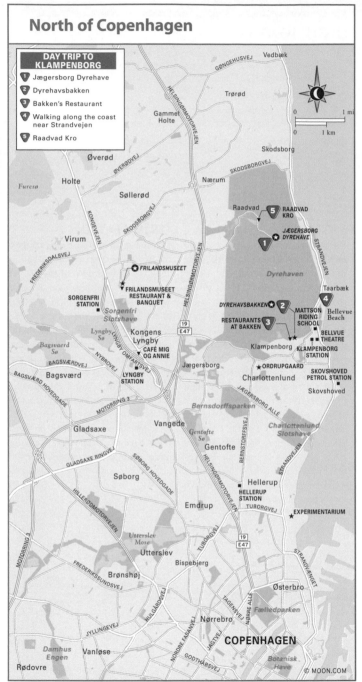

# North of Copenhagen

## DAY TRIP TO KLAMPENBORG

1 Jægersborg Dyrehave
2 Dyrehavsbakken
3 Bakken's Restaurant
4 Walking along the coast near Strandvejen
5 Raadvad Kro

GØNGEHUSVEJ

Vedbæk

HELSINGØRMOTORVEJEN

Trørød

Gammel Holte

Skodsborg

Øverød

ØVERØDVEJ

SKODSBORGVEJ

Nærum

Holte

Furesø

Søllerød

SKODSBORGVEJ

KONGEVEJEN

Raadvad

5 RAADVAD KRO

1 JÆGERSBORG DYREHAVE

Virum

FREDERIKSDALSVEJ

Dyrehaven

HELSINGØRMOTORVEJEN

STRANDVEJEN

FRILANDSMUSEET

FRILANDSMUSEET RESTAURANT & BANQUET

Taarbæk

SORGENFRI STATION

Sorgenfri Slotshave

DYREHAVSBAKKEN 2

4

Bellevue Beach

MATTSON RIDING SCHOOL

BELLVUE THEATRE

Lyngby Sø

LYNGBY OMFARTSVEJ

Kongens Lyngby

3 RESTAURANTS AT BAKKEN

Bagsværd Sø

BAGSVÆRDVEJ

NYBROVEJ

CAFÉ MIG OG ANNIE

Klampenborg

KLAMPENBORG STATION

Bagsværd

LYNGBY STATION

Jægersborg

ORDRUPGAARD

SKOVSHOVED PETROL STATION

BAGSVÆRD HOVEDGADE

MOTORRING 3

Charlottenlund

Skovshoved

Gladsaxe

Vangede

JÆGERSBORG ALLE

Bernsdorffsparken

Charlottenlund Slotshave

STRANDVEJEN

GLADSAXE RINGVEJ

Gentofte Sø

Gentofte

BERNSTORFFSVEJ

SØBORG HOVEDGADE

HELSINGØRMOTORVEJEN

Søborg

Hellerup

HILLERØDMOTORVEJEN

HELLERUP STATION

TUBORGVEJ

Emdrup

EXPERIMENTARIUM

MOTORRING 3

Utterslev Mose

TUBORGVEJ

19 E47

FREDERIKSSUNDSVEJ

Utterslev

Bispebjerg

STRANDVÆNGET

Brønshøj

HILLGÅRDSVEJ

TAGENSVEJ

Østerbro

JYLLINGEVEJ

JAGTVEJ

Fælledparken

Damhus Engen

Vanløse

NORDRE FASANVEJ

Nørrebro

NØRRE ALLE

COPENHAGEN

Rødovre

GODTHÅBSVEJ

Botanisk Have

© MOON.COM

# Itinerary Idea

## A DAY TRIP TO KLAMPENBORG

**1** After breakfast in Copenhagen, take an S-Train to Klampenborg. As you exit the station, go left and enter **Jægersborg Dyrehave**, a large, forested park, where you can take a calming walk in the woods.

**2** Raise your pulse by entering **Dyrehavsbakken** for some old-school fairground fun, including a ride on an octogenarian roller coaster with a wooden frame that arguably cranks the thrill factor as high as any modern alternative.

**3** You can also stop for lunch here at one of **Bakken's restaurants**. There's an extensive array of options—from more traditional restaurants to casual cafés—that cater to various tastes and levels of appetite.

**4** Leave Bakken in the late afternoon, and spend the rest of your day **walking along the coast around Strandvejen**, spotting the exclusive mansions and assorted Arne Jacobsen-designed objects.

**5** For dinner, head to the secluded **Raadvad Kro**, an affordable New Nordic restaurant in an idyllic spot that feels a lot further from the city than it actually is.

# Klampenborg and Around

The Klampenborg suburb, as with many neighborhoods of Greater Copenhagen along the Øresund coast, is a well-to-do area, its status embodied by the big houses, estate agents, and law offices along Strandvejen, a road that's synonymous with affluence in the city. It's not an area that is charmless or exclusive, though. It draws people from across Copenhagen, particularly in the summer, with sandy Bellevue Beach, the historic, working-class amusement park Bakken, and the expansive nature of Jægersborg Dyrehave—all attractive destinations for holiday day trips. A cluster of 1930s buildings and structures designed by Arne Jacobsen, the grandfather of modernist Danish design, can be spotted in the area.

## SIGHTS
### ⊙ DYREHAVSBAKKEN

*Dyrehavevej 62, Klampenborg, 2930; tel. 39 63 35 44; www.bakken.dk; weekends from end of Mar. through Apr.; May-second weekend in Sept., limited opening in Oct., Nov., Dec. noon-11pm or midnight (check the website for exact times); free entry, rides/ amusements from 20kr per turn, passes/*

*multi-ride discounts available including full-pass wristband (269kr, 189 for kids' rides only for one-day pass)*

Dyrehavsbakken, or "Bakken," to use the vernacular which has become its *de facto* official name, is something of an institution in Copenhagen. It's a large, traditional theme park in a centuries-old forest outside the city. It might be the oldest amusement park of its kind in the world, founded in 1583 after a mythical discovery of a natural spring. The area was once owned by nobility and closed to the public. Now it is anything but: the old-fashioned rides and amusements belong to the people, who still attend in huge numbers at the peak of the season, when there are dense crowds and long queues. Visiting Bakken can feel like a time warp, a throwback to the days when your parents took you to the fairground and you bought as many ride tokens as you could with your pocket money. Bakken's payment system can feel as confusing now as fairground tokens did to me when I was a youngster.

Nostalgia is threaded throughout many other aspects of Bakken. The "Korsbæk på Bakken" area is a loving tribute to *Matador*, a legendary 1970s television series set in the fictional town of Korsbæk in the early 20th century. The series is close to the hearts of Danes of all generations. Visitors can walk around period streets and enter shops and establishments true to the era and to the series. And while Bakken has countless rides, the highlight is Rutschebanen, literally "The Roller Coaster," a wooden roller coaster that opened in 1932. The timber of its frame looks like the structure of a half-built church in an old Western movie. Reaching a maximum height of 22 meters (72 feet) and top speeds of around 75 kph (47 mph), it holds its own on the adrenaline front.

candy shop in Dyrehavsbakken amusement park

Other popular rides include the Tornado, which is a steel spinning coaster from 2009; the Ladybird; and the Wild Mouse, both of which are favorite roller coasters for kids. There are spinning coffee cups, dodgems, and of course a horse carousel. Indoors, there are slot machines, cabarets, and circus-style performances.

Bakken enjoys widespread affection and popularity among Copenhageners and people from across Zealand and Denmark, and it can become overcrowded on warm summer days, particularly at the weekend or on Wednesdays, when discounts are given on cash-bought single tickets for rides. Peak times are normally between noon and 2pm, and queues are generally shorter later in the day. Wristbands can be purchased in advance online but still require vouchers to be exchanged for the physical bands at the park's sales and information counters.

It should be noted that Bakken is primarily a summer excursion: the rides are packed away and the stands roll down their shutters at the end of September. Everything opens again for the Danish "autumn holiday" in mid-October when many people are given or take time off work. In December, a festive atmosphere falls over the park like so many layers of snow, as Bakken opens in full Christmas costume on weekends from the second-to-last week in November through Christmas. Check individual days for exact opening hours at these times, and dress very warmly if you're venturing out in the winter months.

## ORDRUPGAARD

*Vilvordevej 110, Charlottenlund; tel. 39 64 11 83; https://ordrupgaard.dk; currently closed for renovation, 2019 opening times TBA; adults 110kr, under 18 free*

Ordrupgaard is a museum that specializes in 19th- and 20th-century French Impressionist and Danish Golden Age art, a period of prodigious creativity in the country inspired by German Romanticism. The museum is considered to house one of Scandinavia's finest Impressionist collections, with works by Monet, Cézanne, Gauguin, and Matisse among others. Danish artists exhibited include Hammershøi among the prominent names: a painter known for poetic, subdued interiors that at times perhaps match the calming atmosphere at Ordrupgaard itself. Set in a beautiful early 20th-century mansion, the museum opened in 1953, and the original building is still used to exhibit the permanent collection of Danish and French works. Monet's *Waterloo Bridge, Women Bathing* by Cezanne, Manet's *Basket of Pears*, and *Sunset* by Rousseau are just a handful of standouts.

In 2005, the museum was extended by prize-winning architect Zaha Hadid, who added a stark glass and concrete element to the original structure. Here, large temporary exhibitions are held, adding to the draw of the museum (this part is as a result often busier than the mansion, which means there is a quieter atmosphere around the permanent exhibitions). As with the permanent collection, there is an emphasis on Impressionism and on the 19th and 20th centuries. Frida Kahlo, Edvard Munch, and Henri Matisse have been featured in the past.

Ordrupgaard is currently closed for renovation and will reopen in 2020, but in the meantime it is possible to visit the museum garden's Art Park, a temporary summer exhibition in the museum's surrounding park (2019 details TBA). Once renovation is complete, the new Himmelhaven section, an underground extension designed by the famous Norwegian architects Snøhetta, will be used to provide new and optimal surroundings for the French Impressionist collection and allow exhibition of more fragile works, such as the pastel colors of Edgar Degas, which have not previously been available for public viewing.

Ordrupgaard is a 40-minute walk from Klampenborg Station. Bus 388 from Klampenborg Station goes to the stop at Vilvordevej, close to the museum, and takes around 15 minutes. You can use the same ticket or Rejsekort journey you used to take the train from Copenhagen, so there is no extra cost. The total travel time from Copenhagen Central Station is approximately 50 minutes.

## RECREATION
### ✪ Jægersborg Dyrehave

*Dyrehaven, Klampenborg; https://eng. naturstyrelsen.dk/experience-nature; open 24 hours; free*

Famous for the herds of deer in the park, Jægersborg Dyrehave ("Animal Park" or "Deer Park") is a 10-square-kilometer (3.8 sq mi) slice of wild Danish countryside in touching distance of Copenhagen. It boasts ancient oak trees, glacial streams, views of the sea and is beautiful year-round, not least during the outbursts of color in both spring and fall. As painters and poets were drawn to this natural park in the past, so are photographers today.

Enter through the red gates near Klampenborg Station and Bakken and head toward Kirsten Piil's spring, the natural water source around which the park was formed. Legend has it that a mysterious woman named Piil

discovered the spring in 1583. The baroque 18th-century Hermitage hunting lodge and oaks three centuries old, as well as ponds, plains, monuments, and wildlife all lie in wait.

It is the deer that are emblematic of the park, with around 2,000 spread throughout its approximately 1,000 hectares (2,471 acres). Different species include fallow deer, red deer, and sika deer. The animals have adapted to the presence of people, so it is possible to see them up close, which provides some great photo opportunities (visitors may not feed the deer or come too close, however, as they must remain wild animals). Deer can be seen in most parts of the park, but it's useful (and interesting) to note that the female red deer, the hinds, and their fawn stay in the southern part, while the stags keep to the north. They normally only mix during the mating season (the rut) in September and October.

In addition to the wealth of deer, birds, and other animals, it's likely you'll see other people, particularly on weekends and during the summer, as well as during the rut, which is a popular attraction. The close proximity of the park to the Technical University of Denmark and residential suburbs mean it's a popular spot for people out running or taking in some fresh air.

There are five walking or bicycling tours within the park, passing attractions including the Hermitage Palace. The five routes are described in the Danish Nature Agency's hiking tour leaflet no. 22, which can be picked up from stands at the entrances to the Dyrehave.

A full guide and map can also be found on the Danish Nature Agency's website (see contact information).

deer in Jægersborg Dyrehave

### Bellevue Beach

*Strandvejen 340, Klampenborg, 2930; open 24 hours; free*

Bellevue is the sandy beach and sloping, grassy park area at Klampenborg that covers a 700-meter-long (2,296 ft) stretch of the north Copenhagen coast close to the southern end of Jægersborg Dyrehave. Look out for the blue-striped lifeguard towers and geometric kiosks: they were designed by Arne Jacobsen, the preeminent Danish designer and architect who lived most of his life in the municipality of Gentofte, where Klampenborg is located, and left a permanent legacy with his buildings. Bellevue remains a popular spot for Danes hoping to catch a ray of sun and take a dip on warm-enough days in the summer, when it can still get crowded, even though its popularity has waned a little since the advent of the Amager Beach Park and bathing facilities at the Copenhagen Harbor during the 2000s. Refreshments are sold at the kiosks, and public toilets can also be found at the beach, which has a lifeguard service during the summer season.

### Strandvejen Coastal Walk

The area around the beach or close to the coastal road in Klampenborg is rich in the influence and legacy of Arne Jacobsen, who lived nearby for most of his life and had a studio and office in the area. Many of the Jacobsen-designed houses were built in the 1930s, early in the architect's career, while some also date from the 1950s. While the clean, minimalistic style associated with Jacobsen is recognizable in most of the buildings, they also reflect how the designer experimented with different methods of construction and types of material.

Some of the highlights of Jacobsen's work can easily be viewed while walking around Klampenborg. You can see the lifeguard towers, the kiosk complex, and the kayak club at Bellevue Beach; the Søholm apartment complex, which includes Jacobsen's former home; the Mattson Riding School,

lifeguard tower at Bellevue Beach

Bellevue Theater and, a couple of miles further south, the striking Skovshoved Petrol Station. Excluding the gas station, a walk taking in these sights can be comfortably completed in much less than an hour; add another 30-40 minutes to include the walk to the gas station at the end. The tour is entirely on pathed sidewalks, although you will need to cross several roads.

Leave Klampenborg Station onto Peter Lieps Vej and turn right, crossing the railway bridge in the direction of the coast. After the bridge, turn right onto Bellevuevej. Immediately on your left you'll see **Mattsson Riding School** (1933-1934)—a hangar-like building in Jacobsen's signature white with a curved roof—on the left-hand side facing the rail tracks. Turn back to Peter Lieps Vej and walk down to the main road, Strandvejen, and turn right. About 100 meters along you'll reach **Bellevue Teater** (1936) (www. bellevueteatret.dk), one of Jacobsen's most famous buildings, unmistakable with its distinctive blue period

lettering and the green ivy covering its broad rounded corners. Cross Strandvejen and head to the beach, where you'll quickly be able to spot the quirky-looking lifeguard towers with splayed legs and horizontal marine blue stripes, and geometric **kiosks** and **Klampenborg Kayak and Canoe Club** (http://klampenborg-kajak.dk), just south of the theater.

No more than 200 meters (650 ft) south of the theater on Strandvejen, roughly opposite to where the beach ends, the **Søholm housing complex** (1951) marks a departure from Jacobsen's white functionalism to a more modernist Danish style, the neatly tessellated brick buildings fitting together in jigsaw patterns. **Strandvejen 413** is the address at which Jacobsen himself lived. Located at the end of the row facing the water, it is unlike the other houses in that it has a small extension that was used as a drawing studio by the architect, who lived there from 1951 until his death in 1971.

From here, your legs will have a bit more of a stretch if you want to finish the walk at the **Skovshoved Petrol Station** (1936). Simply stay on Strandvejen and head south for around 2.5km (1.5 mi). You'll have grassy lawns on one side and the sea on the other and will be able to see Copenhagen in the distance in clear weather. The still-operating gas station is unlike any other you'll have seen: its Art Deco clock, white tiles, and UFO-esque circular roof are quite incongruous with the surroundings. Originally commissioned by Texaco as a new standard model for its gas stations, the design was never put into production. The station at Skovshoved is now a registered historic building.

Returning to Copenhagen, you can avoid having to walk back to Klampenborg by taking the 1A bus from Strandvejen and changing to an S-train on line C at Svanemøllen station, which connects to Nørreport and Copenhagen Central Station. The ticket can be purchased from the bus driver for 48 kroner or you can use the Rejsekort (26 kroner).

# FOOD

## Restaurants at Bakken

*Dyrehavevej 62, Klampenborg, 2930;*
*opening hours as Bakken; prices vary*
*depending on restaurant*

Bakken has 26 restaurants, all of which live up to similar standards while providing for a range of preferences. Perhaps the best known is **Bakkens Perle** (tel. 39 64 31 64; www. bakkensperle.dk; mains 129kr-259kr), a traditional style restaurant that offers a range of steaks and meat-based dishes (and one vegetarian salad) on its evening menu. Danish favorites including herring, fish fillets, and meatballs are available at lunch, and

a buffet is also open throughout the day (lunch buffet 129kr, evening buffet 159kr).

**Al Dente** (tel. 39 63 23 61) is Bakken's Italian restaurant, with pizza and pasta dishes starting at 110 kroner (two courses can be purchased for the standard price of 175kr, three courses for 200 kr). **La Casa** (tel. 39 63 46 04, https://cirkusrevyen.dk/Spisesteder/ La-Casa) touts cold and hot tapas accompanied by Spanish wines or sangria (and Spanish-themed live music). A filling kebab can be had at **Shawarma Hytten** (tel. 22 76 09 01), which also serves falafel and hummus and has a terrace as well as indoor seating. **Jernbane Restauranten** will feel familiar to anybody who has seen iconic TV series *Matador*—a replica of the old-fashioned restaurant in the show where the characters met for a beer and a chat throughout the years. **Elverdybet** (tel. 20 65 30 28; www.elverdybet.dk; sandwiches 50kr-59kr, desserts 28kr-59kr, coffee 24kr-45kr) is a café and ice cream bar partly concealed under a grass-decked roof and located next to the Ladybird kids' roller coaster. It sells meaty sandwiches (and a vegetarian option), *smørrebrød*, and salads as well as burgers, ice cream, banoffee pie, waffles, and other cakes to satisfy the sweet tooth. You can also just stop in for a filtered coffee, latte, or hot chocolate with marshmallows.

## Raadvad Kro

*Svenskevej 52, Kongens Lyngby, 2800; tel.*
*45 80 61 62; www.raadvadkro.dk; Tues.-Sat.*
*noon-3pm and 6pm-9pm, Sun. 10am-5pm;*
*entrées from 125kr, three-course evening set*
*menu 395kr, four-course evening set menu*
*495kr, lunch set menu two courses 295kr*
*three courses 365kr*

Raadvad Kro feels far from the busy

traffic and crowded population centers of Copenhagen. It's set in a tranquil pocket surrounded by narrow lanes, trees, and a small lake. The menu is an uncomplicated take on New Nordic food—shellfish, poached egg, pork with mushrooms and pickled apples, and fish with pumpkin are some examples of menu inclusions. Kids are also thoughtfully provided for with pasta sauce or fish cakes on the junior menu.

## GETTING THERE
### BY PUBLIC TRANSIT

From Copenhagen, taking line C of the S-train or regional train services toward Nivå are the most common ways to reach Klampenborg. From Copenhagen Central Station to Klampenborg Station the journey takes 20-25 minutes and costs 48 kroner for a standard adult ticket, or 26 kroner using the Rejsekort. These trains leave approximately every 10 minutes during the day.

The entrances to Bakken and Jægersborg Dyrehave are within walking distance from Klampenborg station. Turn left out of the station and you'll see the red gate of the animal park. Head through that to enter the forest and continue straight ahead and you'll reach the entrance to Bakken after about 200 meters (650 ft). A northern gate to Dyrehaven is located within walking distance from Skodsborg Station, which is also served by the Nivå regional train (for the same price).

To get to Ordrupgaard from Klampenborg Station, take bus 388 toward Lyngby (exit at Vilvordevej, Ordrupgaard/Klampenborgvej), from where the museum is a 10-minute walk. The bus journey itself takes a few minutes, but there are only a couple of departures every hour. The ticket is the standard 24 kroner (Rejsekort 15 kr). You can also walk the 3km from Klampenborg to Ordrupgaard in approximately 40 minutes. From Peter Lieps Vej outside Klampenborg Station, turn left onto Bellevuevej, veer right after a short distance on Dyrehavevej, continuing on Christiansholmsvej before taking a right turn on to Klampenborgvej (Ordrupgaard is signposted from here). Follow this road for about 2km until you reach the junction with Vilvordevej. Turn on to this road, and the museum is on your left.

### BY CAR

If you are traveling by car from Copenhagen, leave the Inner City crossing the Lakes on Tagensvej and turn right on to Nørre Alle (this is a busy junction, so get in lane early. Follow this road north as it becomes the multilaned Bernstorffsvej/Route 19, keeping right as the road forks, and staying on Bernstorffsvej (the left fork is Route 19). Continue for around 3km and go straight ahead until you reach Vilvordevej, where you will pass Ordrupgaard Museum on your right. Turn right at the junction just after the museum and follow Klampenborgvej to Klampenborg and Bakken's parking area. The 13km journey should take around 30 minutes, depending on traffic and where you start from in Copenhagen.

## TAKE A DETOUR: EXPERIMENTARIUM

*Tuborg Havnevej 7, Hellerup; tel. 39 27 33 33; www.experimentarium.dk; Mon.-Fri.*
*9:30am-5pm (Thurs. until 8pm), Sat.-Sun. 10am-5pm; adults 195kr, children 3-11 115kr;*
*under 3 free*

If you're traveling with kids and feel like extending your fun in the northern sub-urbs of Copenhagen, **Experimentarium** in Hellerup is a nice stop on your way to Bak-ken. The family-focused science museum has eighteen exhibitions spread across three floors, all of which are interactive. There are also daily workshops, demonstrations, and activities, so kids and adults alike can test and learn about physical forces, chemical re-actions, and bodily functions. There are exhibitions about traffic safety, mathematical puzzles, and electricity, but that only really scratches the surface of the wealth of scien-tific discovery and educational value on offer.

Take line B or C of the S-train from Copenhagen to Hellerup Station, a trip that takes 17-18 minutes and costs 24kr standard (Rejsekort: 16kr) for a morning of experimenting before hopping back on line C and hitting up the rides at Bakken.

# Kongens Lyngby

Kongens Lyngby is the commercial center of the suburban Lyngby-Taarbæk Municipality, which neighbors Arne Jacobsen's Gentofte and actually includes the large Jægersborg Dyrehave. Its central shopping street, Lyngby Hovedgade, is suburban and pleasant, but the standout reason for venturing this far from central Copenhagen is the excellent Frilandsmuseet, an expansive open-air museum set in the green countryside, with a huge collection of buildings from Denmark's rural past and an atmosphere to match.

## SIGHTS

### ✪ FRILANDSMUSEET

*Kongevejen 100, Lyngby, 2800; tel. 33*
*13 44 11; https://en.natmus.dk/museums-*
*and-palaces/frilandsmuseet; Tues.-Sun.,*
*May-June 10am-4pm, July-mid Aug.*
*10am-5pm, Aug.-Oct. 21 10am-4pm, limited*
*opening at Christmas and Easter; adult 90kr*
*peak, 75 kr off-peak, under 18 free*

An open-air museum, Frilandsmuseet has both outdoor and indoor exhibits that allow you to escape to Denmark's

agricultural past. You can ride a horsedrawn cart and peruse as many as 50,000 historical artifacts, including tools of the trade used by weavers, millers, and other craftsmen of centuries gone by, and items used by peasants in their homes and by the poor of the workhouse. But the museum's most significant exhibit is the buildings themselves: farms, houses, mills, and shops from various periods and areas of Denmark that were collected and relocated here over the course of 100 years.

There are more than 100 buildings, arranged so as to present Danish life in different parts of the country, and even in other countries and regions with close to connections to Denmark, such as the Faroe Islands and Skåne in Sweden. Opened in 1897 and covering as much as 40 hectares (99 acres), it is thought to be one of the world's oldest and largest open museums: it's possible to spend the best part of a day wandering around its farm buildings, mills (the oldest is a post mill from 1662), and houses and

Frilandsmuseet

their surrounding grounds. Look out for the "station town," with its old gas pump, workshop, garage, and stores showcasing the changes effected by industrialization on small-town life in the late-19th century. The old station building from Øresundsvej on Amager, torn down to make way for the Copenhagen Metro, will eventually be added to this section.

A range of tours with various themes (the lives of farmers, countryside homes, childrens' play and lives, town life in the inter-war period) are offered by the museum for a range of prices starting at 900kr for an hour (plus a 250kr "language fee") for private tours. Call at least two weeks before your visit to inquire about options and arrange a tour. Tours can be canceled with at least three days' notice.

Frilandsmuseet's gift shop has a good range of books, souvenirs and knickknacks as well as toys and candy, including old-fashioned Christmas decorations during the festive season.

# FOOD
## Frilandsmuseets Restaurant & Banquet

*Kongevejen 100, Kgs. Lyngby, 2800; tel. 45 85 34 80; www.frilands-restaurant. dk; Tues.-Sun. May 1-Oct. 22 10am-4pm, Jul. 1-Aug. 12 until 5pm, limited opening at Christmas and Easter; smørrebrød, sandwiches 54-98kr, buffet 285kr-478kr*

Frilandsmuseet's restaurant and café is located in a spacious building within the museum grounds and sticks to Danish tradition in keeping with the surroundings, serving herring and capers, warm *leverpostej* (paté), quiche, and beetroot-marinated salmon among the dishes in its elegant buffet, while curried herring and *flæsk-esteg* roast pork are on the sandwich and *smørrebrød* café menu. It looks a bit formal with white tablecloths and candles, but it is praised for friendly service.

## Café Mig og Annie

*Lyngby Hovedgade 70b, Lyngby, 2800; tel. 45 87 18 34; http://migogannie.dk;*

*Mon.-Fri. 9am-9:30pm, Sat. 9am-8pm, Sun. 10am-8pm; yogurt and fruit bowls 60-70kr, pancakes 60-140kr, sandwiches 125-135kr*

A family-run café that has been a part of the scenery on Lyngby's semi-pedestrianized main shopping drag for the last 20 years, Café Mig og Annie can be found on a leafy corner next to a flower shop, with which it competes for sidewalk space. The food mixes Danish and American café classics: pancakes, fruit and yogurt, bread rolls and cheese, avocado on rye bread, and burgers. Cozy and casual.

## GETTING THERE

### BY PUBLIC TRANSIT

The easiest option for traveling to Frilandsmuseet from Copenhagen is to take the S-train B toward Holte to Sorgenfri Station and walk the final 800 meters (2,600 ft) to the museum. From Copenhagen Central Station, this trip takes around 35 minutes. A standard ticket costs 60kr (32kr using a Rejsekort). To go via the center of the suburb of Lyngby, where there is a semi-pedestrian main street with shops and cafés, leave the train at Lyngby station (one stop before Sorgenfri). This is a 3km (1.8 mi) or around 30-minute walk from Frilandsmuseet.

An S-train and bus combination is also possible (for the same price), bringing you closer to the museum than walking from Sorgenfri station. Taking S-Train E toward Hillerød, get out at Lyngby and take bus 184 or 194 toward Holte. The bus stops outside Frilandsmuseet.

### BY CAR

The drive from central Copenhagen to Frilandsmuseet takes 20 minutes in good traffic. Start out on the same route as for Klampenborg: leave the Inner City, crossing the Lakes on Tagensvej and turn right on to Nørre Alle (a busy intersection: get in lane early). Follow this road north as it becomes the multi-lane Bernstorffsvej/Route 19. Here you diverge from the Klampenborg route. Keep left, taking Route 19 (Tuborgvej). Keep following this road for 9km as it becomes Route 201, taking you through Lyngby, and turn right on to Skovbrynet and left shortly afterward on Kongevejen to reach the museum. The total distance is 15km.

# LOUISIANA MUSEUM OF MODERN ART

**Louisiana Museum of Modern Art** is worth visiting for its location before you get to the spectacular art collections. It's situated in a spacious park in Humlebæk—a small northeast Zealand village between Copenhagen and Helsingør—with a view across the Øresund toward Sweden. Louisiana's location is a reflection of its outlook as a world-class art complex that's still very much grounded in the natural beauty of Denmark. Inside, you'll find six to eight permanent and temporary exhibitions of major international modern and contemporary art, including

# HIGHLIGHTS

✪ **OLD VILLA AND NORTH WING:** The original building of the museum and the glass corridors of the North Wing are home to Louisiana's signature collections (page 173).

✪ **SOUTH WING:** This wing plays host to some of the most exciting special exhibits at Louisiana. A must-see is Yayoi Kusama's *Gleaming Lights of the Souls* (page 174).

✪ **THE SCULPTURE PARK:** A key exhibition at the museum, the park's 60 sculptures blend seamlessly with their coastal natural surroundings (page 175).

works by Alberto Giacometti, Asger Jorn, Pablo Picasso, Yves Klein, and Andy Warhol. Outside, you can lounge on the slopes of the lawn, have a cup of coffee on the terrace of the café, and gaze across the sea or stroll through the museum's sculpture park and landscaped gardens. Louisiana is known by many art and culture lovers as one of Denmark's most beautiful spots, and with good reason.

Humlebæk, the tiny town in which Louisiana is located, is itself a quiet and still place, though it has two harbors: Humlebæk Harbor, just north of Louisiana, and Sletten Harbor, around 2.5km (1.5 mi) to the south. Of these small marina areas, Sletten is the more interesting, with atmospheric lanes and thatched houses along with the highly rated Sletten restaurant in its immediate vicinity. Ten kilometres to the west of Humlebæk, the royal summer residence at Fredensborg weighs in with a serious amount of grandeur, bringing splendor and occasion to this serene corner of Zealand.

Tourist information website www.visitnordsjaelland.dk provides tips on attractions and events in the area, including in Fredensborg and Humlebæk.

# Louisiana Museum of Modern Art

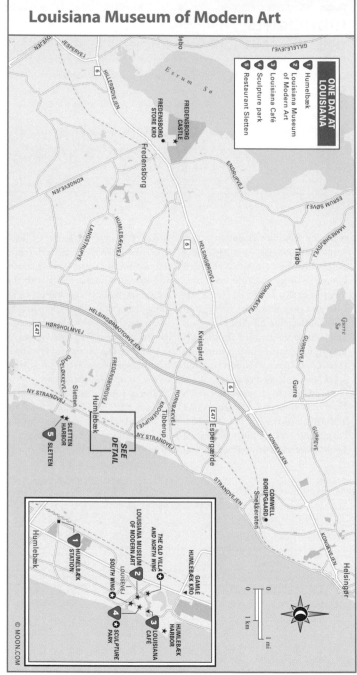

ONE DAY AT LOUISIANA
1. Humlebæk
2. Louisiana Museum of Modern Art
3. Louisiana Café
4. Sculpture park
5. Restaurant Sletten

# Itinerary Idea

## ONE DAY AT LOUISIANA

Louisiana is more than just a museum visit.

**1** Take an early train or bus from Copenhagen to **Humlebæk.**

**2** Spend the morning exploring the **Louisiana Museum of Modern Art**, Denmark's showpiece contemporary art museum. Don't miss the Old Villa and North Wing, check out the special exhibits, and get into a dreamy headspace at Yayoi Kusama's *Gleaming Lights of the Soul* in the South Wing.

**3** Enjoy a Nordic-style lunch and coffee as you gaze at a panoramic view of the Øresund at **Louisiana Café**.

**4** Spend the afternoon wandering around Louisiana's **sculpture park** and enjoying the beautiful rural coastal setting. Download the mobile guide for more information on each of the sculptures that you spot.

**5** Leave the museum and head to the pleasant Sletten Harbor for a seafood dinner at **Restaurant Sletten**.

# Sights

## LOUISIANA MUSEUM OF MODERN ART

*Gammel Strandvej 13, Humlebæk; tel. 49 19 07 19; https://en.louisiana.dk; Tues.-Fri. 11am-10pm, Sat.-Sun. 11am-6pm; adults 125kr, students 110kr, Louisiana members free*

Louisiana is one of the prime modern art museums not just in Denmark, but anywhere. Set on the grounds of an old mansion along the serene northeastern coast of Zealand and overlooking the waters of the Øresund, the clean, square, modernist rooms of the museum house top-class, international contemporary art year-round.

Permanent installations like *Gleaming Lights of the Souls* by Yayoi Kusama will leave all visitors—art buffs or not—in a dream world.

Louisiana's buildings—the original villa and a series of later extensions, renovations, and additions over the years—are themselves considered to be works of art, or to put it in the museum's own words, a "masterpiece of Danish modernist architecture." Founder Knud W. Jensen, bought the original villa with the aim of creating a center for modern art, culture, and landscape away from the noise and bustle of Copenhagen. The modernist approach dates from the 1950s, when Jensen commissioned architects

## LOUISIANA FAST FACTS

- **Number of wings:** 4 (all connected in a ring around the Sculpture Park)

- **Recommended duration of visit:** 3-5 hours

- **Least crowded times:** You'll have more space late on weekday evenings—the museum stays open until 10pm. But that would mean missing out on the beautiful views of the sound (unless it's midsummer), so try weekday mornings instead.

- **Most famous wing:** The North Wing includes paintings by Danish artist Asger Jorn and sculptures by Swiss modernist Alberto Giacometti.

- **My favorite exhibit:** Yayoi Kusama's *Gleaming Lights of the Souls,* which is a beautiful mirrored chamber of endless polka-dot spotlights

- **Underrated gem:** Shilpa Gupta's giant swarm of microphones in the West Wing. Part cloud, part insect plague, it emits a quiet buzzing as you approach. Nearby, a replica of an analogue-style airport departure boards flips numbers and letters in a random sequence, adding to the disorientating sensory effect.

- **Social media:** Visit @louisianamuseum and @louisianabornehus on Instagram to be inspired and to keep up with current goings-on at the museum and children's wing.

to extend the museum by blending its architecture with the surrounding nature. The result is an unobtrusive, minimalistic, low-key, and clean Nordic look: the height of the buildings is constant, meaning that some of them are actually built into the hillside. In keeping with its exhibits, Louisiana is a tribute to modern architectural design.

Characterized by its glass corridors and at-one-with-nature style, the architecture at Louisiana manages to leave a lasting impression without having any features that scream and shout with their visual impact. The lawns and leaves of the Sculpture Park, which is encircled by the museum and also looks out over the sea, is the final element of a stunning and sprawling mosaic and organization of more than 3,500 pieces of post-1945 art from Europe and America.

The arrangement of Louisiana is such that there is no strict order: the aim is not to represent a chronological or categorized progression. Instead, exhibitions are regularly rearranged into new presentations with the intended effect of constantly providing new perspectives from which to experience the museum's huge collection (and as such, it should be noted that works may be found in different locations to their description in this chapter, which refers to the layout of the museum at the time of writing).

Backing up to the shores of the Øresund, the Louisiana Café offers a tranquil place to stop for a sandwich and coffee while breathing in the view. In the 1970s, an auditorium was added that connects to the café. Lectures, debates, and other events are still regularly hosted here, and an amphitheater often hosts small concerts and events, such as during the annual Louisiana Literature festival.

### Tickets and Practical Information

Tickets (adults over 18 125kr, students with valid ID 110kr) can be purchased at the museum. Alternatively, e-tickets can be bought via the Louisiana website and shown either as printouts or on smartphones.

The **Louisiana membership** gives unlimited admission for one year and costs 490kr (full price), 390kr for over-65s, and an astonishingly inexpensive 135kr for people under the age of 27. There are also "membership plus guest" cards, which allows the member to bring one guest (595kr), or up to three (845kr), each time they visit the museum.

Membership provides a number of benefits, including invitations to exhibition openings and special events. Holders can also take advantage of offers in the café and gift shop in addition to the blanket 10 percent members' discount. You also get a free quarterly magazine, although it's in Danish (and not included in under-27 membership).

There's a small **parking lot** outside the museum, and parking is **free**. Alternative parking is allowed at the nearby shopping area, Humlebæk Center, behind the rail station and a 10-minute walk from the museum.

### Visiting Louisiana

Many locals who live in Copenhagen or other areas within easy access of Louisiana make use of the membership card, which allows them to visit as often as they like, dipping in and out of the thousands of pieces on show and 6-8 exhibitions yearly, in addition to the permanent collection. That is less practical, of course, if you're only visiting for a short time or just have a day to see the museum. A few hours is enough to get a real feel of what Louisiana is about, even if you'll never manage to see everything in one visit, and the layout of the museum means you can follow your nose and manage to see each wing in turn. If you are looking to see a particular artist or style in detail, though, it makes sense to plan which wings you want to concentrate on.

## ✪ OLD VILLA AND NORTH WING

In the **Old Villa** and **glass corridors** of the North Wing you will find a large selection of works by **Per Kirkeby**, a mainstay of Danish contemporary artists who passed away in 2018 at the age of 79. Kirkeby's work is primarily displayed in the Villa area. On the **Louisiana Channel** (http://channel.louisiana.dk)—a multimedia website attached to the museum—you will find a recording of an interview between the artist and Louisiana director Poul Erik Tøjner, which was recorded in 2008 when Kirkeby celebrated his 70th birthday. *Weltuntergang* ("The End of the World") (2001) is one of the most affective pieces, its layers of colliding colors reflecting a tumultuous period in the artist's own life.

The **North Wing** of the museum, with its glass corridor and views of the Sculpture Park has a gallery dedicated to the sculptures of **Alberto Giacometti**, one of the most important sculptors of the 20th century. It also plays host to the museum's collection of works by six sculptors—Astrid Noack, Louise Nevelson, Barbara Hepworth, Louise Bourgeois, Sonja Ferlov Mancoba, and Kirsten Ortwed—whose work ranges from classical to modern in style. The view of the gardens through the glass corridors contrasting with the sculptures in the museum is the very embodiment of Jensen's mission. Don't miss the gallery, with its airy, wooden roof work, dedicated to **Asger Jorn**, a tremendous Danish painter.

## ⊗ SOUTH WING

The South Wing, built in 1982, is an exhibition room with a higher ceiling than the preexisting buildings, built into the surrounding terrain to keep the horizontal profile of Louisiana constant and has perhaps the museum's best view of all in the panoramic **Pause Room**.

The South Wing is home to many of the 6-10 **special exhibitions** hosted by Louisiana every year. Some of these are quite spectacular. At the time of writing, a special exhibition to mark 2019's 50th anniversary of the Apollo 11 moon landings includes a collage by American artist Robert Rauschenberg, who was present at the launch itself at NASA's invitation; it encompasses moonlight-exploring works by Romanticist painters such as Caspar David Friedrich and photographers such as Hiroshi Sugimoto, tracking the orbit of the moon as a band of light across the night sky. The exhibition has received rave reviews. Earlier in 2018, German painter Gabriele Münter's life's work was exhibited in the South Wing, as was the art of American "Mr. Cool of Arts" Ed Ruscha (of the 20th Century Fox logo).

One of the permanent exhibits in the South Wing is the spectacular **Yayoi Kusama** installation *Gleaming Lights of the Souls.* You'll definitely spot the queue of people waiting to go inside and lose themselves in the limitlessness of its multicolored hanging polka dots. It's in a room only 4 square meters (43 sq. ft.) in area but feels infinitely bigger.

### EAST WING

The East Wing, also known as the **Graphic Wing**, is used for the exhibition of **drawings** and **graphics** that cannot be exposed to natural lighting conditions (hence its second name).

Old Villa at Louisiana

inside the Louisiana Museum of Modern Art

Completed in 1991, this wing's addition meant that Louisiana's buildings were now connected in something approaching a circle. A curving, underground passage with brick paving, this is one of the most architecturally interesting parts of the museum.

The East Wing also hosts **special exhibitions**: be sure check out the museum's website before visiting for an idea of the aesthetic treats on offer. It was here that Andy Warhol's *Mao Tse Tung* series, in which the Chinese leader is shown in a style reminiscent of Warhol's celebrity portraits, was on display during a 2018 exhibition entitled *Men and Masculinity*. It's a piece that belongs to the Louisiana collection and is worth looking out for during your visit. **Photo, video, and light-based art** are often also found here, and there is also a break from the modern in the form of a permanent collection of **pre-Columbian objects**.

### WEST WING

The West Wing is primarily used to showcase classics from the Louisiana collection. In recent times, **Shilpa Gupta**'s gigantic **Singing Cloud**, a buzzing insect swarm/microphone hybrid that will draw you and repel you in equal measure, has been displayed here. You are also likely to find major

20th-century works from **Picasso**, **Giacometti**, Schlemmer, and others. Other artists included in Louisiana's collection and displayed here include **Sigmar Polke, Morris Louis, Yves Klein**, Alex Da Corte, Franz West, and Marilyn Minter.

### THE CHILDREN'S WING

*Open until 6pm Tues.-Sun., workshops from 11am-5:30pm*

Children are well catered-for at Louisiana. The **Børnehus (Children's House)** has a range of creative and fun activities in facilities spread over three floors. The highlight of the Children's House is the **open workshops**, which get kids creating based on the current exhibitions in the museum: at the time of writing, that meant building space rockets, using clay to form craters, and creating storytelling images of the moon. There's also a monthly **art competition** in which children can enter drawings, sculptures, or paintings inspired by a work they have seen at Louisiana. The winner gets to see their creation posted on the Children's Wing's Instagram page (www.instagram.com/louisianabornehus) as well as an artsy prize.

### ✪ LOUISIANA SCULPTURE PARK

Louisiana's **Sculpture Park**, while part of the main museum, is an attraction in its own right. It is from the Sculpture Park that the unbeatable location of Louisiana and panoramic view can be best appreciated, as can the design of the buildings and their integration into the wooded slopes of the museum grounds. You won't want to miss this part of the museum, which is open year round.

You can spend many hours wandering through it without spotting all of the **60 sculptures**, many of which blend organically into the surroundings (some were created specifically for the site). There's an array of styles among the sculptures, including the jagged **Almost Snow Plow** and metronomic **Little Janey Waney** on the terrace dedicated to sculptor **Alexander Calder,** a bronze alienlike figure by **Joan Miró,** which stands on the lawn in front of the café, and **Henry Moore's** *Reclining Figure No. 5 (Seagram),* which is perhaps the most memorable of the figures gracing the famous view across the Louisiana lawn.

Look out also for a series of works visible from inside the North Wing through the glass corridors. These include surrealist figures such as *Le Grand Genie* by **Max Ernst** and granite sculptures by **Henry Heerup,** which resemble bodies forming themselves as they grow out of the ground.

A personal favorite is a newer addition, 2015's *House to Watch the Sunset* by Swiss artist **Not Vital.** Its reflective steel surface beams back natural greens, browns, and whites during the changing seasons, and the jagged edges of its steps and central column are at once evocative of an M. C. Escher illusion and the trees themselves.

A **mobile guide** to the park, which can be downloaded free of charge from the museum's mobile network, provides valuable insight into the works. The guide can be found on the Sculpture Park section of the Louisiana website, or you can ask to borrow an **iPod** from staff at the entrance to the museum.

## HUMLEBÆK HARBOR

*Humlebæk; tel. 49 19 06 53; https://humlebaekhavn.dk*

Oft-ignored given that Louisiana itself overlooks the sound, Humlebæk Harbor—a stone's throw from the art museum—is a small, quiet corner that exemplifies Denmark's fishing and sailing heritage, with a slight hint of the former's continued presence as an active industry at the location. There's not much in the way of facilities, but the area makes for a pleasant walk and the harbor has a pleasing, natural look with boulders and wood far more prominent than concrete. The harbor celebrated its second century in 2010: it was a part of a slow and painful rebuilding in the years after the bombardment of Copenhagen and destruction of the Danish fleet by the British in 1807.

## SLETTEN HARBOR

*Sletten Havn 1; tel. 20 40 27 72; http://slettenhavn.dk*

In the southern part of Humlebæk, the harbor at Sletten is part of what was once a fishing village, and it remains an idyllic place with around 130 old fisherman's houses, now restored and privately owned. It's possible to take a short walk along the marina (possibly after a meal at nearby Sletten Restaurant), from where there are views across the sound and of the old houses in the village.

## FREDENSBORG CASTLE

*Slottet 1B, Fredensborg; tel. 20 20 10 12; http://kongeligeslotte.dk/da/slotte-og-haver/fredensborg-slot.html; public areas open year round, guided tours of gardens available July 1-Aug. 5, private gardens open to public during same period; free*

Around 10km (6.2 mi) to the west of Humlebæk, Fredensborg Palace, the autumn and spring residence of the royal family was beloved of the late Prince Henrik, husband of Denmark's

Fredensborg Castle

Queen Margrethe—perhaps because of its French-inspired Baroque style. The palace, which is well used by the modern royals, is often the scene of important stately events. Its grounds contain garden, sculptures and fountains of cultural note, and while some areas of the gardens are open to the public year-round, access is best during the summer months, when guided tours are available.

The palace interior and some areas of the gardens (the Private Garden) are normally reserved for royal use, and as such it's not generally possible to visit. During the summer season, however, it is possible to see parts of the castle as well as the Orangery and herb garden as part of daily guided tours. In 2018, guided tours took place from July 1-August 5. The schedule for subsequent years can be checked on the palace website, and tickets for guided tours will be made available via the Royal Palace's webshop (http://shop.kongeligeslotte.dk/billetter-aktiviteter) in the spring prior to the opening season.

Features of the palace interior include the Dome Hall: a setting for banquets and royal functions with a vaulted, domed roof and a characteristic black-and-white star-patterned marble floor. The red-framed windows at the top of the dome provide an atmospheric lighting within the hall, which has held Danish wedding receptions for centuries, including that of the Crown Prince Frederik and Crown Princess Mary in 2004. It is also famous for its window panes, on which tradition dictates that visiting kings and presidents scratch their signatures.

The Baroque Gardens, created in the image of Versailles by 18th-century francophile King Frederik V, consist of broad avenues radiating out from the palace. Boxwood hedges and linden trees line the avenues, and sculptor Johannes Wiedewelt was commissioned by the king to create eight sandstone pieces for the central Broad Avenue (Brede Allé), depicting war trophies and scenes from ancient mythology. There is also an ornamental garden in front of the palace. The gardens and sculptures were restored in 2013 to give them a general resemblance to how the grounds were in Frederik V's heyday.

The Private Garden contains a small bridge, statues of its own, rosebeds, rhododendrons, yellow yarrows, and a half-timbered 1960s playhouse for the royal children. Still reserved for royal use, this part of the palace can sometimes be visited during the summer months, when the Queen is not in residence—as can the Orangery, the vegetable garden that has supplied herbs and vegetables to the royal table since the 1700s.

# Festivals and Events

## LOUISIANA LITERATURE

*Gammel Strandvej 13, Humlebæk; tel. 49 19 07 19; https://en.louisiana.dk/whats-on/louisiana-literature; late Aug.; included in Louisiana museum entry*

Literature festivals are a growing summer phenomenon in Denmark, and Louisiana is on the page of the trend. Its international literature festival—many readings are conducted in English—takes place indoors and outside in late August, combining the atmospheric surroundings with authors' voices and prose.

During a busy four-day festival, around 40 authors from Denmark and abroad take part in readings, panel discussions, and literary events that cover a diverse range of genres and traditions. The 2019 edition is scheduled for August 22-25, and the festival takes place during normal museum opening hours. Previous festivals have included appearances from Paul Auster, Margaret Atwood, Zadie Smith, Patti Smith, Chris Kraus, Tomas Espedal, Karl Ove Knausgård, Alaa Al-Aswany, David Mitchell, and Herta Müller.

# Dining

## Louisiana Café

*Gammel Strandvej 13, Humlebæk; tel. 49 19 07 19; https://en.louisiana.dk/louisiana-cafe; Tues.-Fri. 11am-9:30pm, Sat.-Sun. 1am-5:30pm; buffet lunch 139kr, sandwiches 79kr*

Louisiana Café is perched on the top of the slope, giving a great view across the museum grounds and the coast. Given that it is part of a major attraction, the prices are reasonable—the buffet (139kr for lunch, 169kr for dinner) is fresh, healthy, and Danish, with staples including rye bread, risotto, potatoes, and green salad. Be prepared for long lines at peak times: late afternoons are quieter.

## Sletten

*Gammel Strandvej 137, Humlebæk; tel. 49 19 13 21; https://sletten.dk/forside; daily noon-3pm, 6pm-11pm; entrées from 145kr*

At Sletten Harbor north of Louisiana and Humlebæk Station, Restaurant Sletten shares its owners with Michelin-starred restaurant Formel B in Copenhagen, and the emphasis on high-quality, local ingredients is just as evident here as at the more famous establishment in the capital. Surrounded by fishing huts and with its own view of the Øresund, the New Nordic menu is influenced by both the sea and the cuisine of Formel B: expect wild berries, lobster, and grilled turbot to be among the many delights on the tasting menu. Reserve in advance.

## Gamle Humlebæk Kro

*Humlebæk Strandevej 1A, Humlebæk; tel. 49 19 02 65; www.gamlehumlebaekkro.dk; Tues.-Sun. lunch noon-4:30pm, dinner 5:30pm-9pm; entrées from 145kr*

Gamle Humlebæk Kro is an

Louisiana Café and *Snow Plow* sculpture by Alexander Calder

old-fashioned inn that serves simple, tasty staple Danish dishes including *smørrebrød,* roast pork, and *fiske-frikadeller* (fish meatballs). There's no shortage of history here—the inn has been in place since 1740. Its old-fashioned carpets, grandfather clock, and mounted antlers and animal heads are testament to the traditional feel, as are the checked tablecloths and candlesticks. There's also a large terrace area for outside seating during the summer. Reservations are recommended.

## Accommodations

There are scant places to spend the night in Humlebæk itself, but a couple of good options further afield offer visitors a good opportunity to combine a visit to the museum with other attractions nearby or a trip to Helsingør.

### Comwell Borupgaard

*Nørrevej 80, Snekkersten; tel. 48 38 03 33; www.comwellborupgaard.dk; double occupancy in high season from 1,146kr; 149 rooms*

Comwell Borupgaard, located between Humlebæk and Helsingør, is a hotel with conference facilities in a country-manor type property with modern buildings appended. It has a spa and is a 10-minute walk from the beach. Buffet breakfast is included. All rooms are recently renovated and have a modern, clean style with large en-suite bathrooms, flat screen televisions, and Wi-Fi. Free parking (and electric car charging) is available in the hotel's car park.

**Fredensborg Store Kro**

*Slotsgade 6, Fredensborg; tel. 71 71 21 21;*
*www.storekro.com; double occupancy in*
*high season from 1,320kr; 54 rooms*

With Fredensborg Palace a few hundred yards down the boulevard, it is easy to pick up on the regal countryside vibe at Fredensborg Store Kro, which was originally built in 1723. A bistro restaurant (open daily for lunch from 12pm-3 and Mon-Sat for evening meals from 6pm-10pm) and tourist information desk at reception are among the facilities. Breakfast is not included in room price. Individually decorated, chic rooms have Wi-Fi and en-suite bathrooms and are often furnished with antiques; some of the suites have garden (and palace) views and balconies.

# Getting There and Around

## GETTING THERE FROM COPENHAGEN

### BY TRAIN

The Øresund/Kystbanen trains run by DSB (www.dsb.dk) leave three times hourly from Copenhagen Central Station to Humlebæk and cost 92 kroner for an adult single ticket. The journey takes around 35 minutes. Check www.dsb.dk or www.rejseplanen.dk for departure times. The Rejsekort travel card can be used to pay for the journey, provided you have enough credit, and gives discounts on fares (price is reduced to 53.50kr) if you travel outside of peak times—11am-1pm and after 6pm and on Saturdays, Sundays, and public holidays. However, do note that replacement buses sometimes take over services at weekends, which results in longer and more crowded journeys. Directions will be provided at stations if these are in effect.

Louisiana is around a 15-20 minute walk from the train station along a stretch of main road. The direction is well-signposted (alternatively, follow the many other visitors at peak times). Or you can take the northbound 388 regional bus, across the road from the train station. Get off after one stop, and you'll find yourself right outside the museum entrance. There's no additional cost to use the bus in addition to the train (if using the Rejsekort, do not check out after leaving the train, "re-check in" on the bus and then check out when leaving the bus). Taxis can also be hailed or called at the station. A reliable taxi company is Fredensborg-Humlebæk Taxa (tel. 49 14 46 10); the journey from the station to the museum takes no more than a couple of minutes and should not set you back more than 75kr.

### BY CAR

Head north out of Copenhagen on Strandvejen along the Øresund coast or via the E47 motorway. Louisiana is around 35km north of Copenhagen.

## GETTING THERE FROM HELSINGØR

The Øresund/Kystbanen train from Helsingør to Humlebæk takes 10 minutes and costs 36kr, or 20kr if you are using the Rejsekort, leaving around every 20 minutes. If you're driving, head south on the E45 or route 152 (Strandvejen). You should cover the

10km distance to Humlebæk within 20 minutes.

## GETTING AROUND

The easiest way to travel between Humlebæk and Fredensborg is with direct bus **370**, which leaves from Humlebæk Station and takes a little more than half an hour at the cost of 36 kroner. Unfortunately, this bus leaves no more than once every hour. An alternative method is to make your way to **Kokkedal Station** via southbound **regional trains** (these are often bound for Karlskrona or Kristiansstad in Sweden: don't be put off by this, but make sure you get off at the right place!). At Kokkedal, switch to bus **365R** for Fredensborg. A third option is to head north on the regional train toward Helsingør, get off at **Snekkersten,** and then take local train **930R** to Fredensborg. The total fare is 36kr, and you buy a ticket for the full trip at the beginning of your journey. The Rejsekort (20kr) can be used for all journeys and routes.

# HELSINGØR

**It's impossible to miss the sense** of theatrical occasion as one approaches Helsingør along the northeast Zealand coast, as the colossal Kronborg Castle, immortalized by Shakespeare's *Hamlet,* comes into view. It stands on a spit as if held at arms length from the medieval town that still dominates it, expecting to receive its sound dues, the toll for passing ships on which the city's wealth was founded.

While the UNESCO World Heritage Site, with its Baroque and Renaissance interiors and iconic features, is the town's signature attraction,

# HIGHLIGHTS

✪ **KRONBORG CASTLE:** This iconic castle juts out from the coast, standing rugged and proud over the Øresund. Its evocative courtyard, soaring cannon tower, dramatic royal chambers, and poignant underground chamber of Holger Danske are all experiences not to be missed (page 186).

✪ **M/S MARITIME MUSEUM OF DENMARK:** Denmark's seafaring tradition, housed in an innovatively converted dry dock, deserves a detailed look (page 190).

✪ **SHAKESPEARE FESTIVAL:** See a Shakespeare play in the setting imagined by the Bard himself (page 194).

Helsingør has plenty more to offer, including a broad harbor area with an impressive maritime museum set in a deep dry dock, a new street food market, and a well-preserved old town. Meanwhile, seagulls squawk and sailboats crisscross the water, with the Swedish city of Helsingborg visible beyond on most days: nowhere else is the Øresund narrower than here.

## ORIENTATION

The harbor area, including the maritime museum, Elsinore Street Food, and Kronborg sit to the north of the train station and main bus terminal, which are a short walk of less than 1km (0.6 mi), either along the harborside or through the town itself. Moving inland from the coast, three streets that run parallel to the coast—Stengade, Sct Olai Gade, and Sudergade, as well as the perpendicular Sct Annagade, Sophie Brahes Gade, and Stjernegade—demarcate the old town, which is laid out as it was in the 15th century. This is the best area for exploring the oldest-surviving buildings and streets. The very oldest building in the city, the 13th-century St. Olaf Cathedral, sits at the southeastern corner.

## PLANNING YOUR TIME

Kronborg itself is worthy of a half to a full day, so either a day trip or one overnight stay are a good fit for a Helsingør visit. Your next priority after the castle should be the M/S Maritime Museum of Denmark. And don't forget to spend an hour or two wandering the old city center. It survived a redevelopment of the 1960s and 1970s and retains a layout that has been in place since medieval times.

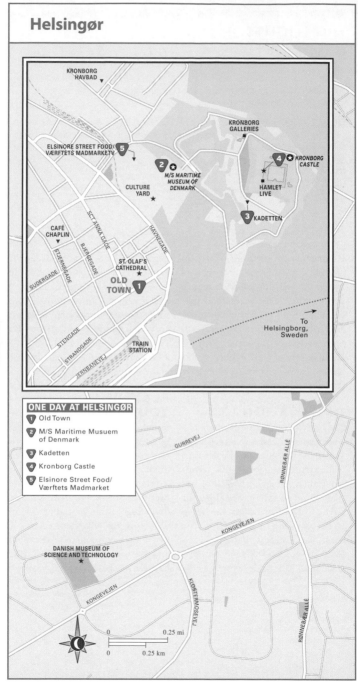

# Helsingør

**KRONBORG HAVBAD**

**ELSINORE STREET FOOD/ VÆRFTETS MADMARKET** 5

**KRONBORG GALLERIES**

2 **M/S MARITIME MUSEUM OF DENMARK**

**CULTURE YARD**

4 **KRONBORG CASTLE**

**HAMLET LIVE**

3 **KADETTEN**

SCT ANNA GADE

HAVNEGADE

**CAFÉ CHAPLIN**

STJERNEGADE

BJERGEGADE

**ST. OLAF'S CATHEDRAL**

SUDERGADE

**OLD TOWN** 1

To Helsingborg, Sweden

STENGADE

STRANDGADE

JERNBANEVEJ

**TRAIN STATION**

## ONE DAY AT HELSINGØR

1 Old Town

2 M/S Maritime Musuem of Denmark

3 Kadetten

4 Kronborg Castle

5 Elsinore Street Food/ Værftets Madmarket

GURREVEJ

RØNNEBÆR ALLÉ

KONGEVEJEN

**DANISH MUSEUM OF SCIENCE AND TECHNOLOGY**

KONGEVEJEN

KLOSTERMOSEVEJ

RØNNEBÆR ALLÉ

0        0.25 mi

0        0.25 km

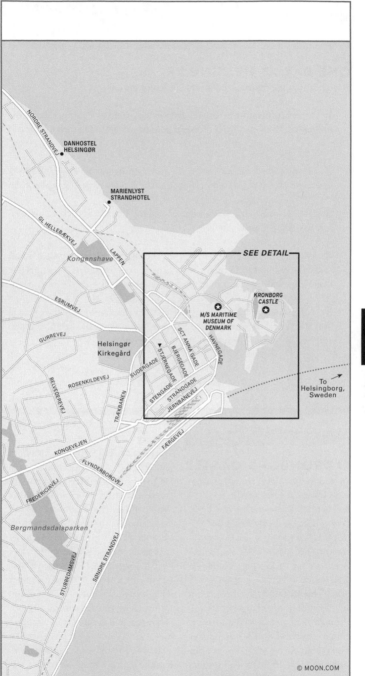

# Itinerary Idea

## ONE DAY AT HELSINGØR

Head north to the mythical home of Hamlet for the day.

**1** After breakfasting in Copenhagen, catch a train to Helsingør. From the rail station, head north and spend an hour or so wandering through the **old town**.

**2** Head toward the harbor—and down under sea level—to the **M/S Maritime Museum of Denmark** for an afternoon of seafaring exploration.

**3** Grab a sandwich at **Kadetten**, located in a lieutenants' school just outside Kronborg Castle.

**4** With your stomach full, step inside the majestic **Kronborg Castle** and spend the rest of the afternoon immersing yourself in Renaissance intrigue. Don't miss scaling the cannon tower for sweeping views of the city.

**5** For dinner, there's no better place than the **Elsinore Street Food/ Værftets Madmarked**. Choose between Brazilian tacos, Belgian crêpes, and fish and chips—or have a little bit of everything.

# Sights

## ✪ KRONBORG CASTLE

*Kronborg; tel. 33 13 44 11; http://kronborg. dk; Jan.-Mar. Tue.-Sun. 11am-4pm, Apr.-May daily 11am-4pm, June-Sept. daily 10am-5:30pm, Oct. daily 11am-4pm, Nov.-Dec. Tues.-Sun. 11am-4pm (last admission is 30 minutes before closing time); June-Aug. adults 140kr, under 18 free, Sept.-May adults 90kr, under 18 free*

There's no mistaking the majesty and significance of Kronborg as you walk through the gateway into a fully enclosed courtyard, which immediately evokes the court machinations of centuries past with its imposing masonry.

### History

The presence of a fortress at Kronborg dates back to the 15th century, when Danish king Eric of Pomerania decided that ships entering the Baltic Sea through the narrow Øresund Strait should pay a toll—known as the Sound Dues—for the privilege. At that time, the other side of the water also belonged to Denmark (it was lost during a series of disastrous wars with Sweden in the 1600s). That meant Denmark was able to control all navigation through the area, which the medieval kingdom quickly monetized.

It was in the stone chambers of Kronborg that a king's residence was established, and in the late 1500s, King Frederik II built the castle into a towering Renaissance stronghold, as it entered a golden era of renown throughout Europe. Its cannons gnashed their teeth at passing ships, and the presence of the authoritative fortress persuaded captains to pay their dues. The king's coffers were thereby filled, allowing Frederik II to endow the castle with spires, towers, sandstone masonry, and copper roofing. Seafarers, merchants, diplomats, and royals sent reports back to their homeland about the majesty and pomp of the court at Helsingør.

A devastating fire in 1629 destroyed art, tapestries, and roofing and signaled the beginning of the end of royal presence at the castle. The loss of Skåne—the region on the other side of the channel—to Sweden in 1658 after a series of costly wars under kings Christian IV (also known for building many of Copenhagen's historic areas) and his successor, Frederik III, greatly weakened Denmark's influence on the strait. The castle was even occupied and plundered by Swedish king Karl X Gustav in 1658-1660.

In later years, Kronborg was used as a military fortress, with new defenses and ramparts built around it. In the 1700s, it became a prison, with soldiers from the military barracks just outside the walls guarding the convicts.

In 1857, the Sound Dues were finally abolished, and in 1938 Kronborg was opened to the public, eventually becoming one of the biggest (literally) attractions on the island of Zealand, with 250,000 visitors annually.

## VISITING THE CASTLE

The castle is a memorable sight, both inside and out, and details such as the cannons outside its far walls still pointing threateningly at Sweden a

courtyard at Kronborg Castle

short distance away and the iron water pump in the courtyard bring its history to life. There's plenty to do and see here, and I recommend taking at least half a day for your visit in order to properly take in and explore the castle and its grounds.

Kronborg has many different parts and areas. Although you'll often move naturally from one area to the other as you walk through the castle, no particular order is better than another. What all visitors will see first, though, is the walk from the harbor, crossing it via two bridges and then turning left to walk around the castle with its wall to the right and earthen defenses to the left. A third bridge takes you across the moat and into the outer battlements of the castle itself, where you'll get a first view of the Renaissance and Baroque influences on its construction, with reliefs, statues, and pillars at the entrance to the main courtyard, a spectacular, walled-in square of sandstone, towers, and narrow rectangular windows. From this courtyard, signposts direct you to all of the attractions within the castle itself.

The opulent **Royal Apartments** are where King Frederik II, who spent a fortune building and furnishing the castle in the late 1500s, lived with the queen, Sophie, whom he married in 1572 (when she was 14 years old). The rooms are not the original ones, which were destroyed in a later fire, and much of the furniture was acquired after Frederik's time, but the chambers have been set out in a reconstruction of the King's design. Look out for a monogrammed shield containing the letters F and S—perhaps the royal, medieval version of a love heart engraved into a tree. There are ceiling-high **tapestries**, which once completely covered the walls of

the ballrooms; sleeping chambers with carved wooden four-poster beds (one each for the king and queen) and an officelike room, the chancellery, where the king's correspondences were kept in cabinets. Some of the more spectacular features elsewhere in the apartments include ceiling paintings that depict members of the royal family and a 62-meter ballroom with an impressively checkered-tile floor.

The **chapel**, built in 1582, survived the fire, occupation, and bombardments of the castle's heyday and is therefore an accurate representation of how it was originally decorated. The ceiling is arched and whitewashed, and the floor a chessboard of tiles, the detailing on the pews and altar ornate, with floral patterns and figures on the ends of the rows.

The **Cannon Tower**, with a view across the water and of the city of Helsingør, is well worth the effort required to climb its 142 stone steps. It is in the southwestern corner of the castle: the entrance is on the far right-hand side as you enter.

From the heights of the tower, you can go straight to the murky depths of the **Casemates**, the damp underground passages where you will find the statue of **Holger Danske** (Ogier the Dane), a legendary knight of Charlemagne, who, it is said, will rise to Denmark's protection in its hour of most dire need. The statue underneath Kronborg, a cast of a 1907 original by H. P. Pedersen-Dan, sits cross-armed and head bowed, as if to underline the magnitude of the castle's symbolism.

Near to the entrance, the year-round photo exhibition "**Hamlet on Location**" pays tribute to actors to have played Hamlet—including Sir Laurence Olivier, John Gielgud, and Jude Law.

view of Helsingør from the Cannon Tower at Kronborg Castle

## TOURS AND PRACTICAL DETAILS

Crowds at the castle increase on weekends and during the summer as well as during the middle of the day: timing your visit to include the last hour before closure is a good way to enjoy a relatively deserted Kronborg. This is a great time for getting a clear view at the top of the Cannon Tower and maximizing spookiness in the Casemates.

For an additional cost, five different guided tours in English are available at Kronborg. The tours range in duration between 60 and 90 minutes, and the price is dependent on number of participants. Places on the tours can be reserved in advance: call 49 21 30 78 or email kronborg@natmus.dk to request prices and information and to make reservations; you can also inquire at ticket sales when you arrive. Two **Hamlet-themed tours** are available at specific times of the year. In the first of these tours, **"In Hamlet's Footsteps,"** the character Horatio—who survives the play's

bloody denouement—acts as your guide, taking you through the narrative of the play and locations where it takes place. This tour goes year-round, except June-August. During the summer, the **"In Hamlet's World"** tour involves a bigger cast—you might find yourself walking into the middle of the action in the courtyard. You will also be guided through the secret corridors and windy bastions to learn about the play's poisonous betrayal, tragic love story, and dramatic rivalries. Both tours are approximately 60 minutes in duration.

Three other tours are available year round (at the time of writing—the program is subject to change): the **"Classic Tour"** of the king's apartments and ballroom, along with the chapel and Holger Danske; and a **"Nooks and Crannies" tour**, taking you to lesser-visited dungeon rooms and unveiling secrets about the castle's history and court life. The **"Royal Housekeeper" tour**, in which preparations for a banquet are presented

## EXPERIENCING HAMLET

Shakespeare's longest play is inextricably connected to Kronborg, the castle at which it is set, even though the Bard himself never visited Denmark and set the play based on his formidable imagination. Many spots at the castle are referenced in the play, and these can be found if you look around (and use your own imagination a little):

- On the castle **ramparts**, Prince Hamlet gets a shock when he meets the ghost of his dead father. You can evoke this scene without having to go into the castle itself, as Kronborg's ramparts are outside the castle wall.

- In Act III, Hamlet and Gertrude's showdown takes place in the **Queen's Chamber** (located within the **King's Apartment** in the real castle), while Polonius listens in from behind a **tapestry**.

- In the **chapel**, in front of the altar, Claudius surrenders and admits to murdering the king.

- The dramatic climax in Act V Scene II, was set by Shakespeare at "a hall in the castle": for this, see Kronborg's **grand ballroom**, located within the castle's royal quarters.

You can also partake in two special castle tours that follow in the footfalls of Hamlet, Claudius, Ophelia, Laertes, and company: **"In Hamlet's Footsteps"** and **"In Hamlet's World."**

In the summer, **Hamlet Live!,** an interactive and immersive experience, takes you through the action of the play and allows you to interact with the characters.

through the eyes of the housekeeper herself, can be booked all year except in June, July, and August.

In addition to these, 30-minute guided **tours of the Casemates** in English take place daily at 1pm and 4:30pm (July-Sept) and 1:30pm (Oct-March). An **"Introduction to Kronborg" tour** is at 11am and 2:30pm (July-Sept), 12:30pm (Oct), and 2pm (Nov-March). Both are included in the ticket price.

There is no restaurant or café within the castle but plenty just outside the entrance and near the ticket office. Bring a bottle of water if you visit during the summer. To purchase entry tickets, look for the last of the orange brick buildings in the barracks area outside of the castle, then turn the corner and head toward the bridge at the entry gate.

## ✪ M/S MARITIME MUSEUM OF DENMARK

*Ny Kronborgvej 1; tel. 49 21 06 85; http:// mfs.dk; Sept.-June Tues.-Sun. 11am-5pm, July-Aug. 11am-6pm; adults 110kr, students & seniors 90kr, under 18 free*

From a distance it's almost invisible, but get up close and you can see right down into the depths of the M/S Maritime Museum of Denmark in its 19th-century converted dry dock. The museum is simultaneously an architectural marvel and a fine telling of Denmark on the waves through the centuries. It was designed by the famed Bjarke Ingels architectural firm and opened in 2013. From the outside, it takes a moment or two to realize the museum is actually a museum, given its appearance as a giant rectangle cut into the concrete of the docks, with glass down its sides and an angular staircase sinking into its

M/S Maritime Museum of Denmark

depths. Inside, the focus is less traditional than it might be at other maritime museums, with fewer models of ships (although these are by no means absent) and more emphasis on telling the stories of Danish and international mariners. Presentation is also untraditional, with lighting, coloring, and display cases made to feel like parts of a ship or of the sea itself.

Quirkier exhibitions include a buoy back-illuminated in a way that makes it look like a disco light and a range of figureheads fixed to the wall like an array of ornaments. Models range from a giant Maersk container ship to frigates and tall ships displayed inside glass cases at far jauntier angles than crews would be comfortable with in real life.

Although there are as many as nine permanent exhibitions, with topics including globalization, life at sea, Denmark's history as a shipping power, and technology and navigation, the museum is relatively compact and can therefore be combined with a day visit to Kronborg. Some of the exhibits are interactive. Guided tours can be arranged at least three weeks in advance: Contact booking@mfs.dk for prices, information, and reservation.

Near the entrance (downward staircase) to the Maritime Museum, look out for the sculpture HAN—a male version of Copenhagen's Little Mermaid statue, echoing the original's size, style, and demeanor—in the harbor area near the museum entrance.

## DANISH MUSEUM OF SCIENCE AND TECHNOLOGY

*Fabriksvej 25; tel. 49 22 26 11; http://tekniskmuseum.dk; Tues.-Sun. 10am-5pm; adults 90kr, students & seniors 80kr, under 18 free*

It looks incredibly unspectacular from the outside, but don't let the gray, cardboard factory warehouse-look mislead you as to what's inside: it's like an aircraft hangar full of transportation and other technology from the last century. With a self-confessed "childlike fascination" with machinery, function, and mechanics, Helsingør's Danish Museum of Science and Technology takes pride in everything from engines to aircraft to twenty-year-old cellphones, which seem as cumbersome to today's teenagers as a Model T Ford. A spectacular model railway, crafted lovingly by local enthusiasts and filling an entire exhibition room, showcases the history of train travel in Denmark until the 1960s, depicting the Roskilde-Copenhagen line along with windmills, a hot air balloon, and early 20th-century factories and with lighting in the room alternating between night and day. There is a lack of information in English throughout the museum, but there's plenty of visual enjoyment to be had. There are vintage bicycles, fire engines, and all sorts of aircraft, from old prop planes to wrecked fuselage to an old Danish Air Lines craft, which you can enter and sit in the cabin. It's also hands-on—there are signs saying which buttons and levers you can try out on the exhibits. There's no heating in the hangar, so it can get cold in winter.

## HELSINGØR'S OLD TOWN

*Sudergade–Strandgade; Sophie Brahesgade–Stjernegade*

Helsingør boasts a well-preserved historical center spanning a small area three blocks by four blocks, no more than 1-2 km (0.6-1 mi) from the harbor. The streets of Stengade, Skt. Olaigade, and Sudergade, which run roughly east to west, are crossed by Sophie Brahesgade, Skt. Annagade, Bjergegade, and Stjernegade in a somewhat north-south direction. The street plan is thought to be the work of King Eric of Pomerania, who also built the original structure of Kronborg in the 14th century. Only one older building, the 13th-century St. Olaf Cathedral, breaks this surprisingly regular pattern.

The names of the streets carry their own stories about the town's history: **Stengade (Stone Street)** was the well-to-do quarter where the first stone houses were built, and **Sudergade** was the shoemaker's street, the word Suder coming not from the Danish, but the Low German word for "shoe."

One "block" south of Stengade, **Strandgade ("Beach Street")** is nearer the coast and was built at some point after the original old town. Streets connecting these two parallel roads include **Gl. Færgestræde (Old Ferry Passage)** and **Brostræde (Bridge Passage)**. The former of these two narrow streets is perhaps the most atmospheric in the entire old town of Helsingør, its cobbled stones still laid on the ground the way they were in the Middle Ages: uneven enough to force you to tread carefully. The buildings, painted a dark yellow-orange in their wooden frames, feel high and enclosing each side of the narrow passageway, such that you start to worry whether someone is about to empty a chamber pot from one of the windows directly above. The open gutter (not in use) that runs down the middle of the street does little to shatter this illusion. This street is so narrow that it's easy to miss: look out for it on the left as you walk along Stengade from the harbor end of town: you'll see the entrance and an old sign painted into the wall reading "Gl. Færgestræde" shortly before you reach the city hall.

Elsewhere around the old town, **old merchant's houses** retain handsome wooden carvings on their colorful facades, and backyards and alleys feel untouched by modernity. **Stengade** is a testament to Helsingør's former position as a strategic location for shipping trade routes, with a number of surviving Renaissance-period houses that bear the influence of the international craftsmen likely to have been involved in construction of Kronborg. Now the town's main shopping street, Stengade also has its fair share of modern and functional architecture, but there are also older buildings, like the Baroque Stengade 64 from 1739, a few meters from Færgestræde. If you have time, explore the surrounding streets for further glimpses of old Helsingør.

## ST. OLAF CATHEDRAL
### (Skt. Olai Kirke)
*Sct. Anna Gade 12; tel. 40 18 68 14;*

*www.helsingoerdomkirke.dk; May-Aug. 10am-4pm, Sept.-Apr. 10am-2pm; free*

The oldest building in the city, St. Olaf Cathedral, dates originally from the 13th century, and the present building was completed in 1559. Remains of the original church's decorations can be seen on the interior north wall. A classic red brick church with a high copper spire, it sits at the southeastern corner of the old city between Stengade and Skt. Olufgade, making it an ideal component of a wander around old Helsingør. Its design has both Gothic and Baroque elements. Inside, there's a 16th-century fresco in one of the nave vaults, which are otherwise whitewashed. The interior is quite beautifully decorated, with ornate chandeliers depicting St. Olaf—the Norwegian king and saint for whom the church is named—and alabaster altarpieces.

a view of St. Olaf Cathedral

# Entertainment and Events

## FESTIVALS
### ✪ Shakespeare Festival
*Kronborg 13; tel. 49 21 69 79; http://hamletscenen.dk; Aug.; ticket prices TBA*

Every year in August the Shakespeare Festival brings *Hamlet* and other Shakespeare plays staged by acclaimed theater companies and production artists to a specially built, open-air theater at Kronborg Castle. A unification of art, cultural heritage, and nature, these plays, are given unique character by the Danish outdoor elements and the cawing of seagulls. With a stunning backdrop of the moat and castle walls rising behind, things can't get much more atmospheric. In 2018 the program included the Chinese opera version of *Hamlet,* called *The Revenge of Prince Zi Dan* by the Shanghai Peking Opera Company, as well as a Shakespeare-based theater concert with dancers and musicians from the Royal Danish Ballet. In 2017, *Hamlet* was performed in an in-house production alongside a Japanese interpretation of a sequel to the character Ophelia's story (in which Ophelia roamed Kronborg as a ghost).

Plays take place in the evening, so bring warm, waterproof clothes: even though it's summer, things can be chilly (and wet). Productions are never canceled, however. The theater has its own bar, which opens at 4pm daily. During intermission, you'll be able to buy drinks and snacks there. You can also preorder a picnic, which can be collected from the bar after 5:30pm and enjoyed outdoors with views of the castle, the sea, and the stage (bring your own blanket). Picnics must be preordered by noon two days

in advance. If you don't opt for the picnic, eat before you arrive.

The festival program and ticket prices are generally announced in spring, and tickets go on sale no later than May 1.

## THE ARTS
### Hamlet Live
*Kronborg; tel. 33 13 44 11; http://kongeligeslotte.dk; June-Aug. daily 10am-5pm; adults 140kr, children free*

Hamlet Live is an immersive and interactive event at Kronborg held daily during the summer. Shakespeare's drama, famously set at Kronborg, is innovatively combined with the attraction itself. As you wander the chambers and courtyards of Kronborg, you'll find yourself plunged into scenes from the play, experiencing firsthand the politics, poison, and sword fights of King Claudius's court and the daily lives of the characters, who are played by trained actors. To get the most out of the experience, interact with the characters and ask about their lives and the secrets lurking in the Kronborg crevices.

Hamlet Live takes place every day during the months of June, July, and August. The performance plays out during the course of the day, with visitors jumping into the story from the moment they walk into the castle courtyard, its events unfolding as you walk around. Exactly who you will meet, and when, is as uncertain as the fate of Ophelia—so there's no need to follow a set schedule. Tickets include entrance to the castle and the Hamlet Live event and are valid for the entire day. Characters speak in English.

The Culture Yard

### The Culture Yard
### (Kulturværftet)

*Allegade 2; tel. 49 28 36 20; https://kuto.dk;*
*Mon.-Fri. 10am-9pm, Sat.-Sun. 10am-4pm,*
*later during events and concerts; ticket*
*prices vary*

The Culture Yard is a cultural house located on the shipyard, a mishmash of glass and brick from where the Kronborg and St. Olaf spires are almost equidistant. Bright, colorful reading rooms on the upper floors have great views of the castle and the bay. The café, Spisehuset, is open from 10am-7pm on weekdays and 10am-5pm on weekends, and has seasonal salads (75kr), paninis (55kr), Mexican bowls (95kr), and good old Danish rye bread, meatballs, and relish (95kr). A library and resource center by day, the 13,000-square-meter (140,000 sq ft) facility hosts hundreds of events yearly, including theater, rock and pop concerts, seasonal events like New Year's celebrations, and special film showings. There are two concert halls, and some events take place on the harbor front itself. Check the website to see what's happening and to buy tickets.

### Kronborg Galleries

*Kronborg; www.kronborggallerierne.dk;*
*see individual galleries for contact details*
*(download brochure from website)*

The Kronborg Galleries are a series of creative spaces located in the former barracks buildings around the castle perimeter. They are often open to the public (look for raised banners outside the entrances) and include shops and arts and crafts workshops featuring a range of specialties including glass, jewelry, ceramics, photography, and painting.

# Food and Accommodations

## ✪ Elsinore Street Food/ Værftets Madmarked

*Ny Kronborgvej 2; tel. 49 20 02 01; http:// vaerftetsmadmarked.dk; daily 11am-10pm, food stands close 9pm; entrées from 65kr*

Opened in 2017 with the aim of bringing locals and tourists together in a public space attractive to all, Elsinore Street Food is a scaled-down version of the larger street food markets of Copenhagen but with the same sense of choice and accessibility. About a dozen stall holders have set up in the high-roofed surroundings of the former Elsinore Shipyard—bits of boat and netting hang from the ceiling to add to the maritime feel. It's a great place to go for an easy and budget-friendly meal and a drink, and options include, but are not limited to, Argentinian steak sandwiches, tandooris, ramen, and gastro-burgers—or you could stick with the shipyard theme and grab a portion of fish and chips.

## Kronborg Havbad

*Strandpromenaden 6; tel. 49 20 20 45; www.kronborg-havbad.dk; daily (from May 1) noon-8:30pm, off peak Thurs.-Sun. noon-8pm; entrées from 105kr*

This is a traditional restaurant in a soulful quayside building close to the harbor and castle area, with seafood and *smørrebrød* a menu cornerstone. A hearty lunch buffet is available.

## Kadetten

*Kronborg 10A; tel. 42 90 10 11; https:// kadetten.dk; daily 10am-5pm; sandwich 95kr, brunch 150kr*

At a second lieutenants' training school just outside the castle (and within the outer entrance) in the Kronværksbyen barracks area, Kadetten is an organic café and socially responsible business, which harvests many of its ingredients from the gardens of military buildings. A particular source of pride to the café, which aims to provide jobs to people with special social needs, is its homemade rye bread made in the style of the rations given to cadets studying at the school in times past.

## ✪ Danhostel Helsingør

*Ndr. Strandvej 24; tel. 49 28 49 49; www. danhostelhelsingor.dk; shared room from 225kr, private room from 395kr*

Located by the sea with a beach at the end of the grounds, this extensive hostel is a preferred location of large school groups as well as independent and older travelers—so there may be noise at times. It's in spacious and welcoming surroundings with a large, main building and several out buildings. It's a short bicycle ride (which can be rented from the hostel) from Kronborg. Breakfast is available, and there is free coffee for guests.

## Marienlyst Strandhotel

*Ndr. Strandvej 2; tel. 49 21 40 00; www. marienlyst.dk; double occupancy in high season from 1,295kr*

This sprawling seaside hotel, just a stone's throw from Kronborg, has a range of room options including some with great sea views. It also has an onsite restaurant, brasserie, bar, casino, and spa.

# Tourist Information

Local tourism organization **Visit Nordsjælland** has a self-service tourist information center inside **The Culture Yard** (Allegade 2; tel. 49 28 36 20; https://kuto.dk; Mon.-Fri. 10am-9pm, Sat.-Sun. 10am-4pm), where information and brochures can be picked up for Kronborg, the Maritime Museum, and other events and attractions. Maps are also available, and free Wi-Fi and computer access is offered here.

# Getting There and Around

## GETTING THERE
### BY PUBLIC TRANSIT

Direct trains leave from Copenhagen Central Station to Hesingør Station (Stationspladsen 2, Helsingør) three times per hour during the day and cost 108 kroner for a standard adult single ticket, or a significantly less expensive 65kr with the Rejsekort. The journey takes 50 minutes, and Helsingør Station is an easy 10- to 15-minute walk from both the historical part of Helsingør and from Kronborg. Check dsb.dk or rejseplanen.dk for departure times. The Rejsekort travel card can be used to pay for the journey, provided you have enough credit. Replacement buses sometimes take over services on weekends, which result in longer and more crowded journeys. If replacement buses are operating, you will be diverted to them directly from train departure points.

### BY CAR

From central Copenhagen, drive north or west and then head north and east on Falkoner Allé/Jagtvej until you reach Lyngbyvej (Route 19). From here, continue north until you are outside of Copenhagen, at which point it will be possible to follow signs all the way to Helsingør by staying on the same route, which merges with the E47 motorway. As you reach Helsingør, follow Kongevejen into town, staying right to continue onto Jernbanevej. This will take you to the old town and harbor area, where you will be able to park close to the attraction. The journey is approximately 50km (30 mi) and should take around 40 minutes.

## GETTING AROUND

Kronborg, the Maritime Museum, Helsingør Old Town, and Helsingør Station are all within a 10-15 minute walk from each other. To get to the Danish Museum of Science and Technology, take bus 802 from the station directly to the museum, which has its own bus stop (standard fare 24kr, 22 minutes). You can also walk there by heading away from the castle, past the station, and toward the outskirts of town on Kongevej for around 3.5km (2 mi) until you meet a large roundabout with the O3 circular road. Take the first road on the right here, then the second left on to Fabriksvej: the museum is around 500 meters (1,640 ft) ahead on the left hand side. It will take around an hour to walk.

# ROSKILDE

**Only 20 minutes from** Copenhagen, Viking capital Roskilde can lay claim to being the most historically significant city in Denmark. This is embodied by the town's two major attractions: the Viking Ship Museum, where an impressive set of preserved longboats overlooks the Roskilde Fjord; and the towering Roskilde Cathedral, with royal tombs that span centuries testament to the longevity of Denmark's royal family.

The town sits at the southern point of the Roskilde Fjord, a 41-km-long (25 mi) waterway that

# HIGHLIGHTS

✪ **VIKING SHIP MUSEUM:** Five Viking longboats were recovered from the waters of the Roskilde fjord and were painstakingly restored. They are the centerpieces around which the story of Viking Scandinavia is told at this museum (page 203).

✪ **ROSKILDE CATHEDRAL:** This brick Gothic church, the final resting place for centuries of Denmark's monarchs, exudes authority over the city's skyline (page 204).

✪ **ROSKILDE FESTIVAL:** Attend this annual music festival, the largest of its kind in northern Europe, for the big headliners, all-hours parties, and an all-around head-spinning experience (page 208).

is an offshoot of the larger Isefjord—the neighboring fjords turning a large part of the map of Zealand blue. The low waters are intrinsically connected to the Viking past, and the discovery of the ancient longboats, which are meticulously preserved and displayed at the ship museum. The fjord has a peaceful air: motorized boats are not allowed due to its status as a nature reserve. The flat, reedy banks and calm shores allow you to look far into the distance on a clear day.

Back in town, Roskilde has nothing of the airs and graces you might expect for a city boasting an enormous cathedral, dozens of buried monarchs, and the title of former capital. It's small enough to visit all the major sights in one day with time to spare, and it is uncomplicated and rewarding. The central shopping streets are a little tired and generic looking, but you'll probably be too busy looking at the cathedral to notice.

If you're here around the beginning of July, expect the downtown area to resemble a Scandinavian Mad Max, as the Roskilde Festival, northern Europe's largest music festival, rolls into town. If you don't have a ticket yourself, it might not be the best time to come. If you decide to brave it, be prepared for a messy city center.

## ORIENTATION

Roskilde Station is located to the south of the city center. The town is compact, and bearing north from the station will inevitably take you to, or very close to, Roskilde Cathedral and the City Park (Byparken) on your way to the fjord. From the station, cross the Hestetorvet square and walk along the narrow Store Gråbrødrestræde and Lille Gråbrødrestræde, or take the more direct Hersegade north from the station to arrive at Algade, a pedestrian high street that runs east-west across the city center. At the western end is Stændertorvet, a large market square with the very noticeable spires of Roskilde Cathedral rising at the northern edge. Directly north of the cathedral, the sloping Byparken, which has tree-sheltered paths and open grassy areas, leads down to the fjord. Roskilde Harbor and the Viking Ship Museum are located on

# Roskilde

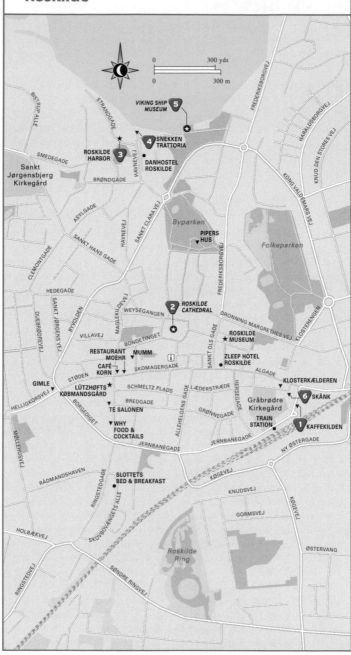

0 — 300 yds
0 — 300 m

VIKING SHIP MUSEUM **5**

FREDERIKSBORGVEJ

BISTRUP ALLÉ

STRANDGADE

HARALDSBORGVEJ

KNUD DEN STORES VEJ

SMEDEGADE

**4** SNEKKEN TRATTORIA

ROSKILDE HARBOR **3**

HAVNEVEJ

DANHOSTEL ROSKILDE

KONG VALDEMARS VEJ

Sankt Jørgensbjerg Kirkegård

BRØNDGADE

ASYLGADE

SANKT CLARA VEJ

Byparken

PIPERS HUS

HAVNEVEJ

SANKT HANS GADE

Folkeparken

CLEMONTGADE

HEDEGADE

FREDERIKSBORGVEJ

SANKT JØRGENS VEJ

BYVOLDEN

MAGLEKILDEVEJ

WEYSEGANGEN

**2** ROSKILDE CATHEDRAL

DRONNING MARGRETHES VEJ

KLOSTERENGEN

DUEBRØDREVEJ

VILLAVEJ

BONDETINGET

ROSKILDE MUSEUM

SANKT OLS GADE

RESTAURANT MOEHR

MUMM

ZLEEP HOTEL ROSKILDE

CAFÉ KORN

SKOMAGERGADE

i

ALGADE

KLOSTERKÆLDEREN

GIMLE

STØDEN

LÆDERSTRÆDE

HERSEGADE

**6** SKÄNK

LÜTZHØFTS KØBMANDSGÅRD

SCHMELTZ PLADS

Gråbrødre Kirkegård

HELLIGKORSVEJ

BORGEDIGET

BREDGADE

ALLEHELGENS GADE

GRØNNEGADE

TE SALONEN

TRAIN STATION

**1** KAFFEKILDEN

MØLLEHUSVEJ

WHY FOOD & COCKTAILS

JERNBANEGADE

JERNBANEGADE

NY ØSTERGADE

RÅDMANDSHAVEN

RINGSTEDGADE

SLOTTETS BED & BREAKFAST

KØGEVEJ

KNUDSVEJ

KØGEVEJ

HOLBÆKVEJ

SKOVBØVÆNGETS ALLÉ

GORMSVEJ

RINGSTEDVEJ

SØNDRE RINGVEJ

Roskilde Ring

ØSTERVANG

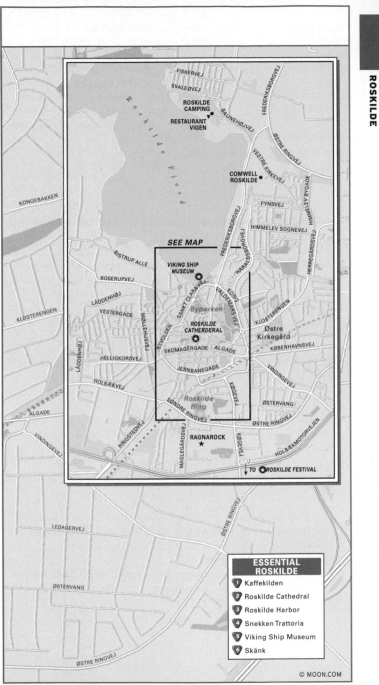

ESSENTIAL
ROSKILDE

1 Kaffekilden
2 Roskilde Cathedral
3 Roskilde Harbor
4 Snekken Trattoria
5 Viking Ship Museum
6 Skänk

© MOON.COM

the southern shore of the fjord, at the edge of the town. It's less than 2km (1.2 mi) and about a 20-minute walk from the station to the museum.

## PLANNING YOUR TIME

It makes sense to spend a full day in Roskilde, split between a half-day at the Viking Ship Museum and the harbor area and half in the city, with around two hours devoted to the cathedral. This allows time to spare to see other peripheral sights. Traveling times from Copenhagen are very short, making a visit easy to plan. Overnight stays are not essential if you have accommodation back in the capital.

# Itinerary Idea

## ESSENTIAL ROSKILDE

Did the Vikings really have undercuts and tattoos? Was Harald Bluetooth, king of Denmark and Norway, really buried at Roskilde Cathedral? Find out on a day trip to Denmark's Viking capital.

**1** After arriving on an early train from Copenhagen, stop into **Kaffekilden** for a coffee and bread roll.

**2** Head first to the **Roskilde Cathedral**, an UNESCO World Heritage Site that is almost impossible to miss as you wander through the city, given its sheer size relative to everything else around it.

**3** After an hour or two of touring the crypts, nooks, and crannies of the cathedral, head to **Roskilde Harbor** for a brisk stroll and great views of the Roskilde Fjord.

**4** For lunch, pop into **Snekken Trattoria** by the harbor. Sit outside if the weather is nice.

**5** Spend the afternoon at the **Viking Ship Museum,** the second most-important site on a trip to Roskilde. If you're there during the summer, book ahead for a tour of the fjord in a replica of a Viking longboat.

**6** Unwind with a beer and a cheese and charcuterie board at **Skänk** before hopping on a train back to Copenhagen.

# Sights

## ✪ VIKING SHIP MUSEUM

*Vindeboder 12; tel. 46 30 02 00; www.*
*vikingeskibsmuseet.dk; daily 10am-5pm;*
*adults 90kr or 130kr depending on season,*
*under 17 free*

In 1962, the remains of five Viking longboats were discovered in a channel at the bottom of Roskilde Fjord. The discovery was hugely significant for study of the seafaring ways of the Vikings, a warrior-farmer people of the era which is defined as lasting from approximately 800-1000 CE. The ships were found together because they had been deliberately sunk to block the channel as part of a defense strategy carried out by Roskilde's Viking-era inhabitants.

The discovery led to a painstaking recovery and preservation process that took decades and resulted in the opening of the Viking Ship Museum in the 1990s. The boats are displayed together in a large exhibition room built over the shoreline, on the beach next to Roskilde's Harbor. You can stand by the glass façade and watch the waters lap the shore beneath your feet as you pause next to the reconstructed longboats, allowing you to get close enough to see the detail in the Viking shipwrights' craftsmanship. The boats vary in size and type, related to their different purposes—one is a warship, one a market transportation ship, one a fishing boat, and so forth. Ranging in length from 3.8 to 17.3 meters (12.5 to 57 ft), the boats look skeletal—their surviving pieces have been recovered, restored, and rebuilt like jigsaw pieces

replica of an ancient boat at the Viking Ship Museum

into their exact original positions in the hulls of the five longboats. Metal framework completes the outline of the vessels, so their full shapes can be appreciated where pieces of the wooden structures have been lost to the centuries spent underwater.

The museum has plenty more to offer than the boats themselves. The basement has a large space for rotating displays, while there are also permanent exhibitions setting out the history, trade, seafaring practices, and culture of the Vikings. Visitors can try on Viking period costume, and there is a small activity area for kids.

Free, guided tours of the museum are offered daily during the summer and occasionally at other times of the year, such as during the school year and Christmas holidays. Conducted by history and archaeology students, the 45-minute tours, which can't be booked in advance, detail the life and use of the ships and what their discovery tells us about Viking maritime culture. Call ahead or check at the museum's information desk for the tour schedule on the day of your visit. A 15-minute film on the discovery of the ships is also shown at regular intervals in English, German, and Danish in the museum's small cinema.

In the outdoor area of the museum, there are various events spread through the summer and holiday seasons, including boatbuilding, blacksmithing, and sailmaking, in which visitors can participate—details of these are published on the museum website in advance, so check what's on during your visit. From May to September, there are daily **boat trips** to the fjord, onboard full replicas of the museum's ships (additional price from 110kr per person, reservations necessary).

## ✪ ROSKILDE CATHEDRAL

*Domkirkepladsen 3; tel. 46 35 16 24; www. roskildedomkirke.dk; June-Aug. Mon.-Sat. 10am-6pm, Sun. 1pm-4pm, Oct.-Apr. Mon.-Sat. 10-am-4pm, Sun. 1pm-4pm, May & Sept. Mon.-Sat. 10am-5pm, Sun. 1pm-4pm; adults 60kr, students & seniors 40kr, under18 free*

Roskilde Cathedral's three spires, Gothic bricks, and collection of chapels are of huge importance to the city. Surrounded by quiet, cobbled streets and historic houses, the cathedral is fronted by a square that just about gives you enough space to see all of the outside of the building in one photo frame. But it's only from the inside—walking through the various crypts, vaults, and staircases, coming face to face with the sarcophagi of Denmark's monarchic past—that the importance of the cathedral really becomes apparent.

A church was first built at the location by Harald Bluetooth, a former king of Denmark and Norway who died around 985 CE. Harald was, according to medieval chronicler Adam

Roskilde Cathedral

sarcophagus of Queen Margrethe I in Roskilde Cathedral

of Bremen, "buried in the town of Roskilde, in the church he himself built to the honor of the Holy Trinity." No traces of Harold's wooden church have ever been found. The structure that still stands today was begun in the 1170s, shortly after the advent of brickmaking in Denmark. Although the body of the building was completed around a century later, chapels and extensions have been added on several occasions throughout the years, giving an array of styles within, incuding neoclassical, Romanesque, and Byzantine.

The cathedral has been the main burial site for Danish monarchs since the 15th century, which makes walking through the crypts and chapels a history lesson in itself, given the tidbits of information about the monarchs that are on display throughout (in both Danish and English) and the evolving styles of the coffins. Look out for the statues at Christian IX's sarcophagus, which are known as "The Little Mermaid's Sisters"—they were sculpted by the same artist, Edvard Eriksen.

There is plenty more to see and admire: the nave and chapel have their own stories to tell, while there is a museum high up within the first floor galleries. Here, the cathedral's history over its 1,000-year lifespan is told through items from a copy of Queen Margrethe I's golden dress to photographs of the devastating 1968 fire that destroyed one of the spires. Most of the information here is in Danish. There is also a scale model of the cathedral from 1730, almost exactly reproducing the church as it was at the time.

Be sure to look up before leaving: above the right side of the entrance you'll see the mechanical clock from around 1500, which is responsible for the hourly chiming of the cathedral bells.

The cathedral has regular opening hours, but do check its website or by calling to make sure it's open before setting out: it is a parish church still used for services and religious ceremonies and can sometimes be closed to visitors.

## ROSKILDE MUSEUM

*Sankt Ols Stræde 3; tel. 46 31 65 29; www. roskildemuseum.dk; Tues.-Sun. 10am-4pm (Wed. until 9pm); adults 50kr, under 18 free*

Roskilde's city museum is in the center of town in two adjoining, listed buildings, a former sugar refinery and a former merchant's house. In the museum, the history of the town is presented. This takes in its golden age as a center of religion and learning, a subsequent fall from grace after the bishopric was moved to Copenhagen, and the 20th century history of Roskilde and today's status as a market town near the capital. Archaeological objects and newer exhibits tell the story, organized across three floors with a natural history section on the ground floor, a Middle Ages section in the middle, and a modern look at of Roskilde on the top floor. There is also a section for children as well as rotating exhibitions, such as a "sneak peak" into archaeological findings from a nearby Iron Age site. Information is provided in Danish and English.

## LÜTZHØFTS KØBMANDSGÅRD

*Ringstedgade 6-8; tel. 46 35 00 61; lützhøftskøbmandsgård.dk; Thurs.-Fri. 11am-5pm, Sat. 10am-5pm; free*

A cross between a museum and a shop, this old-fashioned *købmand* (grocery store) has all sorts of delights on display, from yo-yos and liquorice to shoe brushes and watering cans. The wares are packed into the little shops, and friendly attendants are happy to tell the stories behind the nostalgic items. Some of the replica goods can be purchased as souvenirs and are packaged in paper in 1920s style. Be sure to take a look in the yard behind the

Lützhøfts Købmandsgård grocery store/museum

store, which is an extension to the museum where you can see a collection of crafts from the hands of carpenters, furniture makers, wood sculptors, and clog makers. You can also find refreshments and something sweet in the quaint Te Salonen (Tea Salon) next door (Mon.-Fri. 10am-6pm; Sat. 10am-3pm).

## ROSKILDE HARBOR

*Strandgade 2; www.roskildehavn.dk; free*

Next to the Viking Ship Museum, the small, pleasant harbor area is a popular place for locals to take a walk while stopping for an ice cream or hot dog from the small kiosk. There are plenty of benches to take a rest and enjoy the view of Roskilde Fjord, a 40km-long (25 mi) protected body of water that's home to a variety of bird and plant life. The Snekken Trattoria restaurant and Café Knarr are nearby, if you're feeling hungry. A nice way to head back to the city center is via Kirkegade, a picturesque street with thatched cottages.

## RAGNAROCK

*Rabalderstræde 16; tel. 46 31 68 54; http:// museumragnarock.dk; Tues. 10am-5pm, Wed. 10am-10pm, Thurs.-Sun. 10am-5pm; adults 95kr, under 18 free*

A golden, inverted L-shaped building that looks like it should be the home of some megalomaniac glam rocker, Ragnarock is an ode to all things musical, adding a splash of variety to the primarily nautical, religious, and historical themes of most visits to Roskilde (unless you're here for the Roskilde Festival, in which case music will of course be the order of the day).

The interactive exhibitions take visitors on a trip through the history of modern youth culture, with themes of fan culture, the emergence of different genres, and the relationship between music and dance. You can spin turntables to hear how gramophones work and sample historical music through dozens of headphones attached to a wall. There's even an exhibit that tries to demonstrate what an acid trip looks like. There are many references to Danish music history, but the spirit of the museum will resonate with music lovers from anywhere. A good portion of the information is available in English.

# Sports and Recreation

## PARKS
### Byparken

*Byparken; free*

Byparken stretches downhill between the cathedral and the harbor. It makes for a pleasant outing, regardless of season: there are great views of the fjord to be found among the ponds, treelined paths, and moments of contemplation amid the trickling sound of the streams that run through it. A thatched cottage, Pipers Hus (http://pipershus.dk; tel. 46 36 56 96; daily 10am-10pm), serves food throughout the day, and nearby is a large, grassy slope that is occasionally used for free summer concerts as well as Skt. Hans celebrations.

# Festivals and Events

## ✪ ROSKILDE FESTIVAL

*Darupvej 19; tel. 46 36 66 13; www.
roskilde-festival.dk; last week in June/first
week in July; tickets 2100kr full festival pass
excl. fees; day pass 1050kr excl. fees*

For thousands of young Danes, the Roskilde Festival (commonly referred to simply as "Roskilde") is as much a rite of passage as school leavers' parties and moving out of parents' homes for the first time. Its significance goes beyond that though, with the live music festival attended by people of every generation and Danish artists' careers often taking off after an appearance at the summer event.

The non-profit live music event has around 32,000 volunteers who report for duty each year in return for festival passes. Their work helps to turn the festival area, located in farmers' fields to the south of Roskilde proper, into a temporary city with a population of 120,000—complete with its own rail station, unofficial post office, and expanses of tents visible from the highway. The huge camping area is organized into different suburbs with different subcultures: quiet and clean, full-on partying, and themes. The main musical program is arranged over four days from Wednesday to Saturday, but the camping area is open for an entire week, and early arrivers rush for prime tent locations—a ritual known as "breaking down the fence."

Unpredictable summer weather can wildly change the overall experience from one year to the next (or from one day to the next). In 2017, relentless rain turned the area into a soggy mess. A year later, a week of glorious sunshine left the festival zone looking more like Arizona than Zealand. Regardless of rainfall and temperature, the "orange feeling"—a sense of freedom and openness felt by those camping at the festival, named after the main stage, the Orange Stage—is one of Roskilde's strongest connotations.

### Music

It is actually possible to forget that the primary reason to go to Roskilde is to see live music, and rumors abound of people who never manage to leave the party scenes around the campsites. To do so would be a mistake, however, because as many as 175 acts played on eight stages in 2018, including headliners Nick Cave & the Bad Seeds, Eminem, Bruno Mars, and Gorillaz. Paul McCartney played the Orange Stage (the main stage) in 2015, as did Prince in 2010. Bob Dylan appeared on several occasions during the 1990s and 2000s. There is also plenty of concert time devoted to Danish and Scandinavian acts, so you can discover new music, too.

### Camping

There are several camping options for festival guests, so depending on the amount of background noise you can put up with and the level of sleep and comfort you prefer (although these will never reach the levels of a real bed, particularly by the end of the week), you can purchase add-ons to your festival ticket, which includes the basic camping pass. These camping products are announced early in the year via the website.

Roskilde Festival

### Information and Services

Tickets usually sell out some time before the festival, and one-day options are available, so be sure to monitor the Roskilde Festival website well in advance. The latter normally go on sale in the early part of the year once the line-up, or the main part of it, has been announced. There is also a monthly payment option available through the Roskilde website.

Parking is available at the site, but given its close proximity to Copenhagen it is often easier to arrive via train to Roskilde, then a shuttle bus or special rail service will take you on to the festival area. Roskilde city takes on a markedly different look during the week, as bleary-eyed campers shuttle to and from town to stock up on supplies, bringing the unmistakable festival spirit with them.

# Dining

## DANISH AND NEW NORDIC
### Restaurant Moehr

*Skomagergade 40; tel. 31 73 44 00; http://
moehr.dk; Mon.-Thurs. 10am-11pm, Fri.-Sat.
10am-midnight; smørrebrød from 75kr-95kr,
lunch set menu 275kr, mains & small
dishes from 110kr-135kr, set evening menus
395kr-595kr excl. wine*

In the center of town on the pedestrian shopping drag Skomagergade, Restaurant Moehr has a smart, simple interior and serves well-rated New-Nordic-style dishes and *smørrebrød*. Primarily local ingredients are paired with imported extras such as French chocolate, Spanish ham, or English cheese. Evening guests can combine dishes, which might include (but are not limited to) mussels, scallops, caviar, lobster cream, tenderloin steak, and parsley purée.

## Mumm

*Karen Olsdatters Stræde 9; tel. 46 37 22 01; www.mummroskilde.com; Mon.-Sat. 5:30pm-midnight; 135kr per dish, 4-6 dishes recommended; set menus including wine 785kr-1225kr*

Mumm, tucked away on a quiet side street, serves French and New-Nordic-inspired gourmet food that belies its modest setting. The intricately presented small dishes include salted hake, cauliflower and seafood broth, broccoli with roasted seeds, and mushrooms with mushroom cream, to name a few. These are made with fresh and organic ingredients and seasoned with homegrown herbs in the style favored by leading Danish Michelin-starred restaurants such as Noma. Call ahead to reserve.

## Restaurant Vigen

*Baunehøjvej 5; tel. 46 75 50 08; www.vigen. dk; summer Tues.-Sun. noon-10pm, winter Thurs.-Sun. noon-10pm, kitchen closes 6pm; small dishes from 125kr-150kr, approx. three dishes are equivalent to a main course, small/large evening set menu 550kr/750kr, lunch set menu from 215kr*

Located a few kilometers (about 1.5 mi) north of the city center next to the Roskilde campground, with a nice view of the fjord, Vigen was originally built in the 1930s as a restaurant and dance hall. Its lunch and evening menus are based on locally sourced ingredients and salmon, scallops, halibut, beef tartare, and lobster-based dishes. Call ahead to book.

## Pipers Hus

*Frederiksborgvej 21; tel. 46 36 56 96; http:// pipershus.dk; Mon.-Sat. 10am-10pm, Sun. 10am-5pm; brunch 95kr, salads 105kr,*
*smørrebrød from 62kr, lunch platter 170kr; evening mains 180-255kr*

Housed in a picturesque, thatched cottage in the park (Byparken) with views of the fjord and the cathedral in close proximity, Pipers Hus offers traditional Danish fare for both visitors and locals. The lunch platter includes herring, fish fillet, roast beef with relish, pickled red onions, brie, and rye bread, combining many popular *smørrebrød* elements. In the evening (from 5pm-9pm), the menu switches to à la carte dishes. These include wienerschnitzel, veal brisket with estragon sauce, or steak with potatos and red wine gravy; on Mondays and Sundays a casserole is served with the ingredients of the season. There's seating inside the house and on the terrace, and views of the fjord can be had from both.

# INTERNATIONAL
## WHY Food and Cocktails

*Ringstedgade 28B; tel. 88 34 19 00; www. whyfac.com; Tues.-Thurs. noon-9pm, Fri.-Sat. noon-9:30pm, Sun. 5pm-9pm; dishes from 45kr-140kr, 2-4 dishes constitute main meal, cocktails 85kr*

A Vietnamese fusion restaurant that also serves up specialty cocktails, WHY opened in 2015 and can be found in a quiet yard accessed by a cobbled sidewalk from the main street.

## Snekken Trattoria

*Vindeboder 16; tel. 46 35 98 16; http://snekken-trattoria.dk; Mon.-Fri. 11:30am-10pm, Sat.-Sun. 10am-10pm; weekend brunch buffet 169kr, pizzas/mains 129kr-365kr*

Conveniently located between the Viking Ship Museum and the harbor, this Italian restaurant serves pizzas and pasta along with vegetarian and larger mains and has a good range of Italian wines. There is ample seating inside and the outside section looks out over the fjord.

## CAFÉS AND LIGHT BITES
### Kaffekilden

*Hestetorvet 7; tel. 32 14 60 30; www. kaffekilden.net; Mon.-Fri. 7:30am-9pm, Sat. 9am-9pm, Sun. 10am-7pm; coffee from 22kr, cake from 30kr*

A rustic, cozy-chaired, brick-and-woodwork coffee bar by the station, Kaffekilden is an ideal place to get a caffeine fix if you are arriving after the short train journey from Copenhagen. Cheesecakes, brownies, croissants, and bread and butter rolls are all available to complement your brew.

### Te Salonen

*Ringstedgade 6a; tel. 26 72 22 90; https:// tesalonen-roskilde.dk; Mon.-Fri. 10am-6pm, Sat. 9am-9pm, Sun. 10am-3pm; sandwiches from 89kr, afternoon tea for two 250kr*

Nextdoor to Lützhofts Købmandsgård, you can continue the old-fashioned theme with the quaint Te Salonen, which has an old silver samovar on the counter, 70 types of tea, and delicate antique furniture. Hourglasses ensure

your tea is brewed for just the right amount of time. Tapas and sandwiches are available, but you can also keep things light with afternoon tea for two including a pot of your selection with scones and lemon curd, cakes, and mini cucumber sandwiches.

### Café Korn

*Skomagergade 42-44; tel. 35 12 40 00; https://cafekorn.dk; daily 10am-10pm; evening mains 129kr-239kr, brunches 129kr, light morning snacks 29-39kr, lunch burgers, salads, & sandwiches 129kr-139kr*

Café Korn has spacious seating around a semi-open kitchen area with further seating in "The Stable" in back. There's no shortage of space, and during the warmer season the seating spills on to the street in front of the entrance. The menu includes a range of burgers, sandwiches, salads, and lighter, open-topped sandwiches with meatballs, potatoes, or simply cheese and marmalade (burger orders come with a free refill on fries, if you ask nicely). Tapas platters and steaks are added to the menu in the evening. Service is friendly and informal.

# Bars and Nightlife

## LIVE MUSIC
### Gimle

*Helligkorsvej 2; tel. 46 37 19 82; www.gimle. dk; Tues.-Thurs. noon-midnight, Fri.-Sat. noon-3am, Sun. noon-5pm; see program for ticket prices, some concerts free*

In a low brick building that once housed the city's waterworks, Gimle is a "regional concert venue,"

meaning it receives state support to help develop musical talent. It stages regular concerts and has a bar that opens every day and until late on weekends. Partly volunteer-run, there are two concert rooms that host a broad range of acts and genres. Check upcoming concerts and events on the website: entry is often free.

the name: *klosterkælderen* translates literally to "the monastery cellar."

## BARS

### Klosterkælderen

*Store Gråbrødrestræde 23; tel. 31171114; www.klosterkaelderen.beer; Mon.-Thurs. 2pm-midnight, Fri. noon-2am, Sat. 10am-2am*

As an intimate bar near the station, Klosterkælderen has a great range of 15 craft beers on tap and up to 200 bottled varieties. The on-tap range is rotated regularly, and there are plenty of samples of akvavit schnapps to try—a stingingly sharp Danish spirit. The stone walls reflect

### Skänk

*Hestetorvet 10A; tel. 32 14 32 04; http://4000.skaenk.dk; Mon.-Thurs. 2pm-11pm, Fri.-Sat. 11am-2am*

Skänk is a modern-style wine and beer bar in a room adorned by wooden furniture, barrels, and beams. With eight Danish-brewed craft beers on tap and winetasting from 150kr, it's a pleasant place to while away an afternoon or evening. There's also cheese and charcuterie available, should you want some nibbles with your drinks.

# Accommodations

## UNDER 500KR

### Danhostel Roskilde

*Vindeboder 7; tel. 46 35 21 84; www.danhostelroskilde.dk; shared room from 250kr, private room from 575kr high season, linen rental 50kr; 40 rooms*

Roskilde's Danhostel is in the thick of the fjord action, perched between the harbor area and the Viking Ship Museum. There are pictures of kings on the walls and views of longboats from the windows. With a guest kitchen, laundry room, TV lounge, Wi-Fi, and parking available, the spacious and clean facilities are ample budget accommodation. Breakfast buffet is available.

## 500-1,000KR

### Slottets Bed & Breakfast

*Skovbovængets Alle 4; tel. 20 66 10 40; www.bedandbreakfastroskilde.dk; double occupancy in high season from 575kr; 2 rooms*

In a stately looking mansion built in 1915, this B&B consists of two spacious rooms with shared kitchenette and bathroom facilities. There is access to the quiet, well-kept gardens and a laundry service upon request. Breakfast (125kr) is not included in the basic price.

## 1,000-2,000KR

### Comwell Roskilde

*Vestre Kirkevej 12; tel. 46 32 31 31; www.comwellroskilde.dk; double occupancy in high season from 1,142kr; 159 rooms*

In the northern part of the city with views over Roskilde Fjord, in the "standard small view" room category, Comwell Roskilde is a modern conference-style hotel that was renovated as recently as 2016. Facilities include restaurant, gym, bar, and a game room with table football, darts, air hockey, and a Nintendo Wii, and the breakfast buffet is included.

### Zleep Hotel Roskilde

*Algade 13; tel. 70 23 56 35; www.zleephotels. com; double occupancy in high season from 1,440kr; 73 rooms*

Although it's part of a chain, Roskilde's Zleep Hotel has the appearance of a long-standing part of town and manages to retain an individual feel, owing to its location on the high street in an impressive historic building formerly occupied by another hotel (as evidenced by the façade). It's handsome on the inside, too, with a rococo-style interior. Breakfast (99kr per person) is not included in the basic price.

## CAMPING

### Roskilde Camping

*Baunehøjvej 7; tel. 46 75 79 96; https:// roskildecamping.dk; camping from 195kr, rooms from 400kr, cabins from 550kr*

Camping is located a few kilometers (about 1.8 mi) north of Roskilde city center and with great views over the fjord, so you might spot a passing Viking ship. Roskilde Camping can accommodate tents, caravans, and campers, while cabins are also available. Facilities include a play area for kids and a pier for bathing.

# Tourist Information

### Roskilde Tourist Bureau

*Stændertorvet 1; tel. 46 31 65 65; www. visitroskilde.dk; Mon.-Fri. 10am-5pm (until 4pm Oct.-Mar.), Sat. 10am-1pm*

The tourist bureau is easy to find on the large, central square Stændertorvet, and staff can provide you with all the relevant pointers for seeing the city. You can also pick up free brochures, city maps, and bicycling and hiking maps of the area, as well as purchase the Copenhagen Card (which includes the Viking Ship Museum, Roskilde Cathedral, Roskilde Museum, and Ragnarok).

# Getting There and Around

## GETTING THERE

### BY TRAIN

It is quick and straightforward to reach Roskilde from Copenhagen Central Station. Regional and some Intercity services stop at Roskilde, so there are up to six departures hourly during daytime hours. The journey takes 20-25 minutes, and a single ticket costs 84 kroner or 39 kroner if you are paying with Rejsekort. **Roskilde train station** is located at Jernbanegade 1.

### BY CAR

The easiest route by road is via the O2 ring road to the south of Copenhagen, exiting at national route 21, where signs will direct you to Roskilde.

# GETTING AROUND

## BY BUS

Local bus 203 from Roskilde Station takes you closest to the Viking Ship Museum: get off at the Strandengen (Frederiksborgvej) stop (8 minutes; 24 kroner standard fare, 15kr Rejsekort). Buy a ticket on board or use your Rejsekort. To the cathedral, bus 209 (Stændertorvet) takes you closest, but the journey only takes four minutes (24kr standard fare, 15kr Rejsekort): it might be easier to walk. Between the museum and the cathedral, take bus 204 (the stop closest to the Viking Ship Museum is Sankt Clara Vej (Frederiksborgvej) (3 minutes; 24kr standard, 15kr Rejsekort).

## ON FOOT AND BY BICYCLE

Roskilde is very much a walkable town, particularly if you are sticking to the cathedral and the Viking Ship Museum. The cathedral is a 10-minute walk from the station, mainly along the Algade pedestrian street; the walk from the museum to the fjord, where you'll find the harbor and the museum, takes around 15 minutes through the city park (Byparken).

The town is also comfortably accessible for bicycles, if a little more hilly than Copenhagen. You can bring a bicycle with you on the train from Copenhagen by purchasing the bicycle ticket upgrade at station machines (13 kroner per journey). Bicycles can be rented in Roskilde from Cykelkælderen (Hersegade 34A; tel. 46 32 12 13; Mon.-Fri. 8am-6pm, Sat. 10am-3pm; from 100kr per day).

# DRAGØR

## Dragør is at the southeastern tip

of Amager and is an intimate harbor town that can be reached via a bicycle trip or short bus ride from Copenhagen. A walk through the superbly preserved historical town center, with its windy, cobbled streets and single-story, 19th-century buildings painted in pastel oranges and yellows shows why much of Dragør is protected as a heritage area. There's a summer feel to the harbor, where ice cream stands, local history museums, and the crash of the waves against the dock make you want to sit still until the sun sets. A

# HIGHLIGHTS

✪ **DRAGØR'S OLD TOWN:** Go back in time with a wander around the cobbled alleys of this immaculately preserved old town (page 219).

✪ **AMAGER MUSEUM:** Learn about the local trade and history of Store Magleby at this quaint museum (page 221).

✪ **AMAGER NATURE PARK:** A wealth of outdoor life awaits at the enormous nature reserve area on the western half of Amager (page 222).

3,500-hectare (8,500 acre) nature reserve outside of town is a huge draw, literally and figuratively. This further enhances Dragør's charms, making it a great destination for a day trip from Copenhagen.

## ORIENTATION

Dragør is about 12km (7.5 mi) south of central Copenhagen on the far coast of the island of Amager, which itself is closely connected to Copenhagen by several bridges (much of Amager is part of Copenhagen's municipality). The main road leading into town from the rest of Amager, Kirkevej, terminates at the northwestern corner of the old quarter of this small, compact town, a couple of hundred meters from the harbor. The old town is demarcated by the streets of Kongevejen (which is a continuation of Kirkevej), Strandlinien, Rønne Alle, and Vestgrønningen. The old town itself, much of which is not accessible to vehicles (there's ample parking just outside it), is a windy maze of narrow alleyways and old-fashioned fisherman's houses, off which ivy hangs and the sun glimmers on late summer evenings. There's not much need for orientation in this small area—wander, get lost, and take it all in. You'll easily

find your way out again, even if you don't necessarily want to.

The harbor, old pilot's tower, and Dragør Museum are all directly to the east of the old town, and a flat, grassy area stretches out toward the old fort and a sandy, grassy stretch of beach to the south of the town.

Around 2.5km (1.5 mi) back west along Kirkevej, the village of Store Magleby is probably seen by most visitors before Dragør, as they travel through it to reach the coastal town. The tiny Store Magleby has a handful of streets, the most important being Hovedgaden (literally, "The Main Street"), which leads north from near the church to the Amager Museum at the edge of the town, close to the perimeter of Copenhagen Airport.

Directly west of Dragør, Amager Nature Park is a huge, wild area, taking up almost a quarter of the area of the island of Amager and stretching all the way to the city area in the north. It can be reached via Metro from Copenhagen and by bus, bicycle, and on foot from Dragør.

## PLANNING YOUR TRIP

The close proximity to Copenhagen and small size means that Dragør can be visited almost on a whim: you can

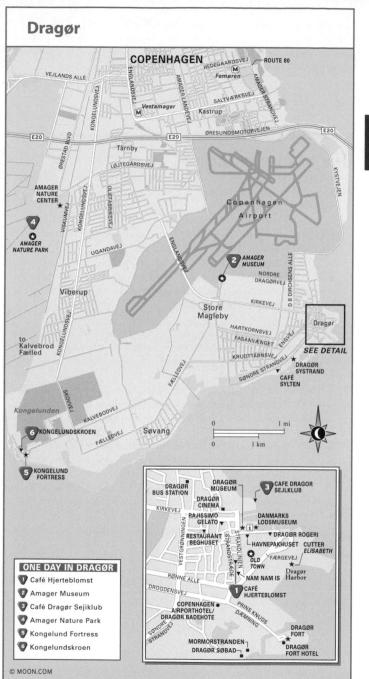

# Dragør

**COPENHAGEN**

VEJLANDS ALLÉ
HEDEGAARDSVEJ — ROUTE 80
Femøren
M
AMAGER STRANDVEJ
ENGLANDSVEJ
KONGELUNDSVEJ
AMAGER LANDEVEJ
SALTVÆRKSVEJ
E20
Vestamager
M
Kastrup
ØRESUNDSMOTORVEJEN
E20
E20
KYSTVEJEN
Tårnby
LØJTEGÅRDSVEJ

AMAGER
NATURE
CENTER

4
AMAGER
NATURE PARK

VISKUMVEJ
KONGELUNDSVEJ
OLIEFABRIKSVEJ

Copenhagen
Airport

UGANDAVEJ

2 AMAGER
MUSEUM

NORDRE
DRAGØRVEJ

Viberup

ENGLANDSVEJ

D B DIRCHSENS ALLE

KONGELUNDSVEJ

Store
Magleby

KIRKEVEJ

Dragør

to
Kalvebrod
Fælled

HARTKORNSVEJ
FASANVÆNGET
ENGVEJ

**SEE DETAIL**

SKOVVEJ

FÆLLEDVEJ

KRUDTTÅRNSVEJ

SØNDRE STRANDVEJ

DRAGØR
SYSTRAND
CAFÉ
SYLTEN

Kongelunden

KALVEBODVEJ

0          1 mi

6 KONGELUNDSKROEN

FÆLLEDVEJ

Søvang

0          1 km

5 KONGELUND
FORTRESS

---

**ONE DAY IN DRAGØR**

1 Café Hjerteblomst
2 Amager Museum
3 Café Dragør Sejiklub
4 Amager Nature Park
5 Kongelund Fortress
6 Kongelundskroen

---

**Detail map:**

DRAGØR
BUS STATION

DRAGØR
MUSEUM

3 CAFE DRAGOR
SEJLKLUB

KIRKEVEJ

DRAGØR
CINEMA

RAJISSIMO
GELATO

DANMARKS
LODSMUSEUM

i

DRAGØR ROGERI

VESTGRØNNINGEN

RESTAURANT
BEGHUSET

STRANDLINIEN
STRANDSTRÆDE

HAVNEPAKHUSET
CUTTER
ELISABETH

OLD
TOWN

FÆRGEVEJ

RØNNE ALLE

NAM NAM IS

Dragør
Harbor

DROGDENSVEJ

1 CAFÉ
HJERTEBLOMST

COPENHAGEN
AIRPORTHOTEL/
DRAGØR BADEHOTE

PRINS KNUDS
DÆMNING

SØNDRE
STRANDVEJ

DRAGØR
FORT

MORMORSTRANDEN
DRAGØR SØBAD

DRAGØR
FORT HOTEL

© MOON.COM

travel to the town, see the old town and harbor, and return within a day. If you want to explore the wilds of Amager Nature Park you will need to plan because of its size, but the park can be even easier to get to than Dragør—the Copenhagen Metro takes you almost to the gate.

# Itinerary Idea

## ONE DAY IN DRAGØR

Centuries-old fishing village Dragør is only a stone's throw from Copenhagen, but get your visit right and you'll feel like you've been to the opposite end of the country—in the nicest possible way.

**1** Start your day in **Dragør's old town** with a morning coffee and pastry at **Café Hjerteblomst**.

**2** After breakfast, walk about 2km (1.2 miles) west to the even smaller village of **Store Magleby**. Visit the **Amager Museum** to learn all about the village's quirky history and Dutch influence.

**3** Head back to Dragør for lunch at **Café Dragør Sejlklub**, where you can enjoy a view of the marina and the Øresund (including the Øresund Bridge) while savoring freshly delivered seafood.

**4** Rejuvenated by lunch, head to the **Kongelunden forest** in **Amager Nature Park** to spend the afternoon biking or walking through the beech and elm woods. Look out for birds (and planes) flying above you.

**5** In the late afternoon, visit the **Kongelund Fortress**, the site of a lookout built during the First World War. You can explore parts of the now-defunct facility, but the best thing to do here is to just sit and enjoy the coastal views.

**6** After all the walking you've done, you're probably famished. Visit **Kongelundskroen**, charmingly located in a traditional Danish *kro* (inn) at the end of the southwestern coastal road, for a hearty, three-course meal of Danish-French fusion food.

# Sights

## DRAGØR
### ✪ OLD TOWN

*Between Toldergade and Rønne Alle, Dragør*

When you wander around the tightly wound old alleys of Dragør's old quarter, life itself seems to stand still. The old town is one of the most well-preserved settlements in Denmark. Founded in the late 1600s and expanded in three periods around 1770, 1830, and 1890, giving a hotchpotch effect, a large number of the buildings and the original layout of the town remain much as they once were, even surviving serious fires in the mid-19th century.

The cluster of 18th- and 19th-century houses nestled in the cobbled alleyways between Kongevejen and Rønne Alle, with their characteristic clay-tiled roofs and mustard-colored walls, comprise the highest concentration of listed buildings in any small town in Denmark, with 76 in total along with a further 5 at the harbor. A good mix of homes and businesses make up the Old Town. In summer, calm descends over the streets in the evening. Clothes hang on lines and windows are opened to let in the evening light, small squares open up around narrow corners, and ivy grows on the walls.

**Guided tours** (info@dragoerturisme.dk; tel. 50 55 44 60) are available in the summer season (June-August), leaving from the tourist information office at the harbor (Strandlinien 2, 2791 Dragør). There are various themes: a classic tour of the

old town in Dragør

city, the escape to Sweden of Danish Jews during the Second World War, or stories of Dragør. Groups can be large or small, and price depends on the number of participants. Call ahead to inquire and make reservations—tours must be arranged in advance.

## DRAGØR MUSEUM

*Havnepladsen, Strandlinien 4; tel. 30 10 88 66; www.museumamager.dk/ udstillingssteder/dragoer-museum; opening hours to be confirmed in 2019; adults 40kr, under 18 free*

By the old harbor in one of the town's oldest houses, which dates from 1753, is Dragør Museum, The museum tells of the town's seafaring and fishing past, including a collection of objects brought home from the seven seas by Danish sailors. Although it's small, there are plenty of items to see, and there's very much a maritime feel with model ships and pictures of historical seafaring scenes. On the first floor, the contents of an entire living room, left to the museum by local woman Leise Schmidt after she died in 2015, give a glimpse into traditional life in the town. There's a touchscreen, which can be used to watch a recollection of Dragør in the 1980s and listen to the town's old-fashioned dialect. The museum underwent renovation in 2018.

## DANISH PILOTS' MUSEUM
## (Danmarks Lodsmuseum)

*Dragør Gl. Havn 11; tel. 30 10 88 66; www. museumamager.dk/udstillingssteder/ danmarks-lodsmuseum; Aug. 14-Sept. 30 Wed.-Sun. noon-4pm; adults 20kr, under 18 free*

Dragør, with its important vantage point looking across the Øresund, has had a pilots' station since 1684, when local mariners began helping vessels to navigate the strait. The Danish Pilots' Museum, a small attraction housed in the two stories of the former station (the current facility is elsewhere on the harbor), is easily located—it is right next to the 16-meter-high (52 ft) pilot's tower (which is not open to the public). The museum showcases everyday life in the pilot's station (in a 20th-century context, not a 17th-century one), with an old-fashioned office and communication equipment, charts, uniforms hanging from a hook on the wall, and lodgings with a small bed and a kitchenette left as it was the day the pilots moved to new facilities in 2006—although it feels as though it's from an earlier era.

## CUTTER ELISABETH

*Dragør Gl. Havn; tel. 30 10 88 66; www. museumamager.dk/udstillingssteder/ museumskutteren-elisabeth-k571; tours Tues.-Sun. noon and 1:15pm, last week in June up to and including first week in Aug.; 100kr*

The cutter *Elisabeth*, moored in Dragør harbor close to the Pilots' Museum, is famous for being part of a scraped-together fleet of private boats used by Danes to assist Jews fleeing Nazi persecution in October 1943. The boats were used to helped hundreds escape to neutral Sweden, with the *Elisabeth*'s skipper, Einar Larsen, helping up to 70 before fleeing himself. The *Elisabeth*, one of the few remaining vessels from the transport operation, was donated to the Amager Museum in 2007 and is now given a prominent place in the harbor.

A 30-foot fishing boat, the now-restored gleaming white *Elisabeth* can be experienced on sailing trips out into the Øresund. These last around one hour and take place only in suitable weather. There is room for 10 people on each tour, and tickets can be bought by the boat itself from around half an hour before departure (cash only).

## DRAGØR FORT

*Prins Knuds Dæmning 2, Dragør Gl. Havn*

Built in the early 20th century on an artificial island to the south of the harbor and connected by a short causeway, Dragør Fort rises like an anomalous green blob across a broad, flat area to the south of the harbor and old city. The 32,000-square-meter (344,000 sq ft) fort was built to protect the coast from hostile advances and was later used as a shooting range by the occupying Germans during the Second World War. The fort was purchased by a private owner in 2001 and converted to the Dragør Fort Hotel—public access is therefore limited, but it is possible to walk around some parts of the grassy fort area (but don't bring a picnic). There are several concrete relics from its previous military use dotted about, including a fire watchman's post and a cannon base; and there is a nice vantage point from which to view Dragør.

# STORE MAGLEBY

The village of Store Magleby, a short distance from Dragør, is also known as the "Dutch Village." There is little trace today of the Netherlands beyond appropriately flat landscape and the presence of Dutch names on some of the church's gravestones, but the settlement was in fact a Dutch colony of sorts from the time King Christian II invited familes from the Netherlands to live in the village in 1521, wanting to improve the quality and variety of vegetables on offer at the palace in Copenhagen. The Dutch farmers were allowed to take over existing farms and land and were given special privileges such as exemption from tax and

military conscription. It is not known to what extent this upset the natives or whether there were recriminations against the new Dutch farmers. Three centuries later, the use of Dutch in the village, by this time mixed with the local Danish and German spoken by priests, was finally phased out.

Despite major fires during the 17th-century wars with Sweden as well as in the 19th century, Store Magleby has retained its original village and road layout (in later years in much of Denmark, many farmers' houses were moved away from villages and closer to the land being worked). No buildings from the original Dutch period remain, but policies to protect the village in recent decades prevented it from expanding through modern developments on its outskirts, so it is possible to gain a sense of how it might once have looked. On Shrove Tuesday, Dutch traditions are upheld as riders gallop through the town on horseback, smashing barrels left out as targets.

## ✪ AMAGER MUSEUM

*Hovedgaden 4, Store Magleby; tel. 30 10 88 66; www.museumamager.dk; July and Aug. 14-Sept. 30 Wed.-Sun. noon-4pm; adults 40kr, under 18 free*

Two old farmyard buildings in Store Magleby are home to the Amager Museum, a collection of cultural relics that illustrate the unique character and culture of the rural area around Dragør, separated from the rest of Denmark by Copenhagen but with a different identity to the capital—not least due to the influx of Dutch farmers in the 16th century. There's a room dedicated to neighboring Dragør, with various items brought back by the town's seafarers: blue tiles from Holland and wooden engravings from England. Elsewhere, there are portraits by local artists and even a small exhibition on tulips, betraying the Dutch connection.

Several examples of Amager's traditional clothing are on display, which is another example of the Dutch culture in the village, since local dress is far less commonplace in Denmark than in the Netherlands or other Scandinavian countries. The clothing is characterized particularly by the wide, flat silk hat for the men, known as the *floshat*. The use of these hats persisted right up until the 1800s and their size even increased—whether this was out of habit or a pride in the Dutch ancestry is unclear. Women wore patterned skirts and blouses and hats that signified whether the wearer was married, a maiden, or in mourning.

The museum also includes an extensive garden, where root vegetables, cabbage, dahlia, and, in the spring, tulips grow.

While the museum is worth visiting any time its doors are open, July is when it really comes to life. Staff in period costume carry out the daily tasks of a preindustrial farm (visiting children are also invited to try old-fashioned outfits). Daily activities vary and can include digging up vegetables, repairing clothes, or weaving, and children are encouraged to learn about what's going on.

**TOP** EXPERIENCE

# ✪ AMAGER NATURE PARK

*Granatvej 3-15; tel. 32 46 10 53; www. naturcenteramager.dk; Mon.-Fri. 9am-3pm, Sat.-Sun. 9am-5pm; bus 33 Foldbyvej (Otto Bachés Alle), Metro Vestamager*

Amager Nature Park is a gigantic nature reserve covering most of the western half of Amager. It is made up of four distinct sections: Amager Fælled (see Copenhagen chapter), Kongelunden, Dragør Sydstrand, and Kalvebod Fælled. The latter is the largest of these, making up 2,000 hectares (4,942 acres) of the total 3,500 hectares (8,650 acres. The entire reserve boasts 25km (15 mi) of coastline, 300 different bird species, 450 types of plants, 20 sites for camping including shelters, and hundreds of cycling and hiking paths. With its vast expanses of moors, marshes, hillocks, ponds, canals, ditches, bird reserves, forests, paths, and shelters, there's enough to keep explorers and nature lovers enthralled for days. Remarkably, these wild, green landscapes are just a handful of Metro stations from the hustle of central Copenhagen; or a bus, hike, or bicycle trip away from Dragør (the park spans the municipalities of both). Lush in summer, it is also beautiful at other times of year, whether under a layer of snow or so rainy and windswept you'll be unable to resist channeling your inner Brontë.

There are a number of ways to access the park, the primary one being via Vestamager Metro station, which is a few minutes' walk from Amager Nature Center. The nature center is an excellent resource, with a café and a tourist information center, and you can borrow a bicycle to get around the park. It is also possible to enter the park at many other points around its perimeter through distinctive red wooden gates, should you want to visit a specific spot far from the nature center. From the inland (eastern) side of Kalvebod Fælled, bus number 33 tracks along the Kongevejen road between Dragør, northern Amager, and Copenhagen. From this road you can hop off the bus at a number of different stops and walk around 500 meters (1,640 feet) west to reach the perimeter of the reserve.

Kongelunden and Dragør Sydstrand are closer to the town of Dragør and easier for shorter visits of at least half a day (I recommend a full day for Kalvebod Fælled, more if you want to camp). They can be reached by bicycle or bus, or on foot if you have a little more time.

## AMAGER NATURE CENTER

*Granatvej 3-15; tel. 32 46 10 53; www.* *naturcenteramager.dk; Mon.-Fri. 9am-3pm, Sat.-Sun. 9am-5pm; bus 33 Foldbyvej (Otto Bachés Alle), Metro Vestamager*

I recommend Amager Nature Center as the starting point and base for exploring and wandering Amager Nature Park. It is close to public transportation connections, and there are parking options outside the gate to the reserve. The center comprises two main buildings, Friluftshuset and Traktørstedet.

At **Friluftshuset**, you can talk with friendly, khaki-clad guides at the tourist information desk, who can advise you on the various walking and cycling routes inside the reserve, shelters for camping (these can also be booked in advance by calling or emailing the center), wildlife to look out for, and which locations are particularly worth searching out at the time of your visit. Bicycles can be rented from the center for the outstandingly inexpensive price of 40 kroner per day, while cargo bikes (50kr per hour) and children's bikes (40kr per day) are also available. Equipment (and guidelines) for campfires and barbequing can also be purchased here.

Friluftshuset also facilitates various activities throughout the year, including short running races, one-hour guided tours (these usually take

Kalvebod Fælled, Amager Nature Park

place at 11am and 2pm on Saturdays and Sundays), obstacle course challenges and the use of picnic areas and sites where barbequing is permitted. Horsedrawn wagon tours (150kr per person), which take around an hour and a half, take place on some Saturdays during the summer. There is space for eight people on the wagons, and children under four can ride for free. Advance reservations should be made via friluftshuset@nst.dk.

**Traktørstedet** (tel. 22 55 32 65; http://traktoerstedetvestamager.dk; Tues.-Sun. 10am-5pm; coffee from 20kr, breakfast platter 95kr, cakes from 30kr, soup, salad 65kr, child's meal 55kr) is a welcoming café with wooden pillars, red-and-white checked tablecloths, and a great view of Kalvebod Fælled to give it a picni-clike feel. The organic menu is fairly extensive, including everything from a continental breakfast to burgers to a kids' meal of rye bread with sausage or vegetarian toppings and fruit. Returnable flasks of coffee and tea can be purchased to take with you onto the commons, as can beer, water, and soda.

To get to the Nature Center from Dragør, take bus 33 (standard fare 24kr; two buses per hour) to Foldbyvej (Otto Baches Allé). From Copenhagen, take the simple fourteen-minute Metro trip to nearby Vestamager station (24kr; frequent departures). It's around 8km (5 mi) from Dragør by bicycle. You can cycle out of town through Store Magleby on Kirkevej, which becomes Englandsvej/Route 221, and you should follow this for around 6km (3.7 mi) until you reach Løjtegårdsvej. Turn left here and continue for less than 2km (1.2 mi): you'll see the signs to the center.

## KALVEBOD FÆLLED

Until the end of the 1930s, the 2,000 hectare (4,942 acres) area that today is known as Kalvebod Fælled was under water. The low-water area was dried out by a dam that was built along what is now the coastline between 1939 and 1943. Rumor has it that the Danish government used the project to keep as many men as possible working, to prevent them being sent to the war industry by occupying Nazi Germany, although this has never been proved. A total of 2,480 hectares (6,128 acres) was reclaimed from the sea (also including part of what is now Amager Fælled to the north) and two pumping stations and a network of channels and ditches were built to dry out the area. These ditches can be seen today in what is now a huge nature reserve, an enticingly close distance from central Copenhagen. It includes an international bird sanctuary; Denmark's largest self-sown birch tree forest, pathways, hillocks, marshes and forests; purple butterflies, edible frogs, blue iris flowers, and herds of sheep and cows.

The **Bird Sanctuary**, in the southwest of the common, is off limits to visitors, but it can still be seen from the vantage point of a series of bird-watching towers on the coastal path that goes around the western edge of the sanctuary (along the dam structure that created it), as well as from a covered viewpoint for birdwatchers (which is a great place to spot kingfishers). This spot is just to the west of **Pinseskoven**, the largest self-sown birch forest in Denmark. The forest was created by seeds that were blown across the Øresund from Sweden in the years after the area was reclaimed. It's an ideal area for camping. The **Birkeholm** area can seem a bit noisy compared to the rest of the reserve—it is not far from a motorway—but is a lesser-visited, open-forested area with places to camp and fish. Svenskehøj and Villahøj were originally built by the military as lookouts during Kalvebod Fælled's time as an army exercise area (it was not completely opened to the public until the 1980s). Now, the two raised areas can be used to observe the park's drainage ditches and are also a good place to spot wading birds such as ruffs. If you've brought a picnic, this is a great spot to enjoy it. To reach this area and the nearby Pinseskoven, follow Granatvej in a straight line southwest from the Nature Center for just under 2km (1.2 mi). If you're looking for a viewpoint a little closer to the Nature Center, try Store Høj, around 750 meters (2,460 ft) west of the information center. This is an easily accessible area with shelters, a lake, and an area for making small bonfires. The top of the hill, with its outlook over the flat moors, is positively melodramatic on a windy day. Between here and the main entrance to the park, you'll find Himmelhøj, a 60-meter-long (197 ft) sculpture in the shape of the hull of a boat, or even an ark. With rocks and places to climb inside, it's a great natural playground for kids.

There are paths and tracks crisscrossing the entirety of Kalvebod Fælled, the Bird Sanctuary excepted, and they are clearly marked and suitable for both boots and bicycles. Four color-coded routes, ranging between 2.5 kilometers (1.5 mi) and 14 kilometers (9 mi) in length, are marked by signposts and can also be followed with a map available for free from Friluftshuset. There are several marked camping areas, as well as four sleeping shelters. These are basic wooden cabins with no amenities in which you can sleep with slightly better cover from the elements than in a tent. As with camping, the use of shelters is free and open year-round, but they must be reserved—contact the center before setting off.

## KONGELUNDEN

Kongelunden is primarily forest at the southern end of Amager and east of Kalvebod Fælled. The woods are shared between deciduous and coniferous areas. It is teeming with flowers, birds, and wild-growing fruits like blackthorn and apples. In the spring you can pick wild chives, and cherry plums can also be foraged. As you wander through the wood, look up to spot a nightingale or a wood warbler; there's also a good chance you'll see an aircraft coming in to land at Copenhagen Airport. Bicycle and walking-friendly paths, bonfire sites, picnic benches, and hundreds of oak and elm trees make this area ripe for outdoorsy fun.

There are three marked and color-coded routes through the forest, all between 2 and 3 km (1.2 and 1.8 mi), including the wheelchair-accessible Collin's Path, which ends in a great view out from the elm trees toward the marshland, the beach, and the sea. Many of the oak trees here are 150 years old, and Kroneegen (the Crown Oak) is 180 years old. It can be found at Collin's Stone, a memorial to Jonas Collin, the councilor who founded the forest in the early 1800s by persuading villagers in Store Magleby to plant trees on some of their land. Also to be found in this area is Knirkebøgen (the Creaking Beech), so-called because of its propensity to moan during high winds. To the north of the Collin's Path area a "tree landscape,"

Landskabstræet, is an area in which 52 different trees have been planted around a path layout that forms the shape of a tree when viewed from above.

In the middle of the forest, Collin's Path is crossed by the Kongelundsvej Road, which bisects Kongelunden. There is a car parking area here: look out for **Løvenskjolds Mindestøtte**, a rectangular monument to a royal hunt master who brought pheasants to the area. The hunt no longer exists, but pheasants still live in the forest. Parking is opposite the monument.

If you are traveling to Kongelunden using public transportation, take bus 33 (from either the bus station in Dragør or from City Hall Square in Copenhagen) and get off at Kongelunden (Skovvej) (standard fare 24kr from Dragør, 36kr from Copenhagen; two buses per hour, duration 40min from Copenhagen, 25 min from Dragør). You'll find yourself in the middle of the forest, a few meters from Collin's Path. You can bicycle here from Dragør in 30-40 minutes and walk in around an hour and a half: take Engvej out of town to the southwest, turn left on to Krudttårnsvej after around 2km (1.2 mi); follow this road for around 2.5km (1.5 mi) before turning left on to Fælledvej; take a right on to Kalvebodvej and then a final right turn on to Skovvej, which takes you into the forest. Alternatively, a path runs from Dragør along the coast through Dragør Sydstrand, and then travels through the forest before continuing to Kalvebod Fælled.

## KONGELUND FORTRESS
### (Kongelundsfortet)

*Kalvebodvej 265; tel. 29 47 67 55; www. befaestningen.dk/besog/kongelundsfort; daily 8am-8pm; free*

A military bunker built during World War I, the Kongelund Fortress is a hefty clump of concrete just south of Kongelunden. The fort, which has a great view of Køge Bay, is an interesting insight into a period when Denmark, like much of Europe, felt the need to protect itself from close neighbors. There's an old radar station, built in 1959, with rickety, metal steps and a lookout post among the Cold-War-looking distressed structure. It is free to walk around and has been renovated with play and barbeque areas, so you can bring along a picnic. There is no access to any of the buildings. There are often activities and events such as paddling, organized runs, and educational talks held by various organizers at the fort. These are often very cheap to take part in. The best place to keep abreast of what's going on is on the fort's Facebook page, www. facebook.com/kongelundsfortet.

To get to Kongelundsfortet, take bus 33 to Sydvestpynten (Kalvebodvej), from where it's a short walk. On foot or bicycle, follow the route as for Kongelunden, but instead of turning on to Skovvej, continue on Kalvebodvej until you reach the fort. Alternatively, follow the coastal path from Dragør to Kongelunden via Dragør Sydstrand—this path passes through the forest close to the fort.

## DRAGØR SYDSTRAND

The closest part of Amager Nature Park to Dragør, this marshy area runs along the south of Amager for around 6km (3.5 mi) and has a coastal path starting just outside Dragør that connects it to Kongelunden. It's replete with salty lagunas, grasses, ducks, and wading birds resting on the flats, and if you're lucky you might spot a seal in the bay or even on the beach. The

## SUMMER IN DRAGØR

Dragør's charm is present year-round, but there's no doubt the area really comes to life in the summer, when the ice cream shops stay open well into the light evenings and visitors come to take in the festive harbor atmosphere. The sounds of masts clinking and the Øresund lapping against the marina are but a few distractions. Some of the best things to do here in the summer include:

- Exploring the wilds of **Kalvebod Fælled**

- Enjoying an **ice cream** while sitting by the **harbor**

- Visiting the **Amager Museum** in **July** when the staff are gussied up in period costume (kids can also try on the old-fashioned outfits)

- Seeing all the bonfires stretching up and down the coast during **Sankthans** on June 23

- Celebrating **Havnefest** in August with the locals by the old port

terrain is sometimes sandy, sometimes grassy, and changes with the effect of coastal erosion. Its flatness makes it a popular spot for morning joggers, although the bracing winds can make even light exercise need a little more energy than usual. It's easy to reach from Dragør: just walk south of the harbor and fort to Batterivej and follow it toward the coast.

The sandy seabed and clean water are suitable for bathing, and the end of Batterivej is also where you will find **Dragør Søbad** and **Mormorstranden** (Grandmother's Beach). The former is a sea swimming facility accessed by a pier (Batterivej 15; tel. 32 89 04 50; http://www.hollaenderhallen.dk; adults 20kr, under 15 10kr). It is open from May to August. The beach, which is sandy with shallow waters and has a volleyball net, is child-friendly, and there's a jetty at its southern end if you want to jump into deeper water. Don't expect the water to warm you up.

# Entertainment and Events

## FESTIVALS
### Dragør Harbor Festival (Dragør Havnefest)
*Strandlinien; tel. 32 53 00 75; http://dragoerhavnefest.dk; Aug.; free*
This small, weekend-long local festival takes place during the summer (normally in mid-August, but this can vary) at Dragør Harbor. Its small size gives a real sense of community.

There's a raft of concerts, with Danish pop and folk artists, local hopefuls, children's entertainers, and covers bands. Kids can try pony rides or get their faces painted, and there are ice cream and food stands.

### Sankthans
*Dragør Harbor; July 23*
*Sankthans*, the Danish version of

Dragør Cinema

Midsummer, does not go unnoticed in Dragør. A bonfire is lit around 10pm on June 23 at the harbor, and there is usually entertainment in addition to the traditional speech and song. In 2018, festivities included a pop-up street food market and a live DJ and bar, despite the unusual event of the bonfire itself being cancelled due to exceptionally dry weather. But the highlight of spending *Sankthans* here is the view from the harborside or coast after the fire has been lit: bonfires can be seen stretching along the coast as well as in Sweden on the opposite side of the strait.

### Dragør Art Festival

*Badstuevælen, Dragør; www.facebook.com/ DragorKunstfestival; July; free*

Dragør's annual art festival weekend first took place in 2009 and is held at Badstuevælen, a square in the old town. More than 30 artists exhibited in the most recent Dragør art festival, with painting, sketching, stone and glass sculpture, photography and handcrafts on show and for sale. The art is exhibited outside under marquees to protect from the elements, and there's a relaxed weekend fair atmosphere.

## CINEMA

### Dragør Cinema

*Jan Timanns Plads 1; tel. 32 53 05 03; www. dragoerbio.dk; tickets 150kr*

The one-screen Dragør Cinema can be found in a quaint building facing a square adjacent to the old town and docks where it was established in 1928 in one of the few buildings in the town large enough to accommodate a big screen. The intimate theater can accommodate 143 guests and screens international box office hits and Danish films.

# Sports and Recreation

## CYCLING

There are no bike rental shops in the town of Dragør, but you can rent one at the Amager Nature Center for cycling in the nature reserve, and many hotels in the area offer bike rentals to guests. Or, you can always rent one in Copenhagen and cycle to Dragør—a trip that takes between 45 minutes to 2 hours, depending on your pace.

### Munkevejen Route 80

*www.munkevejen.dk*

Route 80 is a regional bicycling trail that takes you through almost the entirety of Amager, including some of its natural areas. Cycling the section that goes through Dragør and the wild areas of Amager Nature Park, including Kongelunden, is a great way to see the area.

The 38km (23.5 mi) route starts on the promenade by the Amager Strandpark beach close to the Femøren Metro station. Heading south, it connects to the coastal road, Amager Strandvej, and the cycle path guides you under and around major traffic junctions past the entrance to Copenhagen Airport onto Kystvejen, which follows the outer perimeter of the airport between its fences and the Øresund. This makes for quite a hair-raising and dramatic ride as you bicycle along a long, straight section

with the sea on one side and aircraft roaring in to land just overhead. If you can time it right, it's spectacular at dusk.

After rounding the airport, turn left onto Ndr. Strandvej and follow this road all the way into Dragør, skirting around the Old Town on Kongevejen and Vestgrønningen before continuing out of town on Sdr. Strandvej, which runs alongside **Dragør Sydstrand** (of course, you could decide to stop for a rest in Dragør). It then enters **Kongelunden**, crosses **Kalvebod Fælled** via **Pinseskoven** to the west coast of Amager, and eventually passes close to **Amager Nature Center.** It then makes its way past Field's shopping mall (see Copenhagen chapter) and into Amager Fælled, finally entering the built-up northern end of Amager, and finishing in the Islands Brygge sub-district, across the harbor from central Copenhagen. You'll be cycling mostly on asphalt. The Dragør and Nature Park sections will offer a combination of mild hills and flat sections, windy coastal stretches, and more sheltered areas including forests.

The trail is not signposted, but the route can be found and GPS coordinates downloaded from the Munkevejen website. You should reserve a day for cycling the entire route at a less-than-strenuous pace.

# Dining

## DRAGOR

### DANISH
**Dragør Rogeri**

*Gl. Havn 6; tel. 32 53 06 03; https://
dragor-rogeri.dk; June-Aug. daily
10am-5pm; sandwiches from 49kr, fish fillet
& fries 65kr*

This is a busy fishmonger-slash-café
by the harbor that sells fresh fish with
fries and the sour-tasting Danish relish remoulade. Plenty of types of white
fish, including hake, cod, plaice, and
the signature smoked salmon are popular among locals—you may have to
wait to make your order at the counter.

### SEAFOOD
**Restaurant Beghuset**

*Strandgade 14; tel. 32 53 01 36; www.
beghuset.dk; Wed.-Sat. from 5pm, Sun.-Tues.
private bookings only; à la carte main
dishes 95kr-159kr, 3-5 servings per person
recommended*

Beghuset, within one of the yellow-
washed, tiled-roofed old buildings for
which Dragør is famed, serves a fusion of Danish and French food and
has earned praise from the *New York
Times*. The menu is unsurprisingly influenced by the local fishing tradition,
with oysters on the main menu and a
"sea platter" option included, but there
is plenty of variety.

### CAFÉS AND ICE CREAM
**Café Dragør Sejlklub**

*Strandlinien 1 B; tel. 22 52 15 19; http://
cafedragoersejlklub.dk; Mon.-Fri.
10am-10pm, Sat. 11am-10pm, Sun. 11am-5pm;
entrées from 99kr-125kr, mains 145kr-239kr*

By the pier just off the old harbor, Cafe
Dragør Sejlklub has perhaps the best

Restaurant Beghuset

of all the sea views of any of Dragør's restaurants, and there's plenty of competition. Freshly delivered ingredients are used to make dishes from foie gras terrin to homemade fish and chips. The restaurant also serves as a café with a lunch menu (mains 139kr-239kr) with a French-style platter, falafel salad, Danish *frikadeller* (meatballs), and a burger among the options.

### Rajissimo Gelato

*Kongevejen 19B; tel. 71 49 94 04; http://rajissimo.com; daily 11am-10:30pm (seasonal); ice cream 25-50kr*

Rajissimo also has four branches in Copenhagen, but its outlet in Dragør often sees the longest queues in summers as the popular ice cream takeaway serves its litany of flavors to sweet-toothed visitors. Ice cream is mixed daily; waffle sticks and churros are also available.

### Café Hjerteblomst

*Strandlinien 39; tel. 20 37 96 95; Thurs.-Fri. 10am-5:30pm, Sat.-Sun. 10am-4pm; coffee from 25kr, cakes from 45kr, sandwiches & salads 95kr*

The popular Café Hjerteblomst is full of flowers and free spirit, with a menu—cooked up by exuberant, welcoming owner Linda—that changes from day to day. You can decide what you want in your sandwich or salad based on the fresh ingredients she has. This might include fermented tomatoes, freshly picked herbs, or Italian meatballs. It can all be washed down with a slow-brewed coffee. There's outside seating with a view toward the fort and Øresund, as well as a garden full of plants, flowers, and comfy seats.

### Nam-Nam Is

*Strandlinien 51; tel. 32 53 18 88; hours vary by season; ice cream from 30kr*

Dragør's oldest ice cream shop is known for its crisp homemade waffles and ice cream from famous maker Hansen's. It can be found in an extension on a suitably seaside-looking, large white-and-blue house on the corner of town, facing the sea across a grassy plain. Try the homemade jam on top of your cone.

### Café Sylten

*Søndre Strandvej 50; tel. 30 50 60 19; http://sylten.dk; Wed.-Fri. noon-9pm, Sat.-Sun. 11am-9pm; entrées 75kr-99kr; mains 129kr-179kr*

By the beach away from the busiest section of town, Sylten offers filling café standards including nachos, burgers, sandwiches, salads, and a vegetable stir-fry.

## AMAGER NATURE PARK

### INTERNATIONAL
### Kongelundskroen

*Kalvebodvej 270; tel. 32533157; www.kongelundskroen.dk; Thurs.-Sun. noon-9:30pm; three-course menu 425kr, petit fours 56kr for three*

In a charming setting at the end of the coastal road near the Kongelunden forest and overlooking the sea, Kongelundskroen serves its French-Danish fusion dishes in the traditional-looking setting af a *kro* (inn). You can try wild duck with artichokes, baked cod with winter cabbage, and deer with sundried tomatoes, wild mushrooms, and blackberry sauce, and choose between a three-course set menu or individual dishes. An outside terrace can be used in the summer, and there's a friendly atmosphere inside the homey restaurant, which has a traditional look with patterned wallpaper and low ceilings.

# Accommodations

### Dragør Fort Hotel

*Prins Knuds Daemning 2; tel. 32 53 13 15; http://dragorfort.dk/hotel; double occupancy in high season from 895kr, breakfast 65kr, seven rooms*

In a converted fort on a reclaimed island accessed by a small dam, 400 meters (1,312 ft) from the town and surrounded by a moat, Dragør Fort Hotel's seven rustic rooms—with arched corridors, stone walls, and four-poster beds—can claim a unique setting and an alternative experience to staying in central Copenhagen. Only a small proportion of the fort area has been developed, and much belongs to the hotel, so staying provides an opportunity to see the area that might not otherwise be accessible.

There are only seven rooms, so reserve ahead.

### Copenhagen Airport Hotel/ Dragør Badehotel

*Drogdensvej 43; tel. 32 53 05 00; www. badehotellet.dk; double occupancy in high season from 895kr; 32 rooms*

This three-star hotel has balcony rooms looking toward the Øresund Bridge, marina, and fort. The rooms in the hotel's annex have noticeably less charm than those in the original building. Although it's ostensibly an airport hotel due to its close proximity to Copenhagen Airport, it has a homey feel and is just outside the old town in Dragør, and it's a good option if you want to stay in the town.

# Tourist Information

### Dragør Tourist Information

*Strandlinien 2; tel. 50 55 44 60; www. visit-dragoer.dk/dragoer/dragoer-turistkontor; May-Sept. and during school holidays: May, June, Aug., Sept. daily 10am-4pm, July daily 10am-5pm, school holidays outside peak season daily 10am-2pm*

Dragør's tourist information office can be found in a small house by the harbor and provides information on local sights and attractions and guided tours. Maps of the area are available.

# Getting There and Around

## GETTING THERE

### BY PUBLIC TRANSIT

From Copenhagen, the most direct route is to take bus 350S from Nørreport station directly to Dragør's bus station. This bus travels via Amagerbrogade—Amager's central traffic artery and shopping drag. The standard fare is 36 kroner (20kr with a Rejsekort), and buses depart every 15 minutes at peak times. The journey takes just less than 1 hour. A faster alternative is to take the Metro from Nørreport to Christianshavn and switch to the 350S bus here, thereby cutting out some of the central Copenhagen traffic. This takes about 10 minutes off the journey. The fare is the same.

For Amager Nature Park, the Copenhagen Metro takes you almost to the doorstep: Vestamager station is about 500 meters (1,640 ft) from the entrance to the park and the Amager Nature Center. Bus 33 travels close to other parts of this large nature reserve as well as the Nature Center and is therefore a useful alternative transport option. It terminates in Dragør, so you can also take it from Dragør to get to the park. Taking bus 33 from Copenhagen all the way to Dragør takes 1 hour and costs 36kr; to the Nature Center it's 38 minutes and 24kr (from Copenhagen) and 46 minutes/24kr from Dragør.

### BY BICYCLE

**Munkevejen Bicycle Route 80** (www.munkevejen.dk) is a scenic trail that you can pick up from Islands Brygge near Copenhagen Harbor or from the Amager Strand beach.

Alternatively, head out of Copenhagen via Christianshavn, cross to Amager and head directly south on the main shopping street Amagerbrogade. Follow this road for around 5.5km (3.4 mi), where it will turn right on to Tømmerupvej close to the airport. After 1.2km (0.75 mi), take a left on to Englandsvej/Route 221. From here, there's another 4.5km (2.8 mi) to Dragør, and you can follow the road all the way, passing through Store Magleby as you go. The entire journey will take around 1 hour and is a flat route.

### BY CAR

By car from Copenhagen, the fastest route is via Langebro to Amager, then following Ørestads Boulevard for 3km (1.8 mi) before taking a left turn on Vejlands Alle close to the distinctive Bella Center hotel and conference center, and then, after 1km (0.6 mi), right on to Englandsvej, which you can then follow all the way to Dragør. This 15km (9.3 mi) journey takes 25 minutes.

## GETTING AROUND

### BY BUS

Bus 33 traverses the southern end of Dragør, linking the town's bus station and harbor with Store Magleby and the natural areas to the southwest, including Kongelunden and Kalvebod Fælled. Single journeys cost 24kr or 15kr using a Rejsekort. Journeys to and from the nature park by bus take between 15 and 45 minutes, depending on which part of the reserve you're headed to. Departures are every 30 minutes in peak periods. Use the

Rejseplanen.dk travel planner to plot your route and find departure times.

## ON FOOT AND BY BICYCLE

Dragør itself should be explored on foot—the cobbled alleyways are not suitable for anything else. Bicycle lanes and paths connect Dragør with its surroundings, including Amager Nature Park. The lanes are of good condition and size and are easy to find.

# MØN

## What was once a tough, windy,

and remote corner of Denmark is now a jewel in the crown of its natural attractions. After crossing the bridge from Zealand, an air of calm seems to descend as you travel across the flatlands and rolling fields, through the well-preserved former regional capital of Stege, and all the way to the dramatic white cliffs, Møns Klint, that rise up from the coast. While these are an unexpected geological formation, keeping in mind the flat, sandy coastlines of the rest of the country, the cliffs are far from the only change of track on

# HIGHLIGHTS

✪ **MØNS KLINT:** The White Cliffs of Møn ruggedly define the eastern coast and are visible from forest paths above and shingly beaches below (page 241).

✪ **GEOCENTER MØNS KLINT:** The multimillion-kroner museum at the gateway to the white cliffs is the place to discover the island's geology and the "birth of Denmark," and there is even a dinosaur exhibition (page 241).

✪ **THORSVANG COLLECTOR'S MUSEUM:** Built from scratch over decades by a local restaurateur turned nostalgia buff, this incredible collection of knickknacks will have you feeling wistful for a past you weren't part of (page 250).

✪ **CAMØNO:** This 175km (109 mi), 250,000-step trek across the island takes in forest, field, coast, and starry sky. Its slogan is "the friendliest trail in the kingdom." It does, indeed, exude a sense of welcoming calm and is often strikingly beautiful (page 251).

✪ **MØN IS FARM SHOP AND DAIRY:** Sample the fresh, rich flavors of Møn's locally produced ice cream right at the source (page 257).

✪ **STARGAZING:** Møn has some of Denmark's clearest skies due its small size and proximity to the calm Baltic waters, and there are plenty of ways to participate in some amateur astronomy (page 261).

offer on Møn. Stargazing, abundant birdlife, hiking, and local history, supported by a well-organized, but not overcrowded, tourism infrastructure are all part of what makes Møn a highlight of any Denmark trip.

## ORIENTATION

Møn is a small island, connected to Zealand by bridge on its northwest coast. The road from the bridge heads directly into Stege, the largest town and formerly a municipal capital before administration was moved to the larger island. Northeast from Stege, you'll find the flat, reedy island of Nyord, with its sandy, coastal pathways, tiny town, and octagonal church, via a narrow concrete bridge. Heading

directly east from Stege, you'll pass through the blink-and-you'll-miss-them villages of Elmelunde, Borre, and Magleby before arriving at the coast, where the showpiece geological attraction, the white cliffs at Møns Klint, are located at the top of a gravelly approach road. The southwest of the island is where you'll find the town of Askeby and the smaller island of Bogø. This is the quieter part of Møn, though it has several attractions of its own, including a beachy southern coast.

Route 59 is the main road that connects the island to Zealand. Route 287 links the island from east to west, and from the 287 on the west, you can cross a bridge to Bogø. Driving the full length of the island from east to west

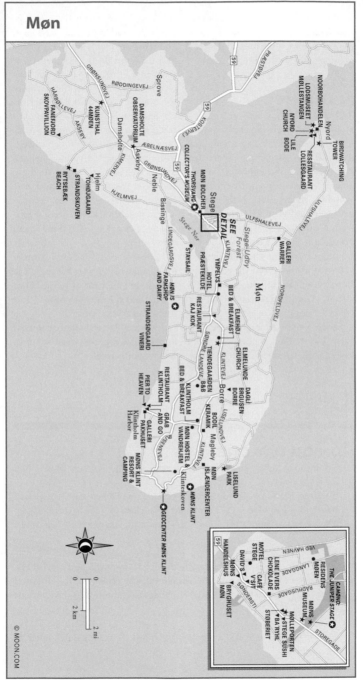

# Møn

**Map labels:**

GRØNSUNDVEJ
RØDDINGEVEJ
Sprove
59
NOORBOHANDELEN
LODSMUSEET MØLLESTANGEN
NYORD CHURCH BODE
LILE LOLLESGAARD
RESTAURANT LOLLESGAARD
GALLERI BODE
Nyord
BIRDWATCHING TOWER
HARBØLLEVEJ
FANEFJORD SKOVPAVILLON
KUNSTHAL 4MØEN
DAMSHOLTE OBSERVATORIUM
AKSEBY
ÆBELNÆSVEJ
GRØNSUNDVEJ
59
KOSTERVEJ
PRÆSTØVEJ
Damsholte
ULFSHALEVEJ
RYTSEBÆK BEACH
STRANDSKOVEN
TOHØJGAARD
Hjelm
KJMTVEJ
Askeby
Neble
MØN BOLCHER
THORSVANG COLLECTOR'S MUSEUM
Stege
SEE DETAIL
HJELMVEJ
Bissinge
Stege Nor
KLINTEVEJ
Stege-Udby Forest
ULFSHALEVEJ
GALLERI WARRER
NORDFELDVEJ
Møn
LINDEGÅRDSVEJ
STAVSAIL
MØN/S FARMSHOP AND DAIRY
PRÆSTEKILDE
HOTEL
YMPELYS
KLINTEVEJ
BED & BREAKFAST
ELMENØJ
RESTAURANT KAJ KOK
SØNDRE LANDEVEJ
ELMELUNDE CHURCH
KLINTEVEJ
Borre
DAGLI BRUGSEN BORRE
STRANDSØGAARD VINERI
TIENDEGAARDEN B&B
RESTAURANT KLINTHOLM BED & BREAKFAST
KLINTHOLM
PIER TO HEAVEN
GRAB AND GO
GALLERI PAKHUSET
Klintholm Harbor
MØN HOSTEL & VANDREHJEM
KLINTEVEJ
BODIL KERAMIK
Magleby
LISELUNDVEJ
KLINTEVEJ
MØN ISLÆNDERCENTER
LISELUND PARK
MØNS KLINT
KLINTEKOVEN
MØNS KLINT RESORT & CAMPING
GEOCENTER MØNS KLINT

**Scale:**
0 — 2 km
0 — 2 mi

**Detail inset:**
59
VED HAVNEN
LANGGADE
RÅDHUSGADE
HANDELSHUS
MOTEL STEGE
LENE EVERS CHOKOLADE
DAVID'S
MØNS MØNS
CAFÉ VSIT
SØNDERSTI
MØNS BRYGHUSET
RESIDENS MØN
MØNS MUSEUM
THE JUNIPER STAGE
CAMØNO
MØLLEPORTEN
STEGE SUSHI
BA RYHL
STØBERIET
STEGE
STOREGADE

© MOON.COM

237

would take around 45 minutes. Møn is small enough to navigate by following your nose most of the time, and there's nothing wrong with asking a passer-by for directions.

## PLANNING YOUR TIME

Møn boasts a rich variety of nature to explore both day and night, and it's ideal for stargazing. There are also charming and enjoyable museums on offer. As such, this nature-abundant, serene island is well suited for a weekend visit. Daytrips by car from Copenhagen, taking in the white cliffs of Møns Klint along with 1-2 other attractions, are also viable and worthwhile, given the relatively small size of Møn and its manageable distance from the capital (about 1.5 hours driving).

Should you, like many Danes, be a keen Tour de France fan, you might enjoy a similar, less physically extreme challenge. Møn's mostly flat landscape can be covered by bicycle in 2-3 days, and there are plenty of routes to follow. However, unlike in cities, there are plenty of roads that do not have bicycle lanes, so travel with care. Since the island is part of the N9 Berlin-Copenhagen bicycle route, there is a ready-made resource for anyone planning to see the island on two wheels, with routes and destinations mapped out. If you have one week to spare and prefer two feet to two wheels, the Camøno trail is an increasingly popular and rewarding way to become intimately acquainted with all the island has to offer.

If you're not visiting primarily to walk or bicycle, having a car makes Møn a lot easier to see, since the island's bus network is not comprehensive.

An excellent website for tourist information for the island is www.sydkystdanmark.dk.

# Itinerary Ideas

## MØN ON DAY ONE

Start your trip to Møn with a visit to the dazzlingly white signature Møns Klint.

**1** Stege, Møn's largest town with a population of 3,800, can be used as a base and is a good place to begin your visit. Head to **Café V'sit** to pick up a homemade organic rye or white bread roll with jam or a boiled egg and a coffee.

**2** Head to **Møns Klint**, which is not far from Stege, and stop at the GeoCenter Møns Klint for some insight into the geology of the cliffs and Denmark's natural history. Children should be enthralled by the dinosaur exhibition.

**3** Pop into the café at the **GeoCenter Møns Klint** for a quick lunch of *smørrebrød*.

**4**  After lunch, take one of the **staircases down to the beach** and spend an hour or two wandering the coastline and admiring the rugged beauty of the cliffs from below.

**5**  After ascending the stairs, try some of the local Møn ice cream (or just grab a coffee) at **the ice cream stand** opposite the entrance to the GeoCenter.

**6**  Head to **Liselund Park**, only 1km (less than 1 mile) or so to the north of Møns Klint for a picturesque early evening walk around the monuments and small buildings.

**7**  End your day with a hearty meal and a pint or two of locally brewed beer at **Bryghuset Møn** back in Stege.

## MØN ON DAY TWO

Take a look into the island's past and present, and experience the meadows and history of Nyord.

**1**  After breakfast at your accommodation, spend some time walking around **Stege**. Don't miss the **Mølleporten**, one of the few medieval town gates anywhere that still marks the limits (or thereabouts) of the town.

**2**  Visit the **Thorsvang Collector's Museum** for a poke around the various treasures and trinkets collected over the decades by the museum's owner, who is a dyed-in-the-wool "Mønbo" (Møn islander).

**3**  Chow down on a hearty, traditional Danish **lunch** at **the museum** before leaving Stege behind for Nyord, a separate island about 8km (5 mi) to the northeast of Stege. There is no public transportation connection between Stege and Nyord, so you'll need to travel by car, bicycle, or on foot.

**4**  Once you've crossed the bridge to **Nyord**, you'll feel like you've switched to a different ecosystem. Spend the rest of the afternoon exploring the island, hiking part of the **Camøno trail** through Nyord's meadows.

**5**  After your hike, you'll be more than ready for a hefty portion of schnitzel at **Restaurant Lollesgaard**, which you can enjoy in their garden if the weather is good.

**6**  If the good weather holds and the night is clear, head to the **birdwatching tower** for a serene night of stargazing.

# Møn Itineraries

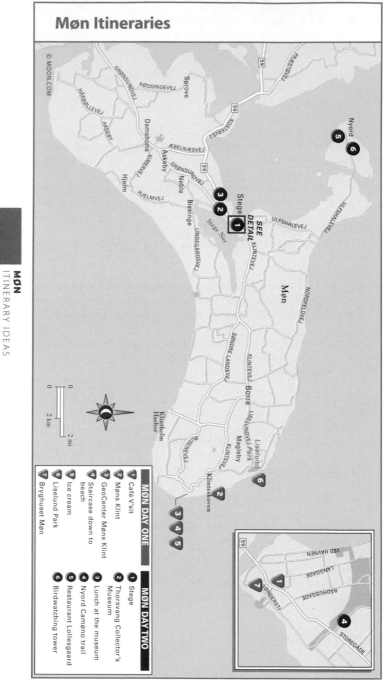

© MOON.COM

0   2 mi
0   2 km

**MØN DAY ONE**

1. Café Vsit
2. Møns Klint
3. GeoCenter Møns Klint
4. Staircase down to beach
5. Ice cream
6. Liselund Park
7. Bryghuset Møn

**MØN DAY TWO**

1. Stege
2. Thorsvang Collector's Museum
3. Lunch at the museum
4. Nyord Camøno trail
5. Restaurant Lollesgaard
6. Birdwatching tower

# Møns Klint and Eastern Møn

The white cliffs of Møns Klint are the island's showpiece attraction and are located on its far eastern coast. Nearby and along the way, the tiny towns of Elmelunde, Borre, and Magleby offer a few sights and other points of interest, as well as places to stay the night.

## SIGHTS

TOP EXPERIENCE

### ✪ MØNS KLINT
### (Cliffs of Mon)

*Stengårdsvej 8, Borre; www.moensklint.dk; 24 hours; free, car park 35kr*

In Denmark, which is a mountainless country, Møn feels almost alpine in places. Climbing from sea level to 143 meters (470 ft) in the space of 1km (0.6 mi), the white cliffs of Møns Klint are melodramatic by Danish standards and seem to rise out of nowhere from the trees of western Møn. The cliffs stretch along 6km (4 mi) of the island's east coast and reach 128 meters (420 ft) above sea level at their highest point. The chalk edifice topped by peaceful forests is one of the country's natural wonders and the pinnacle of the Møn UNESCO Biosphere Reserve.

Adventure movie-evoking beech trees grow right up to the edges of the cliffs in Klinteskoven, the forest above Møns Klint. The leaves of these unusual trees emit a lighter green color as a result of the high content of chalk in the earth. After walking through the forest, take one of Møns Klint's two long, wooden staircases down to the peaceful, pebbly beach and enjoy the awe-inspiring sight of the steep, white slopes above you.

Late spring, summer, and early fall are all great times to visit Møns Klint, which looks spectacular in all three seasons. Denmark's climate is generally unpredictable, and there is no exception on Møn, so come prepared for colder and wetter weather than you might expect. That way, you can only be positively surprised. In winter, tourist services are much more sparse, and wandering around outside can be relentlessly cold, but the bare forests and cliffs retain great natural beauty.

Visitors traveling by car to see Møns Klint can park at the GeoCenter Møns Klint parking lot for 35 kroner. The ticket is automatically issued as you enter the car park, and you can either pay at the information desk in the GeoCenter or at the machine near the entrance.

### ✪ GEOCENTER MØNS KLINT

*Stengårdsvej 8, Borre; tel. 55 86 36 00; www.moensklint.dk; open the last week of Mar. through Oct. 10am or 11am-5pm or*

Møns Klint

# MØN, DENMARK'S FIRST UNESCO BIOSPHERE RESERVE

In 2017, Møn was named as a UNESCO Biosphere Reserve—an area consisting of land, marine, and coastal ecosystems. It is currently the only place in Denmark to have such status, which reflects the presence of most of Denmark's various ecosystem types within Møn's 450 sq km (174 sq mi) biosphere area: woodlands, grasslands, pastures, wetlands, coastal areas, ponds, and steep hills.

The status gives the island extra clout as a world-class natural area and is also recognition of the contribution made by the Mønboer (Møn islanders) to the natural areas on the island: in order to qualify for the UNESCO designation, the area must be considered a place where solutions are found to enable local people and nature to exist in balance. In Møn's case, Stege and the island's villages and farms, with their total population of 10,000, are able to live and work while making sure the ecosystems continue to thrive.

Møn has a series of landscape types, each with its own characteristic animal and plant life and contained within the biosphere zone. These include the cliffs at Møns Klint with ridges and hills created by glaciers at the end of the last ice age, and the landscape around Nyord, which was created by marine erosion and sediment transportation.

There are different types of sea around the island, too, from brackish in the west to saline in the east—hence, the blue-green hue of the shallows at the bottom of Møns Klint, which form a striking contrast with the white of the cliffs.

Up to 18 species of orchids, rare plants, fungi not found anywhere else in Denmark, and semi-endangered birds such as the peregrine falcon and the red kite are further cited by UNESCO's Ecological Sciences for Sustainable Development in its listing of this natural and ecological treasure trove as a listed biosphere.

*6pm (check website for exact times); adults 140kr, children 3-11 95kr, parking 35kr*

A trip to Møns Klint can be substantially expanded by visiting GeoCenter Møns Klint, a child-friendly museum with dinosaur bones, a 3D cinema, virtual-reality glasses, and lessons about glaciers, supervolcanoes, and meteors. The museum also offers geological insight into the local landscape.

The building that houses GeoCenter Møns Klint opened in 2007. It is a modern, boomerang-shaped construction with a café on the terrace that faces the trees of the surrounding Klinteskov forest and Møns Klint. Inside, there's color, sound, interactivity, and plenty of visual stimulation to maximize the attraction and educational value for kids.

Within the high-tech interior, fossils and life-size reproductions of fearsome-looking dinosaurs will spark kids' imaginations, as will the films, taking you not only to the dinosaur kingdom but also underwater among sea monsters as well as into outer space. There's also a virtual-reality installation, in which you can take off and attempt to catch prey from the air.

The exhibition "Where Denmark Was Born," which is in a room dug down into the cliff itself, is built up as a journey through time, presenting the Cretaceous and Tertiary periods and the glaciers of the later Quaternary Period, tying together everything about how Møn's geology was created. As a whole, there is a strong emphasis on interactivity, with both young and old visitors able to get their hands on fossils, make souvenirs, study natural materials, and follow in the footsteps of palaeontologists.

Other highlights include a climbing wall, an "ice cave," and a huge

Liselund Park

collection of belemnite fossils—the museum is attempting to gather the world's largest collection with specimens from the beach at the bottom of the nearby cliffs: visitors are encouraged to put forward their own finds for inclusion in the collection.

Guided tours through the surrounding forest are also available, which can including fossil hunts, ziplines (daily during peak season from noon-4pm; free with entrance), and guides to local plant and wildlife. Options vary according to season, so check ahead or ask at the museum's reception.

Guide tours by mountain bike (daily during peak season from 2pm-4pm; free with entrance) are also available. Guides will present geology, flora, and fauna as you bike through the terrain. Tours are filled on a first-come, first-served basis, but you can reserve a spot by calling ahead, which is recommended. You must be over 12 to join, and helmets are included.

## LISELUND PARK

*Langebjergvej 6, Borre; tel. 55 81 21 78; https://en.natmus.dk/museums-and-palaces/ liselund; 24 hours; free; palace open May 1- Sept. 30 for guided tours at 10:30am, 11am, 1:30pm, 2pm, Wed.-Sun.; adults 50kr, under 18 free*

In the far northeast of Møn, north of neighboring Møns Klint, Liselund Park is like something out of a fairytale. A thatched-roofed cottage, Chinese tea pavilion, Norwegian cabin, lakes, streams, and monuments give this charming park an unquestionably romantic feel—there are few better places to bring a picnic. In fact, the park is a labor of love created by Antoine de la Calmette—a late 18th-century landowner—as a country home for his wife, Lisa.

The park is arguably one of Europe's best-preserved romantic gardens with winding paths, hills, small lakes, trees from far-off lands, and slopes with monuments and pretty buildings. These include a pagoda-evoking Chinese summerhouse, a thatched cottage called the Swiss House, and another house, the Norwegian House, so-called due to its location in a hilly area supposedly reminiscent of Norway's fjords.

The old manor house, Liselund Gammel Slot, is a small country home in the French neoclassical style, built in 1792 (the park itself was purchased from the crown about 10 years before). The rooms, which include nine bedrooms and an impressive entry, have delicate decorations and tasteful colors—oval mirrors, chandeliers, and marble-topped tables. The white building with its thatched roof, light-blue columns, and decorated spire look out over a small waterfall and pond.

If you arrive early in the day (and in season), you can visit the palace where, during the summer months, guided tours are offered—the well-preserved interior is still much the same as that laid out by its 18th-century court decorator.

Although the palace is only open to visitors in the summer, the garden is open year round and admission is free. The park is small enough to walk around in 1-2 hours, and there are gravel paths between the ponds, trees, and buildings.

## ELMELUNDE CHURCH

*Leonora Christines Vej 1, Elmelunde; www. keldbyelmelundekirke.dk; open year-round; free*

The church at Elmelunde is a classic Nordic-style church on the outside, with high whitewashed walls and tiled, pitched roofs, but remarkable on the inside, and where it is notable is its ceiling frescoes. Painted on the Gothic vaultings over the nave and choir by a figure known as the Elmelunde Master, probably in the late 15th century, they were hidden

Elmelunde Church

Møns Klint beach

for centuries following the reformation before being restored in the 1960s. Today, visitors can admire the vinelike floral patterns and chevrons; religious and biblical figures in medieval dress; and animals, including deer, horses, and a human-headed serpent, depicted by the intricate frescoes.

## SPORTS AND RECREATION

### BEACHES

The beach at Møns Klint is a serene sight. Shallow, turquoise water—its color transformed by the chalky sea bed—laps against the pebbles of the beach with thousands of fossils scattered among them, which are preserved for centuries before being released by the advancing geology of the cliffs. The beach stretches across 6km (4 mi) of Møn's east coast, but most visitors walk only the short 1.5km-section (1 mi) between the wooden staircases leading up to Klinteskoven Forest and the GeoCenter. It's not a beach for sunbathing, even on warm days, due to its contours and inaccessibility—Møn has other beaches more suited to this.

There are three wooden staircases close to the GeoCenter that lead from the top of the cliffs down to the beach. The closest of the three, **Maglevand Steps,** is opposite the entrance to the GeoCenter and is clearly signposted, as are the paths into the forest and to lookout points. You can follow any of the staircases up and down, which take anywhere between 15 and 30 minutes to make the descent or ascent, depending on your fitness, the temperature, and the care needed in wet conditions. The **Røde Udfald Steps,** around 1km (0.6 mi) north of the Maglevand Steps, zigzag down the hill and are thereby less steep (until you reach the final section. A third set of steps, **Gråryg Fald Steps,** is south of the GeoCenter. Do not attempt to climb these if you are likely to have any physical difficulties. At the top of the cliffs, windy, forested paths take you between the two staircases—there's no set route. At the

view from Møns Klint Walking Route

bottom, simply follow the curve of the coast and admire the glistening white cliffs, serene atmosphere, and sea air.

## WALKS

### Walking Route: Klinteskoven Forest and the Møns Klint Coast

*Start: GeoCenter*

*Distance: 2.7km (1.5 mi)*

*Hiking time: 1-2 hours*

Walk north from the GeoCenter to Dronningestolen (the Queen's Chair), the highest point on the cliff face 128 meters (420 ft) above sea level. The path is well marked from the starting point and easy to follow through the forest. Continuing about 200 meters (656 ft) north, you will reach Forchhammers Pynt, a second viewpoint with a dramatic vantage over the cliffs. Continue north, passing Klintekongens Ansigt (the Cliff King's Face), a 10 meter (33 ft) outcrop of rock on the cliff face. Turn to the right onto the Røde Udfald Steps, which wind back and forth through the forest and take you down to the beach through leafy wooded slopes until you reach the final descent to the shore. Turn right and walk south along the beach, taking in the clear water and the view of Møns Klint from below. After around 1km (0.6 mi) you'll find yourself at the popular Maglevands Fald Steps, which are steep and almost straight and take you back to the GeoCenter.

## BOAT TOURS

### Sejlkutteren Discovery

*Klintholm Havneby, Borre, 4791; tel. 41 42 90 36; www.sejlkutteren-discovery.dk; Apr.-Oct. 2-6 departures daily, check website or call for daily timetable; adults 175kr, children 3-11 90kr*

You can view the white cliffs from the sea by taking a boat trip onboard the cutter *Discovery,* which is owned by local fishermen and siblings Flemming and Bjarne Larsen. The pair have sailed on the Baltic Sea since the 1980s and sometimes also take their boat out at night for stargazing sessions, if the conditions are right. Call ahead to book your chosen trip—spaces onboard are limited. The two-hour tours have departures daily during the peak season.

### HORSERIDING
#### Møn Islændercenter

*Moenavej 7, Borre, 4791; tel. 55 81 28 10; www.moen-ishest.dk; year-round, tours normally at 11am and 3pm; 500kr per person*

Icelandic horses clip-clop their way through the forest near the cliffs on tours provided by this family-run business. Both new and experienced riders are catered to, and the pace and route are tailored to suit participants, with two guides joining if there is more than one difficulty group—so you might get to try a gallop if you're comfortable enough.

## SHOPPING
### Bodil Keramik

*Sømarkevej 2, Magleby, 4791; tel. 55 81 20 61; http://bodilkeramik.dk; daily 10am-5pm*

This small pottery workshop produces uniquely designed, traditionally made teapots, dishes, bowls, vases, and cups—its walls and stables stacked with locally made pottery, each one hand-thrown on a kick wheel. All products are on sale in the well-stocked shop adjoining the workshop.

## DINING
### Geocenter Mons Klint Café

*Stengaardsvej 8, Borre; tel. 55 86 36 00; http://cafemoensklint.dk; opening hours same as GeoCenter; sandwiches, smørrebrød, and salads 65-75kr*

Unless you've brought a picnic with you to enjoy on the benches outside the museum, in the forest, or even on the beach (all good options), the café at GeoCenter Møns Klint is the only place for lunch. It has a good selection of *smørrebrød,* fruit, pastries, and sandwiches.

## ACCOMMODATIONS
### UNDER 500KR
#### Møn Hostel and Vandrehjem

*Klintholm Havnevej 17A, Borre, 4791; tel. 55 81 24 34; https://moenhostel.dk; shared room from 225kr, private room from 350kr; open February-September*

Located close to Møns Klint in rural surroundings and 3km (1.8 mi) from Klintholm, this large hostel with 29 rooms and 96 beds opened in 2013 after moving from elsewhere on the island, but the building still gives off a retro holiday vibe. Bicycle rentals are available. There is a guest kitchen; breakfast and packed lunches can also be purchased from 75kr. Bed linen must be rented (from 50kr), if you don't have your own with you.

#### Elmehøj Bed & Breakfast

*Kirkebakken 39, Elmelunde, 4780; tel. 55 81 35 35; www.elmehoj.dk; double occupancy in high season from 450kr*

Elmehøj's bed and breakfast opened 27 years ago in a former retirement home, which was built in the 1930s (if you look closely, you can still see the door buzzers in some of the rooms). It has been run as a family business ever since by owner Brit Olifent, who says that the advent of the Camøno has brought an influx of diverse new guests, keeping her as busy as ever. It is located next to Elmelunde Church, famous for its 15th-century frescoes. Facilities include Wi-Fi, a guest kitchen, and clothes-drying room. The 23 rooms (50 beds) are modern, clean, spacious, and comfortable. Linens must be rented (unless you bring your own) for 55kr; breakfast costs 65kr, and packed lunches can be purchased for 55kr.

Elmehøj Bed & Breakfast

### Tiendegaarden B&B

*Sønderbyvej 29, Borre, 4791; tel. 23 47 21 06;*
*www.tiendegaarden.dk; double occupancy in*
*high season from 500kr*

Also popular with Camøno hikers is Tiendegaarden, a B&B set in a handsome old farm house close to Møns Klint—the quiet at night is striking, and it's also a good place from which to stargaze into Møn's famously clear sky. Breakfast costs 75kr and must be ordered by 9pm the preceding evening. There is also a small kitchenette where guests can prepare their own food.

### 500-1,000KR
### Klintholm Bed & Breakfast

*Klintholm Havnevej 4, Magleby, 4791; tel. 55*
*81 24 50; www.klintholm-bb.dk/09; double*
*occupancy in high season from 675kr; 10*
*rooms*

Klintholm Bed & Breakfast is another of the numerous, friendly family-run accommodation options on Møn. This one includes a cozy lounge area with fireplace, outside terrace, and a bar and games room with a pool table. Breakfast is included in the price.

## CAMPING
### Møns Klint Resort and Camping

*Klintevej 544; tel. 55 81 20 25; www.*
*moensklintresort.dk; open Mar. 29-Aug. 26;*
*tent pitch low season adults 106kr per day,*
*children under 12 76kr per day, electricity*
*40kr per day plus tent price 22kr per day*
*low season (March 29-June25, August*
*27-October31), 62kr per day high season*
*(June 26-August 26).*

An extensive campground that also has family and smaller cabins, the well-rated Møns Klint Resort and Camping has three large, clean service buildings with kids' play and sports facilities and a guests' kitchen, as well as a shop and a restaurant. Both tents and caravans are welcome, with space for up to 400 tents, caravans and auto-campers and RVs (caravans/campers/camper vans cost 32 kroner per day to park and 82 kroner per day from June 26th-August 26th). It is close to the countryside and not a bad place at all to see Møn's starry night sky.

# GETTING THERE
## BY CAR
To get to eastern Møn and Møns Klint from Copenhagen and Zealand, take the E47 and exit at junction 41 toward Vordingborg, before following Route 59 to Stege on Møn and then Route 287 toward Borre. From here, signposts will direct you to Møns Klint. The road leads up through the hilly forest and becomes surprisingly steep and gravelly before reaching the top. Here, you can head for the forest path and the steps down to the beach or visit the GeoCenter.

## BY PUBLIC TRANSIT
From Stege, Møn's largest town, take bus 667 to Busemarke (Klintholm Havnevej/Klintholm Harbor) (24 kr, 15 kr with Rejsekort, duration 28 minutes, leaves every 10 minutes during peak season but hourly during winter). From May to September you can change buses here for the number 678, which goes all the way to the stop at the GeoCenter (use the same ticket, around 15 minutes). Note, Rejsekort users should only ever check out at the end of their journey, but always re-check in when making a connection. When bus 678 is not running, you will have to walk (be prepared with walking boots and warm, waterproof clothes), which is a distance of around 6km (4 mi), or arrange for a taxi.

# Stege

Stege has the feel of a market town with a large tourist industry, with a sense that residents are acquainted with each other and well versed in accommodating visitors. The town is charming and nicely maintained, with timbered buildings, narrow streets, and hidden yards around its central market square and the former town hall, as well as at Mølleporten, the old town gate. There's a regular Tuesday market and a string of specialty shops run by local producers. In 2018, the town celebrated the 750th anniversary of its founding with events including open-air theaters, markets, and concerts.

## SIGHTS
### MØLLEPORTEN
*Storegade 75, 4780 Stege*

The 15th-century Mølleporten—literally, the Mill Gate—was once part of the fortifications defending medieval Stege, along with two others like it, which have not survived, and a moat, which is still visible. A sturdy square tower in red brick with white bands of limestone, innumerable transports have passed under its vaulted entrance down the centuries. It gives the impression of loyally insisting on performing the task it was once built for, dutifully watching over the town limits.

### MØNS MUSEUM
*Storegade 75, Stege; tel. 31 66 64 33; www.moensmuseum.dk; May-Aug. Tues.-Sun. 10am-4pm; adults 40kr, under 18 free*
Møns Museum is a modest local history museum archive in

Mølleporten

Empiregården, which is a merchant's house built in 1813 right by the medieval city gate. It has an information desk with resources for the Camøno walking trail. Permanent exhibitions on subjects such as Møn's history from 1660-2000, migration on Møn, and a collection of oil paintings provide a look at local history with a focus on personal stories. There are also rotating exhibitions. One of the museum's most unusual objects is an organlike instrument that is both a normal and a barrel organ and is said to have been used at many special occasions on the island.

## ✪ THORSVANG COLLECTOR'S MUSEUM (Thorsvang Samlermuseum)

*Thorsvangs Allé 7, Stege, 4780; tel. 40 46 91 46; www.thorsvangsamlermuseum.dk; Jan. 17-Mar. 13 Thurs.-Sun. 10am-5pm, except daily Feb. 11-17 10am-5pm, Mar. 14-Oct. 20 daily 10am-5pm, Oct. 21-Dec. 22 Thurs.-Sun. 10am-5pm; adults 60kr, children age 5-18 30kr*

This remarkable local history museum is a collection of odds and ends collected over the course of decades. The owner, now in his 60s, is a local chef who has lived his entire life on Møn. He began collecting the objects now displayed in the museum at the age of seven, and the result is a nostalgic cross between an exhibition and a flea market. The affectionately presented museum is a hoarder's dream, with 18 small shops stocked with 1960s biscuit tins, stacks of crockery, and vintage beer bottles crowding shelves, rooms full of old-fashioned television sets, a garage of Model T Fords, Volvos, and motorbikes in various states of repair; a barber's salon, a carpentry workshop, telephone boxes, a post office....I could go on and on. On the grassy plain out front that also serves as a car park, wooden allotment houses and (inoperational) fairground stalls add to the charm. The staff, mostly retired volunteers, are happy to chat and tell you a bit about the island and the museum's history. A visit here is always memorable and a must-see on Møn.

It would be remiss of you to not stop into the onsite café for lunch to round out your visit of days gone by with a traditional feast. Open between noon and 3pm, there is a buffet of herring fish fillets, salad with curried dressing, relish, and fresh bread available (adults 119kr, children 60kr), or there's coffee and cake for 60kr.

## DAMSHOLTE OBSERVATORIUM

*Grønsundsvej 251, Stege; tel. 38 71 97 18; www.damobs.dk; May-Aug. irregular opening times, rest of the year, 8pm-11pm depending on season; 80kr per person*

This small observatory is run by a society of enthusiasts and was opened in 2016. Much pride is placed on Møn and Nyord's status as an International Dark Sky Community—one that doesn't use poor-quality outside lighting, which can result in glare and light pollution. If skies are clear, the observatory opens for visitors for a couple of hours in the late evening when the sky is darkest, giving you the opportunity to try out some serious telescopic equipment. Remember not to get your phone out or use your flash—you'll reset your (and others') night vision. Always call ahead to request opening before setting out; if conditions aren't right or if no one is coming, the observatory stays shut. A good rule of thumb is if you can see the Milky Way in the sky with the naked eye, you could be in luck. Note that conditions are better in the winter when the sky is darker, and the observatory only opens occasionally in the months of May-August.

# SPORTS AND RECREATION

## HIKING

### ✪ Camøno: The Juniper Stage (Enebæretapen)

*Starting: Møns Museum, Storegade 75, Stege*
*Distance: 15 km (9.3 mi)*
*Time: 2.5-4 hours*

The stage of the Camøno known as the "Juniper" stage begins at Møns Museum in Stege, which also functions as the main tourist information point for the trek, so it's an ideal place to start. Friendly staff will help you plan and prepare for your route. While you're here, take a look at the old merchant's yard behind the museum.

As you leave the museum, you'll turn left and walk rather symbolically through **Mølleporten**, the medieval tower that was once part of the town's fortifications. You'll also pass the excavation of the old moat encircling Stege. Following the road out of town, you'll reach **Stege-Udby Forest**. This wooded area has an easy-to-follow path, bushes and trees, and a small log shelter. At the right time of year, you can pick cherries from the overgrowth by the path.

Emerging from the forest like a hobbit escaping Mirkwood (but without any scary elves), you will have a stunning view across a flat landscape with grazing calves and will be able to look out across Stege Bay's waters. You can stop for organic supplies for your pack and friendly service at **Traneholt Landhandel** (Ulvshalevej 84; tel. 23 29 38 00; www.traneholtlandhandel.dk), where there's a great selection of local produce sold by 10th-generation farmers Christina and Anders.

A long stretch of open countryside follows, where even the sky seems to be stretching its legs and the pathway looks out over the fields, making you feel like a character from *Anne of Green Gables*. This is **Ulvshale Marshes and Heath**. Eventually, the land gives out and you'll find yourself at the **Nyord Bridge**.

The bridge is a simple concrete, single-lane structure with a somewhat retro-looking traffic light. Hikers can walk across the flat bridge and watch flocks of birds soaring above the marshy landscape, while ducks and geese bob in the strait separating Møn and Nyord.

After you reach the **Nyord** side, there's a long, straight section that leads you through the heart of the island and gives you a good feel for how much of it is wilderness. By now, your legs may be tiring, but options are at hand. Turn left onto a dirt trail to find **Hyldevang Shelter**, an octagonal, wooden shelter that is open to the elements and where you can sleep for free (if there's space). You may meet one of the volunteers who help maintain the area. There's a wood-chopping machine for the bonfire, and the **Nyord birdwatching tower** is nearby.

If you are staying over and want (a little) more comfort than sleeping in a shelter in the wild, you could finish the hike into Nyord and rest for the night at **Nyord Cabin** (Nyord Havnevej 10; tel. 23 31 32 70), a white-painted hut with four bunks that can be reserved for 150kr per bunk or 400kr for the whole cabin per night. Call ahead to reserve. Don't expect luxury, but you will find a kitchenette with a kettle and hot plates and access to a patio garden overlooking the sea.

Nyord itself is great reward for finishing the trek. The car-free hamlet, with its fishermen's homes and little harbor with a view of Stege Bay and the Queen Alexandrine Bridge to Zealand is even more idyllic when you've spent several hours walking to get there. There's a designated **Camøno Pause**—a resting spot with toilet facilities and water—here, too, so you can recharge and get ready for the next leg of the Camøno (if you dare).

This leg of the Camøno, at 15km (9 mi), takes 2.5-4 hours, depending on your pace.

## BICYCLING

Møn can be explored by bike with a number of well-signposted routes. Møn's bicycle routes are all well supplied with cafés, shops, and ice cream kiosks, but they are also notable for something that is possibly unique: Denmark's two first bicycle-friendly road churches, **Borre Church** and **Magleby Church**, which offer free water bottle refills, tire pumps, and a rest on the church benches.

### The Berlin-Copenhagen Route
*www.bike-berlin-copenhagen.com*

The **Berlin-Copenhagen N9** bicycle route) traverses Møn (note: it is, for some reason, called **N8** on Møn), and by following this route you will see a great deal of the island. As it's part of a longer route, the N8 can be picked up anywhere on Møn, but if you want to cycle it in its entirety (about 75km or 47 mi), then you should pick it up at Route 287 near the Bogø Bridge, and take it across the southern half of the island. The route eventually turns north on the eastern end, heading back

one of the many hiking paths of Møn

across the northern part of the island and dropping you in Stege.

The best way to plan bicycling on any iteration of the Berlin-Copenhagen route is to use the website's online maps on your smart phone (the website contains a wealth of other resources too, such as downloadable data for GPS devices and written, turn-by-turn navigation), and all routes are also clearly signposted: look for the little white bicycle and route number N8.

### Panorama Routes

*www.visitmoensklint.com/ln-int/moensklint/*
*panorama-routes-moen-day-trips-view*

Møn's three Panorama Routes are good options for those wanting to see Møn by bike. These are designed as sightseeing side trips that can be added to the main Berlin-Copenhagen journey. They include **"On Top of The World—Denmark's Mountain Route"** around Klintholm and Liselund (18km, 11 mi); **"Life Is Sweet,"** circling Stege Cove (21km, 13 mi); and **"Island Hopping—Take The Family Exploring,"** covering the Stege-Nyord stretch (29km, 18 mi). The three routes encapsulate the nature and landscape that make Møn great: the open marshes, chiselled cliffs, beech forests, and expansive shorelines.

The terrain is a mixture of asphalted roads and bicycle lanes with some gravel tracks. Unlike most other parts of Denmark, there

# THE "CAMØNO": A TREK AROUND THE ISLAND

Camøno signpost

The **Camøno** (http://camoenoen.dk) is a 175km-long (109 mi. or 250,000-step) hiking trail across Møn, Nyord, and Bogø. The name is a lighthearted pun that pays homage to the Camino de Santiago trail in Spain. Møn's version is a well-signposted route split into **12 stages**, directing you along country paths, tracks, fern tree forests, and, naturally, to Møns Klint. The trail was established in 2016 and is already becoming one of the island's biggest draws, with 9,000 people stepping onto its paths in the first year alone.

Denmark might not be known for the spectacular geological scenery of the Norwegian fjords or the ice of Sweden's Lapland, but the Camøno and Møns Klint draws compliments from hikers of multiple nationalities. Arriving at Møns Klint is a worthy

are some challenging uphill and undulating sections (notably on the Klintholm panorama route), particularly at the eastern end of the island near Klintholm. To follow the route, look for signposts with the designation "Panoramarute" on the blue road signs. Maps and information can also be downloaded from the website.

### Fri Bikeshop Stege

*Storegade 91, 4780 Stege; tel. 55 81 42 49; www.fribikeshop.dk/cykler-stege; Mon.-Fri. 7:30am-5pm, Sat. 9am-1pm; standard bicycles 75kr daily, electric bicycles and mountain bikes 200kr daily*

Standard, electric-assisted, and mountain bikes can all be rented at this friendly bicycle store in Stege, which has a range of equipment and also makes repairs, if needed. They take a 100kr deposit on rentals. Reservations are recommended from the beginning of spring until the high season ends around September, preferably by email to info4780@fribikeshop.dk; alternatively, you can reserve over the telephone.

## BEACHES AND WATERSPORTS
### Ulvshale Beach

*Ulvshalevej, Stege; free*

This child-friendly, low-water beach on the spit between Stege and Nyord has some nice sand dunes and access for wheelchairs as well as toilets payoff for the long hours of walking; the peaceful sound of the shore directly below a towering wall of white, cream, and yellow chalk cliffs makes the experience an overwhelmingly beautiful one.

**Digital maps** can be downloaded from the Camøno website, and there is a **route planner** and recommendations for different difficulty levels as well. **Physical maps** in Danish, German, and English can also be purchased via the website for 135kr. The website is currently only in Danish, so if your web browser's translator is not getting the message across, **Møns Museum** (Storegade 75, Stege, 4780; tel. 31 66 64 33; www.moensmuseum.dk; May-Aug. Tues.-Sun. 10am-4pm) is the place to go for all the tourist information you will need. The staff is happy to provide advice and words of encouragement.

There are several places along the route where supplies can be bought, including at or near the nine designated break stations known as **Camøno Pauses** where hikers can relax, refill water bottles, and chat with residents and other hikers. These break areas are located about one day's walk from each other and are marked on the maps and with signposts. Many B&Bs sell packed lunches, and the supermarket in Borre (Dagli' Brugsen Borre, Klintevej 381; tel. 55 81 20 04) will even make you a packed lunch if you call in advance and ask.

Some good tips to bear in mind:

- Make sure you have a good pair of **broken-in, waterproof hiking boots**. You won't be making any challenging mountain ascents, but you will be walking for a long time, and your feet will thank you for taking care of them.

- Plan **where to stay** in advance. There are free shelters and cheap camping sites along the route; information on these is available at Møns Museum. Hostels, B&Bs, and hotels on the island are all used to seeing hikers.

- **Ease yourself in** and gradually increase your daily distance. Walking 12-16km (7-9 mi) on the first day is fine; this can then be ramped up to 20km (12mi) per day.

Be sure to say hello to the mønboer (Møn islanders) you pass along your way—people are generally sympathetic to the island's tired feet, the hikers of the Camøno.

and a kiosk. Its blue-turquoise water and white sands can look positively Mediterranean in summer. It has Blue Flag certification, which means quality is assured (dogs are not allowed on the beach).

### Naturen Kalder Kayaking

*tel. 50 96 11 10; www.naturenkalder.com; naturenkalder@gmail.com; various opening hours; tours from 250kr-695kr (children 150kr)*

If paddling is your thing, Møn can be seen from a kayak, with various guided tours available for beginners and experienced oarsfolk. Standup paddleboards can also be rented (two hours 450kr, minimum two persons). It's best to call or email the company directly to reserve and check tour information. Tours can leave from Stege or near Klintholm or Ulvshale, depending on where you will be kayaking.

## SHOPPING
### Ympelys

*Klintevej 110, Stege, 4780; tel. 55 81 30 05; http://ympelys.dk; Apr.-Oct. Mon.-Tues. 10am-5pm, Thurs.-Fri. 10am-5pm, Sat.-Sun. 10am-4pm*

This homey shop is packed with Nordic-style crafts and clothing, starting with a huge selection of handmade candles as wells as ceramics, textiles, clothing, and home goods. Located on the main road heading east just outside of Stege.

### Lene Evers Chokolade

*Storegade 39 (backyard), Stege, 4780; tel. 29 71 15 19; http://lene-evers-chokolade.dk; Fri. 11am-6pm, Sat. 10am-2pm, July 3-Aug. 7 also Tues. 10am-6pm*

With a splendid selection of lovingly made confectionaries, Lene Evers Chokolade is worth stopping by for both the intricate tastes and creative designs of the chocolates. Ingredients include limoncello, figs, berries, rhubarb, coconut, and port. Look out for topical designs—2018 saw both World Cup and Pride chocolates on display.

### Møn Bolcher

*Kostervej 2, Stege, 4780; tel. 55 81 01 01; www.moenbolcher.dk; Mon.-Fri. 10am-4pm, Sat. 10am-2pm*

Danes' favorite candy is liquorice, but the boiled sweets on offer at Møn Bolcher encompass just about every color and flavor going. Think of caramel, rhubarb, eucalyptus, chocolate, peppermint, coffee, blueberry, and pineapple. They can be purchased in a variety of traditional-looking glass jars. Inside the shop, you can watch the "sweet boiler" making the candy, boiling the mix before kneading and forming it into the many eyecatching colors and patterns.

### Galleri Warrer

*Hovedskovvej 20, Ulvshale, 4780; tel. 55 86 10 77; http://galleriwarrer.dk; July-Aug. daily 11am-5pm, Sept.-June Thurs.-Sun. 11am-5pm; free*

The largest gallery on Møn at 1,000 square meters (10,760 sq ft), with art, furniture, ceramics, sculpture, glass, jewelry, and clothing. As many of 50 artists from various disciplines have contributed to the rotating exhibitions. Its location in Ulvshale makes it a convenient stop-off between Stege and Nyord.

# DINING
## DANISH AND NEW NORDIC
### Bryghuset Møn

*Søndersti 3, Stege, 4780; tel. 30 74 04 00; http://detgamlebryghus.dk; daily noon-9pm; burgers from 115kr-225kr, three-course menu 385kr*

In a quiet yard set back from Stege's high street, walking into Bryghuset Møn feels like wandering into a secret alley. There is decking for outside seating in the summer and a spacious, high-ceiling interior that echoes its connection to the local brewery Bryghuset Møn. On the menu is a three-course meal, hearty burgers, steaks, and fish dishes (but few options for vegetarians), any of which can be paired with locally brewed craft beers.

## INTERNATIONAL
### Støberiet

*Storegade 59, Stege, 4780; tel. 55 81 42 67; www.slagterstig.dk/stoeberiet; Mon.-Sat. 8am-9pm, Sun. 1pm-9pm; sandwiches from 70k-100kr , evening buffet 110kr*

Støberiet is simultaneously charcuterie and brasserie. You'll find a traditional butcher's counter in one half of the restaurant, from where you can select a cut of meat to be prepared with your meal. Pair it with side dishes from the buffet and take a seat in the rustic, informal surroundings. The buffet includes herring, fish fillets, cold cuts, and salads, and there are a range of meats to choose from for your main dish, from traditional steaks to more eclectic choices such as kangaroo or crocodile.

### Stege Sushi

*Storegade 30, Stege, 4780; tel. 53 68 85 45; http://stegesushi.dk; daily noon-9pm; set menus from 99kr-359kr*

Stege Sushi was opened in 2016 by two Chinese chefs. The menu is

## EATING MØN IS

Møn's locally produced ice cream comes from cows that live on the island, and the ice cream is 100 percent organic. This means that your ice cream will be made from milk less than eight hours old, giving it a genuine, rich taste, whichever flavor you choose.

As you make your way across the island, you'll find plenty of chances to sample the ice cream. Wherever it's sold, you'll see the characteristic logo—an outline of the island turned into a blob of vanilla ice cream on a waffle. Here are a few places around the island where you can find an ice cream stand:

- **GeoCenter Møns Klint** (Stengårdsvej 8, Borre)

- **Grab and Go** (Thyravej 14, Klintholm)

- **Lille Bod** (Grusvejen 4, Nyord)

- **Møns Handelshus** (Storegade 16, Stege)

- **Tohøjgaard** (Rytsebækvej 17, near Rytsebæk Beach)

- **Daglì Brgusen Borre** (Klintevej 381, Borre)

impressively broad, with a range of freshly prepared maki, nigri, sashimi, and warm dishes. The setting inside the restaurant is mimimalistic and friendly. Takeaway is available.

### CAFÉS AND LIGHT BITES
#### Café V'sit

*Storegade 17A, Stege, 4780; tel. 71 90 98 08; http://cafevsit.dk; Mon.-Wed. 9:30am-5pm, Thurs.-Fri. 9:30am-10pm, Sat. 9:30am-10pm, Sun. 9:30am-5pm; sandwiches 75kr, breakfast items from 20kr, salads 95kr-105kr, tapas from 125kr-250kr per person*

Organic Café V'sit in Stege is open for morning croissants and rolls, sandwiches in the afternoon, or tapas and a glass of wine in the evening. The place is spacious and with plenty of natural light in the morning, and the tapas can also be made to go.

#### David's

*Storegade 11, Stege, 4780; tel. 33 13 80 57; www.davids.nu; Mon.-Fri. 10am-5pm, Sat.-Sun. 10am-4pm; sandwiches from 98k, salads from 99-105kr, tapas 110kr-169kr*

Located on Stege's main street, David's prides itself on its fresh ingredients and has a range of carefully crafted sandwiches including veal with mustard, salmon and crème fraiche, and brie with crispy ham. There are also salads and vegetarian dishes as well as gluten-free options. A cozy courtyard, from where the church spire is visible over the rooftops, makes for a great place to enjoy your lunch on sunnier days.

### ICE CREAM
#### ✪ Møn Is Farm Shop and Dairy

*Hovgårdsvej 4, Stege, 4780; tel. 23 26 38 19; www.moen-is.dk; June-Sept. plus holidays 11am-5pm, rest of year Sat.-Sun. 11am-5pm; from 22kr for one scoop*

Whatever you do, don't miss Møn's locally made ice cream, Møn Is. And where better to sample it than at the source? In the summer, visit the producer's farm shop and dairy, located in rural surroundings where you can enjoy the freshly made flavors and see the animals that provide the raw ingredients. If you enjoy your ice cream enough, you can even thank them. Highly rated flavors include the classic vanilla, pistachio, and coffee with salted caramel.

## NIGHTLIFE
### Ba'ryhl
*Storegade 70A, Stege, 4780; tel. 55 81 75 70; www.baryhlbar.dk; Tues.-Sun. noon-11pm; wine, cocktails from 65kr, beers from 40kr*

Aimed at islanders and tourists in equal measure, Ba'ryhl is both a bar and a café—you can stop for a coffee and panini during the day or enjoy one of the full range of Bryghuset Møn beers or expertly made cocktails in the evening. Informal and welcoming, there are comfy armchairs, board games, and cushions.

## ACCOMMODATIONS
### 500-1,000KR
### Motel Stege
*Provstestræde 4, Stege, 4780; tel. 31 44 40 35; www.motel-stege.dk; double occupancy in high season from 700kr; 12 rooms*

Owned by Brit Olifent, the proprietor of Elmehøj Bed & Breakfast, Motel Stege is located right next to Stege Church and is conveniently close to the bus station and tourist information center. Room options include private and shared bathrooms and some rooms also have their own kitchenettes. There's a large garden where you can put your feet up at the end of a long day's walking or cycling.

### Hotel Præstekilde
*Klintevej 116, Stege, 4780; tel. 55 86 87 88; https://praestekilde.dk; double occupancy in high season from 790kr; 41 rooms*

A hotel, conference center, and restaurant with a golf course right next door. Breakfast is included in the price, and the restaurant serves highly rated,

New Nordic-inspired courses (entrées from 99kr, mains 159kr.349kr).

### Residens Møen
*Langelinie 44, Stege, 4780; tel. 22 36 72 72; www.residensmoen.dk; double occupancy in high season from 825kr; 31 rooms*

Hotel Residens Møn has a selection of diferent rooms, from double rooms to apartments to suites with balconies overlooking Stege Bay and Queen Alexandrine Bridge. The building, built in 1703, is a former navigation college that later became a prison for convicts of means—members of the nobility and even a princess have been incarcerated here. It was opened as a hotel in 2016. The hotel's café offers up popular Danish meals, including ribeye with bearnaise and pork chops with artichoke (mains 175kr-255kr).

### StaySail
*Søndersognsvej 96, Stege, 4780; tel. 20 44 87 46; www.staysail.eu; double occupancy in high season from 575kr; 6 rooms*

A straightforward, overnight option about 7km (4 mi) outside of Stege on the opposite side of the Stege Nor bay—boats and dinghies can be rented for sailing on the bay, and the area around the hotel is generally one from which local natural areas are easily accessed. Breakfast, towels, and linen are included in the price, and evening meals in the hotel's restaurant can also be ordered. Rooms are named after the Dutch terms for different types of ship, and the interior is decorated with model boats and other maritime memorabilia.

## TOURIST INFORMATION
The best and most accessible spot to find broad tourist information, including assistance for the Camøno, is the

Møns Museum (Storegade 75, Stege, 4780; *tel*. 31 66 64 33 www.moens-museum.dk; May-Aug. Tues.-Sun. 10am-4pm, Sept, Nov, Mar-Apr Tues.-Fri 10am-2pm, Sat.-Sun. 10am-4pm).

## GETTING THERE
### BY CAR
From Copenhagen, take the O2 circular road to reach the E20 motorway toward Odense, later merging onto the E47, before taking exit 41 to Vordingborg on route 59. That road will take you all the way to Møn via the striking Queen Alexandrine arch bridge and then on into Stege. The journey should take around 1 hour 30 minutes.

### BY PUBLIC TRANSIT
You can reach Møn by public transit from Copenhagen by first taking the regional train service from Copenhagen Central Station to Vordingborg. There are two trains hourly, and the journey takes 1 hour 6 minutes and costs 106kr. At Vordingborg, you'll switch to the 660R or 664 bus. Buses depart from outside the rail station. Buy a ticket from the driver or use your Rejsekort. The 660R takes 45 minutes and the 664 takes 1 hour to reach Stege. Both buses cost 60 kr or 32kr with a Rejsekort and depart three times per hour.

# Nyord

Nyord is a 5 sq km (2 sq mi) island connected to Møn by a quiet concrete bridge that feels like the backdrop from a scene in a Wes Andersen movie. The island has a calmingly desolate feel, despite its meadows being home to a large and diverse bird population. Black-tailed godwits, ruffs, and dunlins are some of the rarer species that have been spotted here, where waders, terns, ducks, and gulls also all come in numbers to breed. The flat landscape and sandy coastline can be enjoyed on foot—most easily by following the marked Camøno trail—and you might see fishermen wading in the water or sitting in skiffs in the shallow waters off the coast.

Nyord By (the town) has a smattering of streets on the southwestern part of the island (the meadows take up the eastern and northern parts). It feels secluded and remote from Stege,

never mind Copenhagen. The town is miniscule with a population in 2018 of just 36, according to Denmark's official statistics agency. There were a few more than that when I visited on a warm August evening—many of these were surely also visitors, come to enjoy the car-free streets and time forsaken bending roads. If you're lucky, you could find yourself being invited to a summer party at the small harbor, with old-fashioned Danish pop music on the stereo and pork on the grill.

## SIGHTS
### NYORD CHURCH
*Søndergade 1, Nyord By, 4780 www. nyordkirke.dk/forside; open year-round; free*
At the center of Nyord By's handful of twisting, improvised-looking streets is the eight-sided Nyord Church. With a model ship hanging from its ceiling, the traditions bound to this

diminutive place of worship are clear. Built in 1846, the inspiration for architect Jens Otto M. Glahn's design are a little mysterious, with archives not open to the public at the time of writing. However, there are some common characteristics with Middle Age and neoclassical churches built elsewhere in Denmark, as well as in Europe and the Middle East, including Rome's Pantheon, which is a circular church that might just be a distant relative of the one in Nyord.

## BIRDWATCHING TOWER

*Ulvshalevej 401, Nyord; always open; free*

Nyord's approximately 400-hectare (988-acre) meadow and bird habitat has a bird tower by the main (and only) road that cuts through the island. There are open and sheltered areas in the two-tiered birdwatching tower along with a platform for wheelchair users, providing a great view over the meadow. It also has potential as a stargazing spot.

## LODSMUSEET MØLLESTANGEN

*Nyord; open morning to sunset Easter-Nov.; free*

Also worth keeping an eye out for is a brick cabin on the edge of Nyord's town known as "Denmark's tiniest museum": more officially, Lodsmuseet Møllestangen (the Flagpost Pilot's Museum). This micro-museum is filled with posters that tell the story of the old ports and tough stevedores and pilots that worked it. Located on a high spot, this is an ideal place to stop for a rest on your walk around Nyord to enjoy the views of the sea as well as a bit of local history and charm. Visitors are informed not to shut the door on the way out: the latch will lock out subsequent passers-by.

Nyord Church

# ✪ STARGAZING ON MØN AND NYORD

Møn and Nyord are certified dark-sky preserves—areas with restricted light pollution that provide optimal conditions for astronomy. That means there's just as much reason to experience the island at night as there is when it's light. Up to 14,000 stars can be seen in Møn's skies on a clear night (by contrast, no more than 100 can be seen in Copenhagen).

Stargazing on Møn doesn't require a huge amount of preparation, but here are a few tips:

- The summer season is actually the worst part of the year for stargazing, as the short, light nights reduce the visibility of the stars.

- If it's wet, you naturally won't be able to see any stars and can stay home.

- You'll want to bring binoculars, a telescope, or photography equipment, but you won't be able to use a flash.

- Warm clothes are needed—do not underestimate the ability of Danish weather to bring out the chilliness.

- Bring a beach towel to sit on, a lamp, and a bag to carry away your litter.

- Mosquito repellent can be handy in the warmer months.

### BEST SPOTS FOR STARGAZING
In addition to the Observatorium, there are plenty of other spots dotted around the island from where the galaxy views are striking.

- **Birdwatching tower** (Ulvshalevej 401, Stege) on Nyord has wheelchair accessibility, a sheltered section, and is as good for stars at night as it is for wings during the day.

- **Liselund Park** (Langebjergvej 6, Borre) is free to enter and open year-round, so you can crank up the romance levels with a bit of stargazing.

- **Boardwalks at Møns Klint** (Stengårdsvej 8, Borre) are easily navigated from the GeoCenter and lead to some spectacular lookout points. These are great for combining white cliffs and bright stars. Tread carefully in the dark.

- **Rytsebæk beach** on the quiet south coast might give you the Milky Way all to yourself.

# SHOPPING
## Noorbohandelen
*Nyord Bygade 1, 4780; tel. 51 78 04 48; www.noorbohandelen.dk; Easter-October daily 11am-5pm, rest of year Fri. 1pm-5pm, Sat. 11am-5pm, Sun. 11am-4pm*

Eagle-eyed visitors to the Torvehallerne food market in Copenhagen might recognize the Noorbohandelen name, but the specialty spirits vendor is at home on Nyord ("Noorbo" is the word used to describe someone who lives on the island). Herbs and fruit grown on Nyord are used to produce the home-made bitters and schnapps sold here. The spirits can be tasted in the store, decanted from specially designed bottles. Imported whisky, rum, cognac, and grappa are also available. If you stop for a sandwich and coffee, try the locally made Nyord jam and mustard in the Noorbohandelen café.

## DINING
### Restaurant Lollesgaard
*Hyldevej 1, Nyord, 4780; tel. 31 39 99 82; www.lolles.dk; Mar.-Oct. 11am-4pm or 8pm, check website or call for specific day; lunch platter 145kr, sandwich 65kr-85kr*

This Nyord restaurant that opened in 1947 continues the theme of both nostalgia and island life with its traditional kro (inn) style design—stripey wall paper and thick table-cloths. You can also sit in the garden in good weather and be surrounded by trees, flowers, and white wooden tables. The food is a satisfying mix of schnitzels, casseroles, and vegetable quiches.

## GETTING THERE
To drive from Stege to Nyord, simply follow Ulhavevej out of the town heading north and keep going until you reach the Nyord bridge. To find Ulhavevej, leave Stege through Mølleporten, and turn left after 300 meters (985 ft) or so onto Katedralvej. This will bring you to a junction with Ulhavevej. Turn right.

# Klintholm Harbor

The small village of Klintholm Havn, while not an essential part of a visit, is a useful and pleasant spot for passing hikers and cyclists. The harbor itself is quiet with several small fishing boats and other vessels moored. Thyravej, a 200-meter-long (650 ft) road that serves the harbor, has a number of useful amenities including Restaurant Klintholm, an ice cream kiosk (walk to the far end of the road), and **Spar supermarket** ( Thyravej 6) to stock up on supplies for your onward bike or hike.

## SIGHTS
### GALLERI PAKHUSET
*Thyravej, Klintholm Havn, Borre, 4791; tel. 61 75 76 00 or 61 27 61 99; http:// galleripakhuset.dk; May-June Sat.-Sun. 1am-5pm, July-Aug. daily 1pm-5pm, off-season see website; free*

All high ceilings and wooden beams, this summer art gallery exhibits 26 artists from the Møn area and is also dedicated to local crafts. The gallery in an old warehouse at Klintholm Harbor on the south coast also has an antique and second-hand section on its ground floor.

### MEMORIAL STONE
Opposite Spar and Galleri Pakhus there's a discrete, round memorial stone. This is to commemorate the rescue in May 1945 of 370 prisoners from the Stutthof concentration camp near Danzig (now Gdansk) in Poland, after they had been forced on to a barge and left to drift in the Baltic Sea. A German boat tugged the barge into Klintholm, whose residents took in the refugees, saving 351 lives.

### STRANDSØGAARD VINERI
*Bundgarnet 121; tel. 23 24 01 32; July 1-Aug. 12 Wed.-Mon. 11am-5pm, by appointment rest of year*

Located by the lake in the village of Råbylille and surrounded by holiday homes, Strandsøgaard vineyard has a quiet, summer house vibe and a little shop where you can buy that rarest of commodities, Danish wine.

Owner Finn Skaaning is a wine enthusiast who offers tours of his fields and is happy to explain how wine production on Møn works while you taste the Strandsøgaard white wines. There is a well-stocked shop that has a good range of imported wines as well. Call ahead to arrange tours and check opening times, particularly in the off season.

## DINING
### Restaurant Klintholm

*Thyravej 25, Klintholm Havn, 4791; tel. 55 81 92 90; http://restaurantklintholm.dk; May 25-Sept. 3: lunch noon-3pm, dinner daily from 6pm; off-season check website or call for details; lunch buffet 139kr, dinner buffet 189kr*

On the wharf in Klintholm right by the waterfront, Restaurant Klintholm is an affordable seafood eatery with lunch and dinner buffets, which include 18 types of pickled herring. It opened in 2008 in what was once a cold storage for freshly caught hauls. Other buffet items include fishcakes, smoked salmon, and fish salads. There's a large floor with open-plan seating and a terrace looking out over the harbor. The interior is clean and simple with white-painted walls and paintings of Møns Klint.

## BARS AND NIGHTLIFE
### Pier to Heaven

*Klintholm Havneby 24D, Borre, 4791; tel. 51 78 04 48; www.noorbohandelen.dk; open mid-June-mid-Sept. daily from 2pm; cocktails from 70kr, beers from 35kr*

Noorbohandelen's outside summer bar in Klintholm is a fresh place to stop and sip a locally brewed beer or cocktails to the clacking of yacht masts as you take a break on your way around the island. Inside, the "Slyngelstuen" (Rascal's Bar) is a mix of shabby, maritime chic and hip design.

## GETTING THERE

To get to Klintholm Harbor from Stege, take bus 667 (24kr, 28 minutes, leaves every 10 minutes during peak season but hourly during winter).

# Western Møn

## SIGHTS
### KUNSTHAL 44 MØEN

*Fanefjordgade 44, Askeby, 4792; tel. 28 83 24 83; 44moen.dk; June-Aug. Wed.-Sun. 11am-5pm; adults 40kr, students and seniors 20kr*

Contemporary art space 44 Møen is another example of the surprisingly vibrant creative scene on the isle and is based in an old workshop in Askeby. The main exhibit, "Møenlight Sonata," pays tribute to both the starry skies over the island and an apparent penchant for punning. Word plays aside, the gallery also houses contemporary art with a focus on giving breakthrough artists a chance.

## BEACHES
### Rytsebæk Beach

*Rytsebækvej 31, Stege, 4780; free*

In the island's less-visited west, Rytsebæk Beach is a remote, long section of thin sand and stone and is prized by locals. You can reach the beach on foot or on a bicycle, and there is a small car park. The land is flat, so access to the beach is easy. In summer, the bathing conditions are good until late afternoon, when the temperatures start to cool down, and you can go for a walk in the forest while you dry off. About 1km (0.6 mi) to the southwest along the coast, an incredibly quiet and atmospheric beech forest flanks the shore, and there is a great view across the bay.

## DINING
### Fanefjord Skovpavillion
*Fanefjord Skovvej 6, Askeby, 4792; tel. 55 81 73 67; http://fanefjordskovpavillon.dk; summer (late June-mid Aug.) Mon.-Sat.*

*noon-10pm, Sun. noon-5pm, rest of year Thurs.-Sat. noon-10pm, Sun. noon-5pm; brunch buffet 160kr, entrées from 75kr, mains 140-169kr*

This traditional-style bistro in a tranquil forest setting is a great bicycling pitstop, with dishes including salmon and ham salad entrées, steaks with mushroom sauce, and schnitzels. Vegetarian options are available. There is also a bingo night on the second Thursday of the month (when the menu might be subsequently restricted to a plat du jour). The wooden building is a former hunting lodge.

# MALMÖ

## Malmö has been accused of

becoming a pocket-sized Copenhagen, but although the Danish capital's influence can increasingly be felt, in particular through the growing foodie scene, breezy Malmö remains a destination that offers something entirely different—different country, different language, different scale—just a 25-minute train journey across the dramatic Øresund (Öresund to the Swedes). You can even use your Danish transport card to get there and back.

# HIGHLIGHTS

✪ **MALMÖHUS CASTLE:** Wander dungeons and royal apartments, see spiders, and learn about dinosaurs, all in the grounds of one castle (page 275).

✪ **VÄSTRA HAMNEN:** Cycle along the coast, sit by the sea, and enjoy the sight of two wonders of engineering, the Öresund Bridge and the Turning Torso tower (page 277).

✪ **MALMÖ'S PARKS:** Get a lungful of air, stroll in romantic copses, and watch a free concert in an amphitheater: Malmö is the city of parks (page 279).

✪ *FIKA:* Sweden's version of high tea is a national institution. Be sure to take time out of your afternoon for coffee and cake at a cute café (page 284).

Rooted in its history as an international harbor town, Malmö's most attractive areas include a cobblestoned old city and a smart, redeveloping harbor area. Its many parks and proximity to the sea mean you are never far from fresh, bracing air, and a visit to the moat-and-masonry Malmöhus Castle will leave you in no doubt as to the city's role in Swedish and Scandinavian history.

## ORIENTATION

Exiting **Central Station**, where you will arrive by train from Copenhagen or elsewhere in Sweden, the first thing you are likely to notice is the proximity of water in all directions. A network of canals surrounds the historic **Gamla Staden (old city), separating it from the Harbor (Hamnen) District, where the station is located.** You will see one of these canals in front of you as you head out of the station's south entrance.

To the northwest of the station, past **Universitetsholmen**, the small island on which Malmö University

is located, is **Västra Hamnen (West Harbor)**, which was originally part of the still-substantial main harbor and is now a reenergized area with a sea promenade. It's easy to navigate—the 190-meter-tall Turning Torso building, the largest in Scandinavia (it can even be seen from parts of Copenhagen), is right in the center.

To the immediate west of the Central Station, and surrounded by a moat, is the **Malmöhus Castle**. Beyond the castle, to the immediate south, east, and west, **Kungsparken**, **Slottsparken**, and **Slottsträdgården** are among the best of Malmö's numerous green areas, with their rolling slopes, wooded areas, and high stone bridges.

In Gamla Staden itself, as you cross Mälarbron from the station, which leads directly onto **Stortorget (Great Square)**, you'll find an expansive 16th-century marketplace. A statue of King Karl X Gustav, who conquered the once-Danish provinces of Skåne, Blekinge, and Halland and united them with the Swedish Empire in 1658, marks it symbolically.

# CROSSING THE DANISH-SWEDISH BORDER

Traveling between Copenhagen and Malmö means crossing the Danish-Swedish border. Until recently, this was an open Schengen border, but measures in place since 2016 mean that, at the time of writing, Swedish authorities are conducting identification checks on the crossing, and you will therefore need to carry your passport. Even if normal conditions are resumed at some point in the future, always bring your passport or national ID card when crossing the border, as spot checks are theoretically possible. Aside from the border itself, there are a few other things relevant to keep in mind when crossing the Öresund.

- **Border control:** The border control being carried out on the Öresund crossing at the time of writing is in the form of ID checks. That means an acceptable form of ID is required when crossing from Denmark to Sweden, with checks carried out on trains, buses, and by stopping cars. The controls are in the form of spot checks, and their extent varies by location and the general assessment of authorities at the time of travel. Your passport will not be stamped: this is not required regardless of whether your ID was checked on entry.

- **Forms of ID and visas:** Put simply: bring your passport with you. National identity cards from countries that issue these are also accepted. If you need a Schengen visa to visit Denmark, the visa will also be valid for Sweden. In this case, you should carry your passport.

- **Crossing by train:** Border checks are conducted not at Malmö's Central Station but at Hyllie, on the outskirts of the city and the nearest station to the Öresund Bridge. Police officers sometimes board the train to check ID, or you might be required to show it at the temporary border control at Hyllie Station, if you are leaving the train here.

- **Crossing by bus:** Bus passengers are also liable for spot ID checks on arrival on the Swedish side of the bridge.

- **Crossing by car:** Passport control for travelers arriving by car takes place at the Öresund Bridge toll stations at Lernacken at the Swedish end of the bridge. Police have the right to search cars.

- **Currency exchange:** Sweden, like Denmark, does not use the euro, so you will need to exchange or withdraw some **Swedish kronor** (SEK). Exchange rates at the time of writing are: 1 SEK = 0.72DKr = $0.11 = €0.10 = £0.09. Cash can be exchanged at Forex exchange bureaus at both Central Station (Lokgatan 1; tel. 010-211 16 64; Mon.-Fri. 7am-8pm, Sat.-Sun. 10am-6pm) and Trangeln (Rådmansgatan 13; tel. 010-211 16 66; Mon.-Fri. 10am-6pm, Sat. 10am-2pm). If you will be returning to Denmark, consider holding on to your Danish kroner, to save double losses on exchanging currency.

- **Using your phone:** Phones that roam in Denmark will also do so in Sweden, but make sure you've checked ahead with your service provider for your international options before traveling, in order to avoid excessive roaming charges. However, this won't be a problem if your phone has an EU number. The EU abolished roaming charges in 2017, so if you arrive in Sweden (or Denmark) with, for example, an Irish phone, you'll pay the same rates as you do at home (although there can be limits on data usage—check with your service provider). The country code in Sweden is +46. If you want to call Denmark from Sweden, dial +45 or 0045 followed by the Danish phone number in full.

# Malmö

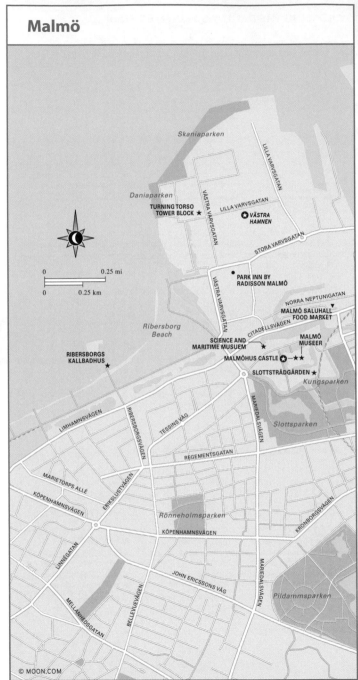

Skaniaparken

Daniaparken

LILLA VARVSGATAN

VÄSTRA VARVSGATAN

LILLA VARVSGATAN

**TURNING TORSO TOWER BLOCK** ★

⭐ **VÄSTRA HAMNEN**

STORA VARVSGATAN

VÄSTRA VARVSGATAN

● **PARK INN BY RADISSON MALMÖ**

NORRA NEPTUNIGATAN

**MALMÖ SALUHALL FOOD MARKET**

Ribersborg Beach

CITADELLSVÄGEN

**SCIENCE AND MARITIME MUSUEM** ★

**MALMÖ MUSEER**

**RIBERSBORGS KALLBADHUS** ★

**MALMÖHUS CASTLE** ⭐ – ★ ★

**SLOTTSTRÄDGÅRDEN** ★

*Kungsparken*

MARIEDALSVÄGEN

LIMHAMNSVÄGEN

RIBERSBORGSVÄGEN

TESSINS VÄG

*Slottsparken*

REGEMENTSGATAN

MARIETORPS ALLÉ

ERIKSLUSTVÄGEN

KÖPENHAMNSVÄGEN

*Rönneholmsparken*

KÖPENHAMNSVÄGEN

KRONBORGSVÄGEN

LINNÉGATAN

JOHN ERICSSONS VÄG

MARIEDALSVÄGEN

*Pildammsparken*

BELLEVUEVÄGEN

MELLANHEDSGATAN

0 ⊢ 0.25 mi
0 ⊢ 0.25 km

© MOON.COM

**MALMÖ**

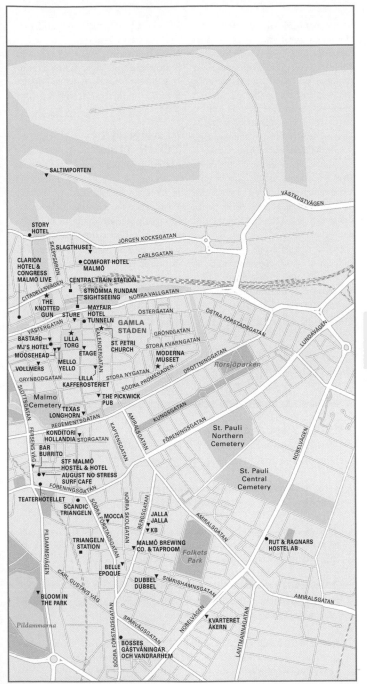

SALTIMPORTEN

VÄSTKUSTVÄGEN

STORY HOTEL

SLAGTHUSET

JÖRGEN KOCKSGATAN

CARLSGATAN

CLARION HOTEL & CONGRESS MALMÖ LIVE

COMFORT HOTEL MALMÖ

CENTRAL TRAIN STATION

CITADELLSVÄGEN

STRÖMMA RUNDAN SIGHTSEEING

NORRA VALLGATAN

THE KNOTTED GUN

MAYFAIR HOTEL

STURE

TUNNELN

ÖSTERGATAN

ÖSTRA FÖRSTADSGATAN

GAMLA STADEN

VÄSTERGATAN

GRÖNEGATAN

LUNDAVÄGEN

BASTARD

LILLA TORG

ST. PETRI CHURCH

STORA KVARNGATAN

MJ'S HOTEL

ETAGE

MOOSEHEAD

MODERNA MUSEET

DROTTNINGGATAN

MELLO YELLO

VOLLMERS

Rörsjöparken

GRYNBODGATAN

LILLA KAFFEROSTERIET

STORA NYGATAN

SÖDRA PROMENADEN

Malmö Cemetery

THE PICKWICK PUB

TEXAS LONGHORN

KUNGSGATAN

REGEMENTSGATAN

AMIRALSGATAN

FÖRENINGSGATAN

St. Pauli Northern Cemetery

NOBELVÄGEN

KONDITORI HOLLANDIA

STORGATAN

FERSENS VÄG

BAR BURRITO

STF MALMÖ HOSTEL & HOTEL

KAPTENSGATAN

St. Pauli Central Cemetery

AUGUST NO STRESS SURF CAFE

FÖRENINGSGATAN

TEATERHOTELLET

SCANDIC TRIANGELN

MOCCA

JALLA JALLA

PILDAMMSVÄGEN

BERGSGATAN

KB

AMIRALSGATAN

TRIANGELN STATION

SÖDRA TOSTADSGATAN

NORRA SKOLGATAN

MALMÖ BREWING CO. & TAPROOM

RUT & RAGNARS HOSTEL AB

BELLE EPOQUE

Folkets Park

DUBBEL DUBBEL

SIMRISHAMNSGATAN

BLOOM IN THE PARK

CARL GUSTAVS VÄG

AMIRALSGATAN

Pildammarna

SÖDRA FÖRSTADSGATAN

SPÅRVÄGSGATAN

NOBELVÄGEN

KVARTERET ÅKERN

LANTMANNAGATAN

BOSSES GÄSTVÅNINGAR OCH VANDRARHEM

MALMÖ

Just around the corner from Malmö's largest square is its most charming, **Lilla Torg (Little Square)**, where some very old buildings are now home to modern bars and restaurants, and people gather on the benches and cobblestones in summer. The third major square in Gamla Staden is **Gustav Adolfs Torg** at the opposite end of the Södergatan high street. A large, public space adorned with sculptures and fountains, the square borders a cemetery adjoined to the Södra Förstadskanalen, a canal you can walk alongside toward the city library and Kungsparken.

On the opposite side of the canal, the central shopping street continues outside of the old city on Södra Forstadsgata, which heads south for around 500 meters (1,640 ft) before terminating at **Triangeln**, the location of a large mall and railway station.

This area has many accommodation options as well as one of the city's major museums, Malmö Konsthall. Southwest from here is the expansive **Pildammsparken**, while **Folkets Park** lies to the east in working-class Möllevången.

## PLANNING YOUR TIME

Malmö's sights are very close to each other, and it is quite easy to be able to navigate around the city on foot. Västra Hamnen is a little further away, though, and taking a bus to and from this area will save time and strain on your legs. The castle and associated museums take an afternoon to explore, as does the old city, so in order to experience Malmö at a leisurely pace, an overnight stay is likely to be a decision you'll not regret.

# Itinerary Ideas

## ONE DAY IN MALMÖ

If you're heading in and out from Copenhagen in a day, this itinerary will help you bring back a piece of Malmö.

**1** After an early breakfast, take the train from Copenhagen's Central Station to **Malmö's Central Station**.

**2** Head straight for the 16th-century **Malmöhus Castle** and spend the morning exploring the varied exhibits inside the castle, from the king's antechamber to the aquarium and dinosaur exhibit.

**3** Have lunch at **Malmö Saluhall food market**, an artisan food market in a converted warehouse near the harbor. You'll have a vast choice of options, but you can't go wrong with a falafel or a bowl of noodles.

**4** Walk off lunch at the expansive **Slottsparken**, one of Malmö's gorgeous green spaces. Meander around the lakes and admire the Castle Mill, a charming windmill.

**5**   Do as the locals do and go for *fika* at **Konditori Hollandia**. The buns and tarts are scrumptious.

**6**   Any remaining afternoon time can be spent walking around the old city as well as the extremely old and equally appealing **Lilla Torg** with its cobblestones and wooden buildings, which is home to a slew of modern restaurants and bars.

**7**   Settle down at **Bastard** for dinner. It's one of the best restaurants the city has to offer. Be sure to book ahead.

**8**   Partake in Lilla Torg's nightlife scene with a drink or two at **Moosehead**.

**9**   If you're staying the night, **Mayfair Hotel Tunneln** is a great choice. The building is steeped in history, but thankfully the rooms are not.

## MALMÖ LIKE A LOCAL

Head outside Gamla Staden and visit the Swedish spots you might not have had time to savor on your first day in town.

**1**   Enjoy coffee and cake for breakfast at **August No Stress Surf Café.**

**2**   See more of Malmö's famed green spaces, and go for a morning jog, stroll, or bicycle ride through the expansive **Pildammsparken**.

**3**   Head to **Saltimporten at the port**—one of the best spots in the city for lunch—for a "meat and two veg."

**4**   Walk off lunch along the **Västra Hamnen** seafront promenade. Stop to take in the goings-on and views of the Öresund Bridge in the distance.

**5**   For a bit of relaxation Swedish style, visit the **Ribersborgs Kallbadhus** public bath for a dip, some sauna time, and light refreshments at the restaurant.

**6**   Across town, it doesn't get much more local than **Jalla Jalla**. End your day with some shawarma or falafel.

**7**   Unwind with a beer at the **Malmö Brewing Co. & Taproom** just down the street.

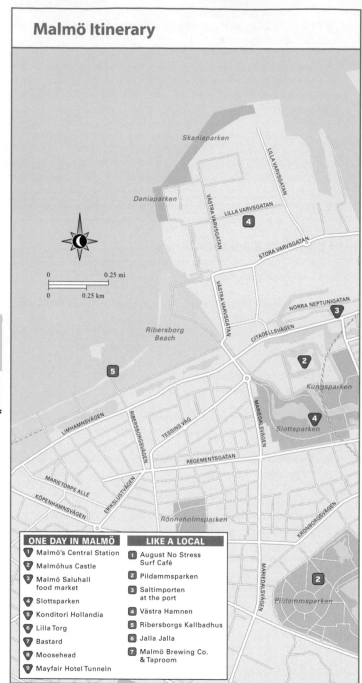

# Malmö Itinerary

Skaniaparken

Daniaparken

LILLA VARVSGATAN

VÄSTRA VARVSGATAN

LILLA VARVSGATAN

**4**

STORA VARVSGATAN

VÄSTRA VARVSGATAN

NORRA NEPTUNIGATAN

**3**

CITADELLSVÄGEN

Ribersborg
Beach

**2**

Kungsparken

**5**

MARIEDALSVÄGEN

**4**

Slottsparken

LIMHAMNSVÄGEN

RIBERSBORGSVÄGEN

TESSINS VÄG

REGEMENTSGATAN

MARIETORPS ALLÉ

ERIKSLUSTVÄGEN

KÖPENHAMNSVÄGEN

Rönneholmsparken

KRONBORGSVÄGEN

MARIEDALSVÄGEN

**2**

Pildammsparken

| ONE DAY IN MALMÖ | LIKE A LOCAL |
|---|---|
| **1** Malmö's Central Station | **1** August No Stress Surf Café |
| **2** Malmöhus Castle | **2** Pildammsparken |
| **3** Malmö Saluhall food market | **3** Saltimporten at the port |
| **4** Slottsparken | **4** Västra Hamnen |
| **5** Konditori Hollandia | **5** Ribersborgs Kallbadhus |
| **6** Lilla Torg | **6** Jalla Jalla |
| **7** Bastard | **7** Malmö Brewing Co. & Taproom |
| **8** Moosehead | |
| **9** Mayfair Hotel Tunneln | |

0        0.25 mi

0        0.25 km

**MALMÖ**
ITINERARY IDEAS

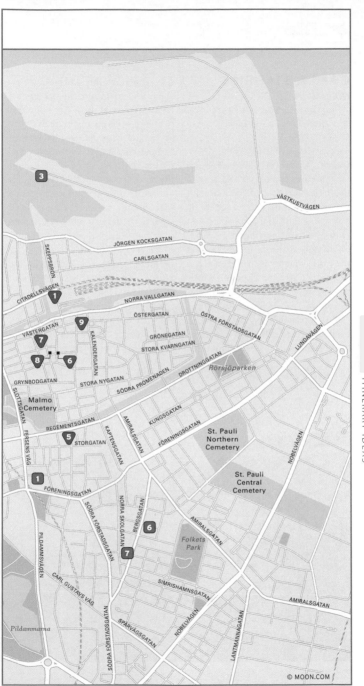

Map labels:

3

VÄSTKUSTVÄGEN

SKEPPSBRON
JÖRGEN KOCKSGATAN
CARLSGATAN

CITADELLSVÄGEN
1
NORRA VALLGATAN
ÖSTERGATAN
ÖSTRA FÖRSTADSGATAN
9
VÄSTERGATAN
7
GRÖNEGATAN
KALENDERGATAN
STORA KVARNGATAN
8    6
LUNDAVÄGEN
GRYNBODGATAN
STORA NYGATAN
SÖDRA PROMENADEN
DROTTNINGGATAN
Rörsjöparken

Malmö
Cemetery
REGEMENTSGATAN
KAPTENSGATAN
AMIRALSGATAN
KUNGSGATAN
FÖRENINGSGATAN
St. Pauli
Northern
Cemetery
NOBELVÄGEN
5
STORGATAN
SLOTTSGATAN
FERSENS VÄG
St. Pauli
Central
Cemetery
1
FÖRENINGSGATAN
SÖDRA FÖRSTADSGATAN
NORRA SKOLGATAN
BERGSGATAN
6
AMIRALSGATAN
Folkets
Park
7
PILDAMMSVÄGEN
CARL GUSTAVS VÄG
SIMRISHAMNSGATAN
AMIRALSGATAN
SÖDRA FÖRSTADSGATAN
SPÅRVÄGSGATAN
NOBELVÄGEN
NOBELVÄGEN
LANTMANNAGATAN
Pildammarna

© MOON.COM

273

# Sights

## GAMLA STADEN
### MALMÖ MUSEER

*Malmöhusvägen 5-8; tel. 040-34 44 37;*
*https://malmo.se/museer; daily 10am-5pm;*
*adults 40 SEK, students 20 SEK, under 19*
*free (Malmö Museer ticket)*

Malmö Museer is the umbrella term for museums located in and around the Malmöhus Castle. The museums within the castle include an aquarium, a dinosaur exhibition, and an art museum (Malmö Konstmuseum) in addition to the historical exhibits within the castle. Nearby is the Science and Maritime Museum. Although a little worn-looking (its entrance is reminiscent of a local library built in the 1980s), it contains several interesting exhibits that are well worth your time.

In summer, visitors can also take the nostalgic Museum Tram (Museilinjen) (included in ticket price) to and from Malmö City Library. Restored with its olive-green livery and Victorian paneling and with uniformed conductors and wooden interiors reminiscent of a boat cabin, the no. 100 tram, built in 1906, dings and whirrs its way from stops outside Malmöhus Castle and the Banérskajen stop by the fishing huts area next to the Science and Maritime Museum. Another restored tram from the era, the no. 20, can also be found plying the route. You can use the tram to get from the castle and museum area to the city center, which is a few minutes' walk away across the Södra Förstadskanal, but it's worth taking just for the fun of the short journey, enjoying the ride

Malmöhus Castle walls

Malmöhus Castle

as the tram passes down a swinging, treelined avenue with Kungsparken's lake to your left.

Malmöhus Castle and the Science and Maritime Museum share opening times and tickets as well as use of the tram. Tickets can be purchased at the information desk just inside the entrance to the castle.

## ✪ Malmöhus Castle

Reedy moats form a citadel reminiscent of Copenhagen's Kastellet. In the middle sits the 16th-century Malmöhus Castle, the oldest Renaissance Castle in the Nordic region where Denmark's coins were once minted when the Kalmar Union briefly brought the Scandinavian nations under a single banner. It was built by the same King Erik of Pomerania who founded Kronborg Castle in Helsingør as he fortified the coasts of the Öresund. The low, deep-red cannon towers and broad moat are the most striking features of the Malmö castle; its appearance contrasts to the thin, almost delicate spires of Kronborg.

The castle's interior successfully conjures up medieval and Renaissance Sweden, with the king's antechamber, all carved furniture, tapestries, portraits, and marble floors on the upper level and, in the dark, stony dungeon, a strong exhibition on the long years of war with Denmark in the 17th century and the history of prisoners incarcerated, and executed, at the castle. This murky section, with its ghost stories and tales (and portraits) of woe, is the highlight—or is it the lowlight?—of a visit to the castle.

You'll find more than just history at the castle. In attached museum galleries, built within the castle grounds in the 1930s as it was restored and prepared to be opened to the public, there are exhibitions on geology and natural history, including a somewhat arresting collection of stuffed animals, some of which are species native to Sweden. There's also an exhibition on dinosaurs and a small aquarium with reptiles, fish, and spiders. In the upstairs section of the galleries, there's a modern art museum with temporary exhibitions and a section on the history of Malmö. All of these extensions are included in the main castle ticket price and provide excellent value and a lot to see, although you needn't feel you should cover everything. Some of the exhibitions don't have English labeling, so take a guide booklet from the information desk (unfortunately, there are no audio guides) and pick and choose what interests you most.

## The Science and Maritime Museum

The Science and Maritime Museum is located just a couple of hundred meters (656 ft) to the west of the castle bridge: just keep walking as you pass the castle, and you'll see it on your right. It contains an entertaining selection of old cars, airplanes, and trains and a submarine in the back yard, which you can enter to experience the claustropbic engine room and look out at Malmö through the periscope. Look out for the corner on the upper floor dedicated to the old Malmö-Copenhagen ferry, rendered obsolete by the opening of the Öresund Bridge in 2000. There's a ticket office, old seats from the boat, a retro price list from the ferry canteen, and a video showing a typical morning for travelers on board, in which a decades-old Copenhagen slips by in the portholes as waiters serve breakfast and coffee to passengers.

Other areas of the museum are dedicated to important scientists from the Skåne region, such as 18th-century botanist, physician, and zoologist Carl Linnaeus, also known as the "father of modern taxonomy." There are collections of various animal skulls and butterflies, and a diorama of the man himself. Astronomer Tycho Brahe, born in Skåne when it was part of Denmark, is one of the region's most famous scientists of all. The "Heaven and Earth" exhibit pays tribute to this with a nice, interactive darkroom in which you can navigate the solar system. Modern inventors are not left out: the "Smart!" exhibit showcases inventions to have come out of Skåne, including pacemakers, nano tachnology, and the humble toothpick.

Overall, there's enough in the science museum to keep you interested for at least 2-3 hours. Just outside (turn left as you exit and take the first street on the left) you'll find **Fiskehoddorna,** traditional-style fishermen's huts, which are also part of the museum. Freshly caught raw fish and shellfish are sold here from 6:30am-1pm every Tuesday through Saturday. Try a piece of herring, smoked salmon, or eel from the sellers, who display their catches in flatbed refrigerators in front of wooden shacks painted in reds and blues.

## LILLA TORG

The most camera-friendly of many handsome spots at the center of the Gamla Staden (Old City) is the cobblestoned Lilla Torg, which is flanked by bars and restaurants in wooden-framed buildings. Created as a marketplace in the 16th century and still a popular meeting spot, Lilla Torg comes alive on weekends as locals fill the nightspots, which include popular places like Moosehead and Mello Yello. In summer, small, free concerts sometimes take place on the square. All around the square, the centuries-old buildings are stunning. Of particular note are the red post-and-beam houses in the southeastern corner that

Lilla Torg

join Skomakaregatan and the neighboring yellow-stuccoed building: the former of these is Malmö's best-preserved timber structure.

## ST. PETRI CHURCH

*Göran Olsgatan 4; tel. 040-27 90 43; http:// svenskakyrkanmalmo.se/st-petri-kyrka; daily 10am-6pm; free*

The oldest building in Malmö, St. Petri Church, which dates from the early 14th century, is open daily for visitors, who can admire its polygonal Gothic spires from the outside and minimalism inside. The Krämare Chapel breaks with this theme with intense vault paintings, the only ones to have survived from the church's medieval heyday.

# OUTSIDE OLD CITY
## ✪ VÄSTRA HAMNEN

*Västra Hamnen; free*

Västra Hamnen was once the city's shipping yard. It has, after heavy investment and redevelopment into a boardwalk and promenade, become a hugely popular destination for locals and visitors. The centerpiece is the towering **Turning Torso**, the highest building in Scandinavia and visible from parts of Copenhagen. The part-boardwalk, part-concrete seafront promenade feels wide open, with grass on one side and the sea on the other. It's a great place to go for a bracing afternoon walk in the cold, and then pop into one of the many restaurants and cafés to warm up with views of the Öresund (bridge included). Summertime can bring a Mediterranean vibe, with music blaring from ghetto blasters and salsa and yoga classes on the promenade. Don't miss **Stapelbäddsparken**, a molded moonscape of a skateboarding park designed by architect Stefan Hauser.

## Turning Torso

*Lilla Varvsgatan 14; tel. 040-17 45 40; www. turningtorso.se; not generally open to the public*

Twisting its way 190 meters (623 ft) into the Öresund coastal sky, the Turning Torso is unlike any other building in either Malmö or Copenhagen, and yet somehow it manages to fit in, like some daydreamy vision of a science fiction Scandinavia. Its white, neofuturist façades bend through seemingly impossible angles, and the center of the building on the roof is not directly above the center on the ground floor. Up close, it's slightly easier, if still not entirely straightforward, to comprehend the fitting together of its nine segments of five-story pentagons. It is a residential building and cannot be visited except through prearranged VIP tours (http://skyhighmeetings. com/en/studiebesok/). However, an app and QR code that can be scanned at the entrance to the building does provide some tourist information. It is well worth passing as part of a walk around the Västra Hamnen area.

St. Petri Church

## MODERNA MUSEET

*Ola Billgrens plats 2-4; tel. 040-685 7937; www.modernamuseet.se; Tues.-Fri. 11am-6pm, Sat.-Sun. 11am-5pm; free*

Contemporary art specialist Moderna Museet Malmö is a part of the state-owned, Stockholm-based Moderna Museet, but it has its own independent exhibition program. Opened in 2009 in a former power station with a distinctive bright-orange extension added on, its perforated façade clashing to agreeable effect with a grey Romanesque archway, it stands out on the quiet Gasverksgatan in the southeastern part of the old city. At a manageable size of 809 square meters (one-fifth of an acre), the exhibition spaces flit between Swedish and international contemporary art. Recent exhibitions have covered early photography, the contemporary history of Chinese restaurants in Sweden and veteran German artist Rosemarie Trockel, while a 2019 exhibition will focus on Andy Warhol.

## THE KNOTTED GUN

*Bagers plats; free*

On the opposite side of Suellshamnen from the Central Station, Carl Fredrik Reuterswärd's iconic pacifist sculpture is an admirable first impression of Malmö, and it's no less pertinent given that some parts of the city have had problems with gun violence in recent times. Officially named *Non Violence*, it is more commonly referred to as the *Knotted Gun*. Reuterswärd created the bronze monument after the assassination of one of the most famous pacifists of all time, John Lennon, in 1980. The barrel of the weathered, oversized Colt Python .357 Magnum turns around on itself; the muzzle, rendered apparently harmless, points toward the sky. There are 22 copies of the work in various locations around the world, but Malmö's is one of only three originals (the others are in New York City and Luxembourg).

# Sports and Recreation

## ✪ PARKS

Malmö is sometimes referred to in Sweden as the "City of Parks" and not without reason. You're never far away from at least one, making it easy to go for a run, a walk, a picnic, or, if you're lucky, to sunbathe. There are lakes, small canals, ampitheaters, broad fields, skateboard parks, and ball courts. It's little wonder the Swedes look so healthy.

### Slottsparken

*Kung Oscars väg; 24 hrs; free*

Running adjacent to Kungsparken and between the castle and the city library, the expansive Slottsparken (Castle Park) does more than its fair share in confirming Malmö as a city rich in park space, splashed with lakes of various sizes and with ample stretches of woodlands. The two most recognizable landmarks are the **Castle Mill**, a large windmill, and Carl Milles's 1950 statue *Man and Pegasus,* with man and his flying horse atop a 10-meter-tall (33 ft) granite pillar overlooking the big lake (Stora dammen). At the lake, you can spot black-headed gulls, herons, and swans. The center of the park is the 2.5 sq km (1 sq mi) Lördagsplanen (Saturday Field), where mini festivals and other events are sometimes held during summer—an Indian culture festival with live music was in full swing on my last visit. There are also rockeries and shaded areas with trees and bushes.

Slottsparken

view of Malmö from Kungsparken

## Kungsparken

*Slottsgatan 33; open 24hrs; free*

Kungsparken is connected to Slottsparken via the Kommendantbron Bridge (the two parks shared the name "Slottsparken" until 1881 and are still often confused). The leafy, calm park with its lake, paths, and idyllic bridges is like a serene, smaller version of New York City's Central Park. Its 8.4 acres boast more than a hundred species of trees. A 19th-century **iron-cast, three-tiered fountain** is the most impressive human-made sight in the park, and a peculiar (very small) **cave** with a snake's head peering down from its apex, spitting water into a stone tray underneath, is a hidden spot for discovery. These are located close to each other near the end of the **Lovers' Alley**, which makes its romantic way east from Trädgårdsbron alongside the canal, flanked by tall, shade-providing trees.

## Slottsträdgården

*Malmöhusvägen 8; tel. 076-890 16 49; www. slottstradgarden.se; 24 hrs; free*

Completing a triumvirate of green areas near the castle with Kungsparken and Slottsparken, Slottsträdgården is an ecological garden reminiscent of a city allotment with its many plant beds and is run by a society of local garden lovers. It has 14 different sections, with both vegetables and ornamental elements: up to 400 types of plants are grown here. Visitors are welcome to walk among the flower beds on the garden paths. It is also home to the **Slottsträdgården Café**, which uses produce from the garden. The café is operated by celebrity chef Tareq Taylor.

## Pildammsparken

*Pildammsparken; https://evenemang2. malmo.se; 24 hrs; free*

At 45 hectares (111 acres), Pildammsparken is Malmö's largest park. The name translates to Willowpond Park, which is an accurate representation of the leafy thickets and two large ponds for which it is known. A domed pavilion with slender columns, Margaretapavillon, is a relic from the grounds of the 1914 Baltic exhibition, from which Pildammsparken sprung. The park was finished in 1926, after it had been used to grow potatoes during the First World War. The pavilion is just west of the largest lake, Pildammarna, which is a great place for a morning jog or afternoon walk (there'll be others out doing the same thing, but there's enough space for everyone). The western section of the park is dominated by a large amphitheater, where free concerts and performances often take place during summer. These are normally listed on Malmö's city website at https://evenemang2.malmo.se.

### Folkets Park

*Amiralsgatan 35; tel. 020-34 45 00; http://malmofolketspark.se; 24 hrs; general entry free (some entrance fees for attractions)*

Located south of the city center, Folkets Park blurs the lines between green space and amusement park. It was partly inspired by Copenhagen's Tivoli Gardens, which can be seen in the design of the Moriska paviljongen (Moorish pavilion). Founded at the end of the 19th century, the park was closely associated with the Social Democratic Party, which bought it in 1891 and sold it to the city 100 years later in 1991. In the intervening years, it was commonly used as a gathering place for workers. Today, the park is a family-oriented diversion with a playground, fairground rides, miniature golf, and a petting zoo (some of these attractions are seasonal). The park hosts small concerts and other activities during the summer. In 2018, a large screen was installed during the World Cup, which proved to be a hit as the Swedish team reached the quarter-finals.

## BATHS
### Ribersborgs Kallbadhus

*Limhamnsvägen, Brygga 1; tel. 040-260 366; summer Mon.-Fri. 9am-9pm, Sat.-Sun. 9am-6pm, winter Mon.-Fri. 10am-7pm, Sat.-Sun. 9am-6pm; single entry 70 SEK*

If you want to take some time out to relax while learning about Swedish culture, then head to the Ribersborgs Kallbadhus public bath. It is a great destination on any visit to Malmö, with a pier location and a distinctive boardwalk. Take a sauna (there are five types) with a sea view, an ice-cold sea bath (known as "winter bathing"), go for a refreshing swim in the summer, or simply get a massage. The restaurant includes a range of fish dishes, salads, and cakes. In true liberated Swedish style, saunas and winter baths are experienced in the nude. There are segregated areas for men and women and one mixed-gender sauna. As with a number of other recognizable Malmö locations, the baths show up in an episode of *The Bridge*.

## BICYCLING

Malmö is superbly equipped for cycling, with broad bike lanes and favorable traffic rules. There has been heavy investment in bicycle lanes in the city since the mid-2000s, providing things like designated parking areas, underpasses designed for optimal visibility, and even apartments with elevators designed to accommodate bikes so they can be stored in homes.

Many of the city's bicycle lanes are separated from roads, so you often don't have to share the asphalt with cars. In traffic, if you are cycling straight ahead through an intersection and a car is turning right across your lane, you have the right of way, so the car should stop and wait for you. Be alert, nonetheless: cars occasionally edge forward or fail to spot cyclists coming from behind. Despite the favorable conditions, it's important to cycle safely at all times, and I strongly recommend always using a bicycle helmet. Almost all bike rental companies offer these. The city's biggest park Pildammsparken, where the wide paths and open spaces mean there is ample space for bikes and pedestrians (but keep things at a leisurely pace), is a prime spot for cycling in Malmö.

### Västra Hamnen to Ribersborgs Kallbadhus

*Start in Scaniaparken*

*Distance: 4km*

*Riding time: 30 minutes*

Västra Hamnen, a redeveloped part of the city, does not suffer from a lack of bicycle lanes found in some other places and is a good place to set out to on a short trip from the center of the city. Parts of the area still have an industrial look, but when you reach the coast you can bicycle along the scenic Ribersborg path or Scaniastigen, where you can view the Turning Torso and the Öresund Bridge and stop for a picnic on the beach or by the promenade. Continuing around the coast in a westerly direction, you will eventually reach the treelined Limhamnsvägen, a beautiful coastal area with a designated bicycle lane that runs alongside a flat grassy plain, sandy beach, and several jetties where you can walk out and take in the sea air. It is also here you will find Ribersborgs Kallbadhus, a public sea-bathing facility that is open year-round. The distance around the coast from Västra Hamnen to the Ribersborg baths is around 4km (2.5 mi).

### Kungsgatan

Kungsgatan, south of the historic center, is a 3km (1.8 mi) stretch of road with long, weaving cycle lanes that undulate under bridges and swerve around trees. There's lots of green space, playgrounds, and fresh air. It's such a pleasant place to ride and is so close to the city that it's worth trying out, even if it's not on a particular route between points of interest.

### Malmö By Bike

*www.malmobybike.se*

Malmö By Bike is a rental service operated by a prepaid card (which must be ordered in advance and delivered to an address in Sweden) that provides access to 500 bikes at 50 stations around the city, with more to come in 2019.

### Donkey Republic

*https://www.donkey.bike*

Donkey Republic is a Europe-wide app that allows you to find, unlock, and rent a bicycle using an app and is available in Malmö.

## TOURS

### Strömma Rundan Sightseeing

*Norra Vallgatan 3; tel. 040-611 74 88; www. stromma.se; ticket booth 10:30am-4pm (seasonal variations apply); from 150 SEK*

Stromma's Malmö canal tour takes advantage of the compact size of the city. The historical center is surrounded by a complete canal loop that provides comprehensive sightseeing tours. The canal tour takes in Kungsparken and Slottsparken, sails close to Malmöhus Castle next to the Old City, and loops into the harbor before returning to its starting point by Centralstation. Seeing the city from this angle, which sometimes requires a low duck as you pass under the old stone bridges, is complemented by guided commentary and anecdotes in Swedish and English. Bring dry and warm clothes if the weather's not agreeable—there's no hiding from the elements on the flat, open canal tour boats.

# Dining

## GAMLA STADEN

### SCANDINAVIAN

**Bastard**

*Mäster Johansgatan 11; tel. 040-12 13 18; www.bastardrestaurant.com; Tues.-Thurs. 5pm-midnight, Fri.-Sat. 5pm-1am; dinner menu small dishes from 55 SEK*

Bastard is an instantly recognizable name on Malmö's culinary scene and lives up to its reputation as one of the best restaurants the city has to offer, not just in terms of quality but also value—its nose-to-tail cooking has previously received a Bib Gourmand award, which is awarded to restaurants that offer exceptional value for money. Bastard offers a fast-paced yet relaxed atmosphere, simple dishes packed with flavor, and a good wine and cocktail list. These put Bastard at the heart of what is good about Malmö's food scene. Book ahead.

**Vollmers**

*Tegelgårdsgatan 5; tel. 040-57 97 50; http://vollmers.nu; Tues.-Sat. from 6pm; menu 1600 SEK*

Vollmers received two Michelin stars in 2018 and is one of three restaurants in Malmö to have been bestowed with the accolade. It emphasizes local ingredients. The dishes are, in the words of the Michelin guide, "refined, inspired, and sometimes original." It's located in an old 19th-century townhouse that's tucked away on a side street a stone's throw from Kungsparken. Book ahead to ensure a table.

**Mello Yello**

*Lilla Torg 1; tel. 040-30 45 25; www.melloyello.se; Mon.-Fri. 1:30pm-1am, Sat.-Sun. noon-1am; entrées from 110 SEK*

Mello Yello is a popular restaurant/bar in a busy location on Lilla Torg that heats up on weekends. Al fresco seating (with plenty of blankets and heaters during winter), Mello Yello features a range of bistro food, including pasta and Swedish-style fish soups, salmon, and cod dishes. However, the prime location pushes prices up a little.

### FRENCH

**Sture**

*Adelgatan 13; tel. 040-12 12 53; http://restaurantsture.com; Wed.-Sat. 5:30pm-midnight; tasting menu from 950 SEK, three-course menu 650 SEK*

Sture opened in November 2016 and was awarded a Michelin star four months later. It is generally considered among Sweden's 10 best restaurants. It has an extensive French wine cellar and a sommelier, Frida Sjögren, who has won national recognition for her talent. The menu mixes French and local ingredients. White asparagus, truffle, foie gras, and langoustine all appear on the menu. Presentation is highly artistic. The restaurant is located in the heart of the old city on a building with a Ottoman-style look with larged arch windows, balconies, and stone pillars on the exterior. Inside, there is a relaxed feel, and the service is highly rated.

## ✪ *FIKA*: THE SWEDISH COFFEE AND BUN TRADITION

Anyone who has spent more than a few days in Sweden will probably be aware of the concept of *fika*, the quintessentially Swedish daily afternoon coffee break—with an all-important sweet nibble—that is just as important as a cup of tea in Britain or an espresso in Italy. The 10-million strong population of Sweden accounts for almost 1 percent of the entire world's coffee drinkers—a surprising statistic that is, in part, due to *fika*.

Pronounced "fee-ka" and used as either a noun or a verb, *fika* is also one of the first contacts with Swedish language visitors are likely to have. Since 2015 or so, the concept has begun to gain traction overseas—much like Denmark's *hygge*.

Although coffee is drunk at other times of the day, it is the crucial afternoon combination of coffee with a delicious, sweet cinnamon bun that makes *fika* the phenomenon it is. People at home, at work, or hiking in the mountains are very rigorous in making space in their schedules for the bittersweet afternoon break. The basic idea is simple and rooted in the Scandinavian commitment to good living standards: it's all about making sure you take some time out of your day to slow things down and not get too caught up in the rush of daily life.

### WHERE TO *FIKA* IN MALMÖ

- **Lilla Kafferosteriet** (Baltzarsgatan 24; tel. 040-48 20 00; www.lillakafferosteriet.se). This coffee specialist has a range of delightful pastries behind the counter.

- **Konditori Hollandia** (Södra Förstadsgatan 8; tel. 040-12 48 86, www.hollandia.se). Thought to be the oldest patisserie in town with a to-die-for range of buns and tarts. It's a great place to *fika*.

### *FIKA* AND CAFÉS
#### Lilla Kafferosteriet
*Baltzarsgatan 24; tel. 040-48 20 00; www. lillakafferosteriet.se; Mon.-Fri. 8am-6pm, Sat.-Sun. 10am-6pm; espresso 25 SEK*

Lilla Kafferosteriet is the perfect place to try *fika*. It's not just any old coffee though. Specialty coffee beans from Guatemala, Indonesia, and Peru, among others, are roasted on site and steamed by specialist baristas. The café can be found in one of Malmö's oldest houses, close to Lilla Torg. Traditional Scandinavian cakes are on offer, such as the dry almond and marzipan *kransekaka* or sugary cinnamon buns, *kanelsnäcka*. There is also a delicious variant of the latter with a custard-and-fruit topping, along with a carrot cake, a range of cheese cakes, and buns and muffins.

### BURGERS
#### Texas Longhorn
*Kanalgatan 5; tel. 040-18 21 40; www. texaslonghorn.se; lunch/brunch Mon.-Fri. 11am-4pm, Sat.-Sun. noon-4pm, dinner Mon.-Tues. 4pm-9:30pm, Wed.-Thurs.*

*4pm-10pm, Fri.-Sat. 4pm-10:30pm, Sun.*
*4pm-9pm; starters from 89 SEK*

Swedish burger chain Texas Longhorn has a couple dozen restaurants spread across the country. The branch at Kanalgatan has a handy location near the central shopping districts and a nice canalside view, making for a pleasant and calming summer city spot to stop for a meal. The simple, order-at-the-bar service is stress-free, and the courteous staff keep comfort at the fore. The burgers are satisfying, and side snacks are a slight variation on the usual—the grilled broccoli is a guilt-reducing alternative to fries. A second Malmö outlet can be found at the Triangeln shopping mall (St. Johannesgatan 1B).

# OUTSIDE GAMLA STADEN

## SCANDINAVIAN

### Saltimporten

*Grimsbygatan 24; tel. 070-651 84 26; www.*
*saltimporten.com; Mon.-Fri. noon-2pm;*
*lunch of the day 95 SEK*

Saltimporten has a somewhat hidden location in the old Frihamnen harbor area behind the Central Station, but it is no secret that this is one of the best spots for lunch in the city. Ingredients are sourced from local producers, and the menu changes daily. The busy hustle more than makes up for the rugged industrial look inside and out. There is excellent value and delicious Scandinavian dishes, which pack as much taste as possible into the "meat and two veg" format. Vegetarian options are also available.

### Kvarteret Åkern

*Nobelvägen 73b; tel. 040-96 96 00; http://*
*kvarteretakern.com; Tues.-Thurs. 5pm-11pm,*
*Fri.-Sat. 5pm-midnight; four-course set*
*menu 395 SEK (vegetarian option 375 SEK)*

Its decor a combination of traditional colors and designs (wallpaper and carpet) and modern kitsch (animal candle holders), Kvarteret Åkern has been praised for its simple Scandinavian food and natural wines. It has a friendly neighborhood feel and can be found to the south of Folkets Park, away from the more tourist-traveled paths of the Old City.

### Bloom in the Park

*Pildammsvägen 17; tel. 040-793 63; https://*
*bloominthepark.se; Mon.-Fri. 5:30pm-11pm,*
*Sat. 10am-2pm, 5:30pm-11pm; two-course*
*lunch menu 395 SEK, three-course dinner*
*menu 495 SEK excluding wine*

Bloom in the Park's status is now well established, having been awarded a Michelin star in 2015. It has a reputation for surprise: there is no menu, and the diner experiences tasting dishes without being given prior information—according to the concept. Allergies are fully catered to, and the menu is presented after the meal. The constantly evolving kitchen and wine cellar reflect season and availability, so each visit is likely to be unique. Located in Pildammsparken overlooking Pildammarna Lake, the black-painted wooden building that houses the restaurant is part of the charm, with a congenial atmosphere filling the minimalistic interior of carefully designed lighting and tasteful paneling.

## FIKA AND CAFÉS

### Konditori Hollandia

*Södra Förstadsgatan 8; tel. 040-12 48 86;*
*www.hollandia.se; Mon.-Fri. 7:45am-7pm;*
*Sat.-Sun. 9am-7pm; tart for five persons*
*195 SEK*

Quaint Konditori Hollandia, which opened in 1903, is thought to be the oldest patisserie in town, and its to-die-for cinnamon buns, cream cakes, and tarts are certainly testament to its years of perfecting the trade. It also has the elegant and charming tearoom look down to a tee, making it a fantastic and atmospheric place for *fika*.

### August No Stress Surf Cafe

*Rönngatan 2A; tel. 040-12 25 25; www. augustsurfcafe.se; Mon.-Fri. 9am-5pm, Sat. 10am-5pm, Sun. 11am-5pm; espresso 25 SEK, desserts from 25 SEK, sandwiches from 85 SEK*

This café is conveniently located on the corner opposite the STF hostel, which puts it in a good place to pick up trade from passing backpackers. With a corresponding surfy theme, August No Stress Cafe has, in fact, a more mature clientele than preconceptions might suggest. It does retain a beach-like relaxed atmosphere, with welcoming staff and a resident dog that walks around wearing a garland. Background music ranges from 1970s disco to Jack Johnson. A range of cakes (25 SEK) and *smörgåsar* (open sandwiches; from 85 SEK) are available. Perhaps the best reason to support the café with a visit is its commendable ambition to "improve tolerance, acceptance, and inclusiveness for people with learning disabilities." August No Stress Surf Cafe provides part-time work to people with Down's Syndrome, including a young man called August, for whom the café is named.

### MARKETS

### Malmö Saluhall food market

*Gibraltargatan 6; tel. 040-626 77 30; https://www.malmosaluhall.se; Mon.-Thurs. 10am-7pm, Fri. 10am-9pm, Sat. 10am-5pm, Sun. 11am-4pm; coffee/pastries from 30 SEK*

An artisan food market in a converted warehouse near the harbor, Malmö Saluhall is an ideal place to stop off for *fika* or a falafel, or for coffee and noodles. Do you have kitchen access at your accommodation? Pick up some premium raw ingredients such as fresh, raw salmon or trout from Söderholmens Fisk or locally grown, organic fruit and veg from Farm Shop. You could also pick out some handmade praline, caramel, and fudge from Chocolatte to take home as a souvenir. Hawaiian poke bowls with lukewarm rice and marinated fish are served up at Påris, and hipster sandwich specialist Poms offers sauerkraut and pastrami, pickled onions, and feta among its fillings. There are plenty more stands besides. The atmosphere is laid back, and summertime brings outside tables into play. Make sure you have a credit or debit card—cash is not always accepted.

### INTERNATIONAL
### Bar Burrito

*Fersens väg 14; tel. 040-615 32 78; https://barburrito.se; Mon.-Fri. 11am-9pm, Sat.-Sun. noon-9pm; from 74 SEK*

Bar Burrito is popular stop for an inexpensive, fulfilling snack. Its rather ordinary-looking interior and display of meats and salads behind the glass counter contains a surprisingly tasty variety of fillings, including pulled pork that's more Mexican than Scandinavian and lightly spiced achiote chicken. Bowls, tacos, and salads are all available as alternatives to the burrito tortilla.

### Belle Epoque

*Södra Skolgatan 43; tel. 040-97 39 90; http://belle-epoque.se; Tues.-Sat. 6am-1pm; dishes from 50 SEK*

Near the lively Möllevångstorget area,

Belle Epoque serves small French dishes that are intended to be shared in a group while you enjoy something from the cocktail list. A mixture of hot dishes, salads, and desserts are included on the menu, which is updated regularly.

### Mocca

*Friisgatan 4; tel. 040-30 11 44; www.
facebook.com/Cafemoccamalmo; daily
9am-7pm; sandwiches from 79 SEK*

One of several good options on the semi-pedestrianized Friisgatan near Triangeln, Mocca's generous salmon sandwiches or lasagna make it a preferable location for lunch or coffee while you're in the central part of the city.

### Dubbel Dubbel

*Simrishamnsgatan 14; tel. 040-12 58
55; www.dubbeldubbelmalmo.se; daily
5pm-10pm; entrées from 69 SEK, dumplings
from 65 SEK*

Dumplings and dim sum are served in authentic bamboo bowls with a Tsing Tao beer or Chinese-inspired cocktail. Dubbel Dubbel is highly popular with locals and influenced by the street-food roots of its Chinese cuisine. Takeaway is available or you can sit inside among the tasteful, Swedish lighting and furniture fused with Chinese square-table, low-stool seating culture. In summer, the backyard garden is open to diners.

### Jalla Jalla

*Bergsgatan 16; tel. 040-623 70 00;
Sun.-Thurs. 11am-2am, Fri. 11am-5am, Sat.
11m-6am; falafel wraps from 35 SEK*

One of Malmö's most popular spots for a late-night shawarma or falafel, Jalla Jalla has an authentic Middle Eastern feel with ingredients such as pickles and halloumi and is easily recognizable from the colorful shop front. The restaurant even makes a brief appearance in hit TV series *The Bridge*.

# Entertainment and Events

## FESTIVALS
### Malmöfestivalen

*Gamla Staden and around; https://
malmofestivalen.se; mid-August; free*

The creaking streets of the old city become awash with colorful sights and exotic tastes during the Malmö Festival, a week-long festival of diverse music, food, and drink events scattered across Gamla Staden. More than a million people attend the traditional mid-August slot every year, making it the largest street party of its kind in northern Europe. The program includes (but isn't limited to) fashion shows, art installations, DJs, dancing and CrossFit competitions, kids' activities, VR, bicycle repair, "pimping" lessons, and good old-fashioned concerts. A huge street food and drinks market fills Gustav Adolfs torg and Södergatan, creating a festival atmosphere in the city streets. Entry is free, and with its sustainability-conscious outlook, good care is taken not to leave Malmö in a mess once the fun is over.

# NIGHTCLUBS AND LIVE MUSIC

## Etage

*Stortorget 6; tel. 040-40 23 20 60; http:// etagegruppen.se/etage; Mon. & Thurs. 11:30pm-4am, Fri-Sat 11:30pm-5am,; cover charge Mon., Thur. free before midnight, 60 SEK after midnight, Sat.-Sun. 60 SEK before midnight, 120 SEK after midnight*

If you plan to go big while in Malmö, Etage is a good place to start. There are two dance floors, a karaoke bar, and a four-table casino. There are six bars in total.

## Slagthuset

*Jörgen Kocksgatan 7A; tel. 040-611 80 90; http://slagthus.se; check program online for events and prices*

Slagthuset is not just a nightclub; it also doubles as a theater, hosting plays, concerts, and stand-up comedy. Located in a former slaughterhouse, from where it gets its name, the high ceilings and minimalist brickwork interior are topped off by details such as using pallets as seating. It gives Slaghuset a hip feel that helps back up its reputation as one of Malmö's most famous night spots.

## KB

*Friisgatan 26; tel. 040-30 20 11; https:// kulturbolaget.se; check program online for events and prices*

KB (Kulturbolaget, to give its official name) first opened in 1982 and has hosted thousands of rock concerts in the intervening years. It also acts as a nightclub when there are no concerts. Check the website for upcoming concerts and ticket availability—you might be pleasantly surprised.

# BARS

## The Pickwick Pub

*Malmborgsgatan 7; tel. 040-23 32 66; www. malmborgen.nu/pickwick-pub; Mon.-Tues. 4pm-11:30pm, Wed.-Thurs. 4pm-12:30am, Fri. 3pm-2am, Sat. 1pm-2am, Sun. 1pm-9:30pm; draught beers from 58 SEK*

A pub in the English tradition, the Pickwick tries with good effect to go for the tavern look, with dark-green color scheme and wood paneling. Any English pub that references Dickens in its name has a decent claim to authenticity in my book, but Pickwick backs this up with a decent selection of ales and beers.

## Malmö Brewing Co. & Taproom

*Malmö Brygghus, Bergsgatan 33; tel. 040-20 96 85; http://malmobrewing.com; Mon.-Thurs. 4pm-midnight, Fri. 4pm-3am, Sat. noon-3am, Sun. 4pm-midnight; draught beers from 45 SEK (small glass)*

Malmö Brewing Co. & Taproom merits recommendation for the four different beers on tap at any one time, including ciders, IPAs, and other brews that are still hard to come by elsewhere. Tours of the on-site microbrewery, which end in a tasting session, are available on Fridays.

## Moosehead

*Lilla Torg 1; tel. 040 12 04 2; www. moosehead.se; Mon.-Fri. 2pm-1am, Sat. noon-1am, Sun. noon-midnight*

There's rustic brickwork interior, antlers mounted on the walls, and a large outside seating area at Moosehead, a tourist-friendly Lilla Torg bar and restaurant with an eclectic menu of beer and cocktails as well as pub food (including an elk burger and a range of Thai dishes). It's a good place to take in the local Gamla Staden action; it heats up on Friday and Saturday evenings.

# Accommodations

## UNDER 500 SEK
### STF Malmö Hostel & Hotel

*Rönngatan 1; tel. 040-611 62 20; www.
swedishtouristassociation.com; shared room
from 230 SEK STF/HI member price, private
room from 550 SEK STF/HI member price,
non-members pay additional 50 SEK per
night*

This is a sprawling hostel with clean dorms and facilities and broader lower bunks on which to spread out. The atmosphere here can be quiet and sterile, but that is made up for by the many friendly guests. The breakfast is expensive at 90 SEK for non-STF (Svenska Turistföreningen, the Swedish affiliate of Hostelling International) members, but it is a good way to start the day: it's a typical continental, buffet style but with a smoothie, overnight oats, and pickled fish added to the menu. A less-expensive "packed" breakfast (30 SEK) is also available. It's conveniently located a short walk from the Central Station and near the central sights.

### Rut & Ragnars Hostel AB

*Nobelvägen 113; tel. 040-611 60 60; www.
rutochragnars.se; shared room from 225 SEK*

Rut & Ragnars is recently furbished, although you might find it hard to tell. It's a distant second choice to STF in the pecking order of Malmö's city hostels. Located a 15-20 minute walk from town, the common areas feel cramped and the toilet and shower facilities are heavily used. Staff are friendly and helpful, and the dorm beds are fitted with curtains, providing extra privacy. Breakfast is not included.

## 500-1,000 SEK
### Teaterhotellet

*Fersens väg 20; tel. 040-665 58 00; www.
teaterhotellet.se; double occupancy high
season from 985 SEK*

Located near the corner of Pildammsparken, Teaterhotellet is a solid budget hotel option close to the city with a hearty buffet breakfast (with a juice presser). The theatrical connection is not immediately obvious, apart from elevator doors being painted like stage curtains, but the functional rooms and efficient service do not leave anything wanting for the price.

### Bosses Gästvåningar och vandrarhem

*Södra Förstadsgatan 110B; tel. 040-32 62
50; www.bosses.nu; double occupancy high
season from 625 SEK*

Located near Triangeln Station and with 36 beds in 17 rooms, Bosses has one-, two-, three-, and four-bed rooms, so small groups can be accommodated in an effective private room for hostel prices. Breakfast is not included.

## 1,000-2,000 SEK
### Mayfair Hotel Tunneln

*Adelgatan 4; tel. 040-10 16 20; www.
mayfairtunneln.com; double occupancy high
season from 1,025 SEK*

Stepping into the Mayfair Hotel Tunneln is a travel experience in itself, given that the building dates in part from the beginning of the 1300s, when the cellar—where breakfast is now served—was built by Danish knight Jens Uffesen Neb. The stepgable Gothic house on top of the cellar was built in the 1500s. History literally drips from the corridors of the hotel, with framed pictures describing the building's and the city's roles in each other's histories. The rooms are anything but 15th century and are well equipped for a peaceful night's sleep. Recommended.

### Story Hotel

*Tyfongatan 1; tel. 040-616 52 00; http://storyhotels.com/studiomalmo; double occupancy high season from 1,190 SEK*

The stylish interior design of the hip Story Hotel is quickly making it a favorite among visitors, as is its location on Universitetsbron, minutes from the Central Station on the bridge toward Västra Hamnen. The rooftop restaurant and bar offers spectacular views over Malmö and the Öresund.

### Comfort Hotel Malmö

*Carlsgatan 10C; tel. 040-33 04 40; http://comfort-hotel-malmo.hotelsinmalmo.com; double occupancy high season from 1,500 SEK*

A three-star option next to the station and the waterfront with breakfast included as well as gym facilities. The location is probably its biggest asset, but the small, modern rooms are more than adequate for short stays in the city, although they lack complimentary tea and coffee. The buffet breakfast is widely praised and can be prepared for you before regular hours if you are checking out early.

### Park Inn by Radisson Malmö

*Sjömansgatan 2; tel. 040-628 60 00; www.parkinn.com/hotel-malmo; double occupancy high season from 1,125 SEK*

This business hotel in a cubic, modernist building at the southern end of Västra Hamnen has an advantageous location if you want to wander around the redeveloped harbor area and visit Malmöhus Castle and its surrounding parks and museums. Some of the rooms have great views of the sea and the Turning Torso. There's a clean, smart look, trimmed throughout with the spectrum of colors used in the hotel's branding.

### Scandic Triangeln

*Triangeln 2; tel. 040-693 47 00; www.scandichotels.com/hotels; double occupancy high season from 1,092 SEK*

The tall, glass-fronted Scandic Triangeln building looks like it might feel more at home on the Upper East Side of New York than in central Malmö. But it provides a good orientation point in (and view above) the central shopping streets. Amenities include a cocktail bar, a gym, and a spa area with saunas.

### MJ's Hotel

*Mäster Johansgatan 13; tel. 040-664 64 00; www.mjs.life; double occupancy high season from 1,120 SEK*

First impressions count at MJ's Hotel, with its entrance on the corner of Mäster Johansgatan and Isak Slagergatan given a glamorous twist with golden pillars and "HOTEL" written in bright lightbulbs reminiscent of the Moulin Rouge. Just a block away from both Stortoget and Lilla Torg, the plush interior and exterior fit with the Old City splendor. Rooms have mahogany furniture and thick carpets or patterned rugs, with marble sinks and copper faucets in the bathrooms.

### Clarion Hotel and Congress Malmo Live

*Dag Hammarskjölds Torg 2; tel. 040-20 75 00; www.nordicchoicehotels.com/hotels;*

*double occupancy high season from 1,038 SEK*

Rising sleekly over the harbor, the Clarion Hotel is perhaps second only to the Turning Torso in dominating Malmö's skyline, and it pulls it off, contrasting and complementing the skyline around the harbor and the castle. Views are excellent from the upper floors—some of the rooms have floor-to-ceiling windows.

# Information and Services

Malmö Tourism (www.malmotown.com) has tourist "info points" scattered around the city, where you can pick up maps and brochures, and staff can help answer your questions. Various locations include Travelshop (Carlsgatan 4A), Triangelns köpcentrum (Södra Förstadsgatan 41), Pressbyrån (Södergatan 11), Fintoan på Gustav Adolfs Torg (Gustav Adolfs Torg), Malmö Konsthall (Skt. Johannesgatan 7), and Moderna Museet Malmö (Ola Billgrens plats 2-4).

In an emergency, dial 112 for ambulance and fire services or 11414 (non-emergencies) for police.

Sweden's postal service is run by Postnord, the same private company responsible for Denmark's. That means that in lieu of regular post offices like the type seen in the United States, United Kingdom, and elsewhere, stamps can be purchased and letters and packages sent at "postal service points," which are desks located in places like supermarkets, convenience stores, and gas stations. These are easily identified: look for the yellow horn and crown symbol on a blue background.

# Getting There and Around

## GETTING TO MALMÖ FROM COPENHAGEN

It's easy to forget that until the year 2000, traveling between Malmö and Copenhagen involved a ferry voyage. These days it's much simpler.

### BY TRAIN

The quickest way is by DSB train (www.dsb.dk) from either Copenhagen Central Station or Copenhagen Airport. Tickets can be bought online, via the DSB app, or by using the Rejsekort travel card. If you go with the latter option, don't forget to check out at Malmö Station. There are only two check-in/check-out points, right at the far end of the concourse by the exit. The trip to Malmö's Central Station is a 25-minute journey from Copenhagen Airport or 40 minutes from Copenhagen Central Station. Tickets cost 89DKr for a one-way ticket, and you can bring a bicycle on the train with a 44.50DKr add-on ticket.

## BY BUS

If you'd rather see the Öresund from a bus, **Flixbus** (www.flixbus.com; from 29DKr single) and **Graahundbus** (http://graahundbus.dk; from 120Dkr return) offer tickets less expensive than the train at the cost of some of the convenience. The latter operator, a play on the Greyhound Bus company, is the more charming option of the two. Flixbuses leave from the Ingerslevsgade bus departure terminal, while Greyhounds depart by the Copenhagen Plaza Hotel, Bernstorffsgade 4. Both of these locations are close to the Central Station, and both companies operate departures from the airport. In Malmö, the Flixbus will drop you off at Central Station and Gråhund at Gustav Adolfs Torg, both central locations. It's not normally possible to transport bicycles by bus.

## BY CAR

Before you begin your drive, remember your wallet: there's a toll to cross the Øresund/Öresund by road, and it's not cheap, at 375DKr for a normal car (up to 6 meters, or 19 ft). Cash and credit cards are accepted. There is a small discount of 30DKr if you purchase in advance on www.oresundsbron.com. From central Copenhagen, take the O2 ring road, which runs close to the harbor near Central Station and south of Vesterbro where it meets Sydhavnsgade. Follow signs for Malmö E20. This road will take you across to Amager via the Sjællandsbroen Bridge. Merge right and continue to follow signs for Malmö E20, crossing Amager from west to east. The sea will come into view, and you'll enter the tunnel section of the Öresund crossing, the 4km (2.5 mi) Drogden Tunnel, you'll emerge onto the artificial island of Peberholm before continuing on the vast Öresund Bridge for the next 8km (5 mi): enjoy the view. Once you reach the other side of the bridge, you'll approach the toll gates. Passport control spot checks take place at these toll stations at the Swedish end of the bridge. Continue on the E20 until you reach the exit for Limhamn/Malmö V. Take this exit and follow into the Swedish city. The entire journey is just over the length of a marathon at 44km (27 mi) and should take around 45 minutes to drive.

## GETTING AROUND
### BY PUBLIC TRANSIT

City buses and trains in Malmö are operated by **Skånetrafiken** (tel. 0771-77 77 77; www.skanetrafiken. se). The most straightforward way to buy tickets is via Skånetrafiken's app, but there are also ticket machines on train station platforms, including at Copenhagen Central Station and Copenhagen Airport). The Skånetrafiken app can also be used to plan journeys.

If you are planning extensive use of public transportation in Malmö, consider buying a timmarsbiljett, which gives unlimited use of the public transit system in the city, including buses and trains. The 24- or 72-hour passes can be purchased for 65SEK and 165SEK, respectively.

A third option is to purchase a reusable Jojo card (20SEK) from Skånetrafiken's counters at Central Station and Triangeln Station. Similar to the Danish Rejsekort, the Jojo card can be recharged with credit as needed. Just check in and out with the card on public transportation. There's a fare discount of 10 percent per journey with the card.

## THE BRIDGE: HOW THE HIT TV SHOW STRENGTHENED THE COPENHAGEN-MALMÖ BOND

Thousands of people cross the Öresund (or Øresund) Bridge every day to commute to work in both countries, and since it opened in 2000, it has revolutionized the economic and logistical link between Copenhagen and Malmö. But if you know it from the hugely successful Scandinoir TV show, called *The Bridge*, you could be forgiven for thinking the Öresund Bridge has an extremely dark underbelly.

Over the course of its four-season run from 2011-2018, the hit series put the nearly 8km-long (5 mi) bridge firmly in the public eye. A joint production between Sweden and Denmark, the series became one of the most successful Scandinavian television exports ever and has also inspired remakes including a US version, also called *The Bridge*, and *The Tunnel*, which revolves around French and British police cooperation.

The dark atmosphere, quirky personalities of the characters, and the shared Scandinavian backdrop have captivated audiences since the show first aired in 2011, beginning with the gruesome, but no less symbolic, discovery of a body in two parts—one on each country's side of the bridge.

Even though the show itself plays out more or less equally either side of the Öresund, about 80 percent of the locations from *The Bridge* can be found in Malmö. This means fans of the show can visit several real locations they will recognize from moments in the series, including:

- The **old Malmö football stadium** (Eric Perssons väg 31), a crumbling, concrete edifice with rusty turnstiles and flaky paint that was originally built for the 1958 World Cup. *Bridge* fans might recognize the location from a tense rooftop scene that involved gang member Julian and rebellious teenager Laura in the second season. With the city's soccer club Malmö FF now having moved to a new stadium, the old ground is slated for demolition, so catch it while it's still there.

- The area around **Barkgatan** and **Möllevångsgatan**, close to **Folkets Park**, is a great place to spot locations from the series. The facades of the Malmö County police stations (different façades were used in different seasons) can all be found here—the buildings are home to offices, health centers, and yoga clubs in real life.

- Falafel restaurant **Jalla Jalla** (Bergsgatan 16) is where Saga receives the call from her boyfriend ending their relationship. It's one of the city's most popular falafel places.

- The **Ribersborgs Kallbadhus** baths (Limhamnsvägen, Brygga 1) are featured in the first season, when Saga and Martin go there to interview a waitress.

- Copenhagen-based **Nordic Noir Tours** (Norra Vallgatan 66; http://nordicnoirtours. com; 300DKr, tours one Sunday monthly, inquiries/bookings via info@ nordicnoirtours.com) shows the series through the eyes of its filmmakers and location scouts, taking you off the beaten tourist track in Malmö. Private tours can be arranged. A similar tour is also available on the Copenhagen side.

Most of Malmö's attractions are close to each other, but public transportation can be useful to save time. From the central Gustav Adolfs Torg in Gamla Staden, bus lines 1, 2, 7, 8, and 35 go to Pildammsparken, an eight-minute journey that costs 25 SEK for a standard single ticket. From Gustav Adolfs Torg to Västra Hamnen, buses 2, 7, and 8 go directly. The ticket price is the same, and the journey is longer at around 23 minutes. Buses leave every few minutes for either journey.

## BY CAR AND TAXI

Driver's licenses valid in Denmark will also be valid in Sweden. If you are driving a rental car, make sure your agreement allows you to cross international borders.

Malmö's traffic is user-friendly and orderly, and there is ample parking. There is a handful of multistory parking garages in the center of the city, with the Triangeln area and Caroli shopping mall (Östergatan 12) both a good bet if you want to get close to the old city. Read more about parking charges in Malmö on the city's parking information website (www.pmalmo.se).

Sweden's taxi market is deregulated, so you can hail cabs and prearrange fixed prices with companies that allow such policies. Arranged prices are entered into taxi meters at the start of your journey. Normally, the step-in fare for a taxi is 40SEK and then 6.16 SEK per minute. A trip from the Central Station to Västra Hamnen will cost around 100-150SEK.

Unlike in Denmark, Uber is legal in Sweden and is therefore an option in Malmö.

## ON FOOT AND BY BICYCLE

Walking and cycling are a breeze in Malmö. There are bicycle lanes, many well away from corresponding roads. Wide paths, coastal promenades, and parks everywhere all contribute to near-optimal conditions.. Take care when cycling in heavy traffic and watch for right-turning cars, which sometimes don't see cyclists and turn in front of them. Always wear a bicycle helmet.

# ESSENTIALS

## Transportation

### GETTING THERE
### FROM THE UNITED STATES

Booking air travel as far as possible in advance is recommended. Traveling directly from East Coast cities such as **New York** or **Miami** is generally the most cost-efficient, with direct, round-trip, economy tickets from these cities to Copenhagen Airport ranging between $300-800.

Skyscanner.com is a good starting point for searching round-trip tickets. Copenhagen Airport is the busiest airport in Scandinavia. **Scandinavian Airlines** (SAS) (www.flysas.com) operate services from a number of U.S. cities, including New York, Boston, Chicago, and San Francisco. **Norwegian** is a low-cost airline that has now opened transatlantic routes, connecting Copenhagen with U.S. cities as far away as Austin, Boston, and Seattle and is very competitive with the traditional carriers on fares.

## FROM EUROPE
### By Air

Budget flights to Denmark are usually less expensive and almost certainly quicker than going anywhere by train or by car, given Copenhagen's awkward location on a smallish island at the northern end of the continent. As such, check all transport options before buying a ticket. Of course, environmental considerations may sway you toward the train, even if other considerations don't. **Ryanair** (www.ryanair.com), **Norwegian** (www.norwegian.com) and to a lesser extent **Easyjet** (www.easyjet.com) all operate low-budget services out of Copenhagen, making much of Europe accessible via a nonstop, relatively inexpensive flight.

### By Train
**Copenhagen Central Station**, (Hovedbanegården, often abbreviated to Hovedbanen), Bernstorffsgade 16–22, is linked to the European network via Stockholm to the north and Amsterdam, Hamburg, and Berlin to the south and east. International tickets can be booked via Denmark's state rail operator **DSB** (tel. 70 13 14 18; www.dsb.dk). If you are planning

an extended trip around Denmark, including some of the other destinations covered in this book, it makes sense to look into the two main European rail passes, **Eurail** (www.eurail.com) for non-Europeans, and **Interrail** (interrail.eu) for European citizens. Both are particularly useful for travelers under 25.

### By Bus
German company **Flixbus** (www.flixbus.com) operates international bus services into Denmark from both Sweden and Germany. **Gråhundbus** (http://graahundbus.dk) has three departures daily serving the **Copenhagen-Malmö route**. Travelers to Copenhagen from within Denmark may do so with **Flixbus** or **Sortbillet** (https://sortbillet.dk). Flixbus and Sortbillet buses arrive at **Ingerslevsgade** terminal, which is actually no more than a parking lane on a side road near the Central Station. **Gråhundbus** drops passengers off at Copenhagen Central Station.

### By Car
Coming by car from either mainland Europe via Germany or from Sweden via the Øresund Bridge remains straightforward, though complications have been added in recent years. Denmark is part of the **European Union's Schengen area**, which allows passport-free travel between member countries—in theory. At the beginning of 2016, the government implemented "emergency" **border controls** on the southern borders with Germany, as did Sweden on its border with Denmark via the Øresund Bridge. Almost three years later at the time of writing, the border controls remain in place. This means being stopped on the border for a spot check

is a realistic likelihood: always carry your **passport** with you.

## Holiday Packages

Copenhagen is a popular destination for all-inclusive holiday packages that bundle airfare, hotels, meals, and entrance fees to some attractions for trips ranging from weekends to full weeks. Various options—budget, luxury, family-friendly packages, and so on—can be found on websites such as **Expedia.com, trivago.com,** and **lastminute.com.** It's important to do due diligence before booking, so you know everything that's included and all upfront and other costs. Weekday packages are often less expensive than those on weekends or public holidays.

## FROM AUSTRALIA AND NEW ZEALAND

It's a long way from Sydney, Melbourne, or Auckland to Copenhagen. Expect layovers and a journey time that give you little to no change out of 24 hours. **Etihad, Emirates, Qatar Airways, Cathay Pacific, Singapore Airlines,** and **Qantas** are some of the major airlines operating these routes, with stopovers in places like Dubai, Hong Kong, Bangkok, and sometimes Munich. The average price from Australia is around US$1,500-1,700, but this can sometimes be reduced if you take a flight with an extra connection or longer layover.

## FROM SOUTH AFRICA

Copenhagen can be reached by flights from Cape Town, Durban, and Johannesburg, but none of them is direct. There's plenty of choice in airlines: **Lufthansa, Emirates, British Airways, Qatar Airways,** and **Iberia** are among the options, stopping over in Doha, Dubai, Munich, or Vienna.

Round trips can be as low as US$650 and range up to US$1,200 for economy flights.

# GETTING AROUND
## BY TRAIN

Copenhagen's public transportation system is comprehensive, consisting of bus and Metro networks as well as an overground metropolitan network known as the S-tog (S-train).

### Metro

The Metro, which currently only consists of two networks, opened in 2002 and does not serve Copenhagen Central Station. It is, nevertheless, very useful, linking the airport with Nørreport, a key hub within the city. Two new lines, adding 24 new stations that include a circular line linking Copenhagen Central, Nørrebro, and the eastern part of the city, will open in 2019 and 2020, and there has been talk of extending the Metro further still in the long term—perhaps even as far as Malmö.

### S-Train

S-trains go through Central Station and run regularly throughout the day from 5am to 12:30am. On weekends, there are all-night services. The S-train's seven lines and 85 stations comprehensively serve the Greater Copenhagen metropolitan area, including Klampenborg, where Bakken is, with the notable exception of Amager.

For travel between Copenhagen and other cities, towns, and regions in Denmark, there is one rail option: state operator DSB. The trains are comfortable and quiet and normally on time but are often looked down on by Danes, possibly due to their high prices. Example fares include Odense

(1hr 36mins, 278kr) and Aarhus (3hrs 13mins, 388kr). Other destinations include Roskilde (29 mins, 84kr), Helsingør (48 mins, 108kr), and Malmö (39 mins, 89kr).

## Planning and Fares

The **Rejseplanen app**, which is available in English, is a must-have for instant planning of journeys that combine all three of the above networks. The prepaid travel card **Rejsekort** is the easiest way of paying fares. It can be bought from machines in stations. The same machines (look out for their neon-blue cladding) can be used to add credit to the cards. Alternatively, single tickets can be bought in Metro and S-train stations and from bus drivers.

When using the Rejsekort, you must "check in" by holding the card over the sensor inside the bus or train at the beginning of your journey. Then, "check out" by using the separate check-out sensor when you are about to reach your destination. If you connect to a different bus/train, you do not check out but must "re-check in" to the second bus or train after switching. You then check out for the entire journey when you reach your destination. The Rejsekort card costs 180kr from machines, of which 100kr can be used as credit.

## BY BUS

There are currently three companies competing for passengers who eschew DSB's more-expensive rail tickets for less-expensive coach services between Danish cities. These are **Sortbillet** (https://sortbillet.dk/, Kombardo Expressen (www.kombardoexpressen. dk) and **Flixbus** (www.flixbus.com). Bus fares are far less expensive than the train, balanced out by the cramped

space and slightly longer journey time. Example fares for a trip from Copenhagen to Aarhus can range from 99kr to 189kr, and from Copenhagen to Malmö (29kr to 89kr, though going by train is preferable).

Within Copenhagen, buses can be used to get almost anywhere in the city and are generally reliable. Primary routes have an "A" in their route number, with the exception of the 5C, an iconic (and often maligned) route that crosses the city. This route was called 5A until 2017, when it got a makeover, new $CO_2$-neutral vehicles, and a new identity. The "A" routes and the 5C run 24 hours a day.

Outside of Copenhagen, local buses are generally simple and convenient ways to cover short distances within towns. Companies awarded contracts by local authorities operate city buses in Denmark (and in Malmö in Sweden), so there's only one type of bus. The Rejsekort can be used anywhere in Denmark in the same way as in Copenhagen, as can the Rejseplanen app for checking departures and planning journeys. Buses usually run at least hourly on principal routes. On Møn, it can be a little difficult to rely on buses alone to get around the island, particularly in the off-season when services are cut back.

## BY CAR

### Traffic and Driving Conditions

As far as major cities go, Copenhagen isn't a bad one to drive in as a newcomer. Traffic, although it can get heavy at peak times (weekdays from 7-9am, 4-5pm, and 3-4pm on Fridays), is generally forgiving: sitting in gridlock for long spells is uncommon.

Driving from Copenhagen to the other destinations in this book is quite straightforward and not at all time consuming by American standards: the most distant location is Møn with a journey time of 1 hour 30 minutes. The major roads and motorways are well maintained, clearly marked, and toll free.

When traveling from Copenhagen to Malmö by car, remember your wallet: there's a toll to cross the Øresund Bridge. This costs 375kr for a normal car (up to 6 meters, or almost 20 ft). Cash and credit cards are accepted. A small discount of 30kr can be had by purchasing in advance from www.oresundsbron.com. There are nine major parking lots spread around central Malmö, including near the city's Centralstation and in the Gamla Staden (Old City). Opening times and prices vary. A good place to check information, prices, and locations is www.pmalmo.se.

## Road Rules

Like all European countries apart from the United Kingdom, driving in Denmark is on the right-hand side. International licenses are not required for residents of EU countries, the United States, Canada, or Australia. Driver's licenses from other non-EU (or EEA) countries are also accepted provided they are printed with Latin letters or accompanied by a translation to Danish, English, or French. International driver's licenses are also valid. It's worth noting that an international license is not a license on its own, and you will still be required to carry your actual driver's license alongside it.

Drivers from most other countries are unlikely to be used to seeing so many bicycles on the road, and you will need to adapt your driving style to accommodate this. Although the bikes have their own lane, they have the right of way on right turns (in other words, when you are turning right, you must wait until all bicycles have passed on your curbside before turning. Not doing so risks an accident, and it will be your fault). The same applies with pedestrians. Right-turning cars must wait for them to clear traffic crossings before making the turn. This isn't the case in many other countries.

## Parking

Copenhagen has four different zones for parking charges, with the three most central and expensive ones encompassing the areas covered in this book. The red zone, which much of Nørrebro falls into, costs 36kr per hour during the day, 13kr per hour in the evening, and 5kr per hour at night. The green zone—the Inner City, Vesterbro, Østerbro, and Christianshavn—costs 19kr per hour during the day, 13kr per hour in the evening, and 5kr per hour at night. Amager is in the blue zone: 12kr per hour during the day, 13kr per hour in the evening, and 5kr per hour at night. There are some time-restricted zones around stations where parking is free but limited to one or three hours: look out for relevant signs here ("Tidsbegrænset zone"). Make sure you set the "parking clock" (a dial stuck to the inside of the windshield) at the time you leave the car, so any inspectors can see how long you've been there.

In Copenhagen, parking fees can be paid using apps including easypark.dk, parkpark.dk, parkman.dk, parkone.dk, plot.dk, and waytopark.dk or from machines on the street.

Frederiksberg, meanwhile, is in a different municipality from the rest of Copenhagen and therefore has different parking charges, albeit paid with the same apps. The first two hours of parking are free in Frederiksberg (so, again, set the parking clock), after which you pay 11kr for the first hour, 27kr for two hours, 48kr for three hours, 69kr for four hours, and 75kr for a day.

There are also several private parking garages, including some that are multistoried and scattered around central Copenhagen, for example near shopping areas. Prices range 12-45kr hourly.

Parking in smaller towns is easier than in Copenhagen, both in terms of finding a spot and being able to park for free, but if you do park in a fee-charging parking lot, the apps used to pay are likely to be the same as the ones used in Copenhagen.

### BY BIKE
Bicycles can be taken on S-trains but are not allowed at the busy Nørreport station or on the Metro during weekday peak times.

# Visas and Officialdom

## UNITED STATES, AUSTRALIA, AND NEW ZEALAND

For American, Australian, or New Zealand citizens, no visa or special documentation is required other than your valid government-issued passport that is valid for six months past the date that you are scheduled to leave the Schengen zone (of which Denmark is a part). The passport must have been issued no more than 10 years ago. A tourist visa or any other kind of visa is not necessary for entering and leaving the Schengen Area for a cumulative 90 days within a 180-day period. This does not necessarily mean 90 consecutive days, but rather 90 total days within a 180-day timeframe. Note that this includes any country in the Schengen Area, not only Denmark. If you plan to exceed the 90-day limit, you will need to obtain a tourist visa or another kind of visa to legally stay in the country. A pre-travel registration system (European Travel Information and Authorisation System or ETIAS) for entry to the Schengen area is expected to be implemented in 2021. Check with the state department or foreign affairs ministry in your home country for more information if traveling in or after 2021.

## EU/SCHENGEN

For citizens in countries that are members of the European Union, you only need a valid passport or government-issued national identity card that is valid during the length of your stay in Denmark in order to enter the country. It is important to have this with you when crossing the land or sea border from Sweden or Germany, as spot checks are possible and you can be sent back if you then do not produce the relevant ID. UK travelers should check regulations post-Brexit.

## SOUTH AFRICA

South African citizens must apply for Schengen visas in order to visit Denmark. The passport must be valid for at least three months after the date of return to South Africa and have two valid, blank and consecutive pages.

Copies of any previous Schengen visas issued within last the three years, even if in another passport, must be presented when applying.

Visa applications for Denmark can be submitted at the **Visa Application Center**: www.vfsglobal-denmark.com/SouthAfrica. It is recommended you apply as early as possible but not more than three months before your planned departure. More information can be found via the **Ministry of Foreign Affairs of Denmark,** http://sydafrika.um.dk.

The Schengen visa will permit you to enter the Schengen Area multiple times for a maximum of 90 days within a 180-day period.

If you are visiting more than one Schengen country during your trip, you must apply for a Schengen visa with the country that is your "main" destination, that is, the one where you'll be spending most of your time.

# Festivals and Events

Long, cold winters have the effect of pushing Danes to fit in as many outside events as possible during the summer months, even if the weather remains unreliable year-round.

## SPRING

Things start to warm up in Denmark in May, when **Ølfestival** brings the city's strong craft beer game and other lovers of fine ales out of winter hibernation. **CPH:DOX** is widely praised documentary film festival that lasts 11 days in March, and it will get you thinking in the meantime.

## SUMMER

Copenhagen comes alive in the summer with what seems a festival every weekend. **Distortion**, at the end of May and beginning of June, turns the streets of the city into a hedonistic mess often bemoaned by residents. The **Roskilde Festival**, though it takes place in a nearby city and not in Copenhagen itself, is the country's most famous festival and the largest live music event in Scandinavia. It brings in the world's biggest

names—Nick Cave and the Bad Seeds headlined in 2018. Bleary-eyed revelers can be seen coming and going in Copenhagen throughout the week, giving the city itself a sense of youthful blurriness. **Copenhell** is a heavy metal festival that takes place in mid-June on Refshaleøen. Festival shuttle buses use service number 666. Copenhagen Jazz Festival is ten big days of big jazz and intimate bar music in early July. By August, things calm down a bit. **Kulturhavn** is a three-day community culture festival on the waterfront, with 100 activities and cultural performances. **Copenhagen Cooking & Food Festival**, Scandinavia's biggest food festival, also takes place in August. In the middle of all this is **Skt. Hans Aften** (St. John's Eve), when the eve of celebration before the Feast Day of Saint John the Baptist is marked in a community spirit and Danes come out to sing in unison and light bonfires. **Copenhagen Pride** is in the middle of August. In Helsingør, the **Shakespeare Festival** brings open-air theater to the real-life location of the events depicted in *Hamlet*. Down the coast, Louisiana Literature is calmer but perhaps no less dramatic, as famous international authors come to the picturesque town of Humlebæk to give readings of their works.

## AUTUMN

Copenhagen Blues Festival keeps the summer music vibe hanging in for a little while longer into autumn. Culture Night (Kulturnatten) is a late-night art and culture festival in October. CPH:PIX, the city's feature film festival is usually on for two weeks in September or October.

## WINTER

Christmas in Copenhagen is almost synonymous with Tivoli, the iconic 19th-century amusement park at the heart of the city that spares no expense, decking itself with fairy lights and Santa's elves, as well as snow, dozens of Christmas trees, and yuletide fun as it throws its doors open for the festive season. Winter Jazz (Vinterjazz) at the beginning of February has intimate concerts—sometimes even held in people's front rooms—as well as events in the city's cafés and jazz bars. Fastelavn, at the beginning of February, is the Danish equivalent of Carnival but has as much in common with Halloween, as kids dress up in funny costumes and hit a piñatalike wooden barrel to win sweets (Danes call this custom "hitting the cat so it comes out of the barrel").

# Conduct and Customs

## LOCAL HABITS

Danes can often come across as taciturn and withdrawn in their meetings with strangers. They commonly avoid making eye contact with neighbors when passing them on steps and are unlikely to acknowledge people sharing public transportation with them, for example. Though this may seem cold compared to, say, the forthcoming nature of Australians or Americans, it should not be taken personally. It is part of Danish culture and makes established friendships feel all the more genuine.

The "Law of Jante," or *Janteloven*, is a code of conduct that has been around for centuries across the Nordic countries and still pervades the Danish subconscious today. The concept can be summed up with a phrase that is not unusual to hear in Denmark: "*du skal ikke tro, du er noget*"—literally, "Don't believe you're anything (special)." That sounds like a way of downplaying someone's success and, for just these reasons it is often maligned by Danes themselves, who call it outmoded and negative. However, it does mean personal success is commonly received with an admirable level of natural humility and dignity.

A good work-life balance is valued highly in Denmark. The working week is normally limited to 37 hours, with office hours from 8am-4pm, and most shops are open from 10am-6pm. The vast majority of supermarkets are open on Sundays, though smaller shops often close on Sundays and sometimes Saturday afternoons. It is also common to finish work early for the weekend on Fridays.

Tipping is not expected in

Denmark, even in expensive restaurants. It is, however, always appreciated—10 percent gratuity is plenty, should you wish to express yours.

## ALCOHOL AND SMOKING

The minimum age for purchasing cigarettes in Denmark is 18 years, and the minimum age for purchasing alcohol is 18 years for beverages with an alcohol percentage more than 16.5 percent and 16 years for percentages less than that. A surprisingly high number of Danes smoke: more than one in five people between the ages of 20 and 24 years smoke daily, according to 2018 figures from the Danish Cancer Society. What's more, the number appears to be increasing. It's unclear what the cause of this trend might be: a partial (but not complete) ban on smoking in bars has been in place for years, and supermarkets are beginning to experiment with placing cigarettes out of sight of customers, thereby preventing advertising in any form. Smoking is still allowed in bars or restaurants with less than 40 square meters (430 sq ft) of floor space, not including staff areas: the old-fashioned pubs known as *bodega*s remain as smoky as they have been for decades.

Given the prohibitive cost of alcohol in Denmark due to high taxes, many lower-income Danes such as students prefer to "pregame" by gathering together at home or at inexpensive, volunteer-run pop-up bars at universities known as *fredagsbarer* (Friday bars). Young Danes sometimes have a tendency to binge drink long into the night, with weekend parties often not finishing until the sun has come up again and everyone has had a *morgenfest* ("morning party").

There are diverse, inventive, hip, traditional, and innovative nightlife venues in the form of nightclubs, cocktail bars, wine bars, and grimy, cheap pubs (the aforementioned *bodegas*) spread all over the city, particularly in the Inner City, Nørrebro, and Vesterbro districts. Nightlife action peaks from Thursday to Saturday, but Copenhagen has something to do every night of the week.

## DRUGS

Recreational drugs including marijuana are illegal to use, purchase, and sell in Denmark, although, as in many countries, you may see people in the general population under the influence. That is particularly the case in Christiania, the nonconformist enclave in the city, which began as a hippie commune in the 1970s and for years openly sold cannabis on its "Pusher Street" market. Police have tolerated this until more recently, when changes in the law resulted in acrimonious battles with Christiania's traders and residents. At the beginning of 2018, a trial began that enabled doctors to prescribe medicinal cannabis for certain illnesses, but there is no appetite among authorities for any law change regarding recreational use.

Using drugs in public can result in a fine from law enforcement. However, you probably won't be fined unless you are disturbing public peace or disobeying law enforcement, or if you are in the wrong place during a spell when police are cracking down on, for example, Christiania. Harder illicit drugs such as cocaine and amphetamines are illegal in Denmark, and being caught with such drugs can lead to prosecution under criminal law.

# Health and Safety

## EMERGENCY NUMBERS

There are two emergency numbers in Denmark:

- 112 is a direct number to emergency services if you require immediate response, for example, an accident or if someone's life is in danger. Use 112 to call an ambulance, the police, or the fire service.
- 114 is a direct number for police across the country, that is, if you have a query but your concern is not urgent.

Operators can in almost all cases speak in English and, in the unlikely scenario that they can't, will quickly transfer you to somebody who can.

## MEDICAL SERVICES

Travel medical insurance is recommended on any type of trip, so arrange this before departure or check what your current health insurance covers internationally. If you need medical attention while in Denmark, you can call 112 for medical emergencies or if an ambulance is needed. Denmark has public healthcare, meaning the government provides free health care to all Danish citizens and legal residents. This is part of a larger integrated health system in the European Union, so if you are an EU citizen, any medical costs that you incur in Denmark can be fully refunded by the medical system in your home country (so keep your receipts).

Regardless of where you are from, if you take ill during your stay in Denmark, you are entitled to free, acute hospital treatment in accordance with normal rules applied in the area. Citizens of the EU plus Iceland, Norway, Liechtenstein, and Switzerland are entitled to acute hospital treatment through the insurance provided by the blue EU health insurance card.

Foreign travelers from countries outside the EU, EEA, or Switzerland have the same rights as Danish citizens when it comes to acute health care, meaning that emergency medical treatment is free of charge in the emergency rooms of public hospitals. Non-emergency medical bills must be paid, however. Prices start from 800kr for consultation.

## PHARMACIES

The Danish word for pharmacy is *Apotek*. Pharmacies are marked with green plus signs and can be found every few blocks in built-up areas and all smaller towns. Law requires a small number of pharmacies to remain open outside of normal business hours. In Copenhagen, Steno Apotek (Vesterbrogade 6; tel. 33 14 82 66; www.stenoapotek.dk), located close to the Central Rail Station, is open 24 hours.

All Danish pharmacists speak English well or adequately and are willing to help you find medications that you need if you are able to describe your conditions or symptoms. If you know the generic name of your prescribed medications, they can sometimes find them for you as well. Unlike in America, things such as generic headache medications and nasal spray are not readily available on the shelves, so you will need to specifically ask the pharmacist for it at the counter.

If you have a serious medical condition, you need to pack your medications in their original containers. Separately, pack other documentation or information that may help you in case of emergency.

## CRIME AND THEFT

Crime rates are low in Denmark, with a drop in crimes reported for the fourth consecutive year in 2016. It does exist, however, including pickpocketing and bag theft. Copenhagen Municipality recorded 30,406 reported pickpocketing incidents in 2016 and 27,442 such incidents in 2017. People in their early twenties are the most common targets, followed by those over 70. Keep your belongings secure when you are in busy places, particularly in and around Copenhagen Central Station and on the Strøget shopping thoroughfare. Although it is sometimes said that you can leave your computer on the table in a café while you go to the bathroom, I advise very strongly against it: always keep valuable items close to you.

Muggings and other forms of assault are also rare but not unheard of: take the same precautions you would in any big city. Don't take unlicensed taxis anywhere at any time.

In 2017 there was an ugly flare-up of violence between organized, crime-linked gangs in and around the Nørrebro neighborhood. More than 25 shooting incidents in the city through the summer and autumn led to increased police presence in the area before tensions were eventually eased, though sporadic incidents have also occurred in 2018. Though this is concerning, it should be noted that gun crime in Denmark remains rare and is extremely unlikely to affect tourists.

The poorer suburbs in Malmö, including Lindängen, Rosengård, and Southern Sofienlund (Seved), have also seen some gang-related violence. However, these areas are located in the south of the city, far removed from Gamla Staden, Västra Hämnen, and other parts where visitors and tourists are likely to find themselves. By and large, both Copenhagen and Malmö are no more dangerous than any other big city.

# Practical Details

## PASSES AND DISCOUNTS

There are savings to be had when visiting museums in Denmark. Some museums are free, such as the acclaimed Islamic art museum The David Collection; others offer discounts on certain days or out of season. The following museums have free entry on specific days: **Ny Carlsberg Glyptotek** (Tuesdays), **Thorvaldsens Museum**, **Nikolaj Copenhagen Contemporary Art Center** (Wednesdays).

Senior citizens and students often qualify for reduced rates on things such as museum entry and transportation, but you'll need to show proof of your student status and/or age.

The **Copenhagen Card** (https://copenhagencard.com) is a prepaid card that provides admission to 86 attractions in the city (as well as outside it) including travel on buses, S-trains, and the Metro throughout the capital region. It also offers discounts at selected restaurants, bars, and on sightseeing tours.

A full list of the discounted attractions can be found via the Copenhagen Card website and app. It's quite extensive, so if you already have a fairly good idea of what you want to see while in the city or are planning to pack in a lot of sightseeing, there is a good chance the card will save you money.

# MONEY
## CURRENCY AND EXCHANGE RATES

Denmark's currency is the krone (krone is singular, kroner is plural); only the krone can be used to pay for goods and services. You may occasionally find businesses that accept the euro, but you should never expect this.

The value of the Danish krone is intentionally kept close to that of the euro by the central bank, Danmarks Nationalbank. At the time of writing, exchange rates were 1 krone = €0.13 = $0.15 = £0.12.

### CURRENCY EXCHANGE

There are several desks at Copenhagen Airport where money can be exchanged. **FOREX Bank** has several branches in Copenhagen, including at the Central Station, in the Inner City (Nørre Voldgade 90; tel. 33 32 81 00), and Østerbro (Østerbrogade 19; tel. 33 91 20 00).

It's worth bearing in mind, though, that Denmark is a relatively cash-free society. Most people make payments using a smartphone app connected to the bank account, **MobilePay,** or with their debit cards. Foreign debit and credit cards can be used to make payments with almost every business and

store in Denmark with the exception of some, but not all, supermarkets.

### BUDGETING TIPS

Denmark is very expensive, particularly for eating and drinking out. Here are some typical prices that you can expect:

- Meal: takeaway pizza/*döner,* 40-60kr; café sandwich, 70-100kr; street food meal, 90-130kr; restaurant, 150-400kr
- Coffee: 25-60kr
- Drinks: beer, 45-75kr; wine, 60-120kr per glass; cocktails, 90-125kr
- Metro or bus journey: single ticket, 24kr, 15kr with Rejsekort
- Entrance fees: 50-150kr
- Accommodation: hostel dorm bed from 180kr; hotel from 400kr per person per night

There are ways to offset these expenses while still enjoying the country to its fullest. Like many Danes, you could alternate inexpensive or free outdoors activities where you take along packed lunches with the more expensive sights. Copenhagen and its surroundings have a raft of great parks and beaches. There's also plenty to see in the Inner City both for window shopping and admiring historic edifices, and there a some great parks for you to stop and relax with a sandwich and coffee.

### BARGAINING

Haggling is not really a "thing" in Denmark. Retailers all have set prices. In thrift stores and charity shops, you may be able to agree on a reduced price with a staff member, depending on the store's policy and the inclination of the person in question. At flea markets, feel free to ask if the price is negotiable (although the answer may well be "no").

## TIPPING

Although not part of Danish culture, tipping is appreciated by workers in Denmark's hospitality sector, so you won't be making a mistake if you want to thank a waiter for good service by leaving a tip. Tipping is not expected, however, as base wages are, in theory, high enough for it not to be necessary. Taxi drivers, hairdressers, or people in other types of service-sector jobs do not expect tips. Anything between 10 and 20 percent will be seen as generous.

## ATMS AND BANKS

ATMs, commonly referred to as *penge-automater* or *hæveautomater* (money machines or withdrawal machines), are commonplace on streets outside of shops and banks as well as within banks. They can also occasionally be found within small stores such as minimarkets: these types should be avoided if possible as they are more likely to levy a withdrawal fee on top of any fee you might already be facing for an international withdrawal.

Check with your bank ahead of time to see if they have any partnerships with Danish banks for waived or reduced fees. If they do not, a fee of around 30-35 kroner is likely to be charged for each ATM withdrawal.

## CREDIT AND DEBIT CARDS

Visa and Mastercard are accepted almost everywhere in Denmark; American Express and Diners Club cards are not always accepted. In general, very few businesses don't accept card payments, and fewer and fewer Danes use cash. Occasionally, you may find a store (for example, some Netto supermarkets) that has a system that doesn't accept cards that don't use Denmark's Dankort debit card payment system. This is rare, however. Any business that caters to tourists will accept card payments, including for small amounts. Surcharges are sometimes imposed on foreign cards. If this is the case, the surcharge must be notified to customers (for example at hotel receptions or on restaurant menus).

## OPENING HOURS

Opening hours can vary between businesses, and seasonal businesses reduce hours during the off-season, but the following hours generally apply:

- **Shops:** Mon.-Fri. 10am-6pm; some close earlier on Saturdays (between 2pm and 4pm), some are open on Sundays
- **Supermarkets:** Mon.-Sat. 8am-10pm; many are open on Sundays, and some close at 11pm or midnight; some convenience stores are open 24 hours
- **Department stores:** 10am-8pm
- **Bars:** Sun.-Wed. 4pm-midnight, Thurs.-Sat. open until 2am-6am
- **Cafes:** 8am-7pm, some café-bar crossovers are open until as late as midnight
- **Restaurants:** noon-10pm, some close later (11pm or midnight)
- **Banks:** Mon.-Fri. 10am-4pm; sometimes they are open Thurs. to 5:30pm or 6pm

## PUBLIC HOLIDAYS

- **New Year's Day** (Nytårsdag): January 1
- **Maundy Thursday** (Skærtorsdag): Thursday before Easter
- **Good Friday** (Langfredag): Friday before Easter
- **Easter Sunday** (Påskedag)
- **Easter Monday** (2. påskedag)
- **Great prayer day** (Store Bededag): fourth Friday after Easter

- **Ascension Day** (Kristi Himmelfartsdag): sixth Thursday after Easter
- **Whitsunday** (Pinsedag): seventh Sunday after Easter
- **Whitmonday** (2. pinsedag)
- **Constitution Day** (Grundlovsdag): June 5
- **Christmas Eve** (Juleaften): December 24 (from noon)
- **Christmas Day** (Juledag): December 25
- **Boxing Day** (2. juledag): December 26

Labor Day, also known as International Workers' Day or Workers' Day (May 1) is not an official public holiday but many employers, especially in the public sector, give employees the day off. In Copenhagen the annual occasion is marked by speeches, workers' songs, and red banners as workers organized by profession or trade union head to the Fælledparken park in Østerbro, where there's a spirited festival atmosphere as people join together to drink coffee and beer and support workers' rights. Denmark's traditions of social solidarity and strong labor unions have helped International Worker's Day prevail as an event that is still going strong in modern, globalized times.

# COMMUNICATIONS

## PHONES AND CELL PHONES

Denmark's country code is +45. All numbers have eight digits (after the country code) and there are no area codes, so it's simple to dial once you're in the country.

If you're coming from outside Europe, check that your handset works on the European GSM 900/1800 network—some Asian and American phones work on different frequencies.

Prepaid, refillable sim cards can be bought at many retailers and supermarkets without showing identification and can also be ordered online for free from companies such as Lycamobile (www.lycamobile.dk), but you will need a Danish address.

Useful numbers:

- **118**: directory assistance
- **113**: international directory assistance

## INTERNET ACCESS

Although the city of Copenhagen doesn't have a public access Wi-Fi, you can log onto Wi-Fi at the vast majority of cafés, restaurants, and hotels, and at many attractions. You may need to ask for a password, although there is often also free access. City buses and intercity coaches also have on-board Wi-Fi, although it's not always reliable.

## SHIPPING AND POSTAL SERVICE

Denmark's postal service is in a sorry state, after it was gradually privatized and subjected to brutal cutbacks and closures, which were branded as modernization. By 2018, there was only one traditional post office remaining in the country—there were 300 in 1999 and 96 as recently as 2010. They have been replaced by so-called "post shops" (*postbutikker*), which are counters at supermarkets run by operator Postnord. Packages are now sent from and can be collected at these counters as well as other package service providers in minimarkets and newsagents. Find your nearest one via www.postnord.dk. Opening hours are normally matched to the store hosting the post desk. Parcel delivery to home addresses still exists but is slow and appears to be getting increasingly unreliable.

Costs for sending packages internationally from Denmark are:

- Weight max. 100g, 30kr
- Weight max. 250g, 60kr
- Weight max. 2kg, 90kr

For registered post, costs on international delivery for packages is the following:

- 500g, 100kr
- 1kg, 170kr
- 5kg, 180kr
- 10kg, 200kr
- 15kg, 240kr
- 20kg, 270kr

## WEIGHTS AND MEASURES

Denmark uses the metric system. Many Danes struggle to name imperial units; others find them quirky. A few basic conversions are as follows:

- 1 kilometer = 1,000 meters, 0.62 miles
- 1 meter = 3.3 feet, 1.1 yards
- 1 liter = 0.26 gallons
- 1 ounce = 28.4 grams
- 1 kilogram = 2.2 pounds

## LEFT LUGGAGE

Luggage storage is available at Copenhagen Airport, where baggage lockers are placed near car park P4. Three sizes are available, ranging from 60kr for four hours to 120kr for 24 hours.

At Copenhagen Central Station, lockers are located at the bottom of the steps inside the western entrance of the station at Istedgade. Luggage storage is open from Mon.-Fri. 5:30am-1am and Sun. and public holidays 6am-1am. The cost is 60kr-70kr for 24 hours, depending on size. There is also staffed luggage storage (65kr-75kr for 24 hours).

## TOURIST INFORMATION

### TOURIST OFFICES

**Copenhagen Visitors Center**

*Vesterbrogade 4A; tel. 70 22 24 42; www. visitcopenhagen.com; Mar.-Apr. daily 9am-4pm, May-June and Sept. Mon.-Sat. 9am-6pm, Sun. 9am-4pm, July-Aug. Mon.-Fri. 9am-8pm, Sat.-Sun. 9am-6pm; Oct.-Feb. Mon.-Sat. 9am-4pm, Sun. 9am-2pm*

This is a smart and user-friendly resource located a few minutes' walk from the Central Station. There's a café and lounge with free Wi-Fi. You can buy the Copenhagen Card, book tours, and use the digital guide or speak to staff, as well as pick up a library of brochures.

### INTERNET RESOURCES AND APPS

The **Rejseplanen app** is essential for planning journeys in Copenhagen and all over Denmark. It tells you the easiest route to your destination, where and how to change, and how much the fare is, and it provides a link to buy the ticket online (this is more expensive than using a Rejsekort). The app is available in English. Train tickets can also be purchased on DSB's app. Google Translate is handy for understanding written Danish, if not for the language's nuances.

### MAPS

Apple Maps and Google Maps are as reliable as ever in Denmark, especially if you need a turn-by-turn GPS when driving, bicycling, or walking around the area. Both are available in offline mode and work well in rural areas like Møn.

# Traveler Advice

## OPPORTUNITIES FOR STUDY AND EMPLOYMENT

Copenhagen is a great city to be a student. As well as the flagship University of Copenhagen, the Technical University of Denmark, Copenhagen Business School, IT University of Copenhagen, and Aalborg University all have campuses here. There are also numerous colleges, including Metropolitan University College, Niels Brock Copenhagen Business College, and University College Capital, which offer a range of bachelor's post-secondary education and academy professional qualifications. Specialist institutions—Royal Danish Academy of Fine Arts, School of Architecture, Copenhagen School of Design, and Technology and Rhythmic Music Conservatory—add to the prestige and choice on offer.

Information about exchange programs at the University of Copenhagen, which is an Erasmus partner university, can be found on the university's website (https://studies. ku.dk/exchange) and it is also worth asking at your home institution about exchange programs with universities in Copenhagen.

Danes have the freedom to live and work in any EU country, but Denmark lacks the option native English speakers often have of being able to find jobs as language teachers. English is taught to a high level in schools, so native-speaking English teachers are in less demand here than in many other countries. Finding work in Denmark can be hard, even if you have experience in your field in your home country: many employers shy away from hiring staff who don't speak Danish, despite the high level of English proficiency among Danes. There are some exceptions to this, notably in the tech industry. For non-EU citizens, employment visa regulations make finding work a daunting prospect.

Less-skilled work in bars and restaurants is more accessible for those hoping to extend their stay in the city, but note that visas are not granted for this, so you will need to have an EU passport.

## ACCESS FOR TRAVELERS WITH DISABILITIES

Accessibility for travelers with disabilities at tourist attractions is still not guaranteed in Denmark, but it is fast improving. Tourist information website visitcopenhagen.com lists sights, restaurants and hotels with good accessibility in its "Accessible Copenhagen" section, at www. visitcopenhagen.com/traveltrade/ copenhagen/accessible-copenhagen.

God Adgang (www.godadgang.dk) is another good resource, listing service providers approved and registered as accessible.

## TRAVELING WITH CHILDREN

With its open spaces and cargo bikes, Copenhagen is a child-friendly capital city. Attractions like Experimentarium and Tycho Brahe Planetarium, as well as GeoCenter Møns Klint on Møn mean there are plenty of stimulating and educational places for kids.

Some of the major museums, such as Louisiana Museum of Modern Art, make sure there is something for kids to do while parents are gazing at contemporary art. In fact, Louisiana has an entire section dedicated to daily activities and workshops for children. Vintage amusement park Bakken is a great day out for children, and Tivoli Gardens is a timeless experience that has a bit of magic about it, not least at Christmas.

Using public transportation with children is made as easy as possible with family areas on trains and reduced tickets, and most restaurants below Michelin-starred class have children's menus.

## WOMEN TRAVELING ALONE

Women should take precautions when traveling alone, especially at night. However there are no specific dangers that set Copenhagen out from other major European cities. Danes are generally reserved in the public sphere, so catcalling is less prevalent than in some other countries. Overall, the prospect of traveling alone as a woman should in no way act as a deterrent for visiting Denmark.

## SENIOR TRAVELERS

Copenhagen can feel like a young city to the point of exclusivity at times, given the stylish, beautiful appearance of so much of its population. However, many museums and attractions are senior-friendly, offering discounts on admission. There are also discounts on public transportation for over-65s. Although it's a cyclist's city (many senior Copenhageners also bicycle), it's compact and easy to get around on foot, too. Outside Copenhagen, public transportation discounts also apply.

Louisiana, perhaps somewhat surprisingly, does not offer a senior discount, but it is otherwise perfectly accommodating. Møns Klint and the Cannon Tower at Kronborg Castle may prove difficult for senior travelers due to the physical demands of climbing hundreds of steps at each attraction.

## LGBTQ+ TRAVELERS

Copenhagen has a strong tradition dating back to the 1970s as a city friendly to LGBTQI people. Denmark was the first country to legalize same-sex civil partnerships in 1989 and unilaterally declassified trans identities as a mental illness in 2016, a step not yet taken by the World Health Organization (WHO). The annual Copenhagen Pride grows in size each year, and the conservative government recently appointed an LGBTQI coordinator and announced investment in promoting equality. The Minister of Justice is the highest-profile of many politicians who are openly gay.

There are plenty of gay-friendly or gay-focused bars and clubs in Copenhagen, particularly in the area around Kattesundet and Studiestræde in the Inner City, underlining why the city is sometimes referred to as northern Europe's gay village.

Homophobia-related incidents do still occur, but there are few places able to compete with Copenhagen on equality, not just because of Denmark's record in public life, but also because of the deep-rooted culture of acceptance and equality.

## TRAVELERS OF COLOR

Multicultural and cosmopolitan, Copenhagen is tolerant to travelers of all races, even though political trends going back to the 1990s have left a lot of non-white Danes feeling not fully accepted. Away from the capital, there is less multiculturalism, but discrimination against tourists remains rare.

# Essential Phrases

Hello: *goddag*
Hi: *hej*
Bye: *hej hej*
Goodbye: *farvel*
See you: *vi ses*
Thank you: *tak*
Thank you very much: *mange tak*
Good morning: *godmorgen*
Good evening: *god aften*
Good night: *godnat*
How much does this cost?: *Hvor meget koster det?*
Where is...: *Hvor er...*
the toilet: *toilettet*
the bathroom: *badeværelset*
the rail station: *banegården*
the museum: *museet*
the beach: *stranden*
the restaurant: *restauranten*
the café: *caféen*
What would you recommend?: *Hvad kan du anbefale?*
I would like to have: *Jeg vil gerne have*
Could I get: *Må jeg få*
the soup: *suppen*

the fish: *fisken*
the sandwich: *sandwichen*
the chicken: *kyllingen*
potatoes: *kartofler*
vegetables: *grøntsager*
pork: *svinekød*
bacon: *bacon*
butter: *smør*
cake: *kage*
coffee: *kaffe*
tea: *te*
milk: *mælk*
water: *vand*
What is your name?: *Hvad hedder du?*
My name is...: *Jeg hedder...*
I come from: *Jeg kommer fra*
How are you?: *Hvordan går det?*
I don't understand: *Jeg forstår ikke*
Do you speak English: *Taler du engelsk?*
Sorry: *sorry/undskyld*
Excuse me: *undskyld*
Look out!: *Pas på!*
Good luck!: *Held og lykke!*
Goodness me!: *Det må jeg nok sige*
Cheers!: *Skål!*

# Index

# List of Maps

# Acknowledgments

My thanks and love to Amalie for accompanying me in Copenhagen and beyond; and to my grandfather, James Dearle, for encouraging me to write and writing to encourage me.

# Photo Credits

# Gear up for a bucket list vacation

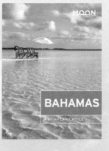

# MOON TRAVEL GUIDES TO EUROPE

# GO BIG AND GO BEYOND!

These savvy city guides include strategies to help you see the top sights and find adventure beyond the tourist crowds.

## OR TAKE THINGS ONE STEP AT A TIME

# More Guides for Urban Adventure

# MAP SYMBOLS

| | | | |
|---|---|---|---|
| ≡≡≡ Expressway | ○ City/Town | ⓘ Information Center | ♠ Park |
| ≡≡≡ Primary Road | ◉ State Capital | 🅿 Parking Area | ⚑ Golf Course |
| ～～～ Secondary Road | ◉ National Capital | ⛪ Church | ✛ Unique Feature |
| ∧∧∧ Unpaved Road | ◉ Highlight | ♣ Winery | ❧ Waterfall |
| ⋯⋯ Trail | ★ Point of Interest | ❏ Trailhead | ∧ Camping |
| ⋯⋯ Ferry | • Accommodation | Ⓡ Train Station | ▲ Mountain |
| ------ Railroad | ▼ Restaurant/Bar | ✈ Airport | ✗ Ski Area |
| ≡≡≡ Pedestrian Walkway | ▪ Other Location | ✗ Airfield | ◯ Glacier |
| ⊡⊡⊡ Stairs | | | |

# CONVERSION TABLES

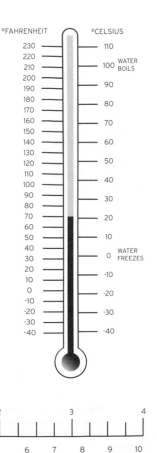

°C = (°F - 32) / 1.8
°F = (°C x 1.8) + 32
1 inch = 2.54 centimeters (cm)
1 foot = 0.304 meters (m)
1 yard = 0.914 meters
1 mile = 1.6093 kilometers (km)
1 km = 0.6214 miles
1 fathom = 1.8288 m
1 chain = 20.1168 m
1 furlong = 201.168 m
1 acre = 0.4047 hectares
1 sq km = 100 hectares
1 sq mile = 2.59 square km
1 ounce = 28.35 grams
1 pound = 0.4536 kilograms
1 short ton = 0.90718 metric ton
1 short ton = 2,000 pounds
1 long ton = 1.016 metric tons
1 long ton = 2,240 pounds
1 metric ton = 1,000 kilograms
1 quart = 0.94635 liters
1 US gallon = 3.7854 liters
1 Imperial gallon = 4.5459 liters
1 nautical mile = 1.852 km

# MOON COPENHAGEN & BEYOND

Avalon Travel
Hachette Book Group
1700 Fourth Street
Berkeley, CA 94710, USA
www.moon.com

Editor: Ada Fung
Project Editor: Lori Hobkirk
Copy Editor: Beth Fraser
Production and Graphics Coordinator: Suzanne Albertson, Darren Alessi
Cover Design: Faceout Studios, Derek Thornton
Interior Design: Megan Jones Design
Moon Logo: Tim McGrath
Map Editor: Mike Morgenfeld
Cartographers: Brian Shotwell, Karin Dahl
Proofreader: Sandy Chapman
Indexer: François Trahan

ISBN-13: 978-1-64049-058-1

Printing History
1st Edition — August 2019
5 4 3 2 1